Religion and Sexuality

THREE AMERICAN COMMUNAL EXPERIMENTS
OF THE NINETEENTH CENTURY

LAWRENCE FOSTER

New York / Oxford
OXFORD UNIVERSITY PRESS
1981

Library of Congress Cataloging in Publication Data
Foster, Lawrence, 1947—
  Religion and sexuality.

  Based on the author's thesis, University of Chicago.
  Bibliography: p.
  Includes index.
    1. Collective settlements—United States—Religious
  life—Case studies. 2. Celibacy—Case studies.
  3. Polygamy—United States—Case studies. 4. Oneida
  Community—History. 5. Shakers—History. 6. Mor-
  mons and Mormonism in the United States—History.
  I. Title.
  HX654.F67   335'.973   80–18104
  ISBN 0–19–502794–9

Printed in the United States of America

Preface

Experiments with communal living, alternative marriage and sexual patterns, and unorthodox lifestyles have occurred throughout American history from the earliest days to the present. Beginning with the Pilgrims and
Puritans, who sought freedom to develop their own distinctive ways of life
in the New World, a host of diverse religious and ethnic groups have attempted to find a haven in America where they could live as they chose.
While immigrant groups continued to bring over their varied traditions,
many native-born Americans also began trying to develop new and more
satisfying communal patterns of their own. Although the opportunities for
social and religious experimentation have never been without limits, extraordinary freedom to explore different lifestyles has always been an important element in the American experience.

Among the most colorful of the efforts to introduce radically new ways
of life in America were those of three controversial religious groups which
originated or peaked in strength during the turbulent decades before the
Civil War. These groups—the Shakers, Oneida Perfectionists, and Mormons—rejected existing marriage and nuclear family patterns. Instead, they
organized new communities around alternative models as diverse as celibacy, group marriage, and polygamy. Like many contemporary religious
cult movements, these groups followed charismatic leaders, challenged the
basic religious and social assumptions of their day, and sought to overcome
the turmoil and disorder they perceived around them by setting up cohesive new communities. These movements were either founded or attracted
many followers in western New York State—an area similar to California
today as a source and magnet for all manner of religious and social causes.

Most writers have treated these three groups and the social ferment out
of which they grew as simply an American sideshow. At best, the individ-

uals who founded or joined the Shakers, Oneida Perfectionists, and Mormons have usually been dismissed as quaint eccentrics; at worst, as psychopaths. Hundreds of books and articles have been written explaining why these groups "failed," or observing that they must have been out of touch with the American "mainstream," whatever that may have been. But I was struck by a different set of questions. Why should thousands of Americans before the Civil War have been so upset about conventional marriage and sex-role patterns that they were prepared to try to change their entire way of life? What did it mean, in personal terms, for a man or woman to give up monogamy and adopt an alternative system such as celibacy, group marriage, or polygamy? How were such systems conceived, introduced, and institutionalized—lasting for more than a quarter of a century in each case? And, underlying all the other questions, could an understanding of the struggle of men and women in these groups provide insights which could help us to come to terms with our current dissatisfactions with marriage and sex roles?

To begin to answer such questions, I immersed myself in the primary manuscript and printed holdings for each group, attempting to recapture at the deepest possible emotional level what it must have been like to have been an early Shaker, Oneida Perfectionist, or Mormon. I worked for two months in the Library of the Western Reserve Historical Society in Cleveland, poring over hundreds of bound Shaker manuscripts, many of them written with all the meticulous care of a medieval scribe. For another two months, I read through microfilm copies of the first twenty-one years of the newspapers published by John Humphrey Noyes and his Oneida Community. And I engaged in more than four months of research in the Library and Archives of the Church of Jesus Christ of Latter-day Saints in Salt Lake City, reading intensively in manuscript and printed sources there. This research and similar work in collections throughout the country has led me to conclusions that differ greatly from those of many previous scholars. In this book, therefore, I have attempted to go beyond the conventional focus on *what* these groups did; I have also sought to explain *why* they did what they did and how successful they were in terms of their own objectives. By trying sympathetically to understand these extraordinary experiments in social and religious revitalization, I believe it is possible to come to terms with a broader set of questions that affect all men and women during times of crisis and transition.

The origin of my interest in alternative systems of family and communal organization goes back to my childhood growing up in a rural barrio in the Philippines. There I first began to realize the great variety and complexity of ways of life and looking at the world. Later, as an undergraduate at Antioch College, an experimental liberal arts school combing both work and study, I was exposed to the peak of the late 1960s social protest and countercultural movements. Many people seemed to be at loose ends, looking for a sense of community yet often not finding it. I began to wonder if other periods of crisis might shed light on our troubled age and allow me to come to terms with unique aspects of my own roots.

During my last year at Antioch, I became increasingly curious about nineteenth-century groups which had experimented with new marriage and family patterns. Under the direction of Robert Fogarty, I contrasted the apparently polar extremes of Shaker celibacy and Oneida Community "free love." At the University of Chicago, Donald M. Scott helped me to expand and focus this work by adding the Mormons and placing these movements into their larger social context. Throughout the entire study, my major adviser, Martin E. Marty, has been of exceptional help. I am deeply grateful for his continuing encouragement and for his incisive suggestions on both stylistic and conceptual issues. My other advisers, Neil Harris and Jerald C. Brauer, also provided invaluable guidance and counsel throughout the research and writing of the original dissertation at the University of Chicago.

Working in the rapidly developing field of Mormon history has been exhilarating. In particular, Jan Shipps, Klaus J. Hansen, and Robert B. Flanders have provided me with both an intellectual and a personal stimulus for which I can never adequately thank them. Their work has served as a model of excellence for my own efforts. Under the leadership of Leonard J. Arrington, Davis Bitton, and James B. Allen, the Historical Department of the Church of Jesus Christ of Latter-day Saints has moved to combine a commitment both to scholarly excellence and to a living faith. I am deeply grateful to them, as well as to individuals too numerous to name who helped in so many ways during the four months when I was conducting my research in the Church Library and Archives in Salt Lake City. Among the many other students of Mormon development whose assistance has been of special value are Danel Bachman, Jay Brandt, Vicky Burgess-Olson, Gail Casterline, Mario S. De Pillis, James E. Elliott, James A. Everett, James L. Kimball, Jr., T. Edgar Lyon, D. Michael Quinn, and David J. Whittaker. As a non-Mormon, I should note that the interpretations presented in this book are my own and do not necessarily represent the views of any of the individuals mentioned above.

One of the most enjoyable aspects of this research has been the enthusiasm and support of librarians and achivists. I have been given exceptional assistance by individuals at the Regenstein Library of the University of Chicago; the Newberry Library in Chicago; the Western Reserve Historical Society Library in Cleveland; the Huntington Library in San Marino, California; and the Library and Archives of the Historical Department of the Church of Jesus Christ of Latter-day Saints in Salt Lake City. I have also received valuable help from librarians at the Beinecke Library at Yale University in New Haven, Connecticut; the Brigham Young University Library Special Collections in Provo, Utah; the Chicago Historical Society Library; the Garrett Theological Seminary Library in Evanston, Illinois; the Library and Archives of the Reorganized Church of Jesus Christ of Latter Day Saints in Independence, Missouri; the Library of Congress in Washington, D.C.; the Sabbathday Lake Shaker Community Library at Sabbathday Lake, Maine; the Shaker Museum Library at Old Chatham, New York; the University of Utah Library Special Collections in Salt Lake City; and the Utah State Historical Society Library in Salt Lake City.

I owe a very special debt of gratitude to my friend Eleanor Melamed, who has read and criticized my work at every stage of its development. Whatever stylistic merit this book may possess is due in large measure to her skillful editing. Robert D. Thomas, author of a fine social-psychological study of John Humphrey Noyes, offered valuable comments on the chapter dealing with Oneida. Regina Morantz of the University of Kansas at Lawrence and D'Ann Campbell of the Newberry Library in Chicago read the entire manuscript and offered important suggestions on its revision. Incisive advice on the final chapter was provided by Robert C. McMath of the Georgia Institute of Technology in Atlanta.

Financial support through a four-year Ford Foundation Fellowship and a University of Chicago Special Humanities Fellowship made possible much of the research and study that has gone into this work.

Permission to use material which first appeared in printed form elsewhere has been granted by *Dialogue: A Journal of Mormon Thought* and the *Journal of Mormon History*.

All quotations used in this book are reproduced exactly as they appeared in the original sources unless I have indicated otherwise. In a few cases, however, I have also inserted a *sic* to remind the reader that a particularly confusing usage is, indeed, an accurate transcription of the original.

The able assistance of my typists, Nancy Cohen, Anita W. Bryant, Genie Vidal, and Jane Holley Wilson, has been much appreciated.

Charles W. Scott and the editorial department at Oxford University Press in New York have given invaluable aid in preparation of the final manuscript.

Finally, special thanks go to my parents, especially to my mother, Portia B. Foster. Her commitment to understanding other cultures and creating a new and more humane way of life in our own society has deeply influenced my own ideals and concerns. This book is dedicated to her.

Atlanta, Georgia   Lawrence Foster
August, 1980

Contents

I have made a ceaseless effort not to ridicule,
not to bewail, nor to scorn human actions,
but to understand them.

SPINOZA

Religion and Sexuality

I

A New Heaven and a New Earth:
The Millennial Impulse and the
Creation of Alternative Family Systems

> The law of marriage "worketh wrath." It provokes to secret adultery, actual or of the heart. It ties together unmatched natures. It sunders matched natures. It gives to sexual appetite only a scanty and monotonous allowance, and so produces the natural vices of poverty, contraction of taste, and stinginess or jealousy. It makes no provision for sexual appetite at the very time when that appetite is strongest. . . . This discrepancy between the marriage system and nature is one of the principle sources [of the sexual tensions and disorders of men and women]. . . . The restoration of true relations between the sexes is a matter second only in importance to the reconciliation of man to God.
>
> John Humphrey Noyes[1]

Writing in 1848 as he was setting up his experimental Oneida Community in central New York State, the unconventional John Humphrey Noyes voiced concerns about marriage, family life, and sex roles that sound curiously similar to those of many present-day Americans. Noyes was convinced that existing marriage patterns were unrealistic, unsatisfying, and harmful. He feared that the family was disintegrating, and with it the whole social fabric. Conventional sexual patterns—or the corresponding efforts to change those patterns—were simply insufficient to deal with the serious social tensions that were developing. Noyes saw no way of working within the system to overcome the disorder he saw around him. Rather than place his faith in the uncertain prospect that the larger society would eventually set family life straight, Noyes chose to devote more than thirty years of his life to creating his own "enlarged family" to overcome the fragmentation he found in his life and in the world around him.

3

John Humphrey Noyes's dissatisfaction with conventional family patterns and sex roles in the pre–Civil War period, shared by many in his time, has many parallels in the present as well. Seldom in American history has the sense of crisis in family life and the whole social order been more intense than in our own time. In fact, some recent observers have gone so far as to speculate that the current strains in marriage and relations between the sexes may presage a breakdown of the family and the development of radically new forms of interpersonal relationships. The rise in the divorce rate, the development of a new women's activism and self-assertion, the increase in experiments with alternative marriage practices and life styles, and the spread of attempts to create alternative communities, all suggest the possibility that a radical rearrangement of traditional attitudes and behavior may be occurring.

How are we best to understand the significance of our present dissatisfactions with sexuality and marriage? What sources can we look to for guidance in this complex and important area? Many have written about our current sexual, marriage, and family concerns, and have suggested a variety of solutions to such problems. Often, however, the deepest understanding of the way in which social change and revitalization occur can be achieved by stepping back from immediate problems and seeking a broader perspective. By looking at how people in another time or place tried to cope with issues similar to those that we now face, we may learn much about our own situation as well. The mid-nineteenth century, when John Humphrey Noyes and a host of other communal experimenters were active, is a particularly fruitful period for such investigation. This period saw unorthodox and illuminating attempts to deal with what scholars have described as the crisis of transition from pre-industrial to more modern forms of family and social life.

To explore such larger social issues, this book will look closely at the origin and early development of three religious communal experiments which grew to importance during the turbulent years before the Civil War—the Shakers, Noyes's Oneida Perfectionists, and the Mormons. Each of these groups explicitly rejected conventional monogamous marriage and instead established functioning communities based on alternative models ranging from celibacy to group marriage and polygamy. These ventures were carefully conceived, skillfully organized, and successfully realized in practice for at least thirty years. The specific solutions developed by these communal experimenters may not provide any direct answers to present-day concerns; the issues with which these men and women struggled, however, suggest much about the process by which rapid social change occurs at both individual and group levels, and reflect many of the social and intellectual tensions of the larger American society.

Initially one is struck by the apparent differences in style and approach among these three groups. The Shakers, with settlements scattered from Maine to Indiana, established celibate, essentially monastic communities in which women shared equally in all aspects of leadership. The Oneida Perfectionists, with headquarters in central New York State, created a system of "complex marriage" or group marriage, sometimes misleadingly called "free love," which resulted in radical changes in sex roles and behavior. And the Mormons, after a turbulent early attempt to introduce polygamy among their following in Illinois, eventually moved to the intermountain West, where they set up an elaborate polygamous and patriarchal system.

As different as these movements were, both from each other and from the larger society, they shared a number of common characteristics which make it appropriate to study them together as a response to nineteenth-century social tensions and the process of rapid social change. All of these ventures were based at first on a similar type of personal, charismatic leadership. The prophet-founders of these groups, as of many similar movements, were individuals who were seen as possessing exceptional powers and qualities that set them apart from their followers and gave them special authority. For whatever reasons, these prophetic figures interpreted their experiences as having cosmic importance. They developed new ways of looking at the world, and they attracted followers who believed that their sense of mission and their ideas were divinely inspired.[2]

The people who joined or participated in these movements also had many characteristics in common. Each of these groups had an Anglo-American ethnic base, drawing its primary membership from native New Englanders and from New Englanders who had moved westward into New York and the mid-West. One of their major sources of strength lay in western New York State, an area which was experiencing rapid economic growth and unstable social conditions before the Civil War—an area similar to California today as a source and magnet for all manner of social and religious causes. And these three groups all were either founded or underwent a crisis in sexual and marital life during the same period, the turbulent 1830s and 1840s.[3]

In addition to developing out of a similar type of prophetic experience and attracting members from similar sources, these three movements shared a similar set of underlying assumptions and attitudes toward the world. They all were convinced that the old order was radically diseased and corrupt, tottering inevitably toward destruction—"the end of the world," in their terms. No purely rational, human means could salvage the larger society; only divine intervention could ultimately set things straight. But human effort would be an integral part of such a divine influx. Rejecting the wicked world, these groups instead set up their own religious communities, based on their own conceptions of the ideal or heavenly model.[4]

That model, in each case, was based on an attempt to "restore" the faith of early Christianity, of "the primitive Christian Church," as they understood it. By beginning to set up a new order based on Biblical ideals, an order which they believed would eventually encompass the entire world, these groups were seeking to overcome the religious and social chaos that they perceived around them. They believed that their efforts would be closely associated with the second coming of Christ and the establishment throughout the world of a millennium of earthly peace and harmony. This millennial faith that the kingdom of God could be established on earth, that the glory of God was immanent in human history, underlies the remarkable beliefs, commitment, and drive of these millennial movements.[5]

A final similarity between these groups is that, like their Puritan forebears, they left an extraordinary range of writings about all aspects of their most personal religious and social concerns. Because they were so meticulous in describing what they were trying to do, how they were trying to do it, and how they felt about their experiences, they provide an excellent illustration of the complex process which individuals undergo when they give up one way of life and adopt a radically different one. Furthermore, since they explicitly and implicitly criticized those patterns of the larger society with which they were in disagreement, these movements also suggest much about the social and intellectual context within which other Americans of the period attempted to deal with pressing problems of sexual, marital, and family organization.[6]

In dealing with the complex and highly personal issues of sexual attitudes and practice in these three groups, I have used two approaches. First, I have read and carefully analyzed the writings of the prophet-founders and other articulate individuals who were committed to these movements. Because such writings may not fully represent the attitudes and behavior of average members, I have also analyzed membership records and other materials which supplement the individual accounts. In the following chapters, the results of this work have been woven into a narrative of how these alternative marriage and family systems were developed, and how individual men and women were able to radically change their ideals and life styles.

Anthropological Perspectives

Such colorful religious and communal ventures as the Shakers, Oneida Perfectionists, and Mormons naturally attracted much popular attention, both in their own time and afterward. Unfortunately, most scholars and popular writers have merely caricatured or patronized these movements. The most interesting issues that they raised have been largely ignored. Typically the groups are said to have "failed" because they were out of touch with the developing economic-industrial order, or because their leaders and members were unstable or psychologically maladjusted, or because they did not fit into the larger American "mainstream," whatever that may have been.[7] Such accounts, often inadequately documented, fail to explain how functioning systems of celibacy, group marriage, or polygamy could have developed before the Civil War and could have attracted so many nineteenth-century descendants of the New England Puritans. How were such alternative family systems conceived, introduced, and institutionalized—lasting for more than a quarter of a century in each case? What were the people who organized or joined these groups trying to accomplish, and how successful were they in terms of their own objectives and the new worldviews that they were trying to develop?

The effort to understand other ways of life with both the sensitivity of an insider and the detachment of an outsider almost inevitably leads toward anthropological perspectives. Studies of millennial and ecstatic religious movements, in particular, show that such ventures are part of a complex effort to create an intellectual and social synthesis for a new society, in their terms "a new heaven and a new earth." Faced with a period of extensive cultural interaction and perceived social crisis, individuals and groups characteristically attempt to return to their roots and reinterpret old values in a new social context. For the Shakers, Oneida Perfectionists, and Mormons these cultural models lay in the faith of early Christianity, as they understood it. Like Perry Miller's Puritans, who also attempted to reinterpret the faith of early Christianity in a new American context, these Yankee millennialists can be viewed as part of an effort to create a distinctive Anglo-American ethnicity. They also provide "an ideal laboratory" in which the process of social change can be viewed at both the individual and group levels.[8]

Perhaps the most complex and fascinating question raised by these millennial groups is how the individuals who founded or joined them made the radical transition in their personal lives from monogamy to celibacy, group marriage, or polygamy. Such change can seldom have been easy, and, as we shall see in the following chapters, in many instances it was extremely painful and disruptive. The early Shakers often would sing, shout, and dance all night until exhausted, in an attempt to overcome their "fallen," carnal natures. The Oneida Perfectionists experienced the most severe emotional and psychosomatic problems as they attempted to introduce and regulate complex marriage. And the Mormons who accepted polygamy often were distraught for days or weeks on end as they wrestled with the question of whether God could really have commanded them to practice something that all their training and emotions told them was wrong.

How are we best to understand such transition periods when an old way of life is dead or dying but a new order has not yet been born? Do the seemingly chaotic experiences of such times of rapid change have some meaning and value in themselves that is not immediately apparent to the outside observer?

One particularly illuminating perspective on such questions is suggested in the work of the anthropologist Victor Turner, especially *The Ritual Process: Structure and Anti-Structure.* Turner begins with Arnold Van Gennep's classic analysis of "rites of passage," or transition, which are found in all cultures at life crisis points such as birth, puberty, and marriage. These rites of passage are marked by three phases: first, a separation, disaggregation, or breakdown of an old status or order; second, an intermediary or "liminal" period when neither the old nor the new standards are in effect; and third, a reaggregation or establishment of a new order.[9]

Turner's most important contribution lies in his analysis of the liminal period of rites of passage. During this phase, a person's status is ambiguous; he is caught "betwixt and between the positions assigned and arrayed by law, custom, convention, and ceremonial." Frequently initiates are represented as possessing nothing, are expected to obey their instructors completely and to accept arbitrary punishment or seemingly irrational demands without complaint. "It is as though they are being reduced or ground down to a uniform condition to be fashioned anew and endowed with additional powers to enable them to cope with their new station in life." In this country, residual forms of such rites of passage can be seen in activities such as fraternity initiations or marriage ceremonies.

Accompanying the temporary ceremonial breakdown of normal secular distinctions of rank, status, and obligation in the liminal period is an intense egalitarianism and sense of emotional unity. There is an overriding feeling of direct personal communion, a blend "of lowliness and sacredness, of homogeneity and comradeship." "It is as though there are here two major 'models' for human interrelatedness, juxtaposed and alternating." The first treats society as "a structured, differentiated, and often hierarchical" system of evaluating men from political, legal, or economic frameworks in terms of "more" or "less." The second, emerging recognizably in the liminal period, "is of society as an unstructured or rudimentarily structured and relatively undifferentiated *comitatus,* community, or even communion of equal individuals who submit together to the general authority of the ritual elders." Turner uses the term "communitas" to distinguish this type of social relationship from an "area of common living."

The distinctive features of the liminal period of individual rites of passage can also be seen in larger and more complex social transitions. However, unlike normal rites of passage in which approved social leaders guide an individual into an already established new status, the prophet-founders of millennial movements face a more difficult task. They must begin to create a new way of life and status relationships at the very same time that they are trying to initiate individuals into those not yet established roles. In short, the desired end point is often unclear, or else is still in the process of being created. Thus, such movements typically go through great confusion and a more severe process of breaking down the old order as they seek to find and develop a new way of life.

The sense of communitas and fellow feeling in such highly committed movements is also extremely intense. Such a state of communitas provides direct personal contact which replaces the institutional constraints that normally separate individuals. And in no area of life are such direct personal relations, freed of all institutional constraints, more powerfully expressed than in sexual communion. Thus it is not surprising that when the anthropologist Kenelm Burridge summarized the transition period in many different millennial movements, he found that a period of sanctioned sexual license or other seemingly bizarre emotional displays frequently precedes "a form of entry into a new condition governed by fresh rules and assumptions." In personal communion with each other and with the divine, leaders and participants alike "seek that inspiration which will guarantee their activities as right and founded in truth."[10]

Although this book will not develop an elaborate theoretical analysis of the relationship between millennial commitment and social change, the perspectives of Victor Turner and other anthropologists do suggest a larger context within which many puzzling features of the transition to alternative marriage forms in these three groups become easier to understand. Taken in isolation, the disorders and excesses of this intermediary period might well appear psychopathological; within a broader context, however, such developments can be understood as part of the birth pangs of a new order, both within the individual prophet-founders of such movements and within the new society which they attempt to create. As Burridge notes: "It is not appropriate to think of a prophet as reduced to a schizophrene or paranoid, someone mentally sick. In relation to those to whom he speaks a prophet is necessarily corrupted by his larger experience. He is an 'outsider,' an odd one, extraordinary. Nevertheless, he specifically attempts to initiate, both in himself as well as in others, a process of moral regeneration."[11]

This study will trace the process of moral regeneration in these three communal groups, highlighting a distinctive type of religious creativity which has implications for any period of crisis and transition. An initial overpowering visionary experience of the prophet-founder leads not to individual psychopathology and withdrawal, but to an active attempt to create a new and more satisfying way of life and looking at the world. The successful prophetic figure finds personal reintegration by establishing his or her own deeply felt ideals as the norm for an entire community. And the followers of the prophet, sharing a deep concern about the ambiguities and inconsistencies of their complex era, find in the new intellectual patterns the promise of authoritative answers to difficult religious and social questions, as well as the basis for a more satisfying community life.[12]

The Social Context

To appreciate the complex challenges faced by the people who organized or joined these millennial groups, we must first place such movements in their larger social and intellectual context. The years from the decade following the War of 1812 to the decade preceding the Civil War—during which these three groups were founded or reached their peak of size and influence—are characteristically described as a time of buoyant optimism and expansiveness. It was the age of "Jacksonian Democracy" when the common man came into his own in politics and public life; of "Manifest Destiny" when the nation surged across the continent to the Pacific; and of "Freedom's Ferment" when Americans, believing that perfection could be achieved on earth, threw themselves into an incredible range of benevolent and reform activities with the confident sense of living in an age of miracles in which all things were possible.[13]

Such an interpretation accurately reflects the period's surface level of drive and boosterism, yet it fails to recognize how such almost compulsive optimism could mask deep anxieties and fears of failure. There was often a darker side to such expansiveness. The revivalists and home missionary societies could talk in glowing terms of gathering in the sheaves for Christ's kingdom, yet a man such as Lyman Beecher could also be motivated by a desire to save the West from "barbarism," and by a deep fear that, should the churches fail to establish order, the new areas might fall prey to chaos. In a rapidly changing society, there was much moral and intellectual confusion. Emerson spoke for many when he declared: "Things are in the saddle/And ride mankind."[14]

Adding to the uncertainties troubling many people was the proliferation of competing religious groups, a situation which one writer has characterized as "American wars of religion," analogous in a modest way to the destructive European conflicts of the sixteenth century.[15] As a brilliant essay by Arthur Bestor has suggested, the very fluidity of this period caused many individuals to feel a sense of urgency that the seeds of future social and religious institutions be planted while society was still malleable, not yet hardened into rigid forms.[16] "Now is the time when the West can be saved; soon it will be too late!" was the cry. Like their Puritan forebears who had fled religious and social disorder in England and attempted to establish "holy commonwealths" in the New World, the New Englanders who moved westward across New York and into the Northwest Territory were faced with the necessity of establishing a new order in the absence of clear guidelines. Theirs was an age of both high promise and great danger.

Of all the areas in which transplanted New Englanders settled, the one in which religious disorder reached its greatest intensity and in which the greatest variety of social experimentation took place was that part of New York west of the Catskills and Adirondacks. This was a "burned-over district"—so called because of the frequency with which the fires of the revival spirit swept through the region. There the Shakers found much of their membership, the Oneida Perfectionists settled, and the Mormon prophet Joseph Smith received his first revelations. Innumerable other excitements of the period—from the revivalism of Charles Grandison Finney and the spiritualism of the Fox sisters to the woman's rights agitation of the Seneca Falls group and the abolitionism of Theodore Dwight Weld and others—also found a home in the Burned-over District and related areas of New England settlement. Whitney Cross's outstanding social-intellectual history of this western New York region describes it as a "storm center," a "psychic highway" upon whose broad belt of land congregated people of predominantly Yankee inheritance, largely from the hill country of New England. These were people extraordinarily given to unusual religious beliefs and to crusades aimed at the perfection of mankind and the achievement of millennial happiness. In the minds of many men and women of the region could be found a strange admixture of skepticism and credulity, pragmatism and superstition, optimism and deep fears.[17]

During the period which saw the completion of the Erie Canal in 1825, the Burned-over District of western New York was rapidly transformed, both economically and socially, and began to show its characteristic tendency toward millennial revivalism. "Ultraism," or the tendency toward extreme religious and social ideas, rose to a peak about 1836. Then came the Panic of 1837, the worst depression experienced by the new Republic to that date. Popular concerns became redirected to a variety of new enthusiasms of the early 1840s. These included the Fourierist communitarian excitements and the Millerite movement which looked to the literal end of the world in 1843 or 1844. Eventually the crusade to abolish slavery, which expanded from its original moral reform base to become a national political movement, would become the focal point for the social concerns of many individuals in the area. Throughout the years before 1850, an atmosphere of intense religious rivalry and competing claims to truth led to great internal tensions in many individuals who desired a secure religious faith and a satisfying basis for social authority.[18]

The fluidity and turmoil in the rapidly developing new Republic before the Civil War—particularly in areas of New England settlement—could not help but place special strains on family life and relations between the sexes. Of course, one may well question whether fundamental structural change was taking place in the family. Recent studies suggest that at least in Western societies, underlying patterns of family organization have changed very slowly over the centuries.[19] Any period of stress is likely to generate a sense that basic social institutions such as the family are threatened with destruction, even if what is actually occurring is only a painful adjustment of old attitudes and structures to new social realities.

Nevertheless, there can be little doubt that many articulate individuals in the antebellum period were concerned about the condition of the family, and that some felt its stability was severely threatened. The historian should refrain from assuming too easily that a one-to-one correlation exists between social reality and a people's perceptions of that reality; however, the deeply felt concerns of vocal individuals certainly do influence behavior and must be taken into account as part of the social conditions of any period. Since current theories of family change and empirical studies of such change in the antebellum period are still in their infancy, here I shall simply suggest a few factors which may have been associated with tensions and readjustments in the family during this period.[20]

The most important forces for change in antebellum family life appear to have been related to increasing economic differentiation, which was based on factors such as the development of commercial agriculture, and nascent industrialization, urbanization, and immigration. As older, essentially rural and local farm patterns of employment changed, men's occupations increasingly took them away from the home into the highly competitive, individualistic world outside. Concurrently, women began to assume a position of almost sole responsibility for managing the home, rearing children, and a variety of other domestic concerns. The gap between the worlds of men and women became wider than possibly at any other time in American history.

Closely related to increasing economic differentiation as a factor requiring adjustments in family life, was the great geographic mobility which developed in the antebellum period. Within little more than seventy-five years following the Revolutionary War, New England settlement, which had been narrowly concentrated along the coast and major navigable rivers, expanded into back-country New England, spread across New York State, and fanned out into the Northwest Territory. At the same time, from the Middle States, Virginia, and the Tidewater regions, people poured over the Appalachian Mountains to settle and develop much of the Mississippi Valley and the South before the Civil War. Economic and geographic expansion proceeded at a pace unprecedented in American experience.[21]

The precise causes of this remarkable expansion, as well as the ways in which it affected family life, still remain uncertain. Nevertheless, such far-reaching economic and geographic changes surely must have had significant consequences for the family. As only one example, the possibility that individuals might separate with greater ease from parental and community ties left them freer to develop their own practices and life styles. Of course, there was still much mobility in kinship and community groups, and many traditional forms of social control remained. However, in the increasing number of cases of individuals who were temporarily or permanently separated from home by many miles, families could hardly maintain as much influence on their children's choice of marriage partners or on the way in which their married lives would be conducted. The growing emphasis in the antebellum period on individualistic "romantic love" as the basis for marriage was parallel in many ways to the increasing individualism of the whole society.[22]

What were the popular and literary reactions to the tensions and challenges of family life and relations between the sexes in this period? Responses varied widely, of course. Many women, for example, celebrated their newly found independence in managing the home domain, and sought to develop within it a variety of new skills and competencies. Others found pressures on them too great, and escaped into psychosomatic ailments and drugs. Still others criticized the limitations placed on women by restricting them to a home role and sought to further expand women's activity in public life. And yet others joined alternative communal ventures which rejected existing family patterns and sought to organize radically new ways of life.[23]

Perhaps the most common response, however—one which underlay or influenced all these others—was the attempt to control potentially anarchic social and sexual tendencies by attributing enormous, even cosmic, importance to "the home." The sense of boundless potentiality and undefined limits that had characterized the 1830s and the 1840s gradually gave way after about 1850 to a period of consolidation and to the introduction of new intellectual and institutional forms of control. This developing Victorian ethos has often been described negatively as repressive, sentimentalizing, and marked by prudish and unrealistic attitudes toward sexual and family matters. It could also be viewed positively, however, as contributing to a new autonomy for women in the home, and as helping to bring about necessary individual and family adjustments to changing social conditions. Behavior that once had been regulated by external community sanctions increasingly came to be guided by internalized values of self-control.[24]

The diverse possibilities implicit in the new ideals are clearly suggested by the "cult of true womanhood" which developed in this period. It stressed the pure, innocent, asexual qualities of the ideal woman, and expected her to curb the base passions of the crude, lascivious man.[25] Most contemporary scholars have viewed this ideal as essentially repressive toward women. Women were theoretically placed on a pedestal, but in fact their activities were constricted and their potential for self-development and influence in the larger society was narrowed. An alternative view, however, sees this stress on domesticity and sexual repression as a form of "domestic feminism." It helped women gain control of their reproductive processes (prior to the development of effective artificial methods of birth control) and gave them an independent power base from which they could actually exercise considerable influence.[26]

In much the same way, the idealization of the nuclear family during this period looks different depending on one's perspective. It has frequently been argued that, with the attenuation of extended kinship and community ties, the antebellum family ceased to be self-sufficient in a preindustrial sense. The increasing complexity of society meant that family and local support networks by themselves were not capable of handling all the economic, educational, correctional, and religious needs of family members. Faced with this situation, the nuclear family turned in on itself, psychologically, for support. In this view, the nuclear family served as a retreat from complexity. It became a psychological bastion which protected individuals from realistic engagement with a society that they found increasingly difficult to comprehend.[27]

An alternative view admits that such psychological withdrawal occurred, but sees it as serving positive functions. When temporary, such withdrawal allowed individuals to regain a sense of identity, security, and power. Strengthened by emotional supports from their families, and aided by the development of larger society-wide institutions such as schools, asylums, prisons, and benevolent societies, individuals could then move back into society to deal with a wide range of pressing issues.[28] Thus, Victorian preoccupations with the nuclear family and with developing internal mechanisms of self-control can be viewed as more than simple repression and withdrawal. Such concerns can also be seen as an essential element helping to produce highly motivated individuals, free of traditional kinship and community restraints, who could contribute to the development of a modern, highly differentiated order.

The Millennial Response

The state of flux and uncertainty in marriage and family relations in the new Republic was clearly reflected in the various millennial movements which expressed such a strong sense of dissatisfaction with the inadequacies and inconsistencies of their transitional age. In fact, nearly all of the mainline and fringe revivalistic movements which developed in the Burned-over District and related areas of New England settlement faced such problems and attempted with varying degrees of success to find solutions to them. Any religion which attempts to encompass the whole of life must inevitably come to terms with the problems of the family and the regulation of relations between the sexes. And never were these issues more pertinent than in the period in which the Shakers, Oneida Perfectionists, and Mormons arose.[29]

In addition to responding to many pressures of its larger environment, religious revivalism contained within itself a tendency to release sexual as well as religious emotions. And such emotions were further heightened in groups which attempted thoroughgoing communal living. Intense and sustained contact between the sexes under such circumstances could lead to enormous pressure to relax the arbitrary sexual prohibitions and rules established by the larger society. It is possible that sexual relations had to be either prohibited entirely or universalized in some fashion in order to sustain the type of total religious and social commitment demanded by these millennial ventures in their early phase of development.[30]

The transitional state of antebellum society and the problems inherent in using the Bible alone as the basis for religious and social order are graphically illustrated by the fact that all three of the millennial groups studied here found support for their unorthodox marriage and family systems in an identical New Testament passage.[31] In the passage in question, Jesus was asked a trick question in an attempt to reduce to absurdity one conception of the afterlife: A woman married one of seven brothers, who died without leaving her any children. So, according to the Jewish law of the levirate, the next brother took her as his wife so that an heir could be raised up to continue the family name. This brother died just as her first husband had. Each of the succeeding brothers who married her in turn also died without leaving her any children. Finally the woman herself died. Which brother would be her husband in the "resurrection," or, very loosely, the afterlife?

Jesus' deft and rather ambiguous response was that the questioner misunderstood the nature of the "resurrected state."

> The children of this world marry, and are given in marriage: but they which shall be accounted worthy to obtain that world, and the resurrection from the dead, neither marry nor are given in marriage: Neither can they die any more: for they are equal unto the angels: and are the children of God, being children of the resurrection.[32]

Ann Lee and the Shakers, following a common Christian interpretation of this passage, argued that no sexual relations would occur in the resurrection. Such carnal distractions would be eliminated there. In imitation of this heavenly model, truly dedicated Christians should practice celibacy on earth. Celibacy thus became the symbol of triumph over sin, the chief factor separating believers from an impure world and allowing them to realize true Christian unselfishness like that of the angels. In setting up their celibate systems, the Shakers considered themselves part of an enlarged family of God. They lived in communal groups called "families," which were composed of some 30 to 150 men and women living under a single roof, but carefully separated in all their activities. Governed under a hierarchical and oligarchic family-style paternalism, the Shakers eliminated only the sexual and individualistic attachments of normal family life so that total loyalty could be devoted to their community and to God.[33]

John Humphrey Noyes, the Yale-trained academician who founded the Oneida Community, disagreed with the Shaker interpretation of this New Testament passage. He pointed out that it said only that "marriage" would be done away with in the resurrected state, not sexual relations per se. And what was "marriage"? Simply a legal, contractual, earthly relationship between a man and a woman, characterized by exclusive sexual privileges and by other rights and responsibilities. The narrow private relationship found in earthly marriage would be done away with in the afterlife, where love would be universalized and expressed equally among all the saints. And, in Noyes's opinion, total love between men and women, both in heaven and on earth, had to include the possibility of physical expression. Oneida "complex marriage" thus was designed to allow the heavenly pattern to be realized on earth. In their "Community home in which each is married to all,"[34] all members lived under a common roof, ate and worked together, attended daily religious-and-business meetings, and eliminated any exclusive sexual attachments. A variety of informal but stringent control mechanisms assured that the resulting system continued to focus the primary loyalty of members on the community and on God.[35]

Joseph Smith and the Mormons, in an equally elaborate explanation growing out of their own "modern revelation," developed yet a different explanation for this same passage. Briefly stated, the Mormon view was that no marriages would be *performed* in the afterlife. Only marriages which had been properly sealed on earth under the authority of the Mormon Priesthood could endure in heaven. Such marriages would become the basis for social status and eternal progression, for Mormons found it impossible to believe that the finest things of this world—marriage and family life—would be done away with after death. Instead, such experiences would be heightened and refined, developing all that was best in earthly social relations. Mormons believed that raising up numerous righteous progeny in the families of the best men was the primary goal of marriage. Polygamy, which was based on the practices of the Hebrew patriarchs, would enable the patriarchal leaders of the Mormons to have the largest families, and thereby gain the most status and power, both on earth and in heaven. Using this elaborate family ideology, the Mormons eventually would successfully colonize much of the intermountain West, providing concrete evidence of their loyalty to their community and to God.[36]

The ability of these three millennial groups to find sanction for their widely divergent marital beliefs and practices in the same Biblical passage reflects both the strengths and weaknesses of the larger Biblical tradition of which they were a part—a tradition associated with Christian millennialism, especially that of the Protestant Reformation. By emphasizing the Bible as the sole source of religious authority and by giving "literal" interpretations to highly ambiguous Biblical passages, millennial groups could jettison the whole religious and social order that had developed over more than a thousand years under the Roman Catholic Church. Thus they were free to innovate radically in belief and practice.

Such innovation had both negative and positive potential. Breaking down old institutions and stressing individual Bible interpretation could lead to great fragmentation. Yet after all the turmoil and confusion was over, reintegration around a more satisfying religious and social center might also be possible. Prophetic Biblical literalism, which ostensibly drew its inspiration from the past, could also serve as a powerful vehicle for the expression of deeply felt present-day needs and concerns. By attempting to reinterpret the faith of the "primitive Christian Church" in a new historical context, such groups were in a sense "backing into the future."[37]

Faced with the inevitable tendency toward fragmentation arising from both its environment and its ideology, a successful millennial movement had to develop powerful new institutional forms to interpret and regulate the permissible range of religious and social variation. The leaders of the Shakers, Oneida Perfectionists, and Mormons dealt with these problems by developing a highly authority-conscious and strongly centralized Church-type structure of government. Community needs were emphasized over those of the individual, although a considerable range of individual variation was allowed as well. Thus, a key to the relative success of these three groups was their eventual development of an authoritative Church structure and a strong, internally coherent social system to overcome the religious and social disorder that their members had found so unacceptable.[38]

The Structure of This Study

The origin, development, and appeal of such unconventional religious movements raise complex issues which can best be addressed by using two different approaches. The core chapters of the following account will use case studies to illustrate the ways in which each of these groups developed and changed. Such an approach makes it possible to capture the idiosyncratic aspects of each movement and to do justice to the specific factors which influenced each group's growth. Case studies alone, however, can not fully capture the larger regularities in each group's development. Therefore, the final chapter of this book will provide a comparative analysis of issues such as the origins of these movements, the ways in which they reorganized sex roles, and their larger significance for the study of social change. By combining the case study and comparative approaches, we shall be better able to understand both the unique aspects and the larger regularities in the development of these remarkable movements.

Within each of the case studies that follow, three main topics will be covered. First will be the formative religious/intellectual experience of the founder or foundress of the movement. In each case this experience led to a new way of looking at the world which he or she felt compelled to share with others. Unlike many creative or eccentric individuals who have little direct influence, however, these individuals were able to attract a following and set up functioning communities around their beliefs. Thus a second major concern in this study will be how such communities were formed and why people were attracted to them. A third issue, underlying these first two, will be how these new ways of life illustrate different approaches to dealing with vital issues of marriage and family relations. Throughout the account, our primary concern will be with the origins and early development of the new forms rather than with the functioning systems themselves, which have already been analyzed by many historians and sociologists.

In the central case studies, approximately twice as much space is devoted to the Mormons as to the Shakers or Oneida Perfectionists. The more extensive coverage of the Mormons is not intended to suggest that they raise more conceptually interesting issues than the other groups. Indeed, because the Shakers and Oneida Perfectionists arrived at such extreme solutions to marriage and family problems, they may highlight certain issues more effectively than do the more conventional Mormons. The special coverage of the Mormons in this account is due to three factors:

First, the size and complexity of the Mormon group creates special difficulties in analyzing and presenting their story. For example, neither the Shakers nor the Oneida Perfectionists suffered any successful schisms during their existence, yet during the first twenty-five years of Mormon development alone, more than twenty-five schismatic groups were formed —several of them important in their own right. Rather than simply creating one community or a network of communities of several thousand individuals separated from the world, the Mormons eventually attracted hundreds of thousands of people to Utah, set up hundreds of settlements, and placed their indelible cultural mark upon the greater part of the intermountain West. To portray the scope of this effort requires special attention to detail and nuance.

Second, and closely related to the first factor, is the richness of the documentation of Mormon origins. The earliest transition periods of the Shakers and the Oneida Community have left few manuscripts, so that much of the documentation of those transitions must be somewhat impressionistic and speculative. By contrast, Mormon manuscript materials are extensive and are now being made available for serious scholarly research. Transitional linkages in the development of the Mormon community and its system of polygamy in the nineteenth century can be shown in the sort of detail that is impossible for Shaker and Oneida Community family patterns.

Finally, unlike the Shakers and Oneida Perfectionists, the Mormons are still a dynamic and rapidly expanding group. Dealing with issues of concern to a living religion—one which has changed greatly during the past one hundred fifty years—leads to special difficulties not present in analyzing the discontinued Oneida experiment or the almost extinct Shaker religion. Although the practice of polygamy is no longer allowed by the main branch of the Mormon Church, the issues raised by the effort to institute a polygamous form of marriage in the nineteenth century have continued to be a source of concern and strain for many present-day monogamous Mormons. I have tried to be fair and thorough in dealing with the many tangled issues relating to nineteenth-century polygamy which have continued to pose intellectual and personal challenges to the more conventional Mormons of the twentieth century.

In their attempts to establish new frameworks for religious and social order, these three millennial movements illustrate the problems and challenges inherent in periods of rapid change and transition. Their marriage and family organization, in particular, provides a striking view of how new cultural patterns can be conceived by a prophetic or charismatic figure and then institutionalized among a much larger following. This book will delineate, as clearly as possible from available evidence, the process by which these remarkable ventures in religious and social revitalization achieved at least temporary success.

II

They Neither Marry
Nor Are Given in Marriage:
The Origins and Early Development
of Celibate Shaker Communities

What is there in the universe, within the comprehension of man, that has so sensible, so quick and ravishing an operation, as a corresponding desire of the flesh in the different sexes? . . . As a gushing fountain is more powerful in its operations than an oozing spring; so that desire of carnal enjoyment, that mutually operates between male and female, is far more powerful than any other passion in human nature. . . . Surely then, that must be the fountain head, the governing power, that shuts the eyes, stops the ears, and stupifies the sense to all other objects of time or eternity, and swallows up the whole man in its own peculiar enjoyment. And such is that feeling and affection, which is formed by the near relation and tie between male and female; and which being corrupted by the subversion of the original law of God, converted that which in the beginning was pure and lovely, into the poison of the serpent; and the noblest of affections of man, into the seat of human corruption.

The Testimony of Christ's Second Appearing, 1808[1]

In the summer of 1770, in a jail in Manchester, England, where she had been imprisoned for taking part in noisy religious services that had allegedly "disturbed the peace," a thirty-four-year-old woman had a powerful visionary experience that radically transformed her life. For nine years, Ann Lee, a poor and unlettered but highly capable and dynamic woman, had experienced a series of exceptionally difficult religious and sexual problems. These had affected every aspect of her life. After suffering four painful deliveries and the loss of all her children in infancy or early childhood, Ann Lee had become increasingly terrified of all sexual intercourse. She had struggled with her impulses, with the importunity of her good-hearted but crude husband, and with the pressure of church authorities who tried to convince her of her conjugal duties. She had frequently spent sleepless nights crying out to God for redemption. And through pentecostal religious activities, which included singing, shouting, and ecstatic dancing, as well as through her lonely individual quest, she had sought to discover the root cause of evil, the foundation of mankind's separation from God.

While she was in jail in Manchester, Ann Lee had a powerful "open vision" of Adam and Eve in carnal intercourse. At last she knew with absolute inner certainty that this act was, indeed, the very transgression which had resulted in the fall of man in the Garden of Eden and the entry of sin into the world. Following this traumatic discovery, Ann Lee had another compelling vision in which the Lord Jesus Christ appeared to her in all his glory. He comforted her and confirmed her sense of mission to spread her new knowledge throughout the world. Convinced that lust was the true source of sin, Ann Lee proceeded to take charge of the little splinter group of Shaking Quakers to which she belonged.[2] However, the group remained stagnant in England, and even their removal to America in 1774 at first did little to increase their membership. Between 1780 and 1784 in the troubled aftermath of the American Revolution, Ann Lee and her followers did attract several thousand potential supporters throughout New York and New England. But in 1784 when Ann Lee died, exhausted by her internal struggles and the intense persecution she had suffered for bearing her blunt and uncompromising testimony against the evils of the flesh, the small group of Shakers appeared to be just another of the many eccentric splinter sects springing up after the Revolution, most of which have been long forgotten today.[3]

Only fifteen years after Ann Lee's death and this relatively unpromising beginning, however, a vigorous network of eleven major Shaker community sites with more than 1600 members had been set up under the leadership of Ann Lee's American followers.[4] A thoroughgoing celibate communal system was flourishing. This system eliminated private property, espoused pacifism, and conducted religious life in self-conscious separation from an evil world. As early as 1803, two Shaker communities could give away thousands of dollars of specie, livestock, and produce to help feed the starving poor who were suffering from cholera in New York City.[5] Both spiritual and temporal success appeared to have come to the Shakers.

This early period was only the beginning of Shaker growth. True to their perfectionist and developmental spirit, the Shakers continued to demonstrate religious, theological, and social innovation and dynamism until the Civil War. A second wave of Shaker expansion led to a network of new communities in the Midwest, and doubled their membership by

1820. And in a final important period of revival and consolidation between 1837 and the mid-1850s, Shaker membership rose to a peak of some six thousand Believers in approximately sixty semi-autonomous communities scattered from Maine to Indiana.[6] By that time, the Shakers had become far more than simply a curiosity visited by innumerable tourists. They had also provided an inspiration to a wide variety of social theorists from Robert Owen to Friedrich Engels and others. These men believed that the success of the Shakers had proved that a thoroughgoing cooperative and communistic system was not simply an impractical dream, but a form of organization that could be successfully established throughout the world.[7]

What accounts for the development of this remarkable celibate, pacifist, and communal religious group during the early years of the United States? How was the transition from monogamous belief and practice to a celibate system achieved? In what ways were relations between the sexes restructured in Shaker communalism, and what were the advantages and disadvantages of such restructuring? And what could have led a significant minority of highly committed and articulate American men and women, as well as many who left no direct record of their thoughts and feelings, to join such a group and make it work, at least for a time?

These will be the primary questions addressed in this chapter. An effort will be made to understand both at an individual and at a larger social level how the transformation to new values and practices was achieved in functioning community life, how a small but intellectually and socially significant group of Americans could have been attracted to this extraordinary religious and communal venture.

English Origins of Shakerism

The roots of Shakerism in England are shrouded in considerable obscurity. Details of the early development are often hazy, recorded in print well over fifty years after the events described. Shaker accounts, however, trace their religious lineage to two sources.[8] One was a sect of revivalistic French Protestants, the so-called Camisard Prophets. In the aftermath of the 1689 revocation of the religious toleration granted by the Edict of Nantes, the persecuted Camisards in the Cevennes Mountains began engaging in extreme revivalistic activities. They shook, shouted, spoke in tongues, and prophesied the imminent destruction of the existing religious and social order. Eventually some of these French Prophets emigrated, settling in London and elsewhere in England.

In Manchester, the French Prophets continued their extreme religious activities and prophesying the imminent end of the world. They taught that the established Church and State were the Biblical Babylon that would be destroyed by God before the coming of a millennium of universal peace on earth. Their call to repentence attracted a small following in England and may well have come to the attention of a number of individuals who later joined the Shakers.[9]

Probably a more important influence on the early Shakers came from the Quakers. The early Quakers had been occasionally given to highly emotional expressions in their religious meetings. Scoffers declared that they literally "quaked" before God. By the mid-1700s, however, English Quakerism had become more respectable and orderly, and was tolerated by the civil authorities.[10] In 1747, a Lancashire couple, Jane and James Wardley, feeling that the Quakers had lost their earlier fire, separated themselves from that group to form their own small religious society. It did not have any established creed or particular structured manner of worship, but was open to the workings of the spirit in the same highly emotional way that the Camisards and early Quakers had been.

Although some later Shakers tended to downplay the importance of the Quaker influence on their development, this influence appears to be a major factor at almost every level of Shaker religious and social belief. The Shakers' debt to the Quakers can be seen in their similar theological framework, liberal approach to Biblical interpretation, elimination of all sacramental forms including Baptism and the Lord's Supper, emphasis on the free workings of the spirit, total pacifism, refusal to take oaths or participate directly in secular government, use of "thee" and "thou," and, above all, the active encouragement of women to participate at all levels of the group as preachers and active members. The influence of the Quaker intellectual framework may even be seen in such later Shaker innovations as their belief in a dual godhead in which male and female elements were combined equally, a belief which was not incompatible with that of the Quakers.[11]

A third influence on early Shaker development was the personality and experience of Ann Lee herself. Ann's personal struggles, both religious and sexual, became transformed into the distinguishing element in the Shaker faith, separating these believers from those in many similar revivalistic groups. Ann Lee joined the Wardley's little society in 1758. But during the approximately nine years following her marriage to Abraham Standerin in 1762, she gradually developed her testimony against the evils of man's fallen, "carnal" nature and became the most influential member in the unstructured group. In the course of those years, she bore four children, all of whom died in infancy or early childhood. Ann's last delivery was exceptionally difficult, requiring the use of forceps. For hours afterward, she showed little sign of life.

After these traumatic experiences, Ann Lee became increasingly terrified and ambivalent about her impulses. She came to avoid her bed as if it were "made of embers," and when she did go to bed, sometimes she shook with such emotion that her husband was happy to leave her alone. At times she would pace the floor all night, trying to keep quiet in order to avoid stirring up her husband's concern and affections. At other times, unable to control herself, she would repeatedly cry aloud to God for redemption. And sometimes she feared to close her eyes lest she wake up in hell. Although naturally robust, she wasted away, becoming weak and emaciated. The period was one of extraordinary emotional turbulence for her.

During this traumatic period, this strong-willed woman gradually developed her distinctive faith, and in the Wardley's little group her testimony against carnal sin became more pointed. A series of overpowering visionary experiences in mid-1770 finally convinced Ann Lee that lust was indeed the root of all evil and corruption in the world—not only in religious matters, but also in economic, social, and political affairs as well. Only by renouncing all "carnal" desires (interpreting the term in its broadest sense) and by deciding to live a life of "virgin purity" could mankind be restored to God.[12]

The attraction of Ann Lee to the Wardleys' small religious society that their neighbors derisively nicknamed jumpers, shiverers, or Shaking Quakers was hardly accidental. One could argue, of course, that the highly emotional and unstructured religious activities of the Shakers provided an outlet for Ann Lee's inner struggles, as well as a supportive group in which she could deal with her problems. But even deeper than her sense that excessive sexual impulses were evil was her sense of the injustice of the role that sexual relations forced upon women. Ann Lee developed an intense concern to correct the imbalance that she perceived in the relations between the sexes. Even when this desire is only partially articulated, it seems to underlie her sense of mission and her concern to help both men and women be restored to God.

Revivalistic religion has always provided both men and women—but especially women—with greater outlets for self-expression and innovation than have the established churches. The Wardleys' little society was no exception. The Apostle Paul may have told women to keep silence in the churches, but in the early Shaker society Jane Wardley was given the honorary title "Mother" to indicate her spiritual role, and she became the effective leader of the group, and confession of sins was made to her. As Ann Lee developed her sense of religious mission and her overpowering conviction that lust was the root of human corruption, she gradually took over leadership from Jane Wardley and was in turn addressed by the group as Mother. Ann Lee's introduction of the belief in the necessity of celibacy for true religious life added a distinctive element to this society; celibacy separated the Shakers from the more common forms of revivalism from which they would otherwise have been virtually indistinguishable.

This band of some thirty Believers had little success in England. Some scholars have seen the Shakers as a by-product of nascent industrialism and the hardship of life in the early factory town of Manchester.[13] Available evidence, however, seems to make this interpretation less than fully convincing. To be sure, the grinding poverty and the evils of early industrialism may have contributed to the Shakers' sense that the old order was radically corrupt and about to be destroyed by God. But early accounts suggest that the most important influence on Ann Lee was her broader sense of religious malaise, and her reaction to her painful sexual experiences. In any case, even if early industrialism may have been related in a complex fashion to the origins of Shakerism, England during this stage of its industrialization did not provide a promising field for the growth of the group. This small band of Shaking Quakers did excite some harsh persecution in England, but, worse, they were generally ignored and attracted few members.

This became obvious to Ann Lee. In 1772, just two years after she effectively assumed control of the Wardleys' society, her associate James Whittaker had a powerful vision of a tree of life with ever-burning leaves in America, representing the Shaker Church that would be established there.[14] Ann Lee also became convinced that in America, a land of religious freedom and promise, her Church would grow and thrive. She was correct. In America her personal convictions could be translated into an organization that was highly successful, spiritually and temporally, given its inherent limitations.

Even if one assumes that economic forces were a major causal factor in Shaker development, the American Shakers may have owed their appeal far more to the stresses of pre-industrial commercial and agricultural development than to problems of the factory system and urbanization. For the most part, Shakers appear to have been small farmers, tradesmen, and handicraft workers, hardworking and independent. The special appeal of the Shaker reordering of male and female roles was related in complex ways to the larger religious and social strains of the young Republic.

Early Growth of the Shakers in America

The America to which a little band of English Shakers led by Mother Ann Lee emigrated in 1774 was a land whose religious, social, and political climates were in a curious way suited to the needs of this young faith. Religiously, America was still influenced by the aftermath of the Great

Awakening of the 1740s which had split the established churches in New England and throughout the colonies, resulting in an unprecedented era of revivals, doctrinal innovations, and divisions. New sects had been spawned, and eventually, a new kind of religious spirit would develop. Economically and socially, the years from the early 1700s had seen remarkable growth followed by stagnation and decline, leading to many strains and tensions between the old order and the new. And politically, America was on the eve of its Revolution and a disruptive war which would bring to birth a new Republic that would attempt to give voice to new ideals of man and society.[15]

When eight Shakers first arrived in New York City on August 6, 1774, however, they were anything but conscious of the many forces which would contribute to their eventual growth. In fact, the very survival of the group itself was in considerable doubt. The Shakers were poor, and had to separate temporarily to find individual employment. Ann Lee's husband, who had followed his wife to America, finally forced the issue of whether she would live with him in a normal marital relationship. Her adamant refusal, which led to their permanent break, must have been a heartrending experience for both of them. As Ann Lee said: "The man to whom I was married was very kind, according to his nature; he would have been willing to pass through a flaming fire for my sake, if I would but live in the flesh with him, which I refused to do."[16] Freed from her husband at last, Ann Lee joined her followers on some land they had purchased near Albany, New York. There for some six years, often discouraged, they eked out a bare living and continued to hope for the spread of their religious message.

The first major Shaker membership breakthrough came in 1780. As one of the small fires in the aftermath of the Revolutionary War, a small revival broke out in 1779 in New Lebanon, not far from the Shaker settlement at Niskeyuna. The leader of the revival was Joseph Meacham, a Freewill Baptist preacher from Enfield, Connecticut, whose father had been converted by Jonathan Edwards, a key figure in the earlier Great Awakening.[17] Feeling discouraged and looking for further light as the 1779 revival waned, Meacham and some of his followers approached this strange group of foreign religionists which was led by a woman, required celibacy, engaged in ecstatic religious services, and professed to be living "sinlessly" in daily obedience to the will of God. Greatly impressed by what he saw, Meacham converted to the Shakers. He brought with him many of his followers, who became the initial American nucleus of the Shaker Church.

The disorder, confusion, and disillusionment of the post–Revolutionary War period, like the aftermath of most wars in American history, was favorable to revivalism and the development of new religious movements.[18] The Shakers had unknowingly settled in an area where the disruption caused by the Revolutionary War was very great, and their early proselytizing ventures took them into similar areas of New England. As foreigners and pacifists, they were persecuted by local American authorities in 1780 for alleged disloyalty. In fact, however, many male Shakers had served in the Revolutionary War, as is indicated by the large number of Shakers who were entitled to receive war pensions.[19] The human coarseness brought out by that conflict must have been deeply disillusioning to many. Even though the Shakers were only beginning their development, they appeared to offer a committed, caring, and ultimately hopeful response to problems that did not seem capable of resolution at the normal political, economic, and social levels.

In addition to the precondition provided by a disordered environment, the appeal of the Shakers in this early phase was due to a number of positive factors within the movement. The leadership of Ann Lee and her early associates was the first great attraction of the Shakers. Even Ann Lee's critics agree that she was a capable, articulate, and dynamic woman, warm and loving to her followers, whom she called her "children." Ann's followers loved her so deeply that they came to believe that in her the spirit of God had been incarnated in female form, just as they believed that in Jesus the spirit of God had been incarnated in male form. Whether Ann Lee herself ever claimed such quasi-divinity is open to question. Her frequent ecstatic utterances, like those of many other early religious leaders, are open to such an interpretation, particularly when she talked about walking with Jesus as her Lord and Lover, or described herself as his Bride. Such statements were viewed by many people of this earlier age as examples of religious excess, of "enthusiasm." Today many people might view some of Ann Lee's utterances as symptomatic of mental disorder.

But if extreme emotionalism had been the primary characteristic of Ann Lee's personality and testimony, her appeal to the other capable and articulate individuals who helped her establish the Society would be hard to explain. Ann Lee was also a strightforward, down-to-earth woman who admonished her followers to put their "hands to work and their hearts to God." She told Believers to do their work as if it would "last a thousand years." When an overawed follower came to her, she told him: "Don't kneel to me. Kneel to God. I am but his servant."[20] And, expressing sentiments that many religious leaders must feel, she once confessed that she was afraid to go in to talk with young Believers because they assumed that whatever she said on any subject came directly from On High. Ann said in frustration that she never claimed to be omniscient in temporal matters. All she knew with certainty was that mankind's recovery to God could only be achieved by giving up all "carnal" desires and practices.[21]

Given the extremely liberal Shaker theology with its emphasis on the symbolic rather than the literal interpretation of Scripture, a different explanation of Ann Lee's alleged divinity is possible. The Shakers traced their belief in direct revelation to the Quaker stress on the immediacy of the spirit of God acting within each individual. Sophisticated Shakers in the early theological treatises appear, therefore, to have viewed Ann Lee as a particularly appealing ideal model. She was seen as embodying God's spirit in a form that was greater than, but not essentially different from, the form that was embodied in each human being. In any case, no matter how individual Believers may have viewed Ann Lee theologically, they expressed a deep and unquenchable love for her and they looked to her as a symbol of the mutual love which was expressed within their religious communities.[22]

Shaker revivalistic activities were a second factor attracting individuals to the Society. Then as now, such extraordinary actions attracted public curiosity and led to extremes of awe or of disbelief. Shaker revivalism might appear exceptional to twentieth-century Americans who are unacquainted with such phenomena, but it was almost indistinguishable from the revivalistic activities of similar groups in hundreds of different cultures throughout history. Among the types of behavior described in Shaker sources were shaking and trembling, shouting, leaping, singing, dancing, speaking in tongues, whirling, stamping, rolling on the floor or ground, crying out against sin and against carnal nature, and a wide variety of even more extraordinary ecstatic, trance, and possession phenomena that few would believe possible unless they had seen them with their own eyes.

Many of these activities seemed to be clearly beyond any conscious human agency, and thus were seen as manifestations of the supernatural. Disbelievers often attributed the manifestations to the Devil; Believers, on the other hand, saw the manifestations as a sign of God's continuing workings in human history and the existence of an authority going beyond the purely man-made. The old order was being shaken, both literally and metaphorically. Human authorities, whether religious or secular, no longer seemed to have any validity, so a return was made to primary and sometimes undifferentiated emotion within a supportive group. The expression of this emotion would lend supernatural sanction to the new order. As a primary Shaker doctrinal source stated, Believers "knew perfectly what those things meant, and felt, therein, the greatest possible order and harmony, it being both the gift and work of God for the time then present; and which bore the strongest evidence that the world was actually come to an end, (at least to those who were the subjects of it,) and the day of judgment commenced."[23]

If such highly individualistic revivalistic phenomena were to result in communal harmony, then institutional order eventually had to be given to the new understandings that had been achieved and validated through group emotional experiences. The propensity of those converted by revivals to "backslide" in the absence of continuing institutional supports is almost a cliché. Possibly the greatest appeal of the Shakers, therefore, lay in a third factor: their carefully planned group life. Eventually it would come to provide a total framework of religious, economic, and social meaning within which individuals could live their faith on a daily basis, not divorced from everyday experience. Such group life was not achieved immediately; rather, it was a gradual and progressive development throughout Shaker history. Even in the earliest phases, however, such total communal life appears to have been held forth as the ideal.[24]

During the early period of Shaker development this concern for establishing institutional order can most clearly be seen in the required confession of sins to elders by new members and old Believers as well. Such confession was a powerful community control mechanism. It was a major factor contributing to the establishment of an oligarchic and familial structure of community life. Required confession of sins by all new members was a means of acquainting Shaker leaders with the character and abilities of incoming individuals. Such confession also could have a therapeutic effect, much as psychotherapy and similar forms of personal counseling have today. Individuals who felt deeply the inadequacies of their earlier lives often received valuable personal counseling that helped them to rebuild their lives around a new center. As a continuing requirement, confession of all sins to designated elders provided an important means of allowing leadership to guide and shape the character of individuals and of the whole Society. And should an individual be tempted to apostatize and "tell all," he would be likely to have second thoughts if he knew that his own sins of omission and commission might well be fully aired in response.

Hostility toward the Shakers

Although some individuals were strongly attracted to the Shakers, many others were just as strongly repelled by the movement. Much of the hostility, brutality, and mobbing suffered by the Shakers during this early period can be understood as an inevitable response to any vigorous missionary effort that tends to interfere with the status quo. But more specifically, the Shakers stirred up hostility because of the outspokenness of their testimony, particularly against the flesh. This testimony frequently was blunt, specific, and coarse. "You are a filthy whore," Ann Lee is said to have rebuked a woman she judged prurient, apparently at first sight.[25] Early Believers, many of them in their teens or early twenties, felt that they were fighting the Devil with no holds barred. "The devil is a real being," Ann Lee declared, "as real as a bear. I know, for I have seen and fought with him."[26]

The Shaker attack on the evils of the flesh implicitly involved actions which their critics viewed as a frontal assault on marriage and all close family ties. For instance, the first Shaker pamphlet, printed in 1790, included a letter from James Whittaker, one of the original English leaders, to his parents. In the letter he excoriated his parents for their carnal propensities, effectively severing any further personal contact.[27] Many individuals, then and later, felt that the Shakers contributed to the breaking up of marriages, the separation of children from their parents, and similar family disharmony. In the nineteenth century, anti-Shaker individuals would attempt to get laws passed in several states to the effect that joining the Society was equivalent to a legal divorce.[28]

The Shakers vehemently denied any intent to break up marriages, and they fought all attempts to link them with such ideas. Usually Shakers tried to bring husbands and wives into their societies together. Nevertheless, there can be little doubt that, in order to establish the primary loyalty of Believers to the group and its larger ends, Shakers went to great lengths to sever all close personal relations between husband and wife within their societies. Then, too, some individuals undoubtedly joined the Shakers as a way out of unsatisfactory marital relationships, since divorces were not easy to obtain in many states. And definite efforts were made to separate children from their parents and rear them communally so that divided loyalties would not interfere with total community arrangements.

In 1853, some seventy-five years after Shaker origins in America, Hervey Elkins wrote a moving statement of his personal reasons for leaving the Shakers after fifteen years in their Senior Order. Elkins spoke with great appreciation of many features of Shaker life, but he sharply criticized "the regime which mildly separates man and wife, parent and child . . . and directs them all to seek a less local, and more general bond of union." "The Shakers are a people who rarely speak in passion, and we would think them sympathetic. But no pity, in their acts or measures, was ever shown to social or earthly ties."[29] In the no-holds-barred atmosphere of the early Shaker movement, the tendency toward breaking up personal relationships must have been even more intense.

In retrospect, such extreme control mechanisms might seem excessive. Nevertheless, these mechanisms were necessary if the Shakers were to maintain any internal cohesion in their celibate system. The Shakers never retreated to the wasteland or the desert to live in cloistered isolation, far from the world. Rather, most of the societies which were "gathered" in the late 1780s and early 1790s were only a few miles away from adjoining communities. Through extensive trading activities and through the continued influx of new members and departure of old ones, the Shakers came in continual contact with "the world." Furthermore, within their communities the Shakers opted to maintain the seemingly irreconcilable extremes of both separation and association of the sexes. Men and women lived together in "families" of 30 to 150 individuals under the same roof, though strictly separated in their activities.[30] Enormous tensions must inevitably have resulted, tensions that had to be dealt with by breaking down individual loyalties and reinforcing general communal commitment. This was particularly true in this early period when the concrete forms of community life had not yet been established.

A second reason for the hostility generated by the Shakers during this early expansive phase was the fact that they were led by a woman, a woman whom many Believers almost deified, even in this early period. Writing in 1780, the apostate Valentine Rathbun noted: "Some of them say, that the woman called the mother [Ann Lee], has the fullness of the God Head, bodily dwelling in her, and that she is the queen of heaven, Christ's wife: And that all God's elect must be born through her; yea, that Christ through her is born the second time."[31] By any standard, a statement of this type was "strong meat." Joseph Meacham's last question in 1780 before joining the Shakers was how a woman could govern or stand at the head of the Church when St. Paul had so explicitly forbidden it. Ann Lee's reply to Meacham (significantly conveyed through a male intermediary) was that "in the natural state, the man is first in the government of the family; but when the man is absent the government belongs to the woman."[32]

In this statement, Ann Lee was suggesting that the relations between the sexes were out of balance, both theologically and socially, and that she was attempting to restore that balance. Meacham accepted this response. But under his later leadership, many Shakers were themselves unwilling to accept his appointment of a female associate, Lucy Wright, to stand at the head of the newly created women's order and eventually of the whole Church. To many Believers, this was too radical a departure from existing religious and social practice. Tact as well as coercive pressure would be necessary to re-educate men and women to the new "gospel" relationship in the Shaker communities.[33]

If even loyal Shakers had difficulty accepting active female participation and leadership, then the extreme hostility of outsiders to this "unnatural" state of affairs is not surprising. Not only was Ann Lee who led the early movement a woman, and a woman widely reported as claiming to be virtually divine, but she was also attacking the basic female duty to "be fruitful and multiply." She seemed thereby to be attacking the validity of family life itself. To many, this seemed an outrageous and perverted state of affairs. Both in England and in America, Ann Lee was frequently accused of being a "witch"; she was seen not simply as misguided or deluded, but as deliberately malevolent.[34] Ann and her followers suffered the most degrading treatment at the hands of anti-Shaker mobs. Frequently she was whipped and beaten. And, in one particularly brutal incident, she was worked over by a bunch of toughs who ostensibly wished to find out if she were really a woman.[35] Such treatment contributed to the excessive zeal sometimes shown by the early Shakers, and helped bring about the premature deaths of all the most capable English leaders of the original movement.[36]

A third factor contributing to the hostility experienced by many early Shakers was the extreme character of many of their revivalistic activities during the period. Although an early convert such as Valentine Rathbun initially could be attracted by such phenomena, eventually he came to have second thoughts about some of the more bizarre involuntary behavior and argued that it was a sign of delusion rather than the influence of the divine.[37] The first Shaker printed statement that discussed the history of the early period in depth noted that, between 1780 and 1787, the peak of Shaker missionary activity, the extraordinary ecstatic and trance phenomena often "appeared to blind spectators like the most unaccountable confusion."[38] The widespread apostate claims that Ann Lee and her followers sometimes appeared drunk may be due, at least in part, to such behavior.[39] The way such phenomena appeared to observers could be widely different from its inner meaning to participants.

The extreme Shaker revival phenomena were heightened by the pressures of the missionary trips, persecution, and poverty of many early Believers. But such phenomena were primarily viewed, both by Shakers and by numerous apostates, as a continuing part of the conscious attempt to mortify and subdue their "fallen carnal natures." Although these phenomena were out of the ordinary, one must not automatically assume that such activities were a sign of individual or group pathology. Anthropological and cross-cultural studies of ecstatic, trance, and possession phenomena show such behaviors to be extremely common in all times and cultures. Such phenomena are by no means necessarily psychopathological, even if they do frequently grow out of disordered individual and social experiences.

According to William Sargant, who has spent the better part of a lifetime studying the physiology of such behaviors in various present-day groups, these activities may often serve a positive personal and social function. Sargant, who worked as a therapist with shell-shocked victims from World War II, found that normal individuals can often profit from the use of abreactive techniques. These techniques bring a distraught individual to a peak of tension followed by collapse within a controlled situation. Through abreaction an individual can overcome emotional blockages that prevent him from functioning normally, and can achieve personal reconstruction around a new emotional center. Interestingly enough, it appears that only schizophrenics and other severely disturbed individuals are unable to respond to such abreactive techniques.[40]

In a related analysis, William Samarin, a linguist who has studied glossolalia or "speaking in tongues," finds that although glossolalia is "linguistic nonsense," it can convey important emotions and it is not necessarily an indication of psychological maladjustment.[41] And I. M. Lewis, an anthropologist, argues that similar social factors tend to be connected with spirit possession and shamanism in other cultures. Such dissociational states frequently provide a means of expression for individuals such as women, the poor, and the young, who are outside normal institutional power structures.[42] In recent decades in this country, these activities have been associated with the hippie, drug, and rock music scene.[43]

Shaker and anti-Shaker accounts bear out many of these contemporary theoretical interpretations. Calvin Green, one of the most important early Shaker leaders and theological writers, spoke of the self-conscious use of ecstatic worship as a means of sublimating sexual impulses:

> There is evidently no labor which so fully absorbs all the faculties of soul and body, as real spiritual devotion & energetic exercise in sacred worship. Therefore there is no operation that has so much effect to mortify & weaken the power of the flesh and energize the soul with the life of the heavenly spirit; as to devote all faculties & life powers under the lead of the spirit & controled [sic] by united open order—In the worship of God. And for this purpose was it established by our blessed Mother [Ann Lee] & spiritual parents. And when the soul is baptized into its life it is a spiritual recreation to all the feelings of soul & body; an enjoyment far superior to any natural recreation, or carnal pleasure—In no earthly pursuit whatever have I ever experienced such delightful feelings or such as would bear any real comparison to what I have felt in sacred devotion.[44]

In their services, Ann Lee is reported to have told brethren and sisters to let themselves go in the spirit: "Be joyful! Joy away! Rejoice in the

God of your salvation."[45] Though the resultant behavior might have appeared bizarre externally, to participants the activities felt good and gave psychic release. Many Believers reported that they felt an ecstatic oneness with each other in a lively meeting of worship.

The accounts of apostates, however, provide the most detailed analyses of the way in which the Shakers utilized ecstatic religious activities both to sublimate troublesome sexual impulses and to transform the character of Believers. In a fair and essentially descriptive account printed in 1782, Amos Taylor observed that "the human frame and construction is such that great effects may be produced merely by, as it were, a mechanical operation on the nerves."[46] He described some of the Shaker ecstatic dancing in which he had participated, which involved "springing from the house floor about four inches up and down, both in the men's and women's apartment, moving about as thick as they can crowd, with extraordinary transport, singing sometimes one at a time, and sometimes more than one, making a perfect charm."[47] Taylor believed that when such activities were prolonged, they constituted a form of sublimation and could easily account for the numerous strange and seemingly supernatural phenomena experienced in Shaker worship.

More important, Taylor described the moral transformation that the total Shaker program could provide:

> However mysterious it may seem, numberless instances can be produced where lyars, swearers, drunkards, extortioners, unclean, unjust, covetous persons, proud, self-willed, heady, high minded, &c. at least many of these characters have all been brought down to confess, and absolutely for a time to leave their ordinary and common vices.[48]

In place of such vices, individuals became devoted to the Shaker faith, which Taylor characterized unfavorably as "one general spirit of downright idolatry" because of their veneration of Ann Lee.

Such character reorientation is one of the most important features of any successful religious movement. Even though the adoption of their distinctive celibacy requirement created many new problems for Believers, the Shakers, like many other revivalistic groups, provided many adherents with a new and more satisfying center around which to organize their lives.

Organizing the Movement

Although Ann Lee and the English Shakers provided the initial impetus for the new religious movement, the actual organization of the scattered groups of Believers into functioning celibate communities was conducted primarily under the American leaders, particularly Joseph Meacham and Lucy Wright. Exhaustion from the persecutions and pressures they had suffered contributed to the premature deaths of Mother Ann and her brother William in 1784, and of James Whittaker, the other capable English leader, in 1787. Before his death, Whittaker, more diplomatic and more organizationally minded than Mother Ann or William, recognized the necessity of gathering the scattered groups of Believers into a united Church order.

Only under Joseph Meacham's leadership, however, did the move from a primarily charismatic to a more routinized organization begin in earnest. To give temporal organizational support to Shaker religious and celibate ideals, Meacham oversaw the establishment of a dual male and female governmental structure which was buttressed by a communistic joint economic order. The shift from English to American leadership was illustrated by the decision to make New Lebanon the first "gathered" Shaker community, the model upon which all subsequent communities would be patterned. New Lebanon was chosen in preference either to Niskeyuna (later called Watervliet), the first headquarters of the English Shakers, or to Harvard (Village), Massachusetts, which Mother Ann had apparently hoped to make her base of operations.[49] Thus, the basic Shaker communal organization which will be described below is properly seen primarily as an American rather than an imported system.

The precise factors which influenced the organizational planning of the new Shaker communities cannot be clearly identified. Probably many features of the new system reflect a pragmatic response to certain characteristic problems which any celibate group would have to face. Nevertheless, the striking similarities between Shaker structures and Catholic dual monastic organization raise the question of whether monastic or other similar communal traditions might have been used as models. Extant literature does not permit any reliable answer to this question. However, the fact that Meacham, Wright, and the American leaders of the Shakers were well educated for their time makes it possible that some conscious borrowing from earlier traditions may have occurred. Certainly the Christian communism described in Acts 2:44–45, which speaks of the early Christians holding "all things common," would always be a continuing ideal for the Shakers.

Joseph Meacham's first major action on acceding to the leadership of the scattered bands of Believers in Christ's Second Appearing, was to begin—carefully, but firmly and decisively—to establish a governmental form and community structure that would make women equal to men at all levels of the Society.[50] Although Mother Ann had attempted to give women a prominent role in her Society, after her death there was a tendency to drift back toward male dominance in the leadership of the group. Meacham sought to counter this tendency. He realized that "there must be a visible parental order to lead the visible spiritual family of Christ," in short, that women must be encouraged to participate fully in the life of the Church community.

To this end, Meacham appointed Lucy Wright as his co-equal to help to establish a women's order of the Shakers that would allow them strict equality with men in their respective spheres and activities. This was a revolutionary departure, "contrary to all earlier rules and views of ecclesiastical Government in the so called Christian world," and many Shakers opposed the move. Shakers may have followed and venerated the charismatic leadership of Mother Ann Lee, but they looked upon the institutionalization of a new authority relationship between the sexes as another matter. In fact, Joseph Meacham's efforts to increase female participation were so controversial that he found it necessary to present by "revelation" his new ecclesiastical organization and Lucy Wright's appointment. With Meacham's encouragement, Childs Hamlin, a moving singer and an impressively spiritual man, declared that "the Order of Mother in Church relation was revealed to him, & that Lucy Wright was the female" prepared by God to assume that role.

Even with this apparent divine sanction, establishment of the new dual order required nearly ten years of strenuous efforts in reeducating Believers. Getting the women to assume a more active role was especially difficult. Mother Lucy worked tirelessly to prepare the sisters to "come forward in their proper sphere, & take their share of the burdens and toils in all needful labors & sufferings, unitedly with their Brethren, as well as to be leaders according to their order in every Department of the Church." Lucy served as a model of the capable, committed woman that the Shakers were laboring to produce. But opposition still remained strong. "In no preceding Dispensation had the Order of spiritual Mother been gained; hence the female portion of humanity never had its due share in the organization & Government of Ecclesiastical Institutions." Quite probably, the so-called "great apostasy" which began in the Shaker orders shortly before Joseph Meacham's death in 1796 was related in part to opposition to the idea of a woman, Lucy Wright, leading the Church.

Despite the many problems, the basic order of the Shaker Church gradually became fully established during this period.[51] This overall structure would remain largely unchanged throughout the history of the group. Supreme authority was vested in the head Ministry at New Lebanon, usually four in number, representing male and female, two of each sex. The head figure of this Ministry had the authority, tempered by the sentiments of the membership, to appoint or replace the other three members of the Ministry, and with them, all the leadership of the various Shaker communities. This was a hierarchical and oligarchic system that critics frequently attacked as "papist," but it worked with great effectiveness throughout most of Shaker history. In more than two hundred years in America, the Shakers have never experienced a successful schism.

As previously indicated, each Shaker settlement was divided into smaller community groups called "families." These families included both men and women who lived under the same roof but were strictly separated in their activities. Each family was relatively self-sufficient, both spiritually and economically. Just as each larger Shaker settlement site had its own Ministry appointed from New Lebanon, so each family ideally had two elders and eldresses to take care of spiritual affairs and two deacons and deaconesses to manage the temporal business. This pattern would prevail throughout all levels of the Society after the initial period of organization: all authority was hierarchical, but on each level, men and women shared equal responsibility in the work of regeneration.

Shaker celibacy made possible this remarkable system which gave women a degree of equality in leadership that even the most militant socialist advocates of women's rights were unable or unwilling to achieve in practice.[52] Celibacy, when combined with communal childrearing practices for the children of individuals joining the Shakers, as well as orphans adopted by the Society, freed Shaker women for an active role in Church leadership at all levels. Shakers justified their arrangements theologically by observing that St. Paul's admonitions to wives to be subject to their husbands, keep silence in the Church, etc., did not apply to women who had given up earthly marriage and were living a life of "virgin purity." In effect, such women were "married to Christ." Their loyalty was directly to God, or, in practice, to the larger community "families" in which the divine pattern was being realized on earth. Freed from the entanglements of the world, Believers could devote themselves fully to God, for, as St. Paul had also said, there is "neither male nor female in the Lord."

In addition to establishing this radical departure from traditional ecclesiastical government, the Shakers under Meacham and Wright set up a cooperative, communistic form of economic organization to buttress their religious ideals. A joint united interest in all things had been an implicit goal under Mother Ann and the English leaders. Consecration of all temporal holdings to the service of the new Church had occurred to some extent, particularly under Whittaker's leadership, as the devotees came together in support of the new faith.

Not until Joseph Meacham took charge, however, was the "gathering" of Shaker Believers into a temporal as well as spiritual union really begun in earnest. Meacham acceded to Shaker leadership and began his organizational work in 1787. Appropriately, that was the same year in which the United States Constitution was signed and order began to be reestablished in the young Republic as well. Between this date and his death in 1796, Meacham set up eleven functioning Shaker centers, composed of numerous smaller "families," in New York and New England. These centers embodied the basic economic forms that would allow the Shaker economic system to function highly successfully throughout the better part of the two succeeding centuries of Shaker life in America.[53]

The process by which new economic institutions and new economic ideals were created by the Shakers has been the subject of considerable popular and scholarly curiosity. Several sophisticated scholarly studies have appeared. Of these, an outstanding example is Edward Deming Andrews's *The Community Industries of the Shakers,* a careful analysis of the central New Lebanon Shaker community. Those desiring a fuller knowledge of Shaker economic development can consult such studies.[54] Here, therefore, only a summary of some of the most important aspects of the new communal organization will be provided, particularly insofar as it relates to Shaker sexual and marital reorganization.

Shaker celibacy, with its subordination of individual sexual life to the larger interests of the community, made possible an equalization of male and female participation in the ecclesiastical system. In addition, celibacy contributed to the success of a communistic system of economic organization in which the good of the individual was subordinated to that of the collectivity. Perhaps because of the desperate poverty from which the English Shakers had come, an emphasis on hard work and economic success had always been an important concern of Believers. They sought to obey Mother Ann's admonition to "put their hands to work and their hearts to God." Believers no longer looked upon productive work as part of the curse pronounced upon Adam. Rather they sought to reintegrate economic and religious life into a harmonious whole, thereby overcoming the exploitative economic individualism that followed the Revolutionary War. By removing the competing demands inherent in separate nuclear family arrangements, the Shakers were able to devote their entire effort to establishing their ideal of the Kingdom of Heaven on earth.

Many Shaker communities were gathered around the holdings consecrated to the group by prosperous small farmers who became Believers. Often these communities were called by the names of the original owners, such as Rufus Clark's family, Israel Talcott's family, and so forth. Other farms were purchased by pooling the resources of a number of Believers. Initially, oral agreements were made by those who consecrated their property to the "joint united interest." However, because of litigation by apostates seeking to reclaim consecrated property, after 1795 written covenants were drawn up to avoid disruption of Church holdings. Even before the formal government of the various Shaker centers had been set up, the economic organization of the Society began to develop.

Far from stifling economic initiative, the "joint united interest" set up by the Shakers appears to have been associated with a high level of economic innovation and commitment. Decentralized economic action was carried out by the various Shaker communities. The basic economic unit was the single Shaker "family" of as many as a hundred or more individuals working cooperatively. Thus the community "family" rather than the nuclear "family" became the productive economic unit. Sometimes several families would unite in an industry or business venture, or maintain a common store or a clearing house for farm or manufactured items. Throughout New York and New England, Shaker businessmen attracted an extensive network of contacts because of the consistently high quality of the many Shaker products. And individual Shakers developed an enormous number of ingenious inventions and improvements that were put to good use in their communities.

Edward Deming Andrews notes that Shaker farm enterprises were organized to operate with an almost military precision, with a clear division of labor in which each member had his or her appointed task at an appointed time. "In these early group activities of the Shakers one recognizes a formative chapter in large scale or 'mass production' enterprise, an anticipation of the corporate businesses which rose later in the machine age in this country."[55] Thus, the Shakers' "amazingly productive economic system" was by no means out of touch with larger American economic developments. Though its response to nascent industrialism was unusual, the Shaker Church contributed in many ways to the successful adjustment of Believers to modern economic realities, while mitigating much of the harshness of the competitive and individualistic economic order that was then developing.

Despite their economic progressiveness and their practice of equality for women in the government of the Society, the Shakers left almost totally unchanged the basic economic division of labor between the sexes that prevailed in America at that time. Shaker women worked in kitchen and dairy industries, in weaving and manufacture of cloth, and in a variety of other types of basically indoor activities characteristically pursued by women of the period. And Shaker men typically were involved in outdoor farm labor in heavy agriculture, as well as in blacksmithing, tanning, and the like. The basic American household division of labor in the nuclear family therefore remained in force in the Shaker communities. Only women's disabilities that were connected with their sexual function in childbearing and childrearing were eliminated.[56]

Why did the Shakers maintain this economic division between the sexes while breaking down many other important divisions in organizational and religious life? Apparently no human society of which we have record has assigned identical productive functions to men and women, although what is considered to be a man's or a woman's occupation has varied widely in different times and cultures. After putting their major efforts into reorganizing other aspects of life, the Shakers apparently did not feel the need to modify the typical American division of labor. This may have been because Shakers saw neither male nor female occupations as being inherently "superior." Men's work and women's work were equal in importance before God. Nevertheless, Shaker women's work was somewhat less varied and interesting than men's work, and this may have caused some dissatisfaction. The testimony of numerous visitors was that in general Shaker women looked less healthy than Shaker men and engaged in more extreme religious activities.[57] Possibly this was related to frustrations arising from the more limiting occupations pursued by Shaker sisters.

Though the Shakers eliminated or minimized differences between the sexes that were explicitly connected with sexual intercourse, reproduction, and childrearing, they firmly maintained that sexual distinctions remained both on earth and in heaven. Such differences could hardly be done away with, for even God was composed of a union of male and female attributes—even God was sexual, a fusion of complementary opposites. Interestingly, groups such as the Oneida Perfectionists and Mormons, in which men were formally dominant, did more to break down the typical American occupational division of labor than did the Shakers, who placed such stress on the equality of men and women in the Church and before God.

Tensions of Transition

The introduction of celibacy, the radical modification of traditional authority relations between the sexes, and the development of a communistic economic system could hardly have been achieved without considerable stresses in the newly developing Shaker communities. Shaker sources admit that there were errors and excesses under both the English and the American leadership. Between 1780 and 1785, there were a number of highly emotional meetings, lasting night and day, the noise of which could occasionally be heard from as far away as two miles.[58] There were thunderings against carnal nature, shaking and trembling, weeping, speaking in tongues, singing, dancing, leaping, shouting, and a variety of seemingly "supernatural" effects.

During the early part of the period from about 1785 to 1797, the revivalistic worship services and attempts to mortify carnal nature became even more intense. Throughout this period, the Shakers almost completely discontinued active proselytizing and shut themselves off from the world in an attempt to establish and regulate their new communal order. Shaker sources admit that the "zeal without knowledge" of some Believers, many of whom were still teenagers, resulted in some actions which the Society would prefer to forget.[59] Instead, the Shakers tried to stress the generally positive consequences of the activities: "Though men of the world have been obliged to acknowledge that the visible fruits [of Shakerism] were good, yet the real internal work from which those fruits were produced, was wholly hid from their eyes."[60]

Shaker sources preferred not to talk about the more extreme physical manifestations attendant upon this "internal work," and little manuscript material bearing on these events survives from the period. The range of activities in which these early Shakers engaged is suggested, however, in the accounts of individuals who left the Society. By far the best of the accounts of this troubled period is the fair, analytical, and meticulously detailed report of the ex-Shaker Thomas Brown.[61] Brown had been a Quaker, but joined the Shakers in 1798 after their revivalistic activities had largely subsided. Both sensitive and curious, Brown investigated almost every aspect of Shaker life for nearly a decade, recording his conversations with Shaker leaders in detail soon after they occurred and explaining the bases for his inferences. Brown's account is a participant-observer report of exceptional quality and scope that contemporary social scientists would be hard pressed to surpass.

According to Brown, Shaker revivalistic tensions peaked between the late 1780s and about 1792–93, not coincidentally the period when the Northeastern Shaker communities were becoming established:

> The exercises of those who were gathering into a family, united interest and order, were extreme beyond conception. They conceived that by the power of God they could labour completely out of their natural instinct implanted in mankind for the purpose of procreation. . . . Imagination was exhausted by inventing, and nature tormented in executing this arduous work. They often danced with vehemence through the greatest part of the night, and then instead of reposing their weary bodies upon a bed, they would by way of further penance, lie down upon the floor on chains, ropes, sticks, in every humiliating and mortifying posture they could devise![62]

As part of such mortifications, according to Brown's careful evaluation of the evidence, some individuals stripped and danced naked to kill their pride. Despite the suppositions of some overly imaginative outsiders, these actions were totally puritanical in conception and effect. The many accounts of alleged licentiousness and debauchery practiced in this period were wholly without foundation. "A few solitary instances of sexual intercourse might be mentioned; but the parties were shut out of union and not received again without confessions and professions of repentence and contrition similar as in other churches."[63]

The more extreme physical manifestations may have been an inevitable concomitant of this troubled transition into new forms, but such behaviors were not desired by the more mature Believers. Joseph Meacham and Lucy Wright, in particular, sought to lead the young Society beyond such extreme activities into a new order. During the transition phase when neither the old order nor the as-yet-unborn new state could provide the basis of authority, the extraordinary manifestations had been essential. As an important early Shaker work noted:

> Divine miracles have generally attended the ushering in of new and extraordinary dispensations of God to a dark and benighted world; because they carry to the minds of the lost children of men, the strongest evidence of the sacred messenger's divine authority. But when that divine authority is once established in the hearts of honest believers, a continuance of outward miracles, for that purpose, is no longer necessary.[64]

In other words, when the basis for the new religious and social order had become securely established in the minds and hearts of Believers, the extreme charismatic gifts and informal leadership could give way to a calmer, more restrained inward faith expressed through daily life under the new system. In his summary of the overall process of transformation, the Shaker leader Calvin Green suggested that the Shaker experience was analogous to that of other Americans of the period: "The first leaders of the Society may be compared to people going into a new country, and settling in the wilderness, where the first object is to cut and clear the land, and burn the rubbish, before the ground can be suitably prepared for cultivation." This difficult process is accompanied by vigorous activity, by much noise, bustle, and confusion. "But when the land is sufficiently cleared, and the rubbish consumed, and the wild vermin have all retreated, and the careful husbandman has securely fenced his field, he can go on to prepare and cultivate his ground in peace. . . . "[65]

Although ecstatic phenomena became less frequent with the reestablishment of order, such phenomena would return with renewed force throughout Shaker history at times of crisis when individuals sought once again to find ultimate sanction for a religious and social way of life that was being called into question.

The Second Wave of Expansion

By 1800 the Shakers in the Northeastern communities had passed through both an initial charismatic phase and a period of institutional organization. Religious unity, internal tranquility, and economic prosperity appeared to have been achieved. Rather than relaxing at this point, however, the Shakers initiated a third phase in their development. A major missionary venture into the Ohio Valley was begun in an attempt to establish new Shaker communities in the area affected by the Kentucky Revival. Between 1805 and 1820, seven new Shaker community sites were established and began to thrive in Ohio, Kentucky, and Indiana. By 1822 there were some four thousand Shakers in all—nearly half of them in the Midwestern communities.[66]

The process of expansion and transformation in this second wave of Shaker settlement was very similar to the first. This development is clearly delineated in *The Kentucky Revival,* the first book ever printed by the Shakers.[67] This book, published in 1807, was written by Richard McNemar, a prominent revivalist preacher who, after converting to the Shakers, was instrumental in organizing most of their Midwestern communities. He was a classical scholar and a powerful debater with a penetrating intellect. His brilliant analysis of the course of the Kentucky Revival examines from a religious perspective the type of transition phenomena described by Victor Turner from a secular vantage point, in strikingly similar terms, as a period of "liminality and communitas."[68]

McNemar describes the pervasive sense of religious and social malaise that preceded the revival. He shows the various ways in which revivalism operated to break down existing institutional and intellectual frameworks. And he analyzes the powerful emotional forces that were released as all distinctions of age, sex, and social rank were dissolved in the intense comradeship of the united worship of God. Yet this sense of the spiritual immediacy, freshness, and awesomeness of direct emotional experience also led to great fragmentation and excess. Different individuals found different and often contradictory messages in the Scriptures. A "hot spiritual war" ensued. Disillusionment was the inevitable result.

Into this field that had been burned over by the fires of revivalism came three of the Shakers' ablest missionaries, Benjamin Seth Youngs, Issachar Bates, and John Meacham. Typically working with individuals or small, receptive groups, these men emphasized the inadequacy of individual Bible interpretation alone as the basis for religious and social truth. Instead, individuals were told that a new communal order and basis of authority were necessary for a holy life. Believers must submit themselves to the authority of the new dispensation as mediated by the

Shaker elders. These elders were representatives of the true Church of Christ "in whom the spirit of truth continually abides." Thus "all who are taught in this manner are strictly and properly *taught of God;* and obeying what they are taught they yield obedience to *Christ."*[69]

In this as in other cases, the Shakers were requiring that their adherents subordinate themselves to a new Church-type authority and communal framework of meaning. Celibacy was their most distinctive control mechanism, setting the Shakers apart from similar revivalistic groups. Celibacy called for a unique depth of commitment and ensured that, both in theory and in practice, the Shaker kingdom could not be of this world. The Shakers were attempting to institutionalize a spirit which can never be fully institutionalized, to create what they hoped would be, in effect, a "continuing revolution."

Well aware of the paradoxical nature of their position, the Shakers nevertheless were able, for a time at least, to achieve a balance between the freshness of individual inspiration and the necessary constraints of a functioning social order. For purposes of this analysis, the chief importance of the Kentucky Revival and the development of Midwestern Shakerism lies in the stimulus it provided for the establishment of Shaker printing. In the earliest charismatic and organizational phases of development, little need was felt for a Shaker literature, since fundamental beliefs could be passed on orally and modified as the experience of the group demanded. By the time of the Midwestern expansion, however, the effects of time and distance made written formulation of beliefs and practices desirable to supplement the still-necessary personal contacts and continuing openness to changing realities.

This was the background of the first great flowering of Shaker publication, a rich outpouring of histories, doctrinal and polemical works, hymnals, and other writings. These were the first mature fruits of Shaker writing and they provide important information on the attitudes of articulate leadership.[70] McNemar's *Kentucky Revival,* first published in 1807 in Cincinnati, Ohio, was the first of the accounts. This book was followed in 1808, at Lebanon, Ohio, by Benjamin Seth Youngs's *Testimony of Christ's Second Appearing.* This was the first and most important Shaker doctrinal work, sometimes called the Shaker "Bible." Thomas Jefferson is said to have praised the book in a letter to Youngs as the best ecclesiastical history that had ever been written.[71]

In 1812, *Millennial Praises,* the first of many Shaker printed hymnals, appeared. It provided an indication of the popular concerns of Shaker membership at the time, and showed that the emphasis on sexual equality was a major theme in popular Shakerism, a theme closely connected with the concern for celibacy. In 1816, a remarkably straightforward and detailed account providing *Testimonies of the Life, Character, Revelations, and Doctrines of Our Ever Blessed Mother Ann Lee,* sometimes called "the secret book of the Elders," was published in an extremely limited edition for the sole reference of the leadership. And in 1818, John Dunlavy's *Manifesto,* the second great Shaker doctrinal work called forth by the Kentucky Revival, was first printed at Pleasant Hill, Kentucky.

These works provide valuable insights into Shaker attitudes toward celibacy and the relations between the sexes, but perhaps the best summation and defense of Shaker sexual and marital beliefs is found in *A Summary View of the Millennial Church* by Calvin Green and Seth Y. Wells. First published in 1823, it is the third and most readable of the early Shaker doctrinal works. Throughout the nineteenth century, the *Millennial Church* served as a primary basis for numerous pamphlet defenses of celibacy, some of which used almost verbatim extracts from the work. The account, therefore, can be used to illustrate both the basic rationale behind Shaker celibacy and the relationship of such beliefs to larger nineteenth-century American social currents.[72]

Like other Shaker writers, Green and Wells emphasized that in the original Adamic state, human sexuality and the faculty of generation arising from it was a positive force, part of the original creation of God which he had pronounced "very good." It was "as simple and innocent, in itself, as the faculty of eating and drinking." But man's transgression had corrupted the very fountainhead of life itself; the human generative function had become subordinate to the inordinate demands of lust. The Shakers interpreted the story of the Garden of Eden in a symbolic, not a literal sense. They believed that although disobedience to a command of God was the *cause* of man's fall, the specific *act* of disobedience was one of carnal intercourse engaged in out of its proper time and season.

In support of this thesis concerning the origin of human suffering, Green and Wells look at the curse pronounced upon the first woman: "I will greatly multiply thy sorrow and thy conception; in sorrow shalt thou bring forth children; and thy desire shall be to thy husband, and he shall rule over thee." Green and Wells argue that this curse placed by God upon Eve must have been in response to the nature of the transgression. That transgression, therefore, must have been a sexual one. This curse of excessive sexual demands upon the woman is seen as a great social problem in antebellum America as well:

> This same curse has been more or less felt by the fallen daughters of Eve to this day. . . . Thus the woman is not only subjected to the pains and sorrows of childbirth, but even in her conception, she becomes subject to the libidinous passions of her husband; . . . This slavish subjection is often carried to such a shocking extent,

that many females have suffered an unnatural and premature death, in consequence of the unseasonable and excessive indulgence of this passion in the man. Thousands there are, no doubt, who are able to bear sorrowful testimony to the truth of this remark.[73]

The marriage ceremony does not alleviate this problem, for lust corrupts even the marriage bond. Man, unlike other animals, has no specific period of the year during which he engages in sexual intercourse. Rather, he indulges this passion at his whim, inside or outside marriage, irrespective of the law of nature and his desire for progeny. As a result, "the lawless passion of lust knows no bounds, is confined to no limits, and subject to no laws." Green and Wells bitterly ask why, if sexual intercourse is such a good thing, those pious divines who try to sanctify the act by a marriage ceremony should refuse to ask their parishioners to do it in public before their very eyes! Shame, they say, is an inseparable part of the act, proof that it is a work of darkness. The inability to establish order in the process of generation is both a symbol and a cause of all other types of social disorder. If sexual behavior could be properly regulated, all other social problems could be brought under control as well.

This analysis, only briefly indicated here, provides interesting perspectives on the tensions between the sexes facing many antebellum Americans. Recent research suggests that, despite the general optimism and expansiveness of the period, a number of special sexual problems may have existed during the years before the Civil War, especially for women. For whatever reasons, it seems indisputable that the desire for smaller families had begun well before the Civil War. In the absence of effective artificial means of birth control (other than abortion), self-control or repression was widely advocated as a means of avoiding the evils of excessive procreation. The Shakers, doubting that such a half-way approach could ever really handle the problem, went one step further than their contemporaries. They advocated eliminating physical connection between the sexes altogether, in effect a rather drastic form of birth control.

But in their practice of celibacy, the Shakers were engaged in considerably more than simply an early faltering attempt at birth control. Had their program been only of this character, it could justly be dismissed as an eccentric attempt to counteract the still-prevalent emphasis on having large families. From the Shaker viewpoint, mankind's recovery to God was a positive process involving total commitment to an ideal and way of life. They felt that the depth of religious commitment which they sought was impossible unless men and women could be freed from the inevitable distractions associated with sexual relations and the nuclear family. Thus, with the possible exception of the earliest period, the Shakers never seriously expected that everyone would join their movement. They recognized the validity of normal procreative life, insofar as it was well lived, but felt that they were living according to a higher standard.[74]

Shaker Membership: Impressionistic Perspectives

What kinds of people were attracted to the Shakers? What concerns and social backgrounds were associated with joining this unusual communal society? Some of the reasons for Shaker appeal have been described in the preceding historical account. This section will further suggest the complex attraction of the Shakers by using the biographical and autobiographical accounts of articulate men and women who became Believers.[75] To supplement this impressionistic picture, a second section will present preliminary findings on the social origins of one Shaker community, the New Lebanon Second Family from 1830 to 1896. By using both autobiographical and group records, a more accurate picture of the characteristics of Shaker membership may be developed.

The complex motives which could lead an individual to join the Shakers are vividly illustrated by the experience of Issachar Bates.[76] Born in 1758 in Hingham, Massachusetts, Bates was married in 1778 to Lovina Maynard from Gary (Gerry?), Massachusetts, where he was then living. By the time he joined the Shakers in 1801, he and his wife had had eleven children, nine of whom were still alive. Following Bates's marriage, he had bought a small farm, but, unable to support his rapidly increasing family on it, he turned to mercantile speculation in a variety of farm products. Eventually his trading ventures failed, in part because of the corruption of his agent, and Bates lost most of his goods. Such economic reverses were not unusual in the rapidly expanding and fluctuating American economy between the Revolutionary and Civil Wars.

In 1795 when he was thirty-seven and had had seven children, Bates began to be afraid of what would happen to his children, both spiritually and materially. His response was to join the Baptists and become a lay preacher. During the next six years, however, he continued to experience extreme emotional swings and remained profoundly dissatisfied with his life. Distraught over his spiritual and material condition, Bates sought to confess his "secret sins" and feelings about the "works of the flesh" to a Baptist elder. The elder, however, refused to hear him for fear that it would lead to the breakup of Bates's family. Instead, he admonished Bates to continue to follow the command of God to "be fruitful and multiply." Bates's wife Lovina likewise refused to listen to his doubts. She ran out of the room when he tried to bring up his anxieties about having more children.

At this point, Bates began to cast around for help, but he got little response from friends when he tried to talk with them about his disillusionment with the works of the flesh, bearing arms, taking oaths, and the snares of superficial worldly concerns. Finally, after four additional children, Bates turned to the Shakers, to whom he was increasingly attracted, to see if they would give his concerns and problems a serious hearing. After he and a Shaker elder shared a lengthy discussion of their mutual concerns, Bates decided to join the Society. Not surprisingly, Bates's whole family militantly opposed this decision at first. Eventually, however, all but his two eldest sons joined the Watervliet Shaker community with Bates. He, in turn, went on to distinguish himself in a missionary career during which he covered some 38,000 miles, largely on foot, and played an important role in helping to start the Midwestern Shaker communities.

Bates's concerns were characteristic of many individuals who joined the Shakers, although he was exceptional in the degree to which he consciously articulated his motives. As the New Lebanon and Sodus Bay membership records show, many people entered the Shaker societies (and many left as well) in family units, sometimes quite large ones. Rearing a large family could be spiritually and physically taxing for both men and women, particularly given the uncertainties of religious and social life in the period. The Shakers offered their adherents a total context of functioning spiritual and temporal community life, and they were willing to deal frankly and honestly with personal problems that many of their contemporaries tried to ignore.

Issachar Bates was middle-aged and had a considerable family when he joined the Shakers, but the biographical sketches and membership records in the collection at the Western Reserve Historical Society show that a majority of individuals joined the Shakers either as children or during adolescence or young adulthood. A sense of uncertainty concerning the general direction and significance of their lives, and not simply sexual confusion or dissatisfaction, appears to have been the conscious concern of most of these people. The Shakers were one of a number of groups to which such individuals might turn to find solutions to their inner uncertainties. Lucy Brown, who joined the Shakers when she was eighteen, shows some of the characteristics of many of these people. Lucy had experienced a relatively satisfying family life, but felt a certain emptiness and uneasiness about her life's direction, as well as a hunger for something more than what her parents and immediate environment could offer her. She was deeply impressed when she visited a nearby Shaker community. In joining the Shakers she was, in effect, stepping out on her own and asserting her individuality and freedom from her parents (much the same reason why many people marry). Although Lucy Brown does not mention any particular family problems, economic difficulties, or sexual anxieties, factors of this sort are frequently described in other accounts as a part of the reason that individuals were attracted to the Shakers.[77]

Significant numbers of young married couples also joined the Shakers. The experience of Lucy Wright and Elizur Goodrich is one such case.[78] Wright, who came from a well-to-do and socially prominent family in Pittsfield, Massachusetts, was married at nineteen to Elizur Goodrich, nine years her senior. They both had a very lofty and idealized conception of marriage and lived together "uncommonly continent" for several months before being converted in the small New Lebanon revival of 1779. Elizur went further and joined the Shakers. After a great deal of resistance, Lucy also joined the Society, but a wide range of rather harsh methods had to be used to wean her affections away from her husband. Elizur finally was sent out preaching, while Lucy remained at Watervliet and, like Mother Ann, reverted to her maiden name. At Watervliet, Lucy had free scope to develop her considerable talents and to embark on the religious career that eventually made her a leader and model for the women in the Society.

The experience of John Lyon of the Shaker community at Enfield, New Hampshire, shows how an individual who was reared by the Shakers might undergo powerful inner experiences which would convince him to stay.[79] Lyon was exceptional, for the majority of those who grew up in the Society eventually left the group, and few recorded conversion experiences as vivid as his. In 1795 when he was about fourteen, Lyon was increasingly disturbed by his developing sexual impulses which he viewed as extremely sinful. He confessed repeatedly to the elders, and generally he tried to follow their advice, but inwardly he was deeply divided and doubted what they told him. In 1802, when he was twenty-one, Lyon had a powerful visionary conversion experience which he describes with remarkable insight. In great inner turmoil, he was alone at work, when "suddenly I was taken from all sense of the things of time . . . apparently the whole heavens were filled, seeming to roll backward and forward, and in every direction." He saw a thin vertical streak of light toward which he walked at the command of a voice, but suddenly he stood next to a great gulf and became "enveloped in a horrible darkness." There was nothing beneath his feet; he was unable to move in any direction, and was in great distress, utterly lost and terrified.

Eventually Lyon discovered that by keeping his eyes firmly fixed on the thin ray of light, he was able to move forward safely through the unknown. But every time he lost his concentration on the light, he was overwhelmed in blackness and terror again. Finally he decided to ask for help. He was instructed in obedience and vowed in his heart that if he survived the experience, he would never disobey his elders again. Then at last he was able to move through the darkness into a bright, lovely vision. After an unknown interval of time, "I heard the same sound which I heard at the commencement of the vision, it came rolling through the heavens, and seemed to fill all things. . . . and I found myself upon my knees, having wet with my tears, a place some ten or twelve inches in diameter." Approximately four hours had elapsed. From that time forth, despite occasional inner conflicts, Lyon was firmly dedicated to the Shakers. He went on to become one of their great leaders.

Any account of Shaker membership based on personal reminiscences would be incomplete without consideration of accounts of apostates and seceders. The New Lebanon and Sodus Bay membership records suggest that many more of the individuals who entered the Society during the nineteenth century "turned off," or left the Shakers, than remained. Some seceders felt strongly enough about their experiences to write accounts which they had printed at their own expense.[80] The majority of those who left, including Valentine Rathbun, Mary Dyer, Eunice Chapman, and William J. Haskett, wrote with a pronounced polemical intent. Others such as Thomas Brown, David Lamson, and Hervey Elkins wrote as skeptical but basically sympathetic participant-observers. The motives which led these people to join the Shakers and later to leave and "expose" them are almost as complex as those of individuals who remained in the Society. Apostate accounts provide fascinating and often quite revealing discussions of important problems largely ignored in Shaker texts.

The experiences of Mary Dyer, the most vociferous of the anti-Shaker writers, show the complexity of apostate motivation, as well as some problems the Shakers faced in dealing with those who did not find celibate life to their liking.[81] Mary joined the Enfield, New Hampshire, community with her husband Joseph and their five children about 1812. Three years later, she left the Society. To recover her children, she instituted several suits, accompanied over the course of thirty years by books and pamphlets attacking the alleged misdeeds of the group.

Mary Dyer's most damaging exposé, *A Portraiture of Shakerism,* appeared in 1822. Much of the book was made up of grossly exaggerated affidavits detailing the alleged misdeeds of the early Shakers. These statements, which referred to events some forty to fifty years previous, showed little except the intense hostility generated by early Shaker missionary activities in New England. The core of the book, however, consisted of reprints of statements made by a galaxy of the most important Shaker seceders and apostates, including Amos Rathbun, Thomas Brown, and Eunice Chapman. These statements culminated with Mary Dyer's own account of her sufferings and trials among the Shakers.

Faced with the implacable hostility and continuing attacks of this capable and contentious woman, the Shakers departed from their normal policy of publicly ignoring apostates. Instead, the Society responded at length to Mary Dyer's charges, implicitly recognizing that many of her criticisms identified underlying points of real vulnerability and stress in their movement. The spirited exchange, *pro* and *contra,* included a statement by Mary's husband Joseph attacking her character and veracity. The barbed comments of husband and wife provided what the Shakers aptly characterized as an account of the Dyers' "domestic broils."

Raking through the numerous allegations and counter-allegations raised in this controversy between Mary Dyer and the Shakers will not be our concern here. Mary Dyer's allegations about hidden Shaker licentiousness connected with "spiritual wives and husbands"—apparently a deliberate misrepresentation of the chaste and straight-laced Shaker "union meetings"—are as unconvincing factually as the equally extreme Shaker claims that Mary had made passes at Shaker leaders and lesbian advances toward one of her roommates. Of far greater significance than such charges is why the Shaker celibate system proved so completely unacceptable to Mary Dyer and other converts who initially had been enthusiastic. It is puzzling that a person like Mary Dyer should have become a "career apostate," a person whose entire life was devoted to trying to destroy a faith that she had once espoused.

From our perspective, Mary Dyer's personal charges against the Shakers tell us little that we did not already know. However, at the time of the printing of her description of the elaborate Shaker control mechanisms with which she clashed, the account was a serious deterrent to potential converts. Mary's primary complaint was that the Shakers had tried to separate her from her husband and her children so that they could all be given a new group loyalty. Her relations with her husband (which had already been severely strained before she joined the Shakers) were further undermined. Three of her children were sent to a different "family." And she was forbidden to talk to or care for the two children remaining in her own "family," who were reared communally. When Mary finally broke with the Shakers, she fought endless battles in her unsuccessful effort to recover her children.

Underlying much of Mary Dyer's anger was her dislike of the loss of privacy and independence that she experienced in Shaker life. For instance, she could not send or receive a letter without first having it approved. And when she felt dissatisfied about something, she was supposed to express those feelings and seek redress only from the elders. She was expected to subordinate her own will to that of the elders, who, in her opinion, acted as though they stood in the place of God. Remaining intransigent, Mary became increasingly isolated and unhappy. Thus, unlike many individuals who joined the Shakers and became docile and obedient members, or others who were able to subordinate themselves initially while gradually working their way into responsible positions, Mary Dyer was unable to adjust. She was invariably at odds with the leadership. Unwilling to let herself be reshaped into the Shaker mold, she would always remain a square peg in a round hole.

The severe restrictions on personal life and independent action which so disturbed Mary Dyer were necessary to make the Shaker system function. In order to sustain their unusual commitment, Shaker leaders deliberately tried to keep the average Believer isolated from the world— physically, socially, economically, and intellectually. Attempts were made to ensure that those who went out into the world on business stayed apart from any but minimal social contacts and thereby as free as possible from worldly contamination. Within the Society, Shaker government showed an almost military regimentation, with every aspect of life minutely regulated. Close personal contact of any kind with those of the same or the opposite sex was forbidden in favor of a generalized "spiritual" love for their co-religionists. Children were raised communally, not by their parents. Occupations were frequently shifted, and privacy was almost nonexistent. Required confession of all sins to the elders further increased the degree of control. Those who accepted such limitations could find many rewards in the well-ordered Shaker system. But those who were unwilling to accept such constraints could find the arrangements oppressive.

Although many people did not find the highly restrictive Shaker system to their liking, few devoted the rest of their lives to exposing the group. Why did Mary Dyer become a "career apostate"? Undoubtedly, her motivation was extremely complex. On the most obvious level, she appears to have been bound to the Shakers because of her children and her continuing ambivalence about her husband who remained happily in the group. But probably at least as important, Mary Dyer, like other apostates such as Valentine Rathbun and Eunice Chapman, appears to have been a frustrated leader. She had genuine talent, as well as a strong sense of personal destiny and self-importance. When her expectations went unfulfilled and she was unable to put her talents to constructive use, she bitterly turned all her energy against the group she felt had frustrated her efforts to create a satisfying life. There is no greater bitterness than that of the person who genuinely believed or wanted to believe, only to have his or her high hopes dashed.

Whatever Mary Dyer's own motives, her experience does suggest many characteristic issues raised by other apostates. Like the somewhat abrasive Mary Dyer, other more sensitive and appealing Shakers who "turned off" also had trouble submitting to the oligarchic Shaker leadership and renouncing individual life and interests in favor of those of the group. Almost without exception seceders found the renunciation of normal marital and sexual life particularly difficult. As Hervey Elkins wrote, many were unhappy among the Shakers because of "an aspiration for something not found in confinement" and a desire to express "the strong affinities of nature."[82] Finally, when individuals did leave the Shakers, many were upset by their loss of consecrated property and were embittered by their difficulties in getting their children out of the Society. Throughout the pre–Civil War period, conflicts and litigation over children whom the Shakers were reluctant to give up to departing parents generated much hostility to the Society.[83] Clearly Shaker communal life was not for everyone.

Shaker Membership: A Quantitative Analysis

An analysis based on leaders and vocal individuals alone would distort the total picture of any group, and particularly one such as the Shakers in which significant differences existed between leaders and the larger membership. To supplement the biographical accounts of believers and seceders sketched above, this section will present a preliminary analysis of the complete membership records for the New Lebanon Second Family from 1830 to 1896.[84] The somewhat less complete records of the Sodus Bay, New York, community will also be briefly considered. Even these detailed records may not do justice to the full range of Shaker membership, since Shaker communities varied greatly in size, sex ratios, and degree of cohesiveness. There were great differences between the Northeastern and Midwestern Shaker societies, for example. Nevertheless, the New Lebanon and Sodus Bay records do suggest something of the types of people attracted to the Shaker communities in close contact with the Burned-over District of upstate New York and related areas of New England.

The life of the New Lebanon Second Family spanned more than a century from the founding of the community in 1790 to its dissolution in 1896. The membership record covers all individuals who entered from 1830 to 1896—the period of the decline of this Family—as well as some individuals who entered earlier. Here information will be analyzed concerning 284 people for whom at least two of three vital dates—birth, entrance, and departure or death—have been recorded. Of this group, 149 were men and 135 were women. However, at any given point in time, women slightly outnumbered the men, since they tended to remain in the community longer than men did. In the Central Bishopric, which included all members of both the New Lebanon and Watervliet societies, there were 312 males to 421 females in 1819. The male/female ratio varied greatly in different Shaker societies and at different periods of time, but apparently in the Northeastern societies it was not until after the Civil War that the heavy preponderance of women would develop.

A total of 171 out of the 284 individuals who entered the Second Family shared a common surname and clear kinship ties with at least one other person who entered the community. Of these 171 people, 98 were males and 75 were females. These individuals belonged to 61 distinct surname groups (including 2 sets of Joneses). Another 11 individuals shared common surnames but could not be positively related by common birth place, entrance date, or location from which they entered. The most common kinship pattern was for two children of 15 years of age or under to enter together. This occurred in 26 cases (8 involved two males, 7 involved two females, and 11 involved a male and a female). Of the 284 individuals entering the Second Family throughout this period, 222 were under 16 years of age. In contrast to the Sodus Bay records in which husband and wife groups with up to ten children were not uncommon, the Second Family attracted few husband-and-wife or other adult kinship units. Particularly during the period of decline in the 1850s and 1860s, large numbers of children were taken in for relatively short periods of time. This information suggests that this community from 1830 to 1896 depended heavily for its membership on custodianship of children who for various reasons could not or did not wish to live with their parents.

The heavy preponderance of such surnames as Baker, Carpenter, Cook, Free, Grey, Hull, Jones, Long, Smith, Taylor, Weed, and White suggests that the ethnic composition of the Second Family was overwhelmingly of English derivation. There were a few exceptions, including the names Brazie, Dubois, Portrus, Van Houten, Apolinaire, and Meixsal. Only 26 foreign-born individuals entered the group, and 20 of these were from England, 3 from Scotland, 1 from Ireland, and 2 from Canada.

Geographically, nearly half of the members were born in New York State (123), followed by Massachusetts (45), Connecticut (20), Vermont (8), Rhode Island (6), and a scattering from 13 other states and the foreign countries mentioned above. Somewhat startling, in view of the stereotype of supposed Shaker rural origins, was the fact that 52 individuals were born in New York City proper, and 15 in Brooklyn! Other large cities in the Northeast and in England also furnished many members. This Shaker community appears to have drawn members chiefly from the Hudson Valley, from areas of New York State that were touched by their extensive trading routes, and from other areas of New England where strong Shaker communities existed or where missionary ventures had occurred. Forty-seven individuals who entered the Second Family were from other Shaker communities, including other families at New Lebanon.

The membership record of the New Lebanon Second Family reveals the internal decay of the Shakers. While the mean age at entry fluctuated between seven and fifteen years for both men and women throughout most of this period, in each decade the length of time that individuals stayed in

Table 1

Length of Stay for Individuals Entering the New Lebanon Second Family

Decade of Entry	Before 1820	1820–29	1830–39	1840–49	1850–59	1860–69
Total men entering	5	14	21	15	43	44
Mean length of stay for men	37.2	31.3	15.3	5.7	4.9	2.1
Total women entering	13	7	17	15	32	44
Mean length of stay for women	39.3	32.1	19.5	9.5	6.5	3.9

the community dropped precipitously for both men and women, as Table 1 shows.

If the length of time that a person stayed with the Shakers was related to the appeal that the group had for him at the time he or she entered, then the decade 1830–39 marks a critical transition period between a relatively strong Second Family and a community that was increasingly losing its appeal. Before 1830, individuals stayed more than thirty years on the average after they entered, often remaining until they died. People who entered during the 1830s stayed, on the average, approximately half that length of time. After 1840, individuals who entered the community stayed less than ten years on the average, and by the 1850s and 1860s, in many cases individuals were staying only a few years or even months before leaving. After 1870, the length of stay was so short that the person who kept the record evidently became frustrated and seldom bothered to note personal information on incoming individuals.

The extraordinary membership turnover in the New Lebanon Second Family can be seen by looking at the aggregate figures in Table 2 showing the reasons why individuals left the community. It is striking that only slightly more than 10 percent of the individuals who entered the New Lebanon Second Family in this period remained in the community for their entire lives. Men and women show similar patterns of movement, except that more men than women left the community. This pattern, if repeated in other Shaker communities, would help explain the increasing disproportion of women in the communities as the nineteenth century progressed.

The fluidity of Shaker membership is even more graphically suggested by the membership records of the short-lived and possibly atypical Sodus Bay community. It lasted from 1826 until 1838, when the

Table 2

Reasons for Departure of Individuals from the New Lebanon Second Family

	Number of males	Percent of total males	Number of females	Percent of total females
Remained in community until death	10	6.7	27	20.0
Left community on own volition	99	66.4	67	49.6
Taken away by parents or relatives	16	10.7	18	13.3
Moved to another Shaker Community	16	10.7	14	10.4
No information	8	5.4	9	6.7
Totals	149	100	135	100

community relocated itself at Groveland, New York, where it continued until shortly before the end of the century. As Table 3 shows, during the eleven years after its founding (the year that Sodus Bay was being set up has been excluded from this overview statement), between 85 and 148 people were living in the community at the end of each year, with a mean figure of slightly over 114 in any given year. During that time, the turnover (total of entries, departures, and deaths) generally ranged between one half and one fourth of the total group each year. Though the

Table 3

Sodus Bay Membership Record

Year	Population at end of year	Number who entered	Number who left	Number who died	Percentage of turnover
1826	72	86	12	2	—
1827	88	31	15	0	52.3
1828	85	19	21	1	48.2
1829	97	29	16	1	47.4
1830	97	32	31	1	66.0
1831	106	23	12	2	34.9
1832	122	25	9 ·	0	27.9
1833	119	12	14	1	22.7
1834	124	26	24	0	40.3
1835	134	23	10	3	26.9
1836	148	28	11	3	28.4
1837	135	9	10	2	15.6

percentage of turnover appears to have been sharply reduced by the end of the first decade, the turnover of even a quarter of the members of a group every year could not help but profoundly affect its life and sense of itself.

If this brief look at two relatively complete Shaker membership records is supported by research on other communities and by further investigation of the development of these two communities, then a number of common assumptions about the Shakers and their development may need to be revised. Most obvious, the fluidity of Shaker membership calls into question any view of the Shakers as an essentially static, isolated, "utopian" community. The make-up of Shaker membership also may have been incorrectly understood. If many nineteenth-century Shakers were born in urban areas, then the assumption that the Shakers came from a sort of rural proletariat is called into question. Perhaps other commonly held assumptions about the Shakers also will have to be reconsidered in the light of more detailed membership studies.

Daily Life among the Shakers

The personal backgrounds and concerns of individuals who became Believers are important but to understand the appeal of the Shakers, their well-ordered communal life must also be examined. This account has focused on complex and often troubled transition periods which are far from characteristic of Shaker life as a whole, even during the early years when visionary and ecstatic phenomena were most common. As early as 1800, visitors to Shaker communities in the Northeast were impressed by the quiet orderliness and simplicity which characterized the group. The antebellum Shakers created and sustained their own modes in music, the crafts, and even architecture, and established a total way of life which still has considerable appeal today. Here this way of life will be briefly presented, with particular reference to the daily work of men and women, the forms of group worship, and the rearing of children.[85]

The everyday work of the Shakers was part of their worship of God, inseparable from abstract beliefs and rituals, in much the same way that daily life and worship ideally are inseparable in a monastic community or any similar institution.[86] Entering a Shaker village, the typical visitor was struck by the order, serenity, and simplicity of Shaker life, and the impressive degree of fellow feeling. One observer noted: "The people are like their village. . . . soft in speech, demure in bearing, gentle in face; a people seeming to be at peace not only with themselves, but with nature and with heaven."[87] No sign of tension or aggressiveness was apparent; there was a pattern of behavior suggesting an element of freedom, grace, and contentment or perhaps the resignation of those who had achieved true inner peace. Even visitors hostile to Shaker religious beliefs often praised their way of life and admitted that the fruits of their religion appeared to be good.

The work which sustained this semi-monastic system was based on an ideal of temperate labor: Shakers always appeared busy doing something, but the work was done at a relaxed pace and the range of assignments was varied and flexible within the overall structure of the needs of each community "family." Individuals were encouraged to develop their special skills and to master new ones as well. Richard McNemar, for example, was a weaver, bookbinder, chairmaker, printer, editor, author, and preacher; Hervey Eads was a tailor, shoemaker, teamster, seedsman, wool carder, tin and sheet-iron worker, dentist, printer, painter, and hatter—as well as author and elder; Elizabeth Lovegrove was a nurse, cook, painter, office worker, seamstress, herb and seedswoman, food processer, and manufacturer of household items. Agriculture and agriculture-related work occupied much of the time of the brethren and sisters. Among the sisters' special activities were work in the kitchen, bakery, work house, dairy, weave shop, and herb house. Although many different tasks were done, with no rigid production schedule, women appear to have had a somewhat less varied range of activities and to have practiced a somewhat more systematic rotation of labor than the men.

A typical Shaker day began early, as it did for other American farmers. As Andrews described it:

> The "order of the day" left little room . . . for vain or idle thoughts. At the sounding of the bell or 'shell,' the Shakers arose early in the morning, between four o'clock and five in summer, between five and five-thirty in the winter. After kneeling together for a moment of quiet prayer, the occupants of each retiring room stripped the sheets and blankets from their narrow cots, laying them neatly over two chairs at the foot, on which the pillows had previously been placed. Fifteen minutes after rising, the rooms had been vacated, the brethren had gone to their morning chores, and the sisters were entering to close the windows, make the beds, and put the room in order. At breakfast time, six, six-thirty, or seven, the chamber work was finished, fires had been started in the dwelling rooms and shops, the cattle fed, the cows milked, and arrangements for the day's industry were all complete.
>
> Before all meals—the early breakfast, the noon dinner, the six o'clock supper—brethren and sisters would assemble, each group by themselves, in appointed rooms, where for a ten or fifteen minute pause which was a kind of "broad grace," they quietly awaited the

bell. Then, in two columns led by the elders and eldresses respectively, and in the order in which they were to be seated, they
proceeded to the dining hall. Taking their places behind the chairs
or benches, the sexes at separate tables, they knelt in prayer at a sign
from the lead, and after a meal eaten in monastic silence, knelt
again before departing directly to their labors. . . .

After the evening chores were done, at seven-thirty in summer and
eight o'clock in winter, all repaired to their apartments for half an
hour, known as "retiring-time," when, on the evenings devoted to
family worship, the Shakers disposed themselves in ranks, sitting erect
with hands folded "to labor for a true sense of their privilege in the
Zion of God." If perchance one should drowse, it was the order to
rise and bow four times, or shake, and then resume one's seat. At the
end of the period, announced by the ringing of a small bell, brethren
and sisters formed separate columns in the corridors, marched two
abreast to the meeting-room, and, after bowing as they entered,
formed ranks for worship.

Assemblies varied with the time and place. In the early years
of the order, and often during revivals, "labouring" meetings were
held nightly, and sometimes during the day. As the society expanded, however, evenings not devoted to union meetings or the
regular religious service were given over to the practice of songs
and exercises. Thus, at New Lebanon in the 'seventies, singing meetings were held on Tuesday and Friday, union meetings on Sunday
and Wednesday, and "labouring" meetings on Thursday and Satur-
days. On Mondays, during this more liberal period, there was a
general assembly in the dining hall, where the elder read letters from
other communities, selections from the news of the week, or some
appropriate book. At the conclusion of such gatherings, to which
strangers were admitted on occasion, the family retired quietly to rest.
The occupants of each room, after kneeling again in silent prayer,
went to bed at a uniform hour—nine o'clock in winter and ten in
summer.[88]

The order and simplicity of such daily activity extended as well into the
products of daily labor. For Shakers, form followed function. No ex-
traneous decoration was added to the simple, spare lines of Shaker buildings, furniture, products for sale, or numerous ingenious inventions—from
the common clothespin to the circular saw, flat broom, or a machine for
paring, coring, and quartering apples. Shaker products expressed in tangible form their distinctive way of life and worship. "Beauty was inherent
in a product fashioned to meet the needs of a life based on contemplation
and dedicated to rectitude of hand and heart."[89]

If daily life was itself a form of worship, nevertheless formal religious
worship also held great importance for the Shakers. Far from being con-

sidered an onerous obligation, the frequent religious meetings, often held in the evenings after a long day's work, were anticipated with pleasure, and viewed in retrospect as a source of refreshment of spirit. Dance and song were recreations which allowed the restrained spirit of Believers to find expression and release. Initially, such activities were often extravagant and highly emotional, with no fixed order or form. As Shaker communities became increasingly organized, however, they also began to create more disciplined and decorous rituals. Songs and dances came to be rehearsed before performance; new marches, steps, and songs were created as earlier free-style worship was transformed into more complex ceremonial forms. A sense of union, order, and fellow-feeling was expressed in lively meetings of song and dance.

While daily work and worship helped unify Shaker life, the rearing of children posed a special challenge to the Shakers' concern for order. Brought into the communities with their parents or else adopted from outsiders, boys and girls were reared in sex-segregated groups, apart from their natural families, by "caretakers" responsible to the elders or eldresses. In education the emphasis was placed on character building and the useful arts, rather than on knowledge and intellectual development, which were considered dangerous to society unless they had first been properly directed. Nevertheless, Shaker schools—which were taught by their best qualified members—soon acquired a deserved reknown. Nor were innocent recreations discouraged. The girls at the Canterbury society, for instance, had gymnastic exercises and a flower garden; the boys played ball and marbles, went fishing, and had a small farm of their own. Picnics, sleigh rides, and nutting and berrying parties provided a departure from the normal routines. Hervey Elkins's frank account of his boyhood at Enfield records lively experiences with interesting companions, mild paternal control, and normal healthful experiences in a beautiful countryside.

Although children were loved and appreciated, they created significant problems in maintaining the artificial restrictions designed to subdue "carnal nature." Difficulties in overcoming "carnal nature" were exacerbated at puberty when Shaker youth often grew resentful of authority and impatient of the many regulations restricting their freedom. Though corporal punishment was largely prohibited by the Shakers, moral suasion —including prayer, supplication, and "keen admonition"—was a formidable force, particularly in combination with the fear inculcated in children of what would happen to them if they left the Society. Despite such training, however, a majority of Shaker children eventually left the Society. The Shaker difficulties in recruiting and maintaining membership—which are reflected in their treatment of children—posed the greatest single challenge to their continued existence. These problems were closely associated with the last great Shaker revival in the pre–Civil War period and the beginning of their long decline.

The Spiritual Manifestations: Crisis and Renewal

The high point of Shaker spiritual and social tensions before the Civil War and the last major effort to revitalize their Society occurred during about a decade of "spiritual manifestations" lasting from 1837 to 1847 or slightly later. The manifestations began on August 16, 1837, when a group of ten-to-twelve-year-old girls meeting for worship in the Gathering Order of the Watervliet Shaker community near Albany, New York, began to exhibit extraordinary behavior. Some shook and whirled, becoming completely oblivious to their external surroundings. A few fell to the ground and broke out into beautiful unknown songs. They told of being led by angels through heavenly places and of seeing Mother Ann Lee, foundress of the Society, who had died more than fifty years earlier.

News of these strange and seemingly inexplicable manifestations which continued to occur created a current of intense excitement throughout the Shaker societies. Within a year most of the closely linked Northeastern Shaker communities and a few of the Midwestern ones were beginning to experience similar and sometimes bizarre and frightening physical occurrences. In an extreme example of a group of young Watervliet boys meeting for worship:

> Some were thrown violently on the floor and all efforts of strong men were unavailing to raise their stiffened bodies. . . . Sometimes they were with those in suffering and torment; they seemed suffocated, as by sulphur fumes; their bodies were distorted and bore every mark of intense agony, while their screeches were terrible to hear.[90]

Thus, in a variety of forms of highly emotional activity, began a complex and tension-ridden decade of "spiritual manifestations," sometimes described as the "spiritualist period" or a "spiritualist" revival.[91] The period brought severe challenges to community order, yet also attempts to revive inner Shaker spiritual life and commitment to their ideals. A rich outpouring of creativity in new forms of worship and ecstatic dance resulted, including hundreds of new songs, of which "The Gift To Be Simple" is perhaps best known. During this period, literally thousands of messages of exhortation and verbal gifts from departed spirits were received which the Shakers considered "words of comfort, gifts of love."[92]

Many historians have found this period of Shaker spiritual manifestations baffling or incomprehensible, just as they have been unable to understand other aspects of Shaker life. Some have viewed the phenomena as the behavior of quaint eccentrics; others have postulated fraud and deliberate manipulation; while still others have suggested mental disorder.[93] Rather surprisingly, few historians have taken seriously the Shakers' own attempts to explain the ecstatic, trance, and possession phenomena which occurred between 1837 and 1847. The importance of the spiritualist period is clear from the extensive Shaker manuscript collection at the Western Reserve Historical Society. Out of a 325-page typescript bibliography of titles in the collection, 80 pages, or more than one fourth of the total, deal directly with this period, while a number of others are peripherally related to it.[94] Many of these manuscripts are beautiful leather-bound books filled with revelations copied with all the meticulous care of a medieval scribe. Since the spiritualist period was of such great importance to the Shakers, it is not surprising that these articulate and sensitive people also provided some sophisticated analyses of its underlying dynamics.[95] In analyzing the earlier periods of Shaker development, the limitations of material have made our generalizations about the tensions and process of change highly conjectural. However, the massive documentation of the spiritualist period allows a somewhat more reliable view of the course of the manifestations.

The context within which the spiritual phenomena occurred is of central importance. In essence, the period was one of religious revival, the last of three or four great revivals in Shaker history. Like the earlier revivals, it was attended by violent shaking, speaking in tongues, and other forms of ecstatic dance and trance phenomena which provided direct experiential support for a new order. Mother Ann Lee herself frequently had been overcome by passion against the evils of man's fallen carnal nature and had gone into trance, abstracted from the world for days at a stretch; she had reported seeing the heavens open and talking with angels and with Jesus himself. Thus for the Shakers strong positive expectations were connected with such revivalist phenomena as those that started again in 1837.

The spiritualist period differed from earlier Shaker revivals in that it was primarily an internal development, rather than an outgrowth of external missionary expansion or a direct response to tensions in the outer society. As in earlier revivals, the spiritualist period began with a sense of declension, rose to a climax of excitement and commitment, and then fell back to a more stable level of commitment.

By the beginning of the spiritual manifestations in 1837, exactly fifty years after the gathering of the first Shaker community in 1787, most of the Believers who had known Mother Ann and the other early leaders personally had died or grown old and feeble. In many communities, there was a growing gap between the very old members and the very young.

Discipline was becoming lax. Curious visitors from the outside world would come to stare with uncomprehending amusement at the strange worship services. The leadership was gradually losing control over the societies and there was a pervasive sense of malaise that led to a longing for intervention by extraordinary or supernatural forces, as in the past, to provide revitalization. If the young were to be successfully inducted into the Shaker way of life, they would have to undergo a powerful, direct, and personal experience of the truth of the Shaker message.[96]

Thus, when the spiritual phenomena began in 1837, they attracted enormous interest. Not only were the Shaker societies experiencing a declension, but there were also great tensions in the outer world, as a period of runaway economic expansion collapsed into the Panic of 1837. The spiritual manifestations spread rapidly and, with encouragement and some direction from the leadership, eventually came to a crescendo between 1841 and 1843—the time differed in different societies—roughly when revivalistic excitements were peaking in the outer world. For the Shakers the most important of these outer excitements were the Millerite expectations of Christ's second coming in 1843 or 1844. The disappointment of these expectations eventually brought many new members into Shaker communities.[97]

By this time Shaker spiritual manifestations were becoming so widespread, with wild behavior and numerous contradictory revelations, that the group was threatened with anarchy. As early as 1842, most Shaker societies decided that the emotionalism of their meetings could not be understood by outsiders, so they closed off their communities to visitors and began to try to put their house in order. Refusing to allow visitors was an extraordinary step in a group that depended upon converts for its existence. Finally, in 1845 a set of Millennial Laws was promulgated.[98] They restored extremely tight discipline, effectively choking off significant further group spiritualist activity. Later Shaker writers looked back on the period with considerable ambivalence. They remembered its positive contributions to the societies, but they also were painfully aware of its excesses.

The spiritual manifestations had both an internal and an external aspect. Externally, as described in the official New Lebanon Shaker account, the operations ranged from those which were "so irresistably violent that it would seem life was in great danger to that which is gentle and scarcely perceptible to the beholder." Most activities took this milder non-trance form in which the emotions were quickened and faith and fellowship were strengthened. The more extreme actions, however, included violent gyrations—turning rapidly upon the toes, bowing, bending, or reeling as though drunk. After these activities, individuals would sometimes fall to the floor and lie helpless, stiff and cold as a corpse, sometimes for days. They might suddenly resuscitate and resume their dance, still abstracted from the world, perhaps speaking with a voice or personality not their own, singing strange, unearthly new songs, or babbling in a euphonious pseudo-language, known popularly as "speaking in tongues." When individuals resisted these trance experiences, they might become temporarily blinded, physically contorted, or possessed of seemingly preternatural strength. Understandably, the Shakers concluded that such actions could not be feigned and must be due to supernatural agency.[99]

Although these phenomena were astonishing and not a little frightening to the participants, these types of involuntary behavior are strikingly similar to related phenomena in other cultures as described by Sargant, Samarin, Lewis, and others. In the Shaker communities, as in other groups, the most severely affected individuals appear to have been girls and boys just reaching puberty, as well as older women. Individuals in these categories are often in some sense frustrated outsiders, unconsciously prone to turn to extra-institutional means of expressing themselves and seeking power, or, alternatively, concerned to find means of accepting or adjusting to a novel and difficult state of being and social reality.[100]

Shaker celibacy and tightly regulated group life made some such emotional phenomena almost essential to validate a social order that was very far from the norm in outer society and far from self-evidently true. In effect, adolescents, converts, or people whose commitment was growing slack had to be initiated (or re-initiated) into a new way of life. Only in conjunction with larger tensions in their communities and in external society, however, did individual tensions in the loosely structured Shaker worship services lead to widespread spiritualist behavior. For the Shakers, the spiritual phenomena contained both a promise and a threat. Spiritual manifestations could contribute to a more vital faith and to revitalization of the group, but if too extreme, those same manifestations could seriously undercut authority and lead to fragmentation.

Since the external aspects of Shaker spiritualism were strikingly similar to ecstatic and trance phenomena throughout the world, to understand the distinctively *Shaker* features of the period we must turn to the content of the messages themselves. The Shakers realized that these messages were of primary importance. In fact, so frequently did the Shakers record only the spirit communications that some writers have seemed largely unaware that such messages generally were received through ecstatic worship and trances. The messages reveal a rich and vivid inner life, by no means simply reducible to body chemistry and sexual frustration, but expressive of the high ideals, hopes, and fears of this committed, gentle people. It should be noted parenthetically that almost no examples of extrasensory perception or evidences of personal survival of death were associated with Shaker spiritualism. Like most spiritualists, the Shakers simply assumed but did not try to prove survival after death.[101]

Two basic types of communications were received: first, personal messages of encouragement, comfort, and evidence of spirit concern for individual members, and second, messages of moral exhortation urging renewed commitment to key Shaker ideals and a strengthening of group life and solidarity. Average members most frequently received personal messages, while the leadership tended to receive messages of general moral exhortation. Both individual and group concerns found expression through elaborate special activities. These included the "Midnight Cry," intricate "Mountain Meetings," and other forms of communal worship—developed primarily after 1842—which led back toward the more patterned worship activities which followed the end of the influx from the "spirit world."[102]

Personal messages of encouragement and comfort were the earliest and continued throughout the period to be the most common form of spirit communication. Typically there were accounts of travel to the spirit world and visits with Mother Ann and the early beloved leaders. Various presents, seen in the mind's eye, would be brought back from these "heavenly parents" to show their continuing concern for their "children" in the temporal world. These presents had no physical existence, but were obviously highly symbolic, even in the accounts of many of the less sophisticated Shakers. "Spectacles of discernment"; "sparkling balls of love"; lamps "to be kept well trimmed and burning so that the enemy may not impede our progress"; celestial wine; silver sacks filled with the bread of life; priceless gems; "six clusters of white plums from the Angel of Peace, with his love and peace written on the leaves that hang to the stems of the clusters"—these and innumerable other "spiritual" gifts were brought back verbally to strengthen the faith of Believers.

Many of the visions were of exquisite loveliness, as was this description a medium of Tyringham, Massachusetts, gave of her guides to the spirit world:

> . . . some had what seemed like filmy gold; others were clad in garments of rich changeable colors, glossy, like silk, while some were enveloped in soft, fleece-like drapery, as white as snow; around their heads were crownlike halos of golden light; some were decorated with diamonds, stars, pearls and other precious gems.[103]

Paradoxically, this vivid visual imagery was occurring among a people who eschewed all private ownership of property and dressed in drab clothing without jewelry, precisely at the time when increasingly stringent regulations against any worldly possessions were being enforced. Eric Rohmann was led to speculate that a sort of "spiritual materialism" may have been operating in many cases, with the Shakers unconsciously compensating for their repressed worldly longings in exquisite visions of the spiritual world to come, where they would obtain surcease from all their strivings.[104]

While messages of personal encouragement and comfort were commonly received by average members struggling to overcome the desires of "carnal nature," the larger group concerns of the Shakers were most clearly reflected in exhortations delivered by the leadership. The first direct participation of a leader as a spiritualist "instrument" occurred on April 22, 1838, about a year after the beginning of the manifestations, when Philemon Stewart, a New Lebanon elder, went into trance. Through him a personality claiming to be Mother Ann spoke at length to an assembled Shaker meeting, exhorting Believers to cast off worldly "superfluities," return to the "true order" of the initial Shakerism, and obey the leadership.[105]

Brother Philemon's statement provided a focus for earlier, more inchoate messages, suggesting that the leadership may have seen the general spiritual awakening in the societies as a heaven-sent means of helping to restore earlier discipline and commitment. While some have seen such leadership involvement as cynical manipulation, this is an inadequate explanation. Since individuals in trance are highly suggestible and have a tendency to objectify their deepest desires, it is not surprising that Shaker leaders, as well as members distraught at the loss of faith in the societies, should express their concerns in trance communications. Even when messages were more obviously of a sermonic than an involuntary character, no cynicism need be postulated, for Shakers felt that the connection between the spiritual and temporal worlds was so close as to be almost inseparable, and ordinary sermons could progress almost imperceptibly into trance communications in the surcharged atmosphere of a lively meeting.[106]

Although a few trance experiences occurred to isolated individuals such as men working in the fields, the vast majority took place in meetings for worship where emotions could be aroused and channeled within a supportive setting. With the mounting collective excitement, new forms of group worship were developed to give freshness and vitality to spiritual life. As in earlier communications, these new forms of worship had a high symbolic content and often did not distinguish clearly between the temporal world and that of aspirations and dreams.

One of the most colorful of the new forms of group worship was the "Midnight Cry," in which a platoon of mediums—six male and six female, with two elders in the lead carrying lighted lamps in their right hands—marched through all the community buildings each night for a period of two weeks. "Every medium wore upon the right wrist, a scrap of scarlet flannel, some two and one half inches wide, and attached to this a written inscription as follows—'War hath been declared by the God of heaven, against all sin, and with the help of the Saints on earth, it shall be slain.' "[107] These activities were interpreted as the actualization of the "searching as with candles" foretold at the beginning of the manifestations. At midnight on one of the nights, the brothers and sisters were awakened with singing:

> Awake from your slumbers, for the Lord of Hosts
>   is going through the land,
> He will sweep he will clean his holy sanctuary.
> Search ye your Camps, yea read and understand
> For the Lord of Hosts holds the Lamps in his hand.[108]

All the Believers dressed quickly and hurried out to join in the marching and singing, before repairing to the meeting house for an hour of active worship. "This strange alarm had a wonderful effect on the minds of those thus suddenly aroused."[109]

Even more dramatic were the elaborate "Mountain Meetings." Mystic names were assigned to the various communities and "Holy Hills of Zion" or "Sacred Squares" were set aside, consisting of an acre of land on or near the highest point in the community, to be specially prepared for twice-yearly meetings in the spring and fall. In the center of the carefully cleared area was a white picket fence encircling a Fountain of Life, which could be seen only by those with spiritual insight. Prior to the meetings, the Shakers purified themselves with fasting and silent prayer, hard work and confession of sins, and dressed themselves in imaginary spiritual garments so they would be clothed symbolically in the virtues of "holiness, innocence, meekness, freedom & peace." Carrying spiritual instruments and spiritual food on which to feast, they marched to the meeting grounds, heard exhortations from the spirits, sang, danced, and finished by sharing a great pantomime feast of spiritual delicacies. It was a joyful and significant occasion, rejuvenating body and spirit.[110]

Although the spiritual manifestations helped in many ways to revitalize Shaker spiritual commitment, the phenomena also contained highly disruptive possibilities. As early as 1839, three leading Shakers, including the venerable Richard McNemar, who had been a key figure in founding the Midwestern Shaker societies, were expelled from the Union Village, Ohio, Shaker community at the behest of a young medium. This medium was perhaps unconsciously acting in support of the leadership of Freegift Wells, who had recently been appointed by the Northeastern Shakers and was involved in a power struggle with McNemar and the old guard Midwestern leaders. Only belatedly were McNemar and his associates reinstated by a directive from the central office at New Lebanon.[111] This unfortunate incident led to the promulgation of rules for testing the validity of spirit communications. They must not be in conflict with basic Shaker beliefs and those affecting policy must be cleared with the New Lebanon ministry.[112]

Nevertheless, the problem continued. As tensions increased between 1841 and 1843, potentially anarchic tendencies appeared. Whereas earlier revelations had been primarily from deceased Shaker leaders such as Mother Ann, later revelations began coming from an extraordinary range of historical figures, including such Biblical ones as Jesus, Mary Magdalene, and St. Paul; popular culture heroes such as Christopher Columbus, George Washington, and Napoleon; outstanding women such as Queen Isabella, Queen Elizabeth, martyred saints of the Middle Ages, and others.[113] Following this period was the "gathering of all nations," in which the Shakers were visited by a motley crew of American Indians, Chinese, Arabs, etc., all of whom acted out popular American clichés of those cultures. Possessed by the spirits of Indians, for instance, Shakers whooped and hollered, war danced, passed the peace pipe, or powwowed.

Such activities began to reduce the spiritual communications to absurdity. Furthermore, the content of the messages themselves appears to have become idiosyncratic, representative primarily of the repressed desires of Shaker membership. A tendency toward cynicism about all spiritual truth and a pervasive spirit of infidelity developed. Attacks were made by mediums on many of the prominent Shaker leaders, many visionists experienced the terrors of hell, and only with great difficulty were some of the manifestations contained within the Shaker communal structure.

Although much of the material dealing with conflicts of this period appears to have been destroyed, there is strong evidence that the sexual tensions of disaffected individuals threatened to break out into overt expression at this time. For instance, a young woman told Frederick Evans that she had had a revelation from Ann Lee that celibacy should be abandoned and they should all move into the higher, married state. Evans, sharp as ever, retorted that they were not followers of Ann Lee! Rather, they followed her principles. If she had fallen from grace, even in the afterlife, her faithful followers would nevertheless continue to follow the truth she had taught on earth.[114]

Faced with such challenges to their leadership and even to celibacy, the only unalterable Shaker tenet, Shaker leaders appear to have recoiled. Rather than channel the vitality of young Believers into renewed external missionary activity or attempt to take advantage of the religious and social ferment of the Burned-over District by setting up new communities, Shaker leaders turned their attention inward and sought to tighten their control over existing communities. They promulgated the Millennial Laws of 1845, the strictest and most rigid in Shaker history. Unlike the earlier Millennial Laws of 1821 or the later ones of 1860, the 1845 Laws were so extreme as to almost parody the Shaker spirit of progressive change and perfectionism. One item went so far as to declare: "Sisters must not mend, nor set buttons on brethren's clothes while they have them on."[115] Such regulations suggest that laxness in obeying the spirit and the letter of the regulations separating the sexes was becoming a serious problem that had to be corrected at any cost.

What was the significance of this remarkable period of spiritual excitement? In retrospect, it was a bittersweet time for the Shakers. The faith of many Believers was deepened and strengthened. Yet the appeal of the Society to new members dropped off sharply. The Society would continue to take in many new individuals, but few of them would stay for more than three or four years. The Shakers were freed from many of their most disruptive members, since almost all of the most severely affected mediums, particularly the young girls, left the Society. Yet other capable individuals such as Hervey Elkins, who could have contributed much as leaders, also left. The failure of the Shakers to regain their lost momentum in the aftermath of the spiritualist period led to deep-seated disillusionment.[116]

Looking back, Giles Avery, a leader who had himself been severely criticized by the mediums, described spiritualism as a "revolutionary element, both in religious and secular society," a two-edged sword with both positive and negative possibilities.[117] Alonzo Hollister urged that each spirit communication be judged separately to see if it were really of God, for many false spirits also had sent messages.[118] For Henry C. Blinn, spiritual manifestations were "not a foundation pillar; but rather a helping hand. . . . The better guide is love, 'Love never faileth.' "[119] Freegift Wells, disillusioned by the dissension in his large Union Village community, a dissension which was associated with its drastic decline, expressed similar sentiments.[120] Perhaps Catherine Allen, eldress at New Lebanon, expressed the ambivalence of leadership most succinctly when she said that, while not in the least doubting the mediums' sincerity, "we agree with the Indian who said: 'Blow breath thro [sic] onion stalk and it smell of onion.' "[121]

The spiritualist period thus may have been something of a pyrrhic victory for the Shakers. Believers made a significant effort at revitalization which helped to sustain the group through more than a hundred years of ensuing membership decline. But the root problems were not overcome. The already faltering Shaker leaders appear to have been somewhat traumatized by the disruptive manifestations. They were unable or unwilling to engage in vigorous proselytizing or undergo extreme revivalistic stresses again. By the 1870s and 1880s, the lively Shaker dancing, which had contributed so much to the vitality of the group, had been largely discontinued. These changes may have been caused by forces beyond the control of the Shakers themselves, such as the decline of the revivalistic enthusiasms upon which the group depended so heavily for members.[122] The changing environment of the nineteenth century—together with the loss of the fervently committed Believers who had known Mother Ann and the early leaders personally—caused the once-vital Shaker societies to go into a gradual decline that not even the spiritual revival of the 1830s and 1840s could reverse.

In summary, Shaker spiritual manifestations during the years between the Revolutionary and Civil Wars were always associated with important periods of growth and transition within the societies. Such phenomena suggest many of the most important problems in the study of religion and social change, as well as the way in which sexuality in its most comprehensive sense is related to such problems. Early Shaker spiritual activities clearly show how fine is the line dividing insanity and social disorganization from ecstasy and the highest visionary reorganization of the individual and society: "Mental disorganization results in psychosis; a creative reorganization underlies the visionary state."[123] Before the Civil War, the Shakers for a time succeeded in achieving a remarkably effective balance between individual creativity and the necessary constraints of their functioning social order.

III

That All May Be One: John Humphrey Noyes and the Origins of Oneida Community Complex Marriage

> Free love with us does not mean freedom to love to-day and leave tomorrow. . . . Our Communities are families, as distinctly bounded and separated from promiscuous society as ordinary households. The tie that binds us together is as permanent and sacred, to say the least, as that of marriage, for it is our religion. We receive no members (except by deception or mistake), who do not give their heart and hand to the family interest for life and forever. Community of property extends just as far as freedom of love.
>
> The thing we have done for which we are called "Free Lovers," is simply this: We have left the simple form of marriage and advanced to the complex stage of it. We have no quarrel with those who believe in exclusive dual marriage and faithfully observe it, but we have concluded that for us there is a better way. The honor and faithfulness that constitutes an ideal marriage, may exist between two hundred as well as two; while the guarantees for women and children are much greater in the Community than they can be in any private family.
>
> Oneida Community *Handbooks,* 1867 and 1871[1]

The unauthorized publication in August 1837 of a remarkable private letter on marriage written by an intense young man of twenty-five marked a turning point in his life. For some six years prior to that date, John Humphrey Noyes had experienced extreme intellectual and emotional turmoil. He had struggled to achieve absolute religious and social perfection, sometimes compulsively reading his Bible twelve to sixteen hours a day. When he finally realized in 1834 that God could not expect the impossible of him, Noyes began to develop new religious and sexual theories stressing the importance of inward attitude rather than outward forms. For three years he wandered quixotically throughout New York and New England, trying with frustrating lack of success to convert the entire world to his highly idiosyncratic and heretical perfectionist religious beliefs. He seemed driven to try to justify his existence by spreading his ideas, but his great efforts led to repeated failures and correspondingly wide swings of emotion. During one particularly trying three-week period in New York City, Noyes reached the verge of total mental and emotional collapse.

Perhaps the most devastating blow to Noyes came when he learned in January 1837 that Abigail Merwin, his first convert, idealized love object, and close associate and supporter, had deserted him to marry another man. The shock was terrific. Shy, lacking in sexual experience, and intensely wrapped up in himself, Noyes poured out his feelings in a letter to a friend. Noyes could not accept the fact that Abigail was gone. Instead, expressing ideas that had been germinating in his mind at least since 1834, he declared that in the resurrected state, which he would have an important part in helping to inaugurate on earth as in heaven, there would be no marriage. The legal partitions between the sexes would be broken down and every dish would be free to every guest. "In a holy community there is no more reason why sexual intercourse should be restrained by law than why eating and drinking should be and there is as little occasion for shame in the one case as in the other."[2]

Extracts from this remarkable letter were published anonymously without Noyes's knowledge in August 1837 in a sensational free-love and anti-establishment newspaper, *The Battle-Axe and Weapons of War*, edited by Theophilous Gates. Not surprisingly, the result was a great scandal among New York and New England Perfectionists—individuals who viewed themselves as free from sin and thus also free to follow their inner feelings instead of outmoded societal conventions.[3] Noyes had been closely associated for three years with this nineteenth-century counterpart to the "counter-culture," including individuals who had been among the most extreme in their sexual and marital experimentation.[4] Although he had not participated directly in the licentious excesses which had occurred, his reputation had suffered because of his associations. Thus when the "Battle-Axe Letter" came out and Noyes courageously acknowledged that he had written it, his assertion that the letter was definitely *not* a call to licentiousness did not convince even his few remaining followers. They deserted him, concluding that he was unstable and unbalanced. Noyes appeared totally discredited and alone.

Only twenty years after this unpromising beginning, Noyes and a group of more than two hundred loyal followers were living in a successfully functioning community at Oneida, New York, which embodied many of the religious and social ideas that had been first publicly broached in the Battle-Axe Letter. During approximately a decade of experimentation and transition to communal life between 1837 and 1847, the new theories gradually were elaborated and tried out in practice in Noyes's home town of Putney, Vermont. Expelled from Putney by pressures from townspeople who were outraged by the Perfectionists' deviation from accepted religious and sexual patterns, Noyes and his followers started over on a permanent and larger basis at Oneida, New York, in 1848. The early years of religious, social, and economic transition were intensely troubled. By the mid-1850s, however, relative tranquility had been achieved and almost all the theories and practices that would make Oneida one of the most distinctive of all American ventures in religious and social reorganization had been at least provisionally established.

Central to these distinctive Oneida communal arrangements was the practice of "complex marriage." This form of group marriage was once described by the journalist Charles Nordhoff as an apparently unprecedented "combination of polygamy and polyandry, with certain religious and social restraints."[5] The system, which lasted at Oneida for nearly thirty-two years from 1848 until 1879, when it was abandoned because of internal tensions and external pressure, served as the basic social focus around which the Community was organized. Under complex marriage sexual partners were exchanged frequently among Community members, under a number of restrictive provisions, one of which prescribed the breaking up of any exclusive emotional attachments (described as "special love"), since such attachments were considered selfish behavior antithetical to communal order. Also underlying the system were a difficult voluntary method of birth control through "male continence"; informal oligarchic Community government and control mechanisms through "mutual criticism," "ascending and descending fellowship," and daily religious-and-business meetings; and a communistic form of economic organization in which the good of the Community was given primacy over individual self-interest. At Oneida, sexual roles were perhaps more radically revised than in any similar American group for which extensive documentation exists. In all, the Community member Abel Easton was exaggerating but little when he described Oneida as "a home the like of which has not been seen since the world began."[6]

What accounts for the development and relative success of such a remarkable "free love" community practicing "Bible Communism" in the Jacksonian Era and after? How did such a system originate, attract capable members, and restructure their religious, social, and economic lives so that the resulting community could prosper over more than a quarter of a century? And what implicit or explicit critique of the marital, familial, and sexual patterns of the larger society did the Oneida Perfectionists make?

These will be the primary questions addressed in this chapter. Although a thorough sociological analysis of how the Oneida Community functioned once it had become established would be of much interest, the primary focus here will be on the historical development of the distinctive beliefs and practices pioneered at Oneida. The historical development of Oneida was closely related to the larger stresses and strains of antebellum society. John Humphrey Noyes's writings present a brilliant and highly original perspective on the problems and prospects of his larger environment. Whitney Cross, the foremost historian of the evangelical religious enthusiasms that spread over western New York before the Civil War, has described Noyes's work as "veritably the keystone in the arch of Burned-over District history, demonstrating the connection between the enthusiasms of the right and those of the left."[7] This chapter will suggest how the larger social critique underlying Noyes's thinking was related to the embodiment of his ideas in functioning communal life.

John Humphrey Noyes and His Religious Quest

John Humphrey Noyes, founder and undisputed leader of the Oneida Community during virtually its entire existence, was born on September 11, 1811, in Brattleboro, Vermont. Like many of the individuals who would later join his communities, Noyes grew up in a family of considerably higher than average intellectual and social attainments. His versatile father John taught school for a number of years, amassed a considerable private fortune through various mercantile ventures, and served as a member of the United States House of Representatives. The Noyes family estate eventually would provide much of the necessary capital base that would underwrite the difficult early years of communal experimentation at Putney and Oneida. Noyes's mother, Polly Hayes, was a strong-willed and deeply religious woman from a prosperous merchant family, and was a second cousin to Rutherford B. Hayes, who later became the nineteenth President of the United States. Polly Hayes had a major influence on the development of young John's sense of religious vocation and mission. She complemented her husband's influence on their son's intellectual development with a strong vein of practical idealism.[8]

The close-knit family environment in which young John Humphrey Noyes grew up would later be reflected in many features of the organizational life of the Putney and Oneida Communities. The family was emotionally ingrown, yet strongly aware of its distinctive talents and capabilities. Noyes's father had four brothers, all of whom, apparently because of shyness, had married close cousins. The elder John Noyes himself had only at long last married Polly Hayes when he was forty. This was the conclusion of an extended and rather desultory courtship which finally came to a close when Polly forced the issue of whether he ever would make up his mind to marry her. Young John also shared his father's intense shyness around women, as well as the resulting tendency to intellectualize relationships with the opposite sex.

In attempting to establish communal life at Putney in the late 1830s and early 1840s, John Humphrey Noyes would build upon the base provided by the family property and would use other members of his own family as the core for the enlarged community "family" that he was attempting to set up. Even before his father's death in 1841, Noyes would begin to break down his mother's resistance to his full leadership of the religious and business affairs of the family. He also proceeded, over his mother's objections, to arrange marriages between two of his sisters and his two closest followers. This family unit, with additions that included Noyes's wife Harriet Holton and brother George, would serve as the nucleus of the initial communal group. The extreme family model so fully elaborated later at Oneida was in many ways an extension of the unusual combination of family closeness and distance that Noyes experienced in his early life.[9]

John Humphrey Noyes first began to develop his special sense of religious mission in 1831 after he was converted in Putney, Vermont, during one of a number of religious revivals inspired by the prominent antebellum evangelist Charles Grandison Finney.[10] The initial result of Noyes's 1831 conversion was his decision to go to Andover Theological Seminary to study to become a minister. A year of the sterile professionalism of the Seminary proved disappointing to the zealous Noyes; he was determined to remain "a young convert forever" and live with his heart fervently fixed on the Millennium. Nevertheless, the experience did expose Noyes to many new ideas which influenced his later theological departures. And contact with a group of young missionary brethren at Andover exposed him to self-improvement practices that provided the basis for "mutual criticism," which later became the primary means of informal government at Putney and Oneida.

Moving from Andover to the more liberal and innovative atmosphere of Yale Theological Seminary in 1832, Noyes gained greater flexibility to develop his religious and social ideas. Perhaps the most striking of these ideas grew out of Noyes's elaboration of the beliefs of Moses Stuart, one of his teachers at Andover. Stuart argued that Christ had predicted that his Second Coming would occur within the lifetime of his then-living followers. Noyes was convinced that Stuart's reading of the Bible account was correct; yet he was equally certain that Jesus could not have been wrong in predicting his imminent return. Noyes thus concluded that the Second Coming must have taken place in A.D. 70 when the Temple in Jerusalem was destroyed and the great Diaspora began. At that time, there was a primary resurrection and judgment in the spiritual world: it marked the beginning of the establishment of the Kingdom of God in the heavens. A second and final resurrection judgment was now approaching: "the church on earth is now rising to meet the approaching kingdom in the heavens, and to become its duplicate and representative on earth."[11]

This seemingly bizarre theory, Noyes's first advance into what he called "positive heresy," had important practical consequences. It convinced him that he could not rely on established orthodoxies, and it gave him the first glimmering of the idea that the development of Christianity was a progressive process, and that the age of miracles and of God's active involvement in human affairs was not past. Though Noyes's theology of the Millennium appeared very different from that of the Shakers, Mormons, and many other contemporary groups, its functional importance was the same: to provide an unshakable conviction that the Kingdom of God could and would soon literally be realized on earth.

The Millennium might, indeed, be imminent. But the *nature* of the millennial society and the *means* by which it would be inaugurated were not immediately evident to Noyes. Rather, these ideas gradually developed as his beliefs and sense of personal mission became clarified. At Yale, Noyes drove himself compulsively, isolating himself and endlessly reading and re-reading the Bible on different topics to determine God's will. He seemed to expect almost superhuman perfection of himself. Finally, following his literalistic bent to its extreme logical conclusion, Noyes became convinced that the extraordinary demands for legalistic perfection that he was making of himself were wrong. God could not expect the impossible. The total perfection that God demanded of all true Christians was a right attitude and inner sense of assurance of salvation from sin, not any outward works per se. "Perfection" did not mean that one was not capable of improvement, but simply that so long as one's attitude and motivation were right, one's acts would follow a pattern acceptable to God. Like Luther and many other great religious reformers, Noyes was inspired by the implicit radicalism of St. Paul, who believed that the spirit not the letter of the law, faith not works, was the chief requirement for salvation.[12]

Once he achieved this intellectual breakthrough on February 1, 1834, Noyes characteristically felt compelled to share his new insights with the world. Not surprisingly, his public declaration that he was "perfect" in the sense indicated above, was misconstrued. Some thought Noyes was crazy. Other felt that his beliefs would lead to antinomian excess, turning people loose to do anything they wanted to do. Unable to convince Noyes to back off from his more extreme assertions, his mentor Nathaniel W. Taylor disowned his precocious former pupil. Noyes's license to preach was revoked, and he was left to depend wholly on his inner resources, without any external institutional supports to validate his sense of mission.

Noyes might have cast away his legalistic attitudes intellectually. But only after three emotionally devastating weeks in New York City in May 1834, during which he plumbed the depths of suffering and came to the brink of mental collapse, did he cut his emotional ties to his earlier legalistic upbringing and begin to clear his heart to rebuild his life on a new and more durable foundation.[13] The immediate precipitant of the crisis was the stress of being left almost completely alone, cast adrift by his old associates. At first he had felt a certain exhilaration and bravado at being freed from old shackles. This soon gave way, however, to a feeling of being near physical death, with labored breathing and internal constrictive pressure, which eventually dissipated. During the day, Noyes went around the city engaging in fruitless disputations with various unsympathetic religious leaders. At night, mental anguish and fear of sleep led him compulsively to walk the streets, including the notorious Five Points area, where he preached to down-and-outers and prostitutes, and sometimes fell asleep in the streets wherever exhaustion overtook him. To break free from "the petty tyranny of fashionable morality" he "drank ardent spirits," though, he later declared, he was never intoxicated. Instinctively he ate and drank whatever he craved, particularly the strongest stimulants such as cayenne pepper.

During this period, his mental anguish became almost unbearable. Noyes came to doubt everything. The Bible, Jesus Christ, even God Himself, seemed to fall away as the basis for truth. "Nothing but my own experience was left me," he wrote, and even that appeared to be a deception. Yet his consciousness of inner strength and an unquenchable hope remained. He said within himself: "If the universe is a blind chaos without God, and the destinies of all beings are to be worked out by their own strength, I have as good right to try what I can do for existence and happiness as any body." With this realization, Noyes asserted his will to achieve victory over evil. "The net gave way, and immediately I found myself again in an atmosphere of confidence and peace."[14]

Noyes had passed through the most intense fires of suffering. He had come through to a new inner resolve and sense of himself that amounted to a second conversion. "The effect of this mental overturn was permanent. It completely emptied me, for the time being, of all the theories which I had previously stored up. I could hardly tell afterward what I believed on any subject, till I had investigated it anew; and from this time forward I have had a deep sense of the necessity of laying the foundations of my belief below the frost of spiritual delusion."[15] At first Noyes's reputation suffered still further, since many of his associates felt he had been deranged, but the overall effect of his New York experience was positive. Throughout his life, Noyes's sensitivity to his own inner conflicts and to the confusion in society would continue to cause him much emotional turmoil, but the outcome was never in doubt later. He had laid the foundations for a personal reconciliation with God and a sense of security from sin which later would be conveyed to the followers who joined him in establishing communal living.

Rethinking Relations between the Sexes

During this period when the basis of his personal life and all religious and social truth seemed uncertain, Noyes also began to question and rethink the basis of relations between the sexes. Shyness around women had always bothered Noyes, and in consequence he thought perhaps more deeply about the nature of sexuality and its proper expression than the average person. Following his expulsion from the ministry in 1834 for preaching the necessity of "perfect holiness," Noyes became deeply attached to Abigail Merwin, his first convert. For a time, she became his loyal supporter and defender in the New Haven Free Church, where he first attempted to establish his authority. Though Noyes at the time viewed their relationship as purely "spiritual," it is clear that the distinction between spiritual and sexual love was unclear; much of Noyes's extraordinary intensity in this period may be seen as part of the sublimation of his sexual impulses.

The conclusions Noyes reached at this time about the proper relations between the sexes paralleled his conclusions about the proper approach to religious and social truth generally. He thought long and deeply about the arguments for celibacy. Gradually, however, he became convinced that the celibate life was an inadequate expression of the full range of human experience. If one had the right attitude, he came to believe, sexual relations, just as other activities in life, would be expressed in an outward manner that would be pleasing to God. Summarizing these early understandings, Noyes declared:

> I then came to the conclusions in which I have since stood, viz., that the outward act of sexual connection is as innocent and comely as any other act, or rather if there is any difference in the character

of outward acts, that this is the most noble and comely of all. This
sentiment covered with any covering but that of the Spirit, is licentiousness. . . . God tells me that he does not care so much
what I do as how I do it. . . . every day sinks me deeper and
deeper in the certainty that these are the principles of God, and of
his heavenly hosts.[16]

Such statements easily could be misconstrued and misused. The excesses of militant Perfectionists forced Noyes to give more serious consideration to how his beliefs in sexual "anti-legality" could be constructively
organized in practice. It was all too easy for emotionally unstable individuals to equate legitimate freedom from external law or outmoded older
standards with the irresponsible antinomian freedom to do whatever they
chose. To do away with external restrictions on behavior without developing new inner standards to replace them would be fatal to the
movement. This was shown by irregularities such as those among the
Perfectionists of Brimfield, Massachusetts.

At Brimfield in 1835, Mary Lincoln and Maria Brown decided to
show that their piety could overcome carnal desires by sleeping chastely
in the same bed with a visiting evangelist. Noyes had been at Brimfield
earlier with that same evangelist, and had sensed that irregularities were
developing even before the "Brimfield bundling" occurred. In fact, he
had felt so threatened by the atmosphere that one evening he had left
Brimfield precipitously, making his way home some sixty miles through
bitter cold and snow to Putney, Vermont, in less than twenty-four hours.
Thus Noyes had not been at Brimfield when the bundling scandal broke;
nevertheless he became associated in the popular mind with such irregularities.

During the four years between his conversion to Perfectionism in 1834
and his attempt to establish a community of his own at Putney in 1838,
Noyes drifted about, geographically and doctrinally. While he sharply
dissociated himself from the bundling at Brimfield and the irregularities
which followed, he recognized how closely his own testimony was related
to such excesses. Having his words "tried by fire," "instead of convicting
me of sin, purged and healed my conscience; but it deepened my sense of
responsibility, and imposed upon my spirit a sobriety and resolution to
resist corruption among professed Perfectionists."[17] As Noyes began to
clarify his position, he moved out to assert his authority and the validity
of his views by attempting to clear Perfectionism of "the disreputable
mysticisms and barbarisms which had begun to discredit it."[18] He met
most of the important eastern Perfectionist leaders, cast off his more
erratic associates, and gradually hammered out the beliefs which helped
him to capture the entire eastern wing of Perfectionism.

The first clear printed presentation of John Humphrey Noyes's sexual and marriage beliefs, and the turning point in his career, came as a result of the unintended publication of a letter that he wrote in January 1837 after discovering that he had lost Abigail Merwin to another man. As late as December 28, 1835, Noyes had tried to minimize their estrangement by writing her of his conviction of their spiritual affinity and that she was destined to be his wife. He further declared that his experiences at New York and at Prospect had brought him to an understanding of "the place which the marriage relation will hold in the coming dispensation."[19]

Those views were starkly expressed in a private letter Noyes wrote to his close friend David Harrison on January 15, 1837. The first part of the letter was a reassertion of Noyes's continued faith in his mission despite the emotional blows he had suffered. Noyes realized that the transition to new social forms which he foresaw would be a painful process: "Between this present time and the establishment of God's kingdom over the earth, lies a chaos of confusion, tribulation, woe, &c. such as must attend the destruction of the fashion of this world, and the introduction of the will of God as it is done in heaven."[20]

The core of the letter, however, was the final paragraph. Because of the importance of this statement in indicating the direction of Noyes's later marriage and sexual thought, it will be reproduced in full here. Using words of startling bluntness, Noyes declared:

> I will write all that is in my heart on one delicate subject, and you may judge for yourself whether it is expedient to show this letter to others. When the will of God is done on earth, as it is in heaven, *there will be no marriage*. The marriage supper of the Lamb, is a feast at which *every dish is free to every guest*. Exclusiveness, jealousy, quarrelling, have no place there, for the same reason as that which forbids the guests at a thanksgiving dinner to claim each his separate dish, and quarrel with the rest for his rights. In a holy community, there is no more reason why sexual intercourse should be restricted by law, than why eating and drinking should be—and there is as little occasion for shame in the one case as in the other. God has placed a wall of partition between the male and female during the apostacy, for a good reason, which will be broken down in the resurrection, for equally good reasons. But woe to him who abolishes the law of the apostacy before he stands in the holiness of the resurrection. The guests of the marriage supper may have each his favourite dish, each a dish of his own procuring, and that without the jealousy of exclusiveness. I call a certain woman my wife—she is yours, she is Christ's, and in him she is the bride of all saints. She is dear in the hand of a stranger, and according to my promise to her, I rejoice. My claim upon her cuts directly across the marriage covenant of this world, and God knows the end. Write if you wish to hear from me. Yours in the Lord.[21]

Not surprisingly, when extracts from this letter were printed anonymously in Theophilous Gates's newspaper, *The Battle-Axe and Weapons of War,* a storm of controversy was the result. Within a month, Noyes had acknowledged that he was, indeed, the author of the letter, but that he had not intended to put those sentiments before the public. Trying to clarify his meaning, he emphatically denied that he had engaged in any improper behavior himself, or that he proposed the platform of his letter for immediate adoption. Properly followed, his approach would not result in licentiousness: "Liberty never metamorphoses the children of God into swine. If any become swine in consequence of learning the law of liberty, they are only hypocrites made manifest."[22]

Not until nearly nine years after the Battle-Axe Letter was published, would Noyes begin the practical introduction of the system among his closest followers. The immediate effect of the publication of the letter, however, was devastating to Noyes's activities. His newspaper, *The Witness,* collapsed as subscribers fell away. His reputation seemed ruined, and his career, such as it had been, seemed finished. Once again, Noyes appeared totally isolated and alone.

Noyes's Marriage and the Move toward Community

The appearance of the Battle-Axe Letter and the repercussions which ensued seemed to mark the nadir of Noyes's career. In retrospect, however, Noyes viewed those events as a providential turning point which presaged his ultimate success. From that time on, he felt that he "was called, even under the heaviest penalties, to defend and ultimately carry out the doctrine of communism in love."[23] In attempting to justify himself and rehabilitate his reputation, Noyes began to settle down and establish the organizational forms which eventually would allow his principles to be realized in functioning community life. Rather than attempting quixotically to convert the whole world to his religious ideas, he turned his sights toward more practical goals. He would seek to realize his social ideas among tested followers in small-scale pilot projects, while continuing to propagate his ideas in the periodical press.

In the wake of the Battle-Axe controversy, Noyes's first important organizational move was to go home and arrange to marry Harriet Holton in 1838. The reasons for this sudden marriage to a woman he barely knew were complex. For Noyes, the essential precondition appears to have been Harriet's demonstrated and unswerving loyalty to him and his ideas. Additionally, she must have seemed "safe" sexually, unlikely to make special demands on him. And, while she was capable and hardworking, she appeared to be totally willing to be shaped according to his desires. Only such a woman would have been likely to have accepted the unusual proposal of marriage offered by John Humphrey Noyes.

That proposal involved a redefinition of the beliefs that Noyes had expressed in the Battle-Axe Letter. Earthly marriage, with its legal and emotional exclusiveness, would eventually be done away with in the resurrected state which was to be realized on earth. Such selfish relationships would be subordinated to the larger and more inclusive concerns of the holy community. Noyes was proposing to Harriet Holton "a partnership which I will not call marriage, till I have defined it."

> . . . we can enter into no engagements with each other, which shall limit the range of our affections, as they are limited in matrimonial engagements by the fashion of this world. I desire and expect my yoke-fellow, will love all who love God, whether they be male or female, with a warmth and strength of affection unknown to earthly lovers, and as freely as if she stood in no particular connexion with me. In fact, the object of my connexion with her will be, not to monopolize and enslave her heart or my own, but to enlarge and establish both, in the free fellowship of God's universal family. If the external union and companionship of a man and a woman in accordance with these principles, is properly called marriage, I know that marriage exists in heaven, and I have no scruple in offering you my heart and hand, with an engagement to be married in due form, as soon as God shall permit.
>
> . . .
>
> I know that the immortal union of hearts, the everlasting honeymoon, which alone is worthy to be called marriage, can never be *made* by a ceremony, and I know equally well that such a marriage, can never be *marred* by a ceremony.[24]

Whatever one might think personally about this extraordinary marriage proposal, it does suggest an acute awareness on Noyes's part of the arbitrary, human character of American marriage practices of his day. Perhaps only in times of extreme social flux, would individuals explicitly articulate the relative character of existing marriage arrangements. For most people in most periods of history, the relationship between emotional expression and the particular social forms within which such expression occurs is largely taken for granted. Noyes and many contemporary millennialists, on the other hand, were sharply aware of the inadequacy of existing marriage forms. Rather than assume that all marriage standards were relative, however, they sought to realize new "divine" standards of their own. For John Humphrey Noyes, the development of such "divine" standards to restructure marriage was a gradual process which was only expressed in clear written form in the late 1840s.

After setting out the premises upon which their marriage would be based, Noyes's proposal to Harriet Holton enumerated the specific reasons why he wanted to marry her. These were given in a flat and unemotional tone, written as a "witness," not an "advocate." Underlying all the other reasons was the idea that the marriage would advance God's work, the work in which Noyes felt he was engaged. Further: "It will set us free, at least myself, from much reproach, and many evil surmisings, which are occasioned by celibacy in the present circumstances." Subsequently, Noyes was to observe ingenuously: "By this marriage, besides herself, and a good social position, which she held as belonging to the first families of Vermont, I obtained money enough to buy a house and printing-office, and to buy a press and type."[25] With that press, which Noyes bought within three weeks of their marriage, he resumed publication of his newspaper, *The Witness,* which for several years appeared to be devoted as much to bearing witness to Noyes's good character as to his views of the will of God.

The Noyes-Holton marriage was thus apparently one of convenience, at least at first. In this time of transition and uncertainty, Noyes was unwilling fully to commit himself emotionally to any individual, even in marriage. Nevertheless, Robert Fogarty's statement that Harriet Holton was the only one of the three women important in Noyes's adult life whom he *"never* loved,"[26] appears exaggerated. Certainly, Noyes does not seem to have loved Harriet in the romantic sense, but he did not really love his followers in such a sense either. The deep respect and abiding affection in which John and Harriet held each other, combined with their mutual and lifelong loyalty in pursuit of larger religious and communal goals, gave to their relationship a dimension beyond the simply pragmatic. In his marriage, as well as in all aspects of the community life which he would develop, Noyes subordinated individual wills and self-interest to the larger communal goals.

Following his marriage, John Humphrey Noyes's next organizational move was to try to assert complete authority over his own family in Putney, Vermont, as well as to establish his leadership over the small group of followers who joined his family at the Putney Bible School which they had started in 1836. Noyes began by securing the loyalty of his younger brother George, as well as of two of his sisters, Harriet and Charlotte, whose marriages he eventually arranged in the early 1840s to two of his closest followers, John L. Skinner and John R. Miller. The Noyes brothers, together with Skinner and Miller, with the later addition of George Cragin, would form the informal governing group of "central members," who charted the development of the Putney and Oneida Communities. Responding to the physical and mental incapacity of his aging, alcoholic father,[27] Noyes also tried to assert his authority over his strong-willed mother. She was upset by the way he was using up the family estate to support his religious projects. Despite the intense psychological pressure applied to her, not until 1839 did she at last fully capitulate to her son as "being to me a teacher and father in spiritual things."[28]

In these instances, as well as in his subsequent community ventures, Noyes demanded total authority and control. As early as 1837, Noyes had declared that "I would never connect myself with any individual or association in religion unless I were acknowledged leader."[29] In later describing his ideal model for the government of his communities at Putney and Oneida, he declared that the Kingdom of God is an "absolute monarchy," with authority coming from the top, yet decisions tempered by the concerns of the membership below.[30] Noyes, of course, would be the supreme leader who benevolently delegated authority to loyal subordinates who would do the concrete work of implementing his ideals. As George Wallingford Noyes observed: "The dogma of Noyes's divine commission became a touchstone in the Putney and Oneida Communities. Those who rejected it were turned away; those who accepted it were bound together in a brotherhood of self-sacrificing quest for the Kingdom of God."[31]

What accounts for this insistence on absolute control which continued throughout the life of John Humphrey Noyes? One initially might suspect psychopathology. This simple answer, however, does not explain why Noyes was able to set up emotionally satisfying communities that played a generally constructive role in their members' lives. Noyes's personal concerns, as well as the appeal of his essentially oligarchic system of government to the articulate individuals who joined his communities, were related to the sense these people had of the extreme disorganization of their larger social environment. Individuals with a sense of religious and social collapse sought to establish some basis for order as the first necessity. A cohesive, unified, and self-contained community life, separated as much as possible from the disorders of the outer world, would allow individuals who felt threatened and disoriented to find a new and more secure basis for their lives.

This interpretation is supported by much of the leading scholarship on Oneida. In his study of the social sources of Oneida membership, Robert Fogarty has argued that, although the religious and social ideas of Oneida might appear radical at first sight, the Community actually grew and prospered because of its "conservatism." It was able to provide a sense of security and a satisfying new set of absolutes to replace the vagaries of revivalistic religion.[32] Noyes himself gave support to this interpretation when he argued that a true "conservative," which he felt that he was, must be prepared to radically change existing belief and practice in order to reestablish a satisfying basis for social life.[33] And a brilliant psychoanalytically oriented study of John Humphrey Noyes by Robert Thomas argues that Noyes's underlying ego-strengths allowed him not only to reestablish his own emotional stability but also to create supports for the lives of his followers as well.[34] Thus, the ability to achieve what Noyes described as "salvation from sin," in both the religious and secular spheres, accounts for much of his appeal, as well as the appeal of other antebellum communitarian experimenters.

The period from 1841 to 1846, when the little community at Putney was in its most plastic state, was also a time of unusual tensions and communal interest in American society in general. Between 1841 and 1844— the depths of the depression generated by the Panic of 1837—Brook Farm emerged out of New England Unitarianism, Hopedale grew out of New England Universalism, and some thirty or more lesser-known and shortlived "secular" Associations were formed under the inspiration of the ideas of the French social thinker Charles Fourier, as reinterpreted by his American disciple Albert Brisbane. The group of Perfectionists which gathered at Putney eventually described itself as an Association, as did Oneida in the early days. This terminology suggests the Fourierist influence upon John Humphrey Noyes's beliefs, which were, in essence, a breakaway from the orthodoxy of New England Congregationalism.[35]

In forming his Communities, Noyes tried to synthesize a new, cohesive unity from the best elements of the great popular excitements of his day. Looking back, he saw the two great efforts at reconstruction in the antebellum period as coming from the religious revivalists, whose great idea was "the regeneration of the soul," and the secular associationists, or socialists, whose great complementary ideal was "the regeneration of society, which is the soul's environment."[36] But Noyes's primary starting point was the religious one, as he indicated in an early critique of the Fourierists:

> . . . we have no hope of perfecting human nature by improving its external conditions. We think the Fourierists have begun at the wrong end. They are trying to build a chimney by beginning at the top; and we think they will fail not because we do not believe that chimneys can and should be built, but because we do not believe that such heavy structures can be durably built on anything but a firm foundation and by beginning at the bottom. The great problems of our relation to God and of the relation of the sexes, which the Fourierists postpone as of no pressing importance, we consider the first to be solved.[37]

To summarize, common values and commitments had to be internalized before durable new social forms for life could be constructed. In retrospect, Noyes concluded that the "Revivalists failed for want of regeneration of society, and the Socialists failed for want of regeneration of the heart."[38] Only by achieving an enlarged unitary family such as the one at Oneida, could all aspects of religious and social life be reintegrated into a cohesive whole.

Following Noyes's order of priorities, the small group of Perfectionists at Putney gradually developed new and more complex forms of social organization to support their religious ideals. As we have seen, the original nucleus of the community had gathered around John Humphrey Noyes's family and a few close associates who had begun to establish the Putney Bible School in 1836. By the time of the formal division of the estate of Noyes's father on February 5, 1841, which provided nearly $20,000 to support community life, a clear economic side to the organization developed as well. On February 22, 1841, a Society of Inquiry was officially established. By the end of March 1843, despite the defection of approximately one third of the members, there were thirty-five persons at Putney—twenty-six adults and nine children—being supported by the common purse and living primarily in three dwellings owned by the Noyes family. Until the commencement of the practice of complex marriage in 1846, no further membership additions occurred.

Between 1842 and 1846, there was a move toward community of property to provide support for the original, primarily religious goals. A Contract of Partnership signed February 26, 1844, introduced a joint-stock principle of property ownership into the Corporation. And on March 8, 1845, this arrangement was superseded by a more elaborate Constitution which moved toward explicit communism of property. Nevertheless, even as late as the Oneida period, full communistic amalgamation of property holdings had not yet occurred. All these arrangements were made on an ad hoc basis, as part of an attempt to find the best way of expressing their religious convictions. As Noyes noted on January 10, 1843:

> A spirit of love naturally led us into a sort of community of goods.
> . . . Our community has no constitution nor written laws. Our object in coming together was not to form a community after the fashion of the Shakers or Fourierites, but simply to publish the gospel and help one another in spiritual things. We found it necessary to investigate many new problems in social economy, but it is difficult as yet to tell what form of social life we shall ultimately take.[39]

The Ideological Underpinnings

John Humphrey Noyes's first move to establish order within himself, and, as a necessary corollary, in the lives of his followers, had been to create loyalty to a common set of religious beliefs, common value premises according to which communal life eventually would be conducted. Religious commitment preceded the formation of communities. Similarly, the theoretical aspects of Noyes's plans for marital reorganization also were developed prior to practice. Noyes stated that during the twelve years between his conversion to Perfectionism in 1834 and his first actual practice of complex marriage on a limited scale in 1846, he had strictly adhered to the normative marriage practices of the world, remaining celibate before marriage and strictly monogamous thereafter.[40] Only when he had set up an adequate value foundation and organizational backing so that he could be relatively confident of success, did he make the break from conventional marriage patterns to those that he considered to belong to the heavenly state.

As we have seen, sexual problems had plagued Noyes and many other Perfectionists in the free-floating, unstructured atmosphere of the 1830s in New York and the Northeastern states. Looking back in 1840, Noyes described the extremes which had resulted. He declared that in dealing with sexual morality,

> . . . the church and the world have swung far beyond the center to the right. Perfectionism took away the restraining force, and some swung far beyond the center to the left. In this case, the church and the world are the cause, for they placed men in a position of unnatural restraint; Perfectionism was the occasion, though innocent occasion; for the abolition of law is an essential feature of the gospel and must not be kept back let the consequences be what they may.[41]

Eschewing the extremes of both the right and the left, Noyes would devote his efforts to restoring a proper balance in the relations between the sexes.

In wrestling with these problems, Noyes was heavily influenced by the writings and approach of the Shakers. This celibate group, which swung even farther to the right than conventional society had in seeking to control human sexuality, provided the most thorough and intellectually impressive contemporary Perfectionist arguments as to how the proper relations between the sexes should be restored. Paradoxically though it may seem, Noyes's sexual theories and even much of his basic theological structure may be viewed, formally at least, as a Shaker heresy.[42] The system which Noyes developed at Putney and Oneida was, in a sense, a form of self-denying "Victorian sensuality," which stood the Shaker system on its head.

Although Noyes developed his own theories without wholesale borrowing from the ideas of other groups, including the Shakers, his affinity for the Shakers' approach is apparent in his frequent respectful, if often critical, use of them as a foil for his own views. Writing in 1848, Noyes observed:

> Forbid sexual intercourse altogether and you attain the same results, so far as shutting off the jealousies and strifes of exclusiveness is concerned, as we attain by making sexual intercourse free. In this matter the Shakers show their shrewdness. But they sacrifice the vitality of society, in securing its peace.[43]

Elsewhere Noyes declared that his approach and that of the Shakers were the only two possible in the resurrected state.[44] And he further said: "If I believed in a Shaker heaven I would be a Shaker now."[45]

But Noyes did not believe in a Shaker heaven. He felt that the Shaker emphasis on sexual shame was morbid and irrational. He declared that both

> . . . the Shaker and the licentious spiritualist are alike in their fundamental error, which is an over-estimate of the importance of the outward act of sexual union. The Shaker, with a prurient swollen imagination of the importance of that act, pronounces it a damnable abomination prohibited to all the saints. The licentious spiritualist, with the same morbid imagination, thinks it right and necessary in the face of all human regulations, to perform it at the bidding of impulse.

In Noyes's view, neither the act of sexual union nor the abstinence from that act had any importance in itself. The goal, rather, was "a healthy development and faithful subordination of the sexual susceptibility." That could be achieved without either "the monkery of the Shakers" or "the extravagances of the licentious spiritualist."[46]

John Humphrey Noyes's contact with the Shakers was not merely abstract or intellectual. Recognizing that celibacy, or "practical Shakerism," was antithetical to his program and could cause a falling away of his own followers, Noyes inveighed against the group and their ideas in his newspaper, *The Witness,* in the late 1830s.[47] In the summer of 1839, Noyes and his new bride visited the Shaker community at Harvard, Massachusetts, where he had a lively, if inconclusive, exchange with them.[48] On March 16, 1849, during the difficult organizational phase at Oneida, Noyes visited the New Lebanon community for the express purpose of informing the elders there "that I was laying the foundations of a society and a system that would sooner or later subvert Shakerism."[49] Later, in a mellower mood, Noyes observed that if only the Shakers had known his method of birth control and scientific propagation, they probably would have adopted his system.[50] Noyes's son Pierrepont remembered that the Massachusetts Shakers frequently visited the Oneida Community in the 1870s, where they performed their dances before the group. And he was struck by his father's long, serious conversations with the Shaker leader Frederick W. Evans, during which Noyes, to his son's surprise, "treated him as an equal and seemed to recognize some spiritual value in an outsider."[51] Throughout this analysis, the influence of the Shaker approach on Noyes's theory and practice will recur as a unifying thread.

Although he was influenced by the Shakers, Noyes's critique of existing marriage practices and his proposed solution to the problem of relations between the sexes were very much his own creation. The burden of Noyes's argument—which originated between 1834 and 1837 and was further expressed publicly and elaborated between 1837 and 1847—is remarkably consistent over the years. The most succinct summary of the views that were published in his newspapers and internalized by his followers in the mid-1840s may be found in Noyes's "Bible Argument Defining the Relations of the Sexes in the Kingdom of Heaven."[52] Written in the early spring of 1848, immediately after he came to Oneida, the "Bible Argument" is a reformulation of Noyes's earlier views, and it almost certainly expresses the ideals which underlay the initial efforts at Putney to introduce the practice of complex marriage in 1846.

The "Bible Argument" was more than simply a recapitulation of Noyes's earlier beliefs. Looking to the future, it also contained almost every important idea for the revision of relations between the sexes that Noyes would implement during the subsequent thirty years at Oneida— including complex marriage, male continence, and scientific propagation. The statement was adopted by the Oneida Association as its declaration of principles, was printed in its *First Annual Report* in 1849, and was boldly sent out to various public officials, including the Governor of New York State. The "Bible Argument" thus provided the pivotal formulation of Noyes's marriage beliefs. It will be further supplemented in the analysis which follows by reference to Noyes's more detailed articles in his newspapers and other writings.

As outlined in the "Bible Argument," the underlying problems with which Noyes sought to deal during his life were fourfold and integrally interconnected:

> The chain of evils which holds humanity in ruin has four links, viz—1st, a breach with God; (Gen. 3:8;) 2d, a disruption of the sexes, involving a special curse on woman, (Gen. 3:16;) 3d, the curse of oppressive labor, bearing specially on man; (Gen. 3:17–19) 4th, Death. (Gen. 3:22–24.) These are all inextricably complicated

[*sic*] with each other. The true scheme of redemption begins with reconciliation with God, proceeds first to a restoration of true relations between the sexes, then to reform of the industrial system, and ends with victory over death. . . . Holiness, free love, association in labor, and immortality, constitute the chain of redemption, and must come together in their true order.

From what precedes, it is evident that any attempt to revolutionize sexual morality before settlement with God, is out of order. Holiness must go before free love. Perfectionists are not responsible for the proceedings of those who meddle with the sexual question, before they have laid the foundation of true faith and union with God.[53]

Since Noyes had already securely established his religious foundations by this time, the "Bible Argument" primarily addresses the second problem—how true relations between the sexes are to be restored. To do this, the earthly institution of marriage, "which assigns the exclusive possession of one woman to one man," must be eliminated. Such marriage treats women in effect as a form of property, and thus has the same harmful effects as other types of selfish ownership of property. The existing marriage regulations of the world are purely arbitrary, not founded in man's real nature. Hence, they lack divine sanction.

All experience testifies . . . that sexual love is not naturally restricted to pairs. . . . the secret history of the human heart will bear out the assertion that it is capable of loving any number of times and any number of persons, and that the more it loves the more it can love.[54]

Noyes describes how the legal marriage restrictions that he and his followers experienced were inadequate:

The law of marriage "worketh wrath." It provokes to secret adultery, actual or of the heart. It ties together unmatched natures. It sunders matched natures. It gives to sexual appetite only a scanty and monotonous allowance, and so produces the natural vices of poverty, contraction of taste and stinginess or jealousy. It makes no provision for the sexual appetite at the very time when that appetite is strongest. By the custom of the world, marriage, in the average of cases, takes place at about the age of twenty-four; whereas puberty commences at the age of fourteen. For ten years, therefore, and that in the very flush of life, the sexual appetite is starved. This law of society bears hardest on females, because they have less opportunity of choosing their time of marriage than men. This discrepancy between the marriage system and nature, is one of the principal sources of the peculiar diseases of women, of prostitution, masturbation, and licentiousness in general.[55]

In later articles in his newspapers, Noyes described the inadequacies of conventional antebellum marriage practices even more explicitly.[56] Briefly, he argued that "marriage," in its present sense, was antagonistic to the "family." By this rather startling statement, he meant that existing patterns of "marriage" which grew out of romantic love, frequently separated a couple geographically, emotionally, and socially from their "family"—that is their parents and larger kinship and community ties. Such marriages based on romantic love contributed to the fragmentation of social relations. As Noyes saw it, love attachments confined to individual couples were "egotism for two," part of the same disruptive and anti-social individualism that was represented by the rampant, economically acquisitive spirit of the antebellum scene.

How were the disruptive aspects of such romantic love to be dealt with constructively? Further individualistic fragmentation—for instance, free love outside a community context—was no solution. Instead of causing community disruption, powerful sexual forces should be given natural channels and harnessed to provide a vital bond within society. Noyes wanted all believers to be unified and to share a perfect community of interests, to replace the "I-spirit" with the "we-spirit." If believers were fully to love each other while living in close communal association, they must be allowed to love each other fervently and physically, "not by pairs, as in the world, but *en masse.*" The necessary restrictions of the earthly period, governed by arbitrary human law, would eventually have to give way to the final heavenly free state, governed by the spirit in which "hostile surroundings and powers of bondage cease" and "all restrictions also will cease." A perfect unity in all respects would result. Each should be married to all—heart, mind and body—in a complex marriage.[57]

This would be achieved by enlarging the home. Loyalty to the selfish nuclear family unit would be replaced by loyalty to the entire community. Noyes inveighed against the harmful effects of growing economic differentiation, which served to split the family. The mother was held in an almost slave-like bondage in the home, while the father toiled in a hectic and uncertain world outside. The family must be reunified. The father must be reintegrated into the spiritual and economic leadership of the home and home economy, and the sexes must work side by side in vital and rewarding labor.[58] One senses that Noyes almost looked for a restoration of the manorial ideal in economic life. At Oneida, such a reintegration of all aspects of life into a unified whole was to a large extent successfully achieved. Religious, economic, social, and even sexual loyalties were raised from the individual to the group level. With a tight organization and a definite separation from surrounding society, Noyes's

Perfectionist followers would be able to create one of the few successful examples of sustained group marriage recorded in history.

New Forms of Social Control: Male Continence and Mutual Criticism

Even as Noyes was developing his unorthodox theoretical approach to relations between the sexes, he faced more mundane and immediately pressing emotional and sexual problems of his followers, problems which necessitated new efforts at social control. In the early 1840s, the most serious sexual difficulty with which Noyes struggled was a triangle involving his followers George and Mary Cragin and Abram C. Smith, leader of a faction of Perfectionists in Newark, New Jersey, which was loyal to Noyes's theories.[59] Smith was locked into a desperately unhappy marriage with a woman whom Noyes described as a "perfect devil." On the other side were Mary Cragin, a coquette and woman who seemingly "couldn't say no," and her husband George, a competent, hard-working, and self-effacing man who apparently only functioned well when working under the guidance of another, stronger personality. When the Cragins visited the Smiths' summer home in Rondout, the results were predictable—a secret liaison between Abram Smith and Mary Cragin. Getting wind of the Smith-Cragin affair, Noyes visited them and severely reproved the guilty parties for their behavior.

Eventually, all three individuals moved to Putney, where they could be under Noyes's immediate supervision. He worked with them, trying to help them overcome the "lusts and affections of the flesh," and work out their emotional difficulties. The Smith-Cragin affair convinced Noyes that his Eden, no less than the original one, must have a wall and a "flaming sword that turned every way" to keep the Devil out.[60] These protections were developed gradually through several new forms of organizational control that were closely associated with preparing the way for the coming of complex marriage.

The first of these controls was "male continence"; the second was "mutual criticism." The source of the theory of male continence, Noyes's unusual form of birth control, can be traced back to 1837, when he read Robert Dale Owen's *Moral Physiology,* an early birth control pamphlet, as well as works of the Shakers.[61] The practical impetus for the development of this new technique came as Noyes attempted to deal with the problems of his wife Harriet. During their first six years of married life, she experienced five difficult childbirths, four of which were premature and resulted in the death of the child. After the last failure, Noyes vowed to her never again to expose her to such fruitless suffering. He decided that he would live apart from her, if necessary, rather than break his vow.

This was hardly a satisfactory solution to the problem. In the summer of 1844, Noyes propounded the idea that the sexual organs had a social function which could be separated in practice from the propagative one. He drew the same basic distinction that Robert Dale Owen had made in *Moral Physiology* between the use of sexual intercourse for "amative" and "propagative" purposes. The first concern of sexual intercourse should be social: to allow the two sexes to communicate and express affection for each other. God created Eve primarily as a "helpmeet" and companion for man, and only secondarily for propagative purposes. Noyes thought that it was extremely important to "establish intelligent, voluntary control over the propagative function."[62]

Noyes thus was highly critical both of unplanned procreation and of the various then-current means to avoid procreation. In his opinion, sexual intercourse when no progeny were desired was analogous to masturbation, less common only because "a woman is less convenient than the ordinary means of masturbation."[63] ". . . after marriage it is as foolish and cruel to expend one's seed on a wife merely for the sake of getting rid of it, as it would be to fire a gun at one's best friend merely for the sake of unloading it."[64] The various current means of birth control—abstinence, artificial aids, and abortion—all appeared unappealing to Noyes. And *coitus interruptus,* the method proposed by Robert Dale Owen, was wasteful of a man's seed and vital powers. In Noyes's opinion: "it is the glory of man to control himself, and the Kingdom of Heaven summons him to self-control in ALL THINGS."[65]

Whatever one's opinion of "male continence," Noyes's term for what is technically described as *coitus reservatus,* the practice certainly did require male self-control. In male continence, a couple would engage in sexual congress without the man ever ejaculating, either during intercourse or after withdrawal. This practice of male continence was a logical outgrowth of Noyes's principles. In his view, regular intercourse is wasteful, sowing the seed where one does not want or expect it to grow.

> Yet it is equally manifest that the natural instinct of our nature demands frequent congress of the sexes, not for propagative, but for social and spiritual purposes. It results from this that simple congress of the sexes, without the propagative crisis, is the order of nature, for the gratification of ordinary amative instincts. . . .[66]

Noyes used several intriguing analogies to defend his unorthodox method of birth control. He denied that male continence was "unnatural." If it was, then "cooking, wearing clothes, living in houses, and almost everything else done by civilized man, is unnatural in the same sense. . . ." ". . . every instance of self-denial is an interruption of some natural act. The

man who virtuously contents himself with a look at a beautiful woman is
conscious of such an interruption. The lover who stops at a kiss denies
himself a natural progression." Noyes was merely drawing the line further
along than a group such as the Shakers, which had only resorted to "the
most imposing of human contrivances for avoiding the woes of undesired
propagation."[67] Indeed, male continence might be described, paradoxically
enough, as a form of "celibate intercourse."[68]

To describe the process of male continence, Noyes used a striking
analogy:

> The situation may be compared to a stream in three conditions,
> viz., 1, a fall; 2, a course of rapids above the fall; and 3, still water
> above the rapids. The skillful boatman may choose whether he will
> remain in the still water, or venture more or less down the rapids,
> or run his boat over the fall. But there is a point on the verge of the
> fall where he has no control over his course; and just above that
> there is a point where he will have to struggle with the current in a
> way which will give his nerves a severe trial, even though he may
> escape the fall. If he is willing to learn, experience will teach him the
> wisdom of confining his excursions to the region of easy rowing,
> unless he has an object in view that is worth the cost of going over
> the falls.[69]

"Our method simply proposes the subordination of the flesh to the spirit,
teaching men to seek principally the elevated spiritual pleasures of sexual
intercourse, and to be content with them in their general intercourse with
women, restricting the more sensual part to its proper occasions."[70]

How well did such an unusual system work? Initial experimentation
by Noyes and his followers suggested that the procedure was effective
in curtailing pregnancies. And after complex marriage began to be introduced in 1846, the technique further proved its effectiveness. During the
twenty-one years between 1848 and 1869, when male continence was
almost the sole sanctioned form of sexual intercourse at Oneida, at most
thirty-one accidental births took place in a community numbering approximately two hundred adults, and having frequent sexual congress
with a variety of partners during that time.[71] Undoubtedly, that low birth
rate can be traced to the practice of having women past menopause induct
young men into male continence and having older, more experienced men
induct young women. But the effectiveness of male continence as a means
of birth control in a regulated community setting is incontestable. There
were fewer pregnancies with male continence than there would have been
with the pill.

The psychological effects of the system are more ambiguous. Unfortunately, approximately twenty-five years ago, an extensive body of diaries,

journals, and other personal papers of Community members which might shed light on this matter apparently were destroyed. And those items which were fortuitously saved are not currently available to most outside scholarship, nor likely to become so in the near future.[72] As a result, evaluation of the psychological effects of male continence must be based primarily on the printed sources put out by the Community—the books, pamphlets, and especially the newspapers. These are often remarkably frank in discussing ideals and problems of all sorts.

From the printed sources, it appears that there were indeed serious problems connected with the introduction and dissolution of Community life, including male continence and complex marriage, which male continence helped make possible. But if these difficult transition periods are excepted, male continence and other forms of Community control do not appear to have been excessively burdensome. Even in the troubled late stages of Oneida's history, a careful medical study of the health of the Community by Noyes's son Theodore showed *less* incidence of "nervous disorders" than in the society at large, although the relationship of such disorders to male continence is not clear.[73] Noyes himself felt that a slightly higher than average level of sexual tension was not necessarily harmful.[74] His son Pierrepont dimly recalled a quality of restrained romantic excitement pervading and invigorating Community life, an atmosphere that Abel Easton described as a sort of "continuous courtship."[75] Finally, the practice of male continence for many years evidently did not lead to impotence. When Noyes instituted his experiment in "scientific propagation" in 1869, many men who had long practiced male continence deliberately sired children.[76]

Despite the disclaimers, it is difficult to believe that there were no significant problems connected with male continence. Probably even with unusually strong religious commitment, proper training, and stringent enforcement procedures, few men could have found the technique "easy," as Noyes declared it was for "spiritual men." Hints in Noyes's writings and exhortations, for instance, suggest that masturbation, and associated antisocial withdrawal from Community life, may have been a minor problem at times, but the record is inconclusive. According to Maren Lockwood Carden's figures, the rate of secession from Oneida for men was approximately twice that of the women, though it was only two or three per year on the average.[77] Although this could have been due to dissatisfactions with male continence or a variety of other aspects of Community life, probably the higher figure for men simply reflected the greater ease that they found in reestablishing their independence in the outside world. Whatever the difficulties associated with male continence, most Oneida men evidently preferred it to celibacy, the only other alternative, which seems to have been practiced by a few men of the Community.[78]

Although male continence was described almost wholly in terms of male perspectives and concerns, leading Robert Thomas to conjecture that Noyes developed the technique more to satisfy his own psychic needs than to alleviate his wife's problems,[79] the practice apparently had the unintended side effect of enhancing women's enjoyment of sexual intercourse. In describing his early experimentation with male continence, Noyes stated: "my wife's experience was very satisfactory, as it had never been before."[80] The medical historian Norman Himes opined "that the Oneida Community stands out historically as perhaps the only group experiment, at least in the Western World, placing great emphasis upon the full satisfaction of the woman, and this in a culture dominated by male attitudes."[81] And the sex researcher Havelock Ellis concluded that some women did reach orgasm when male continence was practiced.[82]

If negative side effects of this unusual birth control practice are at best conjectural, is it still possible that individuals who accepted it did so because they were psychologically abnormal? Maren Lockwood Carden makes the acute, if only partially accurate, observation that John Humphrey Noyes never was able "to commit himself fully to any idea, action, or person."[83] She also suggests that Community members must have had an unusual "psychological makeup" which allowed them to be attracted to this demanding and controlled system.[84] Unfortunately, Carden fails to produce convincing evidence, in either her dissertation or her book, to support this latter thesis. Oneida Community publications also fail to show that Community members had any unusual character structure in common. The detailed psychological critiques of Oneida members that were given in mutual criticism sessions and reported in the Community newspaper show the full range of human types, with almost every conceivable character strength and weakness.[85]

To be sure, Noyes's followers were a highly selected group of people. As Robert Fogarty has shown in his analysis of the social sources of Oneida membership, the individuals attracted to the Community frequently were in an emotionally unsettled state when they entered. They sought surcease from inner turmoil and external uncertainties, particularly those associated with the vagaries of revivalistic religion. Oneidans found Noyes's system appealing because it helped them reestablish order and become resocialized to a more secure and satisfying way of life.[86] But this is true of converts to almost any religious or secular cause which seeks to radically restructure the beliefs and lives of its followers. The burden of proof for any argument that these Perfectionists had a special "character structure"—whether ideal or psychopathological—rests on the person who makes it. Had the Oneida Community been unbalanced, either in character types or in occupational backgrounds and abilities, it seems unlikely that it could have functioned successfully for more than thirty years.

Male continence should not be simply dismissed as aberrant, therefore, but rather should be investigated as a serious if unusual form of sexual organization. In just such a way, an anthropologist would investigate and attempt to understand the functions of any form of social organization, however bizarre it might appear. Viewed within its cultural context, male continence may perhaps best be seen as an extension of certain characteristic Victorian attitudes, a sort of "Victorian sensuality," showing an exaggerated concern for control. The image one has of the later Oneida Community is of a group of ideal Victorian gentlemen and ladies playing croquet on the lawn in front of the great Community Mansion House, the whole scene being simply an extension of the ideal Victorian home.[87] Pierrepont Noyes remembered that the children at Oneida, who were reared communally in the Children's House, became conscious of their sexual drives at a later age than most children in external society.[88] And, except during its foundation and breakup, Oneida's relations with the external society remained very good. Noyes's practice might appear bizarre, but his ideals represented a fusion of characteristic elements from the larger American culture into a harmonious new synthesis.

Male continence may have represented an accentuation and synthesis of certain characteristic Victorian attitudes which sought internalized control of sexual expression. The primary importance of the technique was practical, however. Noyes declared that the "Oneida Community in an important sense owed its existence to the discovery of Male Continence" and that the principle underlying that practice "has been the very soul of its working constitution."[89] Male continence undercut the emotional and physical exclusiveness of couples. It prevented the complications which having children would have posed to establishing the primary loyalty to the Community in all things. And it allowed a degree of sexual pleasure, coupled with stringent self-control and self-denial not found in artificial methods of birth control. Few would be tempted simply to make a "hobby" of the practice and withdraw from the normal round of Community life into exclusive emotional and sexual attachments. In short, male continence was a necessary precondition for the practical establishment of complex marriage as Noyes envisioned it.

The second form of social control which helped to prepare the way for complex marriage and the close community life associated with it was the practice of "mutual criticism," sometimes called "free criticism" or simply "criticism."[90] Mutual criticism served the same function for the late Putney Community and for the Oneida Community that confession of sins to the elders did for the Shakers. It provided the basic means of encouraging the desired character development and commitment to the Community and its principles. The idea of mutual criticism went back to Noyes's experiences at Andover. There he had participated with a group of students preparing to be missionaries in frank criticisms of each other's character, for the purpose of improvement. The individual to be criticized remained silent, except to correct obvious errors of fact, while the other members of the group, one by one, plainly and honestly told him his faults.[91]

During the difficult transition to complex marriage and more intense communal life at Putney in the winter of 1846–47, when new ideas and practices were being developed and emotional tensions were high, Noyes introduced a form of group criticism similar to that which he had found so valuable at Andover. This mutual criticism provided a kind of many-sided mirror, reflecting an individual's strengths and weaknesses so that he could see how others responded to him and could improve his personal relations within the Community. Mutual criticism brought faults and irritating personality characteristics into the open rather than let problems fester in secret.

Looking back, the Community newspaper noted the cathartic effects of this process during the winter of 1846–47 when the Perfectionists at Putney felt that they were "in the day of judgment."

> Criticism had free course and it was like a fire on the tender life.
> . . . It was painful in its first application, but agreeable in its results. One brother who had a vivid memory of his sensations, says, that while he was undergoing the process he felt like death, as though he was dissected with a knife; but when it was over, he felt as if he had been washed. He said to himself, "these things are all true, but they are gone, they are washed away."[92]

In like manner, at the group level the old order was passing away; the Community was being prepared for social integration around new beliefs to be internalized by each individual.

At Oneida, because the size of the group had increased and many members were not well acquainted, the practice was modified in several ways. Initially:

> Instead of subjecting volunteers for criticism to the scrutiny of the assembly, the Association appointed four if its most spiritual and discerning judges, to criticize all the members. The critics themselves were first criticized by Mr. Noyes, and then gave themselves to their work, from day to day for three weeks, till they had passed judgment on every character in the Association. Their method was first to ascertain as much as possible about the character of the individual about to be criticized, by inquiring among his associates,

and then after discussing his character among themselves, to invite him to an interview, plainly tell him his faults, converse with him freely about his whole character, and give him their best advice.[93]

Later on, members formed classes of ten or fifteen, and each separate group carried through a course of mutual criticism of all its members. Various other approaches also were tested, including public criticism of individuals by the whole family at their evening meeetings.

As mutual criticism developed, it became the chief means of Community government. The Oneida Community, which considered itself an enlarged family, was also like a family in having no formal government, statutory regulations, or fixed forms. Rather, its arrangements were informal. Noyes quoted with approval Charles Nordhoff's opinion that mutual criticism would be an excellent means of discipline in most families.[94] Recognizing the close connection between mental and physical health, Noyes also encouraged the use of criticism to cure physical ailments. To Noyes, mutual criticism sometimes seemed to be almost a panacea, combining the best aspects of many different possible forms of government—monarchy, aristocracy, and democracy.[95] When mutual criticism was coupled with the removal or restriction of sexual privileges, it provided an extremely powerful means of strengthening loyalty to the Community.

First Steps toward Group Marriage at Putney

Having thought through his goals and set up the organizational mechanisms to inculcate his religious and social views in the Community, John Humphrey Noyes finally was in a position to initiate a carefully considered move out of traditional monogamous marriage into a complex, group form. The impetus for the realization in practice of what had until then remained an unrealized ideal was the increased intimacy of ever closer association and the resulting mutual attachment networks that were growing up. Noyes's attraction to Mary Cragin was the trigger for the first actual departure from monogamous marriage. On an evening in May 1846, the two went for a long walk together and Noyes, with Mary's encouragement, took some liberties in personal intimacy. Rather than give way to his impulses, which were strong, Noyes maintained self-control. True to form, he sought sanction for his beliefs before putting them into practice. When the two of them returned home, Noyes called a meeting between them and his wife and George Cragin. After a searching talk, and strong opposition from Cragin who initially felt that he was being cuckolded again, the four agreed to give each other "full liberty" within the group.[96]

From this beginning, the circle of attachments was gradually enlarged. In early November 1846, the Noyes, Cragin, Skinner, and Miller families signed a declaration of principles which declared: "All individual proprietorship either of persons or things is surrendered, and absolute community of interests takes the place of the laws and fashions which preside over property and family relations in the world." Noyes was to guide and direct "the family thus constituted."[97] A consolidation of households followed this declaration. The Noyeses and Cragins moved to the Campbell house, and the Skinners and Millers joined the Leonards at the Noyes homestead. The new arrangements would be elaborated and extended slowly. Not until the mid-1850s, however, approximately a half-dozen years after the removal of the group to Oneida, would the system be fully established in an entire community.

During the early stages of this move into the practice of complex marriage, strict secrecy, or what Noyes called "Bible Secretiveness,"[98] was maintained as much as possible. The new practices were revealed only to those deemed able to understand and support them. Only by maintaining such a cover could the difficult internal problems and conflicts generated by the new arrangements be worked out satisfactorily. Some of Noyes's followers such as John R. Miller initially found it difficult to accept the idea that the move was really a principled one.[99] Despite the effort to maintain secrecy, a surprising number of indications of the new departures found their way into the Community's newspaper. During the winter of 1846–47, Noyes could not refrain from directly revealing the facts of the new system to a small number of Perfectionists outside Putney as well. Only a year later at Oneida, he would write his "Bible Argument," a statement far more open than any of those ever put out by the early Shakers or Mormons when they were attempting to institutionalize new marriage practices. During the five years between 1846 and 1851, Noyes dropped his editorship of the Community newspaper, so that he could devote his full efforts to organizing his new system of complex marriage.[100]

The explicit communal affirmation of the new marriage system was made in a meeting of the Putney Perfectionists on June 1, 1847. As reported in the *Spiritual Magazine,*[101] the Community newspaper, Noyes asked if it was not now "the time for us to commence the testimony that the Kingdom of God has come?" He declared: "Separate households, property exclusiveness have come to an end with us." In the discussion which followed, it was concluded that, although the existing arrangements fell short of the heavenly ideal (no marriage), the Community nevertheless represented an outpost of that Kingdom. The Putney believers therefore unanimously affirmed that *"The Kingdom of God Has Come."*

Not surprisingly, the transition to a model radically different from that of existing society resulted both in internal tensions among the Putney Perfectionists and in external tensions with their neighbors. The extent of the internal tensions connected with the new arrangements is suggested by numerous exhortations in the *Spiritual Magazine* to unity, obedience, self-control, and the like. Equally telling was the development of a variety of psychosomatic illnesses, which Noyes attempted to treat, with varying degrees of success, through mutual criticism and faith cures. In their excitement at the idea that the Kingdom of God had actually arrived, unsuccessful attempts were made to treat organic illnesses as well.[102]

The greatest threat to the establishment of the new marriage arrangements, however, came when external hostility was fueled by information that leaked out as a result of dissension within the group. It was almost inevitable that rumors of the new practices should first circulate in distorted form and eventually receive direct confirmation from some of the Putney Perfectionists themselves. The Perfectionists complicated their situation by attempting to draw into their circle two girls, Emma and Helen Campbell, along with Helen's fifteen year old friend, Lucinda Lamb. The anxieties of the parents and relatives of these girls added explosive new hostilities to those that the Perfectionists already faced. As a natural result, the group came under closer scrutiny.

Two less-than-fully-loyal Perfectionists precipitated the crisis. One of them correctly surmised what was happening; the other learned from Noyes himself what was going on. The two men reported their information to anti-Perfectionist leaders in Putney and to the State's Attorney in Brattleboro, and Noyes was indicted by a Grand Jury on two specific counts of adultery. Rather than stand trial for the charges or remain in Putney to face the mounting clamor of the townspeople, Noyes left the state, forfeiting his $2,000 bond. Finally he went to New York City. He and his followers, several of whom soon joined him in New York, remained unrepentant. Noyes wrote to John R. Miller that he would continue to advocate his ideas, even should he eventually suffer the loss of all his personal property, imprisonment, or death. Yet he would not brave public opinion unnecessarily. Exactly what he or his followers would do remained an open question.

Reorganizing Relations between the Sexes at Oneida

The departure of the leadership of the Putney Perfectionists late in 1847 might easily have marked the end of this unusual effort at reorganizing marriage and community life. Instead, after a brief period of confusion, early in March 1848 the chief loyalists from Putney began regrouping around Perfectionist holdings in the Oneida Reserve in central New York.

At Oneida, the unorthodox religious and social forms pioneered in the Putney Community were further refined and organized. Increasing attention was devoted to a third concern—the establishment of a form of economic organization which would allow for communal self-sufficiency. By 1857, when the Community for the first time showed a financial profit, Oneida's distinctive religious, social, and economic forms were virtually set. Only Noyes's experiment in "scientific propagation" remained to receive practical implementation in the late 1860s.

After Noyes and his closest followers left Putney in 1847, the initial concern was to find a new base for communal operations. Several locations were considered, but Noyes wisely decided to settle his followers on the holdings of Jonathan Burt, a Perfectionist living in the Oneida Reserve. Burt's land was well located in the geographic center of New York State, a few miles from the Erie Canal. This area was the strongest Perfectionist center in the state, and thus could provide a valuable source of members and supporters. By January 1849, the original nucleus of Putney Perfectionists had expanded to 87; by February 1850, the number had risen to 172; and by February 1851, the total reached 205.[103] The group at Oneida would rise to a stable level of approximately 250— or some 300 in all at Oneida and its sister community at Wallingford, Connecticut, after the consolidation of the various peripheral communities that were founded in the late 1840s and early 1850s. Although a few accessions to the group and a few defections from it would continue to occur, 84 of the 109 adults who joined in the first two years either died in the Community or lived there until the breakup.[104]

This impressive degree of membership stability was connected with the carefully selected character of the group. Members were deliberately chosen on the basis of complete loyalty to Noyes's leadership and dedication to his Perfectionist ideals. Members represented a wide range of occupational skills, emotional types, and personal interests necessary for the Community. They came from most of the areas of New York and New England where sizable pockets of Noyes's Perfectionist followers lived, and many of them were relatively affluent.[105] By 1857, the members had invested almost $108,000 in the Oneida Community and its branches. Only with such a large capital backing could the Community have continued to function despite a loss of $40,000 during the ten lean years before it finally achieved financial stability at Oneida.[106] Many other communities of the antebellum period failed because, unlike Oneida, they lacked adequate organizing principles, capable leadership, a diversified and dedicated membership, and sound financial backing.

Even with so many factors in its favor, the Oneida Community's early years were very difficult, both physically and emotionally. The innovative spirit and dedication which contributed to the success of the Community during those early years may be seen in the drastic reorganization of male and female roles that took place at this time. Many of the modifications in activities, such as setting women to work alongside the men constructing buildings and doing other outdoor labor, were primarily pragmatic responses to the requirements of establishing a functioning community. Certain other modifications were also of this character. Women cut their hair short for practicality's sake and, partially for the same reasons, wore an unusual outfit comprised of a mid-length skirt over pants, similar to the attire later popularized by Amelia Bloomer.[107]

The decision to allow men or women to assume roles normally associated with the other sex was not made for pragmatic reasons alone, however. There was an explicit intellectual rationale as well. Noyes sought to do away with artificial distinctions between the sexes. His goal was to reintegrate men and women into a cohesive community-home through vital labor together. As a result of these concerns there was greater flexibility in job assignments and less sex-stereotyping at Oneida than in society at large.

In a contemporary analysis of the Oneida Community from a feminist perspective, Marlyn Hartzell Dalsimer described five categories of work at Oneida and how women were integrated into each of those areas. The five occupational areas were:

> 1) traditional women's work, e.g., kitchen, housekeeping, laundry, sewing and mending, nursing, early childhood care, and nursery school teaching. In these areas of work women dominated as both workers and supervisors; they made most of the decisions in these work "departments";
>
> 2) light manufacturing and community support activities, e.g., fruit canning and packing, silk-spooling, traveling bag manufacture, print shop, bookkeeping, and phonography. In these activities women predominated as workers and were supervised by both men and women;
>
> 3) industry, e.g., the animal-trap business and machine shop, and various departments of specialization including dairy work, dentistry, transportation, and gardening. In these economic activities, men predominated as both workers and supervisors, but a few women worked in these areas too;
>
> 4) heavy farm work, carpentry, saw milling, lumbering, sales work and peddling. Community men and hired laborers did all these tasks; and,
>
> 5) ideological administration. John Humphrey Noyes dominated this department with the aid of a few men and women he personally selected to assist him.[108]

Dalsimer's analysis of the Oneida division of labor was based on her concern for achieving absolute occupational equality, and thus she was critical of the extent to which the choice of jobs at Oneida still followed traditional sex-stereotyped patterns. If one places Oneida within its nineteenth-century context, however, one is struck by the extent to which the Community broke down or undercut traditional male and female occupational patterns and authority relations. At Oneida, a conscious effort was made to include both men and women in most departments, women served in some departments in positions of authority over men, and there were almost no departments in which women were prohibited from working. It is true that, except during crisis periods, women did not do heavy farm work and the like, but men also sought to avoid such tasks, and eventually the Community hired outside laborers to do the most onerous hard labor and routine work. Likewise, women did not peddle goods outside the Community, but this limitation appears to have been due to external social convention rather than because the Community explicitly prohibited such activity for women. In short, women at Oneida typically gravitated toward traditional female occupations, but few occupational possibilities were formally closed to them.

Men at Oneida also engaged in a wide variety of tasks that had traditionally been assigned to women, from washing dishes and cooking to rearing children, knitting, and sewing their own clothes. Noyes sought to create an efficient system which would allow both men and women to participate as fully as possible at all levels of communal life. Male continence freed women from the burdens of unwanted procreation, and communal childrearing freed them from many of the normal strains of child care. Thus women were able to do almost everything that men did, including participate in group criticism sessions and daily religious-and-business meetings. Few societies in history have broken down the conventional distinctions between the sexes as fully as did the Oneida Community.

This significant revision of sex roles and the rise in women's status at Oneida might seem paradoxical in the face of John Humphrey Noyes's explicit belief in the superiority of men over women. Although Noyes emphasized the necessity of a reciprocal relationship of mutual respect between the sexes, he made it clear that man's primacy over woman was part of the very nature of the universe. The male-female relationship was even said to mirror that of the Father and the Son in the Godhead. St. Paul had said: "The head of every man is Christ, and the head of the woman is the man, and the head of Christ is God." Noyes concluded: "The female capacity is in its very nature negative. Weakness makes way for strength. Deficiency embraces fullness. Hence the Father takes precedence of the Son. 'My Father,' says Christ, 'is greater than I.' "[109] Sexual role distinctions were minimized but not eliminated at Oneida, and women were encouraged to express their distinctively "feminine" skills and talents.

Women could achieve higher status at Oneida in spite of Noyes's formal belief in the inequality of men and women, because Noyes was not primarily concerned with male and female authority patterns, but with establishing his own personal authority over all his followers, both men and women. So long as Noyes's male and female followers unquestioningly acknowledged his paternalistic, God-like authority, he was prepared to be flexible in delegating that authority and making changes for the benefit of both sexes. No single way of organizing relations between men and women was sacrosanct; the underlying spirit rather than any specific external form was Noyes's concern. Men and women at Oneida shared a common personal and religious commitment that cut across normal social restrictions. Woman's primary responsibility was not to her husband or to her children, but to God, an article in the Community's newspaper declared.[110] This meant that the conventional juxtaposition of male superiority and female inferiority no longer had much significance within the Community. As St. Paul had said, there is "neither male nor female in the Lord." If some women were, in fact spiritually superior to men—as they recognizably were—they should exercise more authority at Oneida than *those* men.

Thus, instead of stressing gender as the basis for authority at Oneida, life in the Community gradually came to be governed by a philosophy of "ascending and descending fellowship," in which those of higher "spirituality" exercised more authority than those of lesser attainments.[111] Noyes was at the top, along with a handful of the most spiritual men who oversaw most major decisions. These men cooperated closely with the most spiritual women, who in turn were above the less spiritual men, who were above the less spiritual women, and so forth. Since those who were seen as more spiritual generally were older than the less spiritual, age was implicitly a factor in the determination of status in the Community. Because it was considered desirable to associate with those higher in the ascending fellowship, individuals of higher status had access to a greater range of sexual contacts than did members of lower status. Children appear to have entered into this hierarchy of ascending and descending fellowship at puberty and sexual initiation, and at least during their teens and twenties they were expected to associate sexually with older, more spiritual men and women. Since spirituality was the basis of authority at Oneida, Noyes was forced to reverse the popular argument of the world that women were more spiritual than men.[112] Thus, Noyes's radical religious views were associated in a complex way with the radical revision of sexual roles at Oneida.

The Institutionalization of Complex Marriage

The primary factor contributing to the revision of relations between the sexes at Oneida was the institutionalization of the complex marriage system throughout the entire Community. This was a difficult and often extremely painful process. Lack of access to first-hand records describing this transition phase from an internal perspective makes any analysis conjectural, but the Community newspapers give enough information to reconstruct at least partially the general lines of development. Even at Putney, with a small and carefully tested group of followers, the introduction of complex marriage had been difficult and only partially achieved. But at Oneida, under trying living conditions and with many new Community members who were only minimally acquainted with each other and with the new practices, the difficulties must have been enormous. Internal and external tensions inevitably resulted.

The essence of the complex marriage system which Noyes was seeking to institute among his followers was the elimination of "selfishness"— the subordination of individual self-interest to the larger and more inclusive interests of the Community, which in turn was dedicated to achieving God's will. Even individual sexual loyalties, usually formalized through "marriage" in the external society, had to be given up. Sexual loyalties instead were raised to the Community level, to the "enlarged family." The resulting ties were at least as binding and demanding as those of ordinary worldly marriage. Tendencies toward "special love" (exclusive romantic attachments) were rigorously discouraged. Any special individual attachments to offspring, or any close friendships between members of the same sex were similarly broken up. Because of the fragmentation that Noyes and his followers had experienced, they placed great emphasis on the achievement of unity and communal cohesion.

In most instances, the "green-eyed demon jealousy" was exorcized through Community pressure and free criticism. More difficult cases frequently involved the suspension or limitation of sexual privileges until the ostracized individual began to shape up to Community standards. In some cases, individuals who became overly attached to each other were separated by sending one person off to the Wallingford, Connecticut, sister community for a time. In at least one instance, a couple which could not be separated in their "special love" for each other, were instructed by Noyes to find other individuals and have children by them—and they obeyed.[113] Abel Easton, a Community leader, expressed the basic rationale behind such actions when he declared: "No matter what his other qualifications may be, if a man cannot love a woman and be happy in seeing her loved by others, he is a selfish man, and his place is with the potsherds of the earth. There is no place for such in the 'Kingdom of Heaven.' "[114]

It was understandably difficult to institutionalize such a system. Noyes compared the transition process over which he and his trusted associates presided to the condition of an army sent into a foreign territory. When sent for military purposes alone, it is "placed under the rules of martial discipline, which have reference to hostile surroundings and are very restrictive." "But an army sent for the purpose of introducing civil institutions and settling a foreign territory, ought to pass, as soon as it can do so safely, from the restrictions of martial law, to the conditions of permanent civilized life."[115] This latter state was Noyes's goal in his attempt to introduce the Kingdom of Heaven on earth. By the mid-1850s at Oneida, he had largely achieved communal stabilization.

With this martial image in mind, one can more easily understand the significance of many of the articles of moral exhortation which appeared in the newspapers of the Putney and Oneida Communities between 1846 and 1853. During this period, endless articles exhorted Community members to total and unquestioning obedience, unity, love, harmony, right devotion, and the like. Others urged them to overcome jealousy, backbiting, shame, bashfulness, and similar problems. The tone was, indeed, a martial one, and one article was appropriately entitled "The Soldier Spirit." Psychosomatic illnesses and faith cures were frequently discussed, and several cases of temporary insanity and suicidal tendencies were mentioned. There were even some problems with "spiritualist" communications which could have become a threat to Noyes's authority had they become more organized. Shortly before the expulsion from Putney, John Miller, Noyes's trusted associate, wrote that he felt like Moses before the Red Sea parted: he knew that God would find a way to lead them through, but he had no idea how.[116] Throughout the period before 1853, the atmosphere was often tense, and the direction of the Community sometimes appeared unclear. As the *Oneida Circular* recalled:

> The years 1850, '51, '52 were years of external trial to the community. First came the conflict with internal "evils," such as insubordination, disloyalty, and pleasure-seeking, culminating in the withdrawal of several families which seemed at times to jeopardize the very existence of the community.[117]

In 1849, about a year after the founding of the Oneida Community, Noyes—who typically tried to remove himself from conflict situations which he could not handle—moved with a nucleus of some of his most loyal Putney followers to a small community outpost at Willow Place in Brooklyn, New York. He lived there most of the time between 1849 and 1854, when John Miller, who had been the primary leader at Oneida, died. During those years, and particularly after he once again formally took over the editorship of his newspaper in 1851, Noyes wrote with a sense of surprising distance from his communal ventures. In his column "Ideas from the Communes," for instance, he seemed to write with an observer's detachment about his own Associated Communities at Oneida, New York; Wallingford, Connecticut; Newark, New Jersey; and Cambridge and Putney, Vermont.[118] Noyes wrote that the Brooklyn Community where he was living, and not Oneida, was the real center of his efforts.[119]

One has the sense that in this period, Noyes, deeply afraid of failure or loss of control, was hedging his bets. Faced with uncertainty in his communal ventures, he seemed to be returning to his first concern— getting his ideas before the public through his newspaper. He left the difficult task of translating those values into communal life to capable subordinates who had internalized his values. This pattern would persist throughout the life of the Oneida Community. Between 1842 and 1880, Noyes spent only about half of his time at Putney and at Oneida, and he typically left at times of major stress.[120] In retrospect, this appears to have been the best thing he could have done. Few prophets have sufficient wisdom to know when to step a little aside after they have established the value foundations of their communities, and leave the pragmatic problems of implementing their ideals to capable subordinates. As a distant figure above the battle, Noyes and his ideas could serve as a unifying force in times of conflict.

External pressures also contributed to Community tensions in this period. In 1850 and 1851, Grand Juries in Oneida and Madison counties, on whose boundaries the Community was located, heard complaints about the Perfectionists from their enemies, probably including seceders. The Madison County Grand Jury adopted a "wait and see" attitude. The Oneida County Grand Jury at Utica, however, called Community men and women to testify early in 1851, asking obscene and insulting questions about their most personal experiences. The exemplary deportment of Community members, who answered the questions freely and honestly, maintaining dignity and perfect manners, helped to defuse the hostility. Nevertheless, this intense pressure and harrassment caused the leaders at Oneida actually to consider other possible areas where they could relocate the Community. But a petition encouraging the Perfectionists to remain in the area gained overwhelming public support, and influential local power figures interceded on their behalf.[121]

The success of the Oneida Community in resisting such pressures was undoubtedly due in part to what they had learned from their problems with the residents at Putney. At Putney, hostility peaked when a local girl, Lucinda Lamb, was encouraged to join the Perfectionists against her parents' wishes. When the Oneida venture was begun, Community members showed greater circumspection. They scrupulously avoided direct efforts to convert local residents, and made it plain that they were simply trying to mind their own business. As early as 1850, the Oneida Community publicly stated that it was not actively seeking new members, although it continued to attract new people who were familiar with Noyes's writings. After 1856, the Perfectionists stopped considering applicants for admission with rare exceptions.[122]

The exigencies of successfully establishing complex marriage thus necessitated a move away from Noyes's desire to convert the entire world, toward the more restricted goal of establishing a tightly knit, internally unified community. At Putney, as George W. Noyes noted, the primary problem had been to break free from the bonds of conventional morality and attitudes; at Oneida, after they had broken through that initial barrier, the goal was to reestablish order and avoid the potentially disintegrative effects of the subtle spirit of pleasure-seeking.[123] Such an order could not easily be established if there were many new people joining the Community or leaving it all the time.[124]

Internal tensions over the new complex-marriage practices continued to pose severe problems. On October 3, 1850, a rare public airing of internal Perfectionist disharmony over the new marriage system occurred when a letter from a believer from Wisconsin was prominently featured in the Community newspaper.[125] Bitterly he asked "from the depths of my soul" why the Oneida Community should insist on maintaining unorthodox sexual practices which only alienated many potential converts to holiness—individuals who were otherwise in agreement with the group. In reply to this eloquent and deeply felt plea, John Miller simply asserted that their sexual theory was a part of the demands of God; it could not be accepted or rejected on opportunistic grounds. Another Community member suggested that a certain recklessness in following the truth, regardless of the possible consequences, was necessary in overcoming personal selfishness to achieve the Kingdom of God on earth. These statements were by no means adequate responses to the entire question raised and they did not show the thoroughness with which Noyes usually refuted the opinions of his detractors.

The explicit discussion of these highly divisive issues was virtually unprecedented in Noyes's newspapers. The feeling of opposition to complex marriage, as well as the less than wholehearted support that Noyes was receiving on this issue from even his loyal subordinates, is apparent in this exchange. It is quite possible that John Humphrey Noyes's decision to resume formal editorship of his newspaper in 1851 was in part an attempt to avoid losing control over *both* his newspaper and his communities in the face of deep-seated opposition to his policies.[126]

The Temporary Discontinuance of Complex Marriage

The peak of the early difficulties over the institutionalization of complex marriage, and the beginning of the resolution of those problems, apparently came between March and August of 1852. There is compelling evidence that during those six months complex marriage was temporarily discontinued at Oneida. The obvious external reason for this abrupt change was an all-out newspaper crusade launched by a New York religious paper, *The Observer*. A number of other newspapers also took up the hue and cry, and in a sustained and well-organized campaign, attacked Oneida as an offense to public morals.

On March 7, 1852, evidently in response to this pressure, the *Circular* made an unexpected announcement. Although the Perfectionists felt that their course had received "vindication in reason and conscience," they nevertheless recognized that their "liberty on this subject is looked upon with jealousy and offense by the surrounding society."

> And in view of the fact, we have decided to forego it and withdraw from the position we have held. It may be understood that the Oneida Association, and all Associations connected with it, have receded from the practical assertion of their views, and formally resumed the marriage morality of the world, submitting themselves to all ordinances and restrictions of society and law on this subject. This definite concession to public opinion, made in good faith, we trust will be satisfactory and give peace.

The statement went on to say that this step was intended only as a temporary retreat that would last until there would be a "change of public feeling" which would gradually extend the "area of freedom" tolerated. By its action, the Community was graphically demonstrating that it was "not attached to forms," even to its own. "To be able to conform to *any* circumstances, and *any* institutions, and still preserve spiritual freedom" was the goal of the Perfectionists. There was also a certain sense of looking back at a chapter of a story that was already completed. In some important sense, the Community had let its "previous activities pass into history." The Community's new efforts would be devoted to the establishment of a free press and to what must appear a most puzzling objective, indeed—the "abolition of death."[127]

What is one to make of this remarkable statement? To begin with, there is every reason to believe that the practice of complex marriage was, in fact, discontinued during this period. Although "Bible Secretiveness" might sanction speaking in a sort of code language or not telling a hostile public the whole truth, Noyes and his followers were invariably honest when they made direct factual assertions. Their word was their bond. Furthermore, numerous articles over the next six months either directly or indirectly support the contention that complex marriage was temporarily discontinued at this time.[128] Had it continued to be secretly practiced, Community dissidents probably would have passed on that information to a hostile press. And it seems significant that when the Oneida Community finally gave up complex marriage forever in 1879, the language and constructions used were in several instances almost verbatim repetitions of the 1852 statements.[129]

Looking back at that last discontinuance of complex marriage in 1879, which was said at the time to be only a temporary move, Abel Easton noted that:

> On more than one occasion previously, in the presence of sickness in the family or of persecution or other causes, John H. Noyes proposed that the Community as a body consider itself under criticism, and proclaim a fast from conjugal freedom; making a time of earnest self-examination and spiritual improvement, and proving their power of self-control in refraining from, as well as using, their freedom. Such seasons of fasting sometimes lasted a few days or *six months,* and they were strictly observed by all. Their right to exercise freedom as a principle was no more abandoned in the public suspension of complex marriage than it was in their former more private experiences of temporary suspension. It was rather an assertion of their right, either to use their freedom or to yield to expediency; they elected to yield until such time as they deemed it expedient to do otherwise. At the same time, they had pledged themselves to the public, and having assumed that pledge, of course considered themselves bound to observe their promise until they were prepared to renounce it as publicly as they had professed it [emphasis added].[130]

The period from the beginning of March to the end of August 1852 is the only time in the history of the Oneida Community when there is any indication of such a six-month suspension of complex marriage. And if such a suspension in fact took place in 1852, it would appear to have been both a response to external pressure and a reaction to a sense of internal malaise for which communal penance was necessary.

A further key to the motivation behind this apparent retreat from complex marriage is Noyes's enigmatic observation that for a time the primary efforts of the Community would be devoted to the "abolition of death," rather than to marriage reform. A later article reasserts this primary concern, clearly indicating that "death" was being used in a special sense: If this attack on "death" be madness, yet there is a method to it.[131] In fact, when Noyes speaks of trying to "abolish death," he usually is referring to his efforts to overcome sickness and ill-health, especially mental and emotional disorders. Such psychologically related ailments are the first which must be eliminated if the "King of Terrors" is eventually to lose his hold over the mind and spirit of man.[132]

Thus what Noyes may be saying here, in his own special code language to be understood by his followers but not by the outside world, is that for a time, the severe mental and emotional problems (many of them associated with the introduction of complex marriage) are to be the primary concern of the Community. This interpretation is also supported by the number of articles appearing in this period on such topics as nervousness, faith and unbelief, insanity, spiritualist excesses, inattention, the uselessness of self-condemnation, problems of insubordination, and the like. The Oneida Community appears to have been deliberately retrenching, performing an internal and external penance which would prepare a solid foundation for a second and successful effort to reintroduce the practice of complex marriage later.

Noyes was also faced with the threat of internal insubordination and even apostasy during this period. The problems of "bridling sensuality" and placing such drives at the service of the larger purposes of the Community are discussed in numerous articles. Noyes himself did not always appear to be contributing to the solution of such problems when he wrote in enthusiastic terms of God being "married to matter" and the like.[133] A concrete threat of outright apostasy also existed. In late March and early April, two articles appeared on Judas Iscariot,[134] who "was not merely an unprincipled traitor, but a positive rival of Christ." The articles make it clear that a high Community member was seen as playing the role of Judas.

In these articles, the Community Judas is portrayed as one whose sin was that of "covetousness"—of affections. His character is contrasted to that of the Mary who impulsively anointed Christ with expensive ointment. This Mary, and her Community counterpart, "had little worldly prudence. Her love exceeded her discretion. She was found at Jesus' feet, absorbed in his discoursing," abandoned

> . . . to the attractions of her heart—a dangerous susceptibility in the case of misplaced affections, but her glory as a follower of Christ. This led her, at the loss of dignity, into that wonderful gratitude and love, which Christ promised should be recorded of her as a memorial of praise to all generations.

But Judas, with his base, uncomprehending heart, could not appreciate Mary's "tribute of affection," and so betrayed Christ for a paltry thirty pieces of silver to the public authorities.

There can be little doubt as to the identity of the Community members whose relationship was obliquely discussed in these articles. Almost certainly, George Cragin, a member of the central committee and one of Noyes's earliest followers, stood in the place of Judas; his wife, Mary Cragin, was represented by the wayward Mary whose devotion to Christ brought her everlasting glory; and, of course, John Humphrey Noyes, God's special representative, served symbolically as Christ. Full documentation of this complex triangular relationship of Noyes and the Cragins, which apparently led to George Cragin's temporary estrangement from Noyes, will not be provided here.[135] Some of the probable general outlines can be indicated, however.

John Humphrey Noyes's relationship with Mary Cragin had always had strong overtones of idolatry, the sort of "special love" which he so discouraged in his followers. It must have been galling to George Cragin to be for all intents and purposes supplanted by Noyes in his wife's affections, especially when both the Noyeses and Cragins were living together in Brooklyn between 1849 and 1851. After Mary Cragin died in a boat accident in July 1851, Noyes was almost inconsolable. For over a year, nearly every issue of his newspaper contained fulsome tributes to her character, examples of her writing, and the like. In 1853, Noyes's *Bible Communism,* the final important summation of his sexual and marriage theories, was dedicated obliquely to her memory:

> To Mary of Nazareth, the blessed of all generations, who so beautifully yielded to the will of heaven, though it contravened the fashion of this world, and, at the hazard of her good name, and of all earthly affections and interests, became the mother of Christ, and so the mother of Christianity, this work is respectfully and loyally dedicated.[136]

The recognition that Noyes continued to be emotionally involved with Mary Cragin, even after her death, could certainly have disturbed George Cragin. Furthermore, there were also clear conflicts between the small, relatively comfortable, elite Brooklyn group which printed the newspaper, and the larger group of struggling Perfectionists at Oneida which provided their financial support. The fact that Noyes apparently slipped his emotional moorings after Mary Cragin died did little to maintain Community confidence in him or his ideas. It should be noted, however, that Noyes was extremely sensitive to external conditions and needed to validate the truth of his own ideas by seeing them accepted by his followers. Thus his emotional instability at this time could well be seen primarily as a reflection of the disorder then present in his communities, rather than simply as his individual problem.

In an attempt to overcome these personal and communal conflicts, Noyes launched a wholehearted effort to reestablish common values among his following—values that could provide a rationale for their existence. His newspaper printed repeated exhortations to unity, and also systematically reprinted articles from the mid-1840s which he had originally written to prepare the minds of his supporters for closer communal living and complex marriage at Putney. Individual and communal purification was stressed as part of a larger effort to achieve God's objectives on earth.

These and other measures apparently proved effective. On August 1, 1852, an article by George Cragin reaffirmed his total submission to God's will (as mediated through Noyes).[137] In the next issue, an article on "The Character of Peter"[138] noted that although Peter's denial of Christ might appear culpable, Peter had nevertheless come back to become Christ's "devoted follower." Throughout August a new optimism was evident in the newspaper. The tone rose to a radiant crescendo in the August 29th issue, with articles such as "The Resurrection King," "The Light Shineth in Darkness," and "The Heart Satisfied." Most important, that same issue contained Noyes's "Theocratic Platform" which apparently served to announce to the world the reestablishment of complex marriage and close communal life at Oneida. Among the planks of the platform were: "Abandonment of the entire fashion of this world—especially marriage and involuntary propagation," "Cultivation of free love," and "Dwelling together in association or complex families."[139]

Although emotional tensions within the group continued to exist, by the end of 1852 the worst was over, both for Noyes and for Oneida. With the basic value premises and marital forms established, the primary effort of the Community was increasingly turned toward developing successful and satisfying economic arrangements. After the death of the overworked and exhausted John Miller in June 1854, Noyes returned to Oneida to take personal charge. Recognizing that he had overextended himself in attempting so many different communal ventures, Noyes consolidated the six associated groups into two communities at Oneida and Wallingford.

This action, and the development of a successful line of animal traps for sale, succeeded in putting Oneida on its financial feet by 1857 for the first time in its history. An increasingly secular and relaxed tone prevailed in the Community newspaper. In place of the interminable abstruse theological essays of earlier years, the newspaper broadened its coverage to include numerous chatty articles on Community affairs; discussions of economic matters, including articles such as "Christ: A Business Character";[140] and accounts of Noyes's extraordinarily diversified interests, ranging from botany to world politics and social life. The transition process at Oneida was largely complete. Noyes and his followers had passed "from the restrictions of martial law, to the conditions of permanent civilized life," and were now free to enjoy the fruits of their labors.

Daily Life at Oneida

The introduction of complex marriage had been accompanied by considerable turmoil, but for more than twenty years after the successful establishment of the new system in the mid-1850s, it provided a secure structure within which an appealing and generally satisfying life was possible. The details of the way in which the Community functioned during this period will not be discussed at length here. Those interested in these aspects of Oneida can turn to the Community newspapers or to works by Maren Lockwood Carden, Pierrepont B. Noyes, Robert Allerton Parker, and Constance Noyes Robertson.[141] This section will simply provide a glimpse of daily life at Oneida.

The Oneida Community functioned as an enlarged family in which everyone had a variety of different roles. The physical home for this enlarged family was the imposing Mansion House within which almost all the life of the Community was carried out. Noyes described its importance: "The organic principle of Communism in industry and domestic life is seen in the common roof, the common table, and the daily meetings of all the members."[142] Reminiscences of Pierrepont Noyes and Harriet M. Worden —entitled *My Father's House* and *Old Mansion House Memories,* respectively—also suggest the way in which the house served as a symbol of the Community, providing a sense of security and unity.

Originally a large frame building, the Mansion House was rebuilt in the 1860s on a magnificent scale, as an impressive Victorian Gothic structure made of brick. As a result of additions over the years, it eventually sprawled around the quadrangle, surrounded by lawns landscaped with an impressive variety of trees. In keeping with the emphasis on the greater importance of communal over individual concerns, the inside of the house contained a number of small private and semi-private rooms for sleeping and other purposes, supplemented by a large and attractive library, several communal sitting rooms which provided comfortably furnished centers for Community life, and a large hall, which despite its size, had an appealing intimacy. A writer from the New York *Tribune* of May 1, 1867, reported:

> A handsome hall, furnished with chairs and small tables, is occupied by members in the evening, in the same manner that a family gathers around the hearth. . . . At each table are lamps; the women knit and sew, and I saw a man knitting. Meanwhile, one will read a daily paper, or letters from friends, or short addresses. Then they

will talk over their affairs. In this way their evenings are spent until bed-time.[143]

The large hall of the Mansion House served many functions. Perhaps the most important activities carried out there were the religious-and-business meetings held each evening, and attended by all adult members of the Community. The Oneida Community had no formal religious services on Sunday or on other days, and the religious and moral concerns of the group were often raised in the evening meetings, particularly in the extemporaneous "Home Talks" by John Humphrey Noyes. In addition, other activities were planned, ranging from spirited dancing to Community-produced plays and musical events, and other skits and special productions which helped to vary the normal routine and keep the Community lively. New talent was encouraged to develop and perform. Community life could hardly be characterized as a dour, gloomy pursuit of ascetic perfection. Pierrepont Noyes remembers: "The grown folks seemed almost as bent on being happy as they did on being good. Everyone worked; almost everyone seemed to have time for play, or perhaps I should say recreation."[144]

The flavor of daily life in the Community is captured in many articles in the Community newspapers, but the following overview of a "typical" day perhaps best describes the routine at Oneida on a day when visitors were allowed to come (usually only on weekends). Note that the Community itself operated on a two-meal-a-day breakfast and dinner system. With the exception of the account of the influx of visitors, the following article could be a description of almost any day at Oneida during the two decades from the mid-1850s to the mid-1870s:

Five o'clock! Stillness reigns from attick to cellar. Six o'clock! The whistle sounds. Little bare feet pattering along the main hall on their way to the children's room to be dressed—the first glad sound of morning. Laughing voices ringing through the empty halls and corridors arouse the sleepers from their dreams. Half an hour and there is a noise of footsteps, some light and some heavy, constantly hurrying up and down the long stairway from the Mansard; the noise of chairs and tables hastily shoved about, and the rumble of bedsteads in the many chambers around the house. Another half hour and the women are at their several callings—bed-making, sweeping halls, tidying up the parlors, mopping and dusting the library, and putting things to rights generally. Meanwhile a trio of active cooks are getting breakfast for the fifteen "titmen" of the family, who file out of the dining room at seven o'clock. Some of the men go to the shop, some are out on the farm, some are at the barn, one or two are in the printing office, a few are reading in the library, and the rest are in their rooms until eight o'clock when the whistle calls them one and all to breakfast.

By the hour of nine the people are scattered to their various assignments—trap-shop, machine-shop, silk-room, business-office, printing-office, kitchen, dining-room, laundry, company-room, etc. The children with their guardians start off for the lot east of the road, and the people who remain are tending our youngest, or making their clothes, or taking care of the various concerns of the household. Company comes in on the train at ten—a slight bustle ensues. Just at noon a few more are added, and subsequently more bustle. Cooks and waiters are stepping lively to get dinner in readiness at one o'clock. At twelve the bell rings, and the older children go to school, and the younger ones to bed. Stillness reigns for the next two hours. At three the whistle calls to dinner; there's a thronging toward the dining-room and the two hundred discuss the viands temptingly laid out. Dinner over, and many resume their labors until six o'clock, when the family are all again at home.

People are meeting in the court, vestibule, or in the sitting-rooms to tell the latest news; young and old mingle in croquet on the lawn, or at dominoes in the house, as the case may be. Many are reading, or studying, or writing; the children are frolicking below stairs; it is a time of rest and relaxation, and the home feeling predominates. All concentrate in the Hall at eight for a family meeting; some interesting topic draws out the enthusiasm of all who are present. Meeting closes at nine, and people disperse, some to the sitting room downstairs, some to the south sitting-room; some to the nursery kitchen, and some to their own bedrooms. At ten o'clock the house is still. The watchman goes quietly round on his mission; he locks the doors—puts out the lights—darkness and tranquility till morning.[145]

Thus for more than twenty years, life at Oneida would follow its basically tranquil course, based on an enlarged family model in which almost all necessary activities were carried out within the Community itself.

Stirpiculture and the End of Complex Marriage

The story of life at Oneida would not be complete without a postscript concerning Noyes's venture in "scientific propagation," or, to use the term that he coined for his eugenics experiment, "stirpiculture." By 1868, the Community had securely established itself and Noyes was prepared to take one further step in his efforts to institutionalize what was in effect his "continuing revolution." The ideal of scientific propagation had first been proposed in print by Noyes as early as 1848.[146] In 1868, Noyes decided that certain Community members would be allowed to have children, subject to the approval of a stirpiculture committee, which he initially headed. During the decade following the formal start of the experiment in 1869, forty-five live children were born under these regulated arrangements. Most participants selected their own mates and applied as couples, but probably one fourth of all unions actually were suggested by the committee.[147]

Just as Noyes's maintenance of a press to disseminate his ideas to the world was part of his effort to prevent the Community from becoming excessively inward-looking, the stirpiculture experiment was part of an attempt to avoid complacency and communal stagnation, as well as to expand the practice of the Community beyond the limits of the effectively celibate system which had hitherto prevailed. Ironically, this very effort to strengthen and revitalize the Community and its ideals eventually became a major factor contributing to the destruction of that Community. As first practiced, stirpiculture demanded the total subordination of individual attachments to the good of the whole. Inevitably, however, the stirpiculture unions tended to introduce divisive special affections into the Community, thus leading almost imperceptibly back toward the selfish forms of this-worldly marriage.[148]

Despite the good intentions which underlay the stirpiculture experiment, it and the other sexual practices of the Oneida Community eventually became a major factor in the complex organizational and emotional conflicts which eventually led to the breakup of the group. The declining ability of the aging and increasingly deaf John Humphrey Noyes to lead the Community set the stage for the breakup, and the difficulty of the situation was compounded by the inability of other leaders successfully to fill Noyes's place. Connected with and underlying this was a decline in the commitment of the group to their original religious ideals. A younger generation lacking direct experience of the early struggles of the Perfectionists showed an ever more skeptical and secular inclination. Without a strong commitment to common values, it became more and more difficult to justify the intense self-sacrifice necessary to make the Community's distinctive organization work. Actions by the governing central committee members came to be viewed as arbitrary and lacking in any other rationale than self-interest.

As common values broke down, specific sexual tensions that had always been potentially present began to be very divisive. Young people and Community members of lower status, began to chafe under the system of ascending and descending fellowship, which limited the sexual contacts of those of lower status. Additionally, the stirpiculture experiment made it clear that only those deemed fit would be permitted to have children. This created further resentment within the group. With a high degree of commitment to basic ideals, such frustrations could perhaps have been minimized. In the absence of such commitment, however, an internal power struggle and factionalization resulted. When an external campaign against the Community was launched by Professor John W. Mears at Syracuse in the mid-1870s, the weakened Community was no longer confident of its mission and the loyalty of its members.

In the face of an increasingly uncertain internal and external situation, in August 1879 the Community leaders acted gracefully to terminate their distinctive sexual arrangements while their venture could still be counted a success. In discontinuing thirty-three years of unorthodox Perfectionist marital practice, the Community announced that they were placing themselves "not on the platform of the Shakers, on the one hand, nor of the world, on the other, but on Paul's platform which allows marriage but prefers celibacy."[149] The Community also stated, in what may well prove a fitting epitaph:

> The past history of the Oneida Community is at least secure. Its present social position and its future course, whatever they may be, have no power to change the facts of the past; and the more these are studied, the more remarkable they will appear. These things prove, as does also their present course in giving up that phase of their communal life which has caused offense, that the Communists have not been the reckless bacchanalians a few have represented them. The truth is, as all the world will one day see and acknowledge, that they have not been pleasure-seekers and sensualists but social architects, with high religious and moral aims, whose experiments and discoveries they have sincerely believed would prove of value to mankind.[150]

Noyes in Retrospect

What is the larger significance of John Humphrey Noyes's life and the distinctive communal ventures that he helped to found? One is struck initially by Noyes's self-conscious awareness of the arbitrary human basis for social order. Writing in 1853 about the "principles" that he and his followers held, Noyes observed: "Our fundamental principle is religion."[151] Note that Noyes does not say anything in this statement about the specific *content* of their religious principles—including specific beliefs about God, Christ, or other topics—but refers only to the *form* of those beliefs. In effect, he is saying that his followers believed in *"having* a religion," that is, in having a common basis of belief. This spirit of solidarity and unity might be an absolute—or to put it differently, some basis of social order had to be accepted as a given—but the content of religious and social practice could be altered drastically, depending on circumstances. Cor-

respondingly, Noyes could clearly see that none of the varied ways of relating men and women to each other sexually in a possessive marriage
relationship had any ultimate validity. The ideal state, he felt, must be
something more.

Although realizing on both the emotional and the intellectual levels
that existing social patterns were inadequate and subject to change, Noyes
did not make the common mistake of lesser minds and hearts and simply
conclude that "anything goes." Instead, he almost compulsively sought a
new set of common assumptions and basis of unity to restore the possibility
of healthy human relationships. Since he had a strong sense of personal
destiny and was unwilling to try to conform to the shifting and unreliable
patterns of society around him (one does not try to stay on board a sink-
ing ship), Noyes sought to create a form of unified community life which
would demonstrate the validity of his views. As he put it in 1837: "God
has set me to cast up a highway across this chaos, and I am gathering out
the stones and grading the track as fast as possible."[152]

Unlike many lesser reformers and religious leaders, Noyes insisted that
the intellectual or creative person must accept responsibility for the social
consequences of his beliefs. Noyes would not break down existing social
patterns until he felt that he had something better to offer and was convinced that he stood a reasonable chance of introducing the new ways
successfully. In the twelve years between 1834 and 1846, he worked to
establish the basis for new ideals and practices within himself and among
his followers. Only after he and his followers had internalized this new
basis for morality did Noyes lead the way out of the marriage customs of
the "apostasy" and into those of the "resurrected state." Throughout this
effort, Noyes always sought to maintain a harmonious balance between
"the two great principles of human existence," "solidarity" and "liberty,"
which, though they appeared antithetical, "like the centripetal and cen-
trifugal forces of nature," were in fact "designed to act upon human life
in equilibrium."[153]

Although it is the idiosyncratic social life at Oneida that has principally
attracted the attention of popular and scholarly writers, Noyes's primary
importance is as a brilliantly original social thinker and synthesizer. For
more than forty years, Noyes and his followers struggled with problems
of social order and disorder, both in theory and in practice. They made
the transition to a radically new way of living and they made that new
way of life work for more than twenty years. Noyes's observations from
his own experience on the problems and prospects of transitional periods
of human life, rank with the analyses of the best modern social theorists.
But one must be able to penetrate his unusual religious and intellectual
framework—to have "eyes to see" and "ears to hear."

Noyes's statement concerning the true "conservative" provides a fitting summary of his career. He wrote:

> The truth is, all present institutions are growths from an imperfect society and are adapted only to a transition state. This is true of religious as well as political institutions, marriage as well as slavery. The spirit of heaven in order to fulfill its full development in this world requires that we be ready to forsake all institutions adapted to the selfish state of society, and to expect something new and better. A truly conservative man therefore will be ready for change. He will not violently or unwisely attack any present institutions, but he will be ready and on the lookout for change.[154]

John Humphrey Noyes and his communal experiments deserve the kind of serious scholarly attention that they have only recently begun to receive.

IV

A New and Everlasting Covenant of Marriage: Joseph Smith and the Origins of Mormon Polygamy, 1831-1844

> The whole subject of the marriage relationship is not within my reach or in any other man's reach on this earth. It is without the beginning of days or the end of years; it is a hard matter to reach. We can feel some things with regard to it: it lays the foundation for worlds, for angels, and for Gods; for intelligent beings to be crowned with glory, immortality, and eternal lives. In fact, it is the thread which runs from the beginning to the end of the holy Gospel of the Son of God; it is from eternity to eternity.
>
> Brigham Young[1]

On July 12, 1843, one of the most remarkable nineteenth-century American experiments in reorganizing marriage and family life first received detailed written sanction. According to records of the main body of the Church of Jesus Christ of Latter-day Saints, better known as Mormons, it was on that day that Joseph Smith, the Church's dynamic thirty-seven-year-old prophet-founder, privately dictated a revelation in the Church's headquarters in Nauvoo, Illinois. This revelation called for a restoration among the Mormons of polygamous marriage practices similar to those of the Biblical patriarchs Abraham, Isaac, and Jacob. These new standards were set within the larger context of a conception of marriage, growth, and development as lasting throughout eternity. The "new and everlasting covenant" thus revealed to a small group of Smith's closest followers was conceived as a key element in his new religion.[2]

Not surprisingly, many Mormons had difficulty accepting the new standards. From its founding in 1830, the Mormon Church had provided many Americans of Puritan descent with a compelling new faith that satisfied their intense quest for true religious authority and seemed to restore the ancient gospel spirit of Christianity in all its fullness and purity. Since early Mormons were strong believers in the conventional monogamous standards of their day, the initial promulgation of polygamous marriage beliefs, even within the restricted circle of Joseph Smith's closest followers, led to misunderstandings and a severe crisis within the Church. Little more than a year later, the beloved prophet of the Church and his brother Hyrum were murdered in a jail in Carthage, Illinois, while awaiting trial on charges arising, in part, from dissatisfactions connected with the new marriage beliefs and practices.

This tragic denouement might have been expected to cripple the young Church and cause it to abandon its nascent form of family organization. Instead, quite the opposite occurred. By 1852, less than a decade later, the main body of Mormons, led by Brigham Young, had successfully completed a heroic trek to the intermountain West to escape persecution and were beginning to establish themselves securely in their mountain Zion. In Salt Lake City, on August 29, 1852, they announced to the world their commitment to plural marriage as an integral part of their religious and social organization.[3] By that time, acceptance of polygamy was in large measure a *fait accompli* among the Mormons. For nearly forty years until intense Federal pressure and internal Mormon dissatisfactions with polygamy combined to necessitate its official abandonment in 1890, plural marriage was advocated as the ideal form of family organization in the Utah Territory and adjacent areas of Mormon settlement. Even though many Mormons only accepted polygamy with reluctance, the practice became an important component of life within a large area of the intermountain West upon which the hardworking Mormons placed their indelible cultural imprint.

The origin and early development of polygamous beliefs and practices among the Mormons suggest many complex questions. What could have led the prophet Joseph Smith to conceive of such a form of family organization? Equally important, why did he apparently come to feel, as his closest followers repeatedly asserted, that the acceptance of plural marriage was essential to the continuing development of his Church? How did Smith's followers—most of them reared in a strict monagamous tradition and highly critical of any sexual irregularities—react to the beliefs, and why did many of his most committed followers come to support the belief and practice? Finally, and perhaps most important, how did plural marriage work in Utah during the period before external persecution interfered significantly with its natural development? What were the positive values, as well as the problems, associated with this form of social organization? And what, if any, explicit or implicit critique of the contemporary American family did Mormon plural marriage offer?

Despite the voluminous literature pro and con, these questions and the larger question of the significance of plural marriage in the total Mormon religious and social worldview have barely been touched. In this chapter, I shall try to suggest the social, intellectual, and political matrix within which plural marriage was put forward before the death of Joseph Smith in 1844, as well as some of the unresolved questions connected with the attempt to introduce such new cultural patterns in nineteenth-century America. The following chapter will describe the complex effort to institutionalize polygamy under Brigham Young's leadership and the way in which the system of plural marriage functioned in early Utah.

Four Approaches to the Origins of Mormon Polygamy

To begin to understand how polygamy developed, we must first look briefly at the four hypotheses that have most frequently been used to explain the origin of the practice. Each of these hypotheses appears to some people to be the self-evident explanation for the origin of plural marriage, yet none of them by itself satisfactorily explains all the evidence.

The complexity of the problem facing the scholar is suggested by the fact that one whole branch of the Mormon Church, the Reorganized Church of Jesus Christ of Latter Day Saints (RLDS), has generally denied that Joseph Smith had anything to do with the practice. Instead, polygamy is seen as a corruption of the Church by Brigham Young or by other unspecified individuals. Smith himself is said to have been innocent of the evil ideas and practices attributed to him by the Utah Mormons.

While one may sympathize with the intense hatred of polygamy shown by the Reorganized Mormon Church, the popular RLDS position on this issue is historically untenable. Overwhelming evidence exists that Joseph Smith not only introduced polygamous beliefs into the Mormon Church, but that he almost certainly engaged in polygamous practice himself. This evidence includes contemporary letters, diary accounts, and circumstantial evidence from Mormon believers, including a handwritten letter from Joseph Smith; contemporary manuscript and printed accounts by Mormon apostates and anti-Mormons who were in a position to know what was happening in Nauvoo; and a large body of retrospective testimonies and affidavits by Smith's plural wives and closest associates. These accounts are supported by statements from most of the early leaders of the Reorganization and by the official RLDS paper, the *True Latter Day Saints' Herald*. In its first issue, on January 1860, the *Saints' Herald* repeatedly criticized Smith for introducing polygamy into the Church, but claimed that he had repented of his error before his martyrdom.

Despite the wide range of biases represented by these different sources, the degree to which they agree on the basic details of early polygamy is impressive. The allegation that the testimonies and affidavits which the Utah Church later released to support its position were fraudulent is simply not supported by the evidence. Nevertheless, in spite of the limitations of the popular RLDS position, it is correct in implicitly recognizing the limited extent of polygamous belief and practice in Nauvoo, and in stressing the importance of Brigham Young's role in introducing and institutionalizing polygamy among the main body of Mormons who went to Utah. Even though Joseph Smith conceived and started polygamy, Brigham Young made it work.[4]

A second partially unsatisfactory explanation of the origin of Mormon polygamy is the one accepted by most non-Mormons and anti-Mormons. This is the hypothesis that Joseph Smith was just an oversexed individual —a lusty, good-natured libertine, perhaps—who was trying to rationalize his amorous propensities.

This is too simple. To be sure, no serious scholar would deny that sex drives influenced the introduction of polygamy. Smith was unquestionably a handsome, dynamic leader with great physical and intellectual vitality— a man not afraid to break with convention. Many of his statements reveal a basically positive attitude toward sexual expression, as well as the difficulty he sometimes had in keeping his impulses in check. But this is not enough to account for the introduction of polygamy. Many men have had strong sexual impulses; few of them have tried to develop a complete system of polygamy. Smith, like many other men, could have found easier ways of gratifying his sexual impulses than by setting up an elaborate polygamous system. Something far more complicated than simple rationalization or conscious fraud is involved here. Even knowledgeable apostates recognized Smith's underlying seriousness of purpose and his larger sense of prophetic mission. Available evidence shows that Smith began to formulate polygamous beliefs at least as early as 1831, ten years before any significant attempts to introduce the practice can be identified. Why did he wait so long if all he was after was personal sexual gratification? At the very least, his actions suggest that if this was a rationalization, it was a very complex one indeed.[5]

A third hypothesis concerning the origin of plural marriage is the one usually advanced by the now-monogamous Utah branch of the Mormon Church. This group has generally argued that Joseph Smith was commanded by God to introduce plural marriage. He was just obediently doing his best to carry out the inscrutable demand of the Almighty, a demand he may well have felt to be an onerous obligation. An angel with a drawn sword commanded him to enter into the practice and he was constrained to obey or lose his prophetic powers. To Mormons who hold this view, simply saying that God commanded the introduction of polygamy some-how seems enough to explain why and how it occurred.

Although this may well be an accurate reflection of the way in which many of the Morman rank-and-file reacted to the command, it does not do justice to the complex process by which Smith himself received and interpreted revelation. Even if one accepts the validity of the Mormon revelatory framework, one still must ask why the Lord should have given the command to Smith at that particular time and place. Typically, Joseph Smith received revelation only in answer to concrete intellectual or social problems that he or his followers were facing. He would lay such problems prayerfully before the Lord or, alternatively, as seen from a secular perspective, he would place the problem in his unconscious mind. When his heart "burned within him" with a definite answer to the particular problem, he would proceed to deliver that answer as a revelation, though not necessarily in written form or at the precise time that the insight came to him. Thus, even someone who adopts a sophisticated Mormon view of Joseph Smith's revelatory process would still have to ask what the intellectual and social roots were for the revelation on plural and celestial marriage.[6]

A final set of explanations for the origin of polygamy involves various types of psychological reductionist approaches. These characteristically treat Joseph Smith as a deeply disturbed individual, perhaps with paranoid obsessions. In the last year of his life, for example, Smith was head of his own private army, a candidate for President of the United States, the secret "king" of his Kingdom of God, and the "husband," in some sense, of dozens of wives. Out of touch with reality, so the reductionist arguments run, Smith created his own fantasy world, one facet of which was polygamy.

These approaches also are not fully satisfactory. Note, in the first place, that none of the possible psychological reductionist arguments concerning Joseph Smith has ever been systematically and convincingly developed by a competent psychiatrist or psychologically sophisticated historian. Furthermore, the psychological reductionist approaches almost inevitably tend to be based on the assumption that no sane, rational person could possibly want to introduce polygamy as the norm for a society. Is it fair to assume, however, that deviance from certain cultural norms is necessarily a sign of pathology—particularly during a period of rapid social change when the norms themselves are being called into question? Available evidence clearly shows that Smith and his followers strongly identified with the cultural patterns of the Biblical Hebrews. They thought of themselves as a "New Israel" and sought to revive many of the values and practices of that earlier way of life, including polygamy. Can this simply be dismissed as a case of pathology, unless one is prepared to argue that the practices of the Biblical Hebrews were pathological or that any thoroughgoing attempt to translate different cultural values into one's own experience is inherently pathological? Geniuses frequently do not accept the everyday assumptions of their contemporaries. The religious and social creativity of such individuals cannot be explained simply by attaching a derogatory label to it.[7]

Joseph Smith's Sense of Religious Mission

All the preceding explanations of the origin of plural marriage contain elements of truth, yet none of them captures the whole picture. The historian Jan Shipps has suggested that in order to understand Joseph Smith we must attempt to see him as a whole person and comprehend the total context within which he was operating, with all its complexities and ambiguities.[8] Based on a careful study of original sources, an attempt will be made in this chapter to reconstruct the goals that Joseph Smith was trying to accomplish, the problems that he faced, and the degree of consistency that he showed in terms of his stated objectives.

There can be little doubt that Joseph Smith was a religious genius. Like geniuses and creative figures in all fields, he attempted to fuse the raw materials of his experience into a new synthesis that would have meaning both for himself and for his contemporaries. Joseph Smith began as a barely literate farm boy living in a socially marginal family in western New York. During less than fifteen years between the founding of his religion and his death, he elaborated a complex system of religious belief and organization purporting to be a restoration of the original gospel faith of "primitive Christianity." He attracted tens of thousands of followers, as well as a group of able and committed leaders. And he founded a series of new communities including Nauvoo, Illinois, which grew within five years to become the second largest city in that state,[9] and provided a social and religious blueprint for what was later to be achieved in Utah. The introduction of polygamous belief and practice must be viewed within the larger context of Joseph Smith's total attempt to reintegrate religious and social values into a harmonious whole. What was the driving dynamic behind this intense and sustained effort at culture building?

Central to Joseph Smith's sense of prophetic mission was his millennial vision of a corrupt, diseased old order tottering inevitably toward destruction. After its demise, there would be a glorious restoration of the true religious and social practices of the "kingdom of God" on earth, a veritable "new heaven and new earth" purged of the evils of the old order.[10]

Every account of the genesis of young Joseph's religious concerns stresses his profound dissatisfaction with the cacophony of religious claims which surrounded him, a cacophony which was part of the almost explosive growth, expansion, and development of the United States in the antebellum period.

As we have seen, western New York where Joseph Smith grew up and received his first revelations was a particularly troubled region which was repeatedly "burned over" by the fires of religious enthusiasm. Into this area, which was undergoing rapid economic growth, came many displaced New Englanders who became attracted to an extraordinary range of crusades aimed at the perfection of mankind and the achievement of millennial happiness. The atmosphere of intense religious rivalry and competing claims to truth led to great internal tensions in sensitive individuals who desired a secure religious faith.

Joseph Smith's family was deeply affected by this religious and social disorder. The Smith family had always manifested a strain of visionary discontent. They had moved frequently, never achieving economic security, and showed a strong religious concern and sense of family destiny while not finding satisfaction in any of the available institutional frameworks. Young Joseph was described as a generally pleasant and outgoing ne'er-do-well who spent much time hunting for hidden treasure—an activity, incidentally, which was common to other young men in the area as well.[11] Yet underneath the nonchalant and outgoing exterior, conflicts seethed. Looking back on his experiences, Joseph declared: "So great were the confusion and strife among the different denominations, that it was impossible for a person young as I was and so unacquainted with men and things to come to any certain conclusion who was right and who was wrong."[12]

This inner tension demanded some sort of resolution. At least as early as 1823, young Joseph began experiencing a series of visions—or what might be described as waking deams of unusual force and vigor which totally reoriented his life.[13] He became convinced that all existing religions were wrong and that he had been specially called by God to restore the primitive gospel faith of early Christianity in all its immediacy and purity.

This sense of mission initially expressed itself through what Smith described as his "translation" by religious inspiration of inscriptions on golden plates that he claimed to have found in a large hill near his home. This "translation" purported to be an ancient religious history of two peoples of Hebrew extraction who had migrated to the American continent about 600 B.C. It detailed their many conflicts and apostasies which culminated about A.D. 400 in the destruction of the lighter-skinned Nephites by the darker-skinned Lamanites, ancestors of the American Indians.[14]

Although non-Mormon archaeologists have not found this account historically persuasive, this epic story of two great cultures in conflict and of a direct Biblical linkage between Old World and New had immense appeal in an early nineteenth-century America seeking a sense of its historical roots and a uniquely American identity.[15]

Joseph Smith's intense identification with the ancient Hebrew culture which he claimed to describe was perhaps the most striking feature of the Book of Mormon. As a contemporary observer in a New York magazine noted:

> The author lives with the whole strength of his imagination in the age he portrays. It is difficult to imagine a more difficult literary task than to write what may be termed a continuation of the Scriptures that should not only [avoid] all collision with the authentic sacred work, but even fill many chasms that now seem to exist. . . .[16]

Equally striking was the way in which this earlier culture was related to nineteenth-century America. Alexander Campbell, one of the leaders of a religious group for whom the Mormons were proving a major rival, paid the young prophet a backhanded compliment in 1831 when he declared that in the Book of Mormon, Smith reproduced

> . . . every error and almost every truth discussed in New York for the last ten years. He decides all the great controversies—infant baptism, ordination, the trinity, regeneration, the fall of man, the atonement, transubstantiation, fasting, penance, church government, religious experience, the call of the ministry, the general resurrection, eternal punishment, who may be baptized, and even the question of free masonry, republican government, and the rights of man.[17]

Campbell was astute in recognizing the way in which the Book of Mormon answered many of the key questions that concerned New Yorkers of the period. In retrospect, the book can also be seen as providing the framework for much of subsequent Mormon development, even though new elements of Church doctrine and organization would also be gradually unfolded through Joseph Smith's continuing revelations of the 1830s and 1840s.[18]

Intellectual Origins of Polygamy before Nauvoo

The early development of plural marriage can be closely correlated with three major periods of religious and social creativity in the Mormon Church. The first of these periods came in the late 1820s and early 1830s when the intellectual and organizational foundations of the new religion were established. In the early 1840s a second period of significant doctrinal and social departures took place. The third and final period included the time following Smith's death, the exodus from Nauvoo, and the establishment of the main body of Mormons in Utah in the late 1840s and early 1850s which set the foundations for the "Great Basin Kingdom."

The early development of plural marriage paralleled these larger developments in the Mormon Church. The first phase in the development of plural marriage appears to have begun at least as early as 1831, and to have continued through 1838–39 in Kirtland, Ohio, and several locations in Missouri where the Mormons settled. This period saw the intellectual genesis of the new beliefs, and possibly some early faltering attempts at practice. During the second phase, in Nauvoo between 1840–41 and 1844, Smith began an effort to introduce polygamous beliefs in the whole Church, and he initiated the practice of polygamy among some of his closest followers. A third phase, to be considered in the following chapter, led to the establishment of plural marriage as the highest ideal of family organization for the entire Church, although only a minority of the membership ever engaged in polygamous practice.

Joseph Smith's driving concern to overcome the religious confusion both within and outside himself must almost certainly have led to reflections on the family and sexual disharmony prevalent in the socially troubled region of western New York in which he grew up in the 1820s. The problems associated with rapid economic expansion, mobility, and competing value systems had already produced widespread marital experimentation in this region. Nearly all the new religious groups in the area were involved to some extent with unorthodox marriage ideals and practices. Such movements as the Shakers and Oneida Perfectionists were only the tip of the iceberg of dissatisfaction with prevailing marriage, family, and sex roles. Much of the less-structured marital experimentation in the area was referred to by the pejorative generic term "spiritual wifery," a catchall suggesting rationalized infidelity. Joseph Smith, with his wide-ranging interests and travel throughout the region, must have been familiar with both the problems and the experimentation, and he must have thought about the way in which personal relationships between men and women should be handled.

Recognition of the personal tragedies brought about by sexual disorder and family disorganization was one of the earliest themes in the Mormon faith. The Book of Mormon declared that "fornication and lasciviousness and every kind of sin" were running rampant, and that "a hundredth part" of these evil proceedings could not be described in its account.

> For behold, I, the Lord, have seen the sorrow, and heard the mourning of the daughters of my people, . . . in all the lands of my people,

because of the wickedness and abominations of their husbands.
. . . Ye have broken the hearts of your tender wives, and lost the
confidence of your children, because of your bad examples before
them; and the sobbings of their hearts ascendeth up to God against
you.[19]

This concern with sexual sins and the evils of family disorganization is
a recurring motif in the Book of Mormon. Indeed, the restoration of family
ties was implicit in the commission Joseph Smith said he had been given in
his vision of September 21, 1823—when, according to his account, the
angel Moroni told him that he would bring forth the Book of Mormon. It
was said then that Elijah would restore to Joseph Smith the Priesthood
powers of the true Church before the Second Coming. "And he shall plant
in the hearts of the children the promises made to the fathers, and the hearts
of the children shall turn to their fathers. If it were not so, the whole
earth would be utterly wasted at his coming."[20] This statement suggests
the problem of restoring ties of religious and social continuity which underlay Smith's concerns and claims to authority throughout his life, including the development of the rationale for marriage-sealing ceremonies
for "time and eternity" and earthly polygamy.

Given Joseph Smith's strong identification with the Old Testament patriarchs as cultural models, his intellectual problems with their practice
of polygamy are not surprising. Americans of Smith's day were not inclined
to look kindly on polygamy, even in the Bible. Interestingly, the Book of
Mormon contains five separate denunciations of polygamy. The practice
was linked with the "fornication," "whoredoms," and various problems of
family disorganization which appear to have so disturbed Joseph Smith.
David and Solomon were attacked for having many wives and concubines, "which thing was abominable before me, saith the Lord." The people were commanded not to do "like unto them of old."[21]

These harsh attacks on polygamy might appear ironical in view of the
later Mormon adoption of the practice. The apparent paradox partially
disappears, however, when one considers the passages closely and places
them within the dispensational framework of the Church. The most important of the anti-polygamy passages declares: "Wherefore, my brethren, hear me, and hearken to the word of the Lord: for there shall not
any man among you have save it be one wife; and concubines he shall
have none: For I, the Lord God delighteth in the chastity of women. And
whoredoms is [are] an abomination before me. . . ." This apparently
clear cut prohibition is qualified by a significant proviso: "For if I will,
saith the Lord of Hosts, raise up seed unto me, I will command my people:
otherwise, they shall hearken unto these things" [my emphasis].[22] This
passage would appear to leave open the possibility that God through

Joseph Smith might eventually issue a new command if it would contribute to the propagation of numerous progeny in righteous families. The argument that polygamy was a means of a man's begetting numerous progeny would be a key part of the rationale for plural marriage in Utah.

The standard Mormon interpretation of this passage in the Book of Mormon is that it simply refers to a specific time when polygamy was interdicted for practical reasons, and that it is not a blanket condemnation of the practice. A blanket condemnation would necessarily have to be applied to the great patriarchs of the Bible such as Abraham, whose conduct God evidently approved, and would therefore be self-contradictory. The key to understanding this interpretation lies in the Mormon concepts of progressive revelation and different dispensations. Behavior permitted in one dispensation might not be permitted in another. Mormon writings declared: "The Mosaic dispensation was one of practices; the Christian Church was one of principles; while the Latter-day work differs from either yet includes both."[23]

In pragmatic American fashion, the Mormon religion thus combined Biblical literalism with a dispensational interpretation of history to free itself for continuing religious and social innovation, a type of innovation that Jason Briggs described as "walking backward towards the future."[24] As Orson Pratt noted in 1869: "Domestic relations were governed according to the mind and will of God, and were varied according to circumstance, as he thought proper."[25] The problem in this and other cases was that the distinction between the mind of God and the mind of Joseph Smith was often uncertain at best.

As the references to polygamy in the Book of Mormon suggest, the interpretation of ambiguous passages with *doubles entendres* poses constant problems in dealing with the early history of the Mormon Church. It is difficult to know whether a statement about polygamy actually means what it appears to mean. Almost all early public statements relating to the topic were couched in a special language, the significance of which could be grasped only by those who knew its inner meaning. So controversial were the new beliefs that they could not at first be revealed to rank-and-file members of the Church, let alone to the outside world. Although polygamous marriage appears to have been practiced before the recording of the revelation in 1843 and although a fairly extensive polygamous system was set up following the exodus to Utah, until 1852 the leaders of the Saints always officially denied that they sanctioned any such belief or practice. The casuistry involved in these denials seemed justified to Mormon leaders because they felt that the perversions ascribed to them by rumor bore no resemblance to the regulated practices that they were trying to introduce.[26]

Whatever the ethics of such secrecy, it was a practical necessity. Persecution of the Saints was already enough of a problem without public knowledge of polygamy to add fuel to the fire. Other groups had also maintained secrecy about unorthodox marital practices. Earlier, the Shakers had closed themselves off from the world while they were organizing their initial celibate orders. John Humphrey Noyes at first maintained "gospel secrecy" about his system of "complex marriage" at Putney and Oneida. So, too, Joseph Smith and his followers realized that their plural marriage ideas were too controversial to be introduced openly. Probably our knowledge of the development of polygamy before Nauvoo will always remain rather conjectural. From Nauvoo on, however, a more nearly reliable picture can be provided.

Although the intellectual and practical development of Mormon polygamy before Nauvoo cannot be reconstructed with any degree of certainty, Joseph Smith appears to have first seriously considered the possibility of introducing plural marriage at least as early as 1831. According to the retrospective Mormon view—which may be partially an extrapolation from internal evidence in the 1843 revelation—Smith first became convinced that polygamy should be reintroduced while he was making his inspired revision of the Old Testament, particularly Genesis. While engaged in this work, he became impressed by the "evident approval of God to the plural marriage of the ancient patriarchs." In answer to one of his pleas for information concerning God's view of marriage, he then received the sanction for a plurality of wives "under certain limitations and special conditions," although full details were not then revealed to him. This view is supported by a number of statements of close associates from the period.[27]

That Joseph Smith was considering the possibility of plural marriage as early as this period is also suggested by a recently published revelation dated July 17, 1831, that he allegedly gave to seven elders near the boundary west of Jackson County, Missouri. This revelation obliquely implies that plural marriage eventually would be reintroduced in some form. The present copy of the revelation, in the handwriting of W. W. Phelps who was present on the occasion, dates from the 1850s or 1860s; however, references to the revelation by a knowledgeable contemporary apostate, Ezra Booth, only five months after its alleged delivery, tends to confirm its authenticity.[28]

The relevant portion of the revelation states:

> Verily, I say unto you, that the wisdom of man, in his fallen state, knoweth not the purposes and privileges of my holy priesthood, but ye shall know when ye receive a fulness by reason of the anointing;
> For it is my will, that in time, ye should take unto you wives of the

Lamanites and Nephites that their posterity may become white delightsome and just, for even now their females are more virtuous than the gentiles.

In a note appended to the revelation, W. W. Phelps adds:

About three years after this was given, I asked brother Joseph, privately, how "we," that were mentioned in the revelation could take wives of the "natives" as we were all married men? He replied instantly "In the same manner that Abraham took Hagar and Keturah; that Jacob took Rachel, Bilhah and Zilpah; by revelation—the saints of the Lord are always directed by revelation."[29]

This document suggests that within two years of the founding of his Church, Joseph Smith had at least considered the possibility of introducing a form of polygamous practice. Like many of Smith's other revelations, this one is not important doctrinally. It was not considered of enough significance to be formally brought to the attention of Brigham Young until 1861. Yet the revelation typifies many of Smith's concerns in this early period. It attempts to relate two different cultures, Biblical Hebrew and native American, in a new synthesis within a larger American restorationist framework. The statement appears to foreshadow, at least in part, temple ceremonies later to be adopted in Kirtland and Nauvoo, some of which were connected with plural marriage. Although this statement suggests that Smith contemplated the eventual reintroduction of a form of Biblical polygamy in nineteenth-century America, this account clearly indicates that in 1831 he did not believe that the time to begin the practice of the principle had arrived.

The critical description of this revelation by Ezra Booth in the *Ohio Star* of December 8, 1831, reveals some of the further social factors associated with Mormon marital changes in this period. Booth did not grasp the implications that the revelation might have for polygamy. Rather, he emphasized the difficulties the Mormons were having when an individual was converted to the faith but his or her spouse did not join, and remained adamantly opposed to the Church or to coming to the Mormon place of gathering.[30] How were unsatisfactory marital alliances to be terminated when Mormons lived or traveled in many different states and encountered a plethora of state marriage and divorce laws?

Faced with this problem, the Mormon Church of the 1830s began to assume responsibility for the marriage and divorce of its own members. Sometimes the Mormon arrangements were not fully in harmony with local marriage regulations or mores. For instance, the question of whether Joseph Smith, who was not a formally ordained minister, could solemnize marriages, evidently provoked some controversy in the mid-1830s. Sidney

Rigdon, another prominent early leader, actually was indicted (and acquitted) for "solemnizing marriages without a license" in 1835.[31] In November 1835, at the marriage ceremony of Newell Knight and Lydia Goldthwaite, Smith reportedly "remarked that marriage was an institution of heaven, instituted in the garden of Eden; that it was necessary it should be solemnized by the authority of the everlasting Priesthood."[32]

If the Mormon Church were to gain the independent control of its own destiny that it sought, it had to be able to control the marriage and divorce practices of its members. Such control was also a necessary precondition for the establishment of polygamy, since that form of marital practice was illegal in the states in which the Mormons settled. Only the Church could regulate such alternative family forms. Innovation in other areas of marriage and family life may also have been encouraged by the increasing Mormon independence of civil regulations.

Whatever the causes may have been, fundamental changes in the attitudes of Mormon leaders toward marriage appear to have begun in the early and mid-1830s. As early as March 1831, in Kirtland, Ohio, Joseph Smith gave a revelation commanding three followers to proselytize the nearby Shaker village at North Union (the present Shaker Heights). Although the venture itself proved inconclusive, this revelation suggested many characteristic Mormon marriage beliefs, including the idea that marriage was a sacred ordinance of God.[33] Explicit steps to link religion with civil relations marked a major departure from the tradition out of which the Mormons had come. The Mormons were moving away from the New England Puritan view of marriage as a strictly civil contract, and back toward the pre-Reformation approach which treated marriage as a sacrament.

The innovative Mormon re-sacralization of marriage was vividly expressed in W. W. Phelps's statement in 1835, which alluded to the idea that marriage relations existed in heaven:

> We shall by and by learn that we were with God in another world, and had our agency: that we came into this world and have our agency in order that we may prepare a kingdom of glory; become archangels, even the sons of God where the man is not without the woman, nor the woman without the man in the Lord. . . .[34]

More than five years later in Nauvoo, Joseph Smith would begin to teach that the divine form of marriage "sealed" couples together for eternity, forging a key link to weld the faithful together in a family relation. Translated into temporal practice, this belief would make possible the development of earthly polygamy among the Mormons.

If Smith began considering the possibility of introducing polygamy as early as 1831, it would not be surprising if some early attempts at practice should have occurred. Whether pilot efforts took place in Kirtland, Ohio, and in Missouri remains a moot point.[35] Many of the allegations of polygamy in this period may well reflect nothing more than the confusion of individuals who heard rumors that new practices were to be introduced. Some accounts may be evidence that a few individuals "ran before being sent," entering polygamous relationships prematurely on their own initiative. Possibly some of the early adultery cases in the Church may have been of this character.

Smith was well aware of the necessity for extreme caution in this delicate matter. He had a canny sense of how fast he could move. Speaking to Brigham Young in Kirtland, Smith once commented that "if I were to reveal to this people what the Lord has revealed to me, there is not a man or a woman that would stay with me."[36] The Bible did not provide detailed guidelines as to how polygamy was to be practiced. Thus, it is not surprising that the development of Smith's thought in this and in many other areas of revelation appears to have been a gradual process, building "precept by precept, and line upon line." By the time plural marriage was announced publicly in 1852, many of the problems in its early development had been overcome. The retrospective views of key participants, writing as much as fifty years after the events they described, may well attribute greater order to the early development of polygamy than had really existed at the time.

Although solid contemporary evidence for the practice of polygamy before Nauvoo is extremely rare, rumors of polygamous beliefs and practices were quite common in the 1830s. The Mormon historian Stanley Snow Ivins has collected more than one hundred thirty allegations concerning Mormon polygamy before 1841. Many of these admittedly are unreliable, speculative, or second-hand, but others seemingly are based on more substantial evidence.[37] An RLDS source implies that problems with polygamy may have existed in the Church as early as 1833.[38] And a Mormon writer, Mosiah Hancock, speaking of the Kirtland period, said: "My father made some things known to me concerning those days, and the part he took with the Prophet in trying to assist him to start the principle. . . ."[39]

By 1835 enough rumors were circulating that a resolution explicitly denying that the Mormons practiced "polygamy" was introduced under the auspices of W. W. Phelps and Oliver Cowdery into the 1835 edition of the Doctrine and Covenants. It declared:

> Inasmuch as this church of Christ has been reproached with the crime of fornication, and polygamy, we declare that we believe that one man should have one wife, and one woman but one husband, except in case of death, when either is at liberty to marry again.[40]

It it unclear whether Joseph Smith favored this resolution, which was unaccountably presented while he was absent on a brief trip. Although the primary object of the resolution appears to have been to staunch damaging rumors of polygamy, it may also represent opposition to polygamy by several of those closest to Joseph Smith.[41]

Following the dedication of the Kirtland Temple in March 1836, rumors of polygamy appear to have become more widespread.[42] Such rumors were only a minor factor among the complex causes of dissension in the late Kirtland and Missouri periods, however. With Missouri Governor Lilburn W. Boggs calling for either the expulsion or the literal "extermination" of the Mormons, the group had little time for minor worries. Nevertheless, rumors of polygamy did add to Mormon problems.

A resolution adopted by the presidents of the Seventies Quorum of the Church on April 29, 1837, declared that fellowship would be withheld from any elder "who is guilty of polygamy or any offense of the kind."[43] In an editorial comment in November 1837 in Kirtland, Ohio, and in July 1838 in Far West, Missouri, the *Elder's Journal* responded to "questions which are daily and hourly asked by all classes of people" concerning the Mormons, including "Do the Mormons believe in having more wives than one?" The answer was an unequivocal "No."[44] And, in a letter of Joseph Smith's from Liberty Jail in Missouri, in which he defended himself against charges the gentiles had made against his people, he wrote at length denying that Mormon communitarian efforts were connected in any way with a "community of wives."[45]

The most serious criticism of Joseph Smith connected with polygamy in this period appears to have been based on his alleged liaison with Fanny Alger, an attractive young girl who worked as a servant in his household in the mid-1830s. Later Mormon writers believed that she was "without doubt the first" or "one of the first" of his plural wives.[46] A major charge in Oliver Cowdery's excommunication trial in Far West on April 12, 1838, was for defaming Joseph Smith's character by falsely alleging that he had committed adultery, and Cowdery's letters show that "the girl" in question was Fanny Alger.[47]

Cowdery's anger appears primarily to have been aroused not by the relationship itself but by Joseph Smith's allegation that Cowdery's indiscreet talk about Smith's activities involved a deliberate untruth. The ethical problems arising when two distinct standards of truth had to be maintained during the early development of plural marriage would continue to create bitterness and misunderstandings in Nauvoo as well. Given Cowdery's network of friendships in the Church, it would not be surprising if a part of the dissatisfaction of other prominent Mormons who left the Church in Far West, Missouri, was also associated with nascent polygamous belief and practice.[48]

Initial efforts to introduce plural marriage—if that is what was happening—thus got off to a slow start. Summarizing his analysis of the development of polygamy in this period, the Mormon historian Max Parkin writes:

> It appears that polygamy was a secret practice in Kirtland in the 1830s and the Church, or rather the Church's Prophet, neither had the intention of making it a public matter nor at that early date making it a principle of the Mormon faith . . . within the Church, the conflict of the period was accentuated by the few who understood the new principle, and by others who mispracticed it.[49]

Whatever the early development of plural marriage may have been, not until Nauvoo would the latent tendencies lead to the formal introduction of polygamous beliefs and practices at the highest level of the Church as part of a radical effort to create and establish a total way of life.

The Pivotal Period in Nauvoo

The period between 1839 and 1844 that the Mormons spent in Nauvoo, Illinois, under Joseph Smith's leadership was pivotal in their history. Nauvoo saw the climax of the earlier phase of Mormon development and set the pattern of new doctrinal, social, and political approaches which would be further developed and tested in Utah. In Nauvoo, Smith made his most concerted effort to realize his conception of the Kingdom of Heaven on earth. No aspect of life was left untouched.

The period abounds in paradoxes. From one perspective, Nauvoo was a typical Jacksonian boom town, representative of the raw potentiality, enthusiasm, crassness, and tensions that characterized the era. Yet at a more fundamental level, the Mormons in Nauvoo were attacking and attempting to overcome the rampant, exploitative Jacksonian individualism which surrounded them. They were seeking a total solution, more akin to medieval ideals in which religious and social life were inextricably intertwined, and the good of the community took precedence over individual "self-interest." Mundane "secular" life would be re-sacralized and integrated into a new organic unity which in turn had its place and meaning in the cosmic order.[50]

The introduction of new marriage and family patterns was an important part of this total effort. In some respects, plural marriage may be seen as an outgrowth of characteristic American values, in particular, an attempt to restore earlier patriarchal patterns in marriage that were under attack in the period. At the deepest level, it was a fundamental protest against the careless individualism of romantic love, which seemed to threaten the very roots of family life and social solidarity. Plural marriage was conceived as a means of strengthening kinship relations and social solidarity. Nevertheless, the introduction of plural marriage exacerbated the already severe internal and external problems facing the Mormon Church, leading to the death of Joseph Smith and the temporary disorganization of his religion.

A variety of social, intellectual, and political factors made possible the introduction of plural marriage on a limited scale in Nauvoo. The key emotional thread running throughout this period was a sense of increasing tension and imminent crisis. This encouraged self-sacrifice, increasing intellectual and practical isolation conducive to excess, and an almost obsessive emphasis on unquestioning loyalty to the Priesthood as the cardinal virtue.

In 1838–39 the Mormons started over again in Illinois, after fleeing attacks in Missouri that surpassed in brutality any of the outrages that would later be perpetuated by border ruffians on "Bleeding Kansas." This and previous persecution had established a crisis mentality. Although the Mormons at Nauvoo initially were well received by their neighbors, Mormon group loyalty soon began to lead to tensions with the surrounding areas. Determined not to be pushed around any more, the Mormons secured a city charter that, if freely interpreted, made Nauvoo virtually independent of the state.[51] An all-Mormon militia of more than two thousand men called the Nauvoo Legion was established, provoking fear in nearby non-Mormon regions. And the tightly organized Church, which presided over what became temporarily the second largest city in Illinois and which appeared to hold the balance of power in the state, managed to alienate both political parties. Within this context of escalating tension and increasing separateness, the inhibitions which normally discourage radical innovation in the larger society became less significant and major doctrinal and social changes could occur. As separateness encouraged innovation, so innovation in turn encouraged separateness by providing doctrinal and practical bases for evolving singularity.[52]

Closely connected with the tensions between Mormons and outsiders as a factor which made it possible to introduce new doctrinal and social patterns were the social tensions within the Mormon community itself. Nauvoo was a boom town, growing within five years from a few hundred people into a city with over eleven thousand inhabitants. Like many such boom towns, it was plagued by a host of problems attendant upon rapid growth. Visitors commented on the extremes of wealth and poverty in the city, as well as on the Mormon efforts to overcome those problems.[53] With thousands of immigrants from the Eastern states and from England entering the city each year, the induction of new members into the distinctive Mormon beliefs and cultural patterns presented a major challenge. The city was close to the marshy malarial bottoms along the Mississippi River, and there were frequent and numerous deaths. According to one historian, as many as fifteen hundred to two thousand people may have died during the six years that the Mormons lived in Nauvoo. While this estimate is undoubtedly too high, there were few families in Nauvoo that were not intimately acquainted with disease and death.[54]

Probably the most important internal dislocations were an unforeseen side effect of the Mormon missionary effort. While this program brought in vitally needed convert-settlers and capital, it also placed severe strains on marital relationships. On the one hand, men were frequently called with little notice to go "without purse or scrip" on extended missionary trips which necessitated long periods of temporary celibacy. Parley P. Pratt spoke for many Mormon missionary husbands when he wrote from England in 1840 to his wife Mary Ann: "Why must we live separate? Why must I be forever deprived of your Society and my dear little Children? I cannot endure it, and yet I must."[55] Only an intense personal commitment to the larger objectives of the Mormon group enterprise could have induced so many men like Parley P. Pratt to sacrifice their normal family lives.

Although the demands on Mormon missionary husbands certainly were considerable, the pressures on their wives were even greater. Of necessity, they were left behind, often pregnant or with young children to care for, as they faced the problem of trying to support themselves somehow. The case of Eunice B. Shurtliff was typical. In 1842, her husband Luman recorded a letter from her in his journal, to give "a small understanding of the trials, labors, sufferings and hardships of the sisters, and especially the wives of traveling elders." Eunice wrote that she was four months pregnant, had been severely sick for three months, and could not get credit to purchase food at the store. ". . . I have no husband to talk with or comfort me these long nights. . . . You know when Jane was born and you were gone from home . . . I had to get along the best I could. Luman, I do not think it is your duty to stay there and leave me in such circumstances. Come without fail."[56] The plight of yet another woman, whose husband was absent for the exceptionally long period of five years, was tellingly described as a temporary "widow-hood."[57] Under these conditions, the marital dissatisfactions of both men and women must have pressed for resolution.

Thus there may well have been a relationship between the significant expansion of the Mormon missionary program in 1837, which included the founding of an English mission, and the subsequent effort by Joseph Smith to introduce new marriage and family beliefs and practices. Nor is it surprising that the twelve apostles, who spearheaded the missionary program, were the principal leadership faction supporting Smith in these efforts, and would eventually oversee the introduction of polygamy into the Church as a whole. Faced with lengthy separations from their wives and families, these men may well have been attracted to the idea of formalizing and consummating emotional attachments that developed with women whom they met in their proselyting work. Likewise, wives of these missionaries must sometimes have wished for a husband who was not frequently absent for long periods of time, and who could provide them with economic security.

In short, even without any religious or intellectual rationale, an idealization of family and married life, a longing for stable and permanent relationships, and a deviation from conventional marital arrangements would probably have occurred. Indeed, it is surprising that despite these tensions Nauvoo was generally agreed to be a well-kept and "virtuous" town. Significant marital variation seems to have occurred only in the upper hierarchy of the Church.

The Revelation on Plural Marriage and Eternal Family Relationships

All the contradictory tensions and potential of Nauvoo eventually seemed to become embodied in Joseph Smith himself. After the devastating apostasy of John C. Bennett in 1842, Smith became increasingly suspicious of the loyalty of even his closest associates, and he attempted to concentrate all positions of power in his own hands. He served simultaneously as Prophet and President of his Church, Mayor of the city, Major-General of the Nauvoo Legion, and chief economic planner for the city and the Church, as well as in many other capacities—enough to tax the talents of many a lesser man. As tensions rose to a climax in 1844, Joseph Smith also began a seemingly quixotic campaign for President of the United States. At the same time he apparently had himself secretly crowned King of his evolving political kingdom.[58] Faced with an enormously complex set of interlocking problems, Smith increasingly behaved as though he were only willing to trust his own resources; he sought through his own powers alone to find solutions to all the difficult problems facing him.

It was in the context of this rapidly increasing tension that Smith chose to present in Nauvoo doctrines that had long been germinating in his mind. Apparently foreseeing the possibility of his eventual martyrdom, Smith became obsessed with teaching even his most controversial ideas to his close associates, lest those ideas die with him. On January 22, 1843, in a mood of aggressive fatalism, he reportedly declared: "God Almighty is my shield; and what can man do if God is my friend? I shall not be sacrificed until my time comes; then I shall be offered freely."[59] Given such an attitude, a strong-willed man may be capable of remarkable actions.

Joseph Smith appears to have had such a strong sense of his prophetic mission that he could convince himself that his own deepest perceptions were divine in origin and he could consider himself responsible only to God for his actions. Other Mormons, however, would not have been willing to leave behind familiar moral standards and commit themselves to an unknown and untested new way of life without clearly defined guarantees or sanctions.

Some writers have suggested that Smith's personal "charisma" was sufficient to induce his followers to adopt new marriage and family practices. This is an inadequate explanation. Certainly Smith did possess unusual personal magnetism, but his appeal lay at least as much in his prophetic role as in his person. An intellectual-doctrinal framework of great power and appeal, as well as a variety of impressive new temple ceremonies, had to be created to induct Smith's followers into the new beliefs and practices.

Anthropologists are familiar with rites of passage in various cultures; these occur in certain socially prescribed circumstances and forms. What Joseph Smith did was more complex; he created a whole new framework of meaning for his followers. This framework included elaborate new beliefs and rituals which would lead his followers out of their present state and initiate them into a largely unknown new condition of being. In effect, Smith was attempting to demolish an old way of life and build a new social order from the ground up.

Not surprisingly, Smith encountered difficulties with this venture. Only following his martyrdom, when his personal motivations were no longer in such hot dispute among most Mormons, could his new beliefs and practices be introduced into the whole Church.[60] In the antebellum period in America, the absence of adequate institutional means to deal with pressing problems allowed various reform ideas to assume unusual practical influence.[61] In turbulent Nauvoo, which in many ways was a microcosm of the America of that time, ideas came to play an exceptionally significant role in events. Therefore, Joseph Smith's ideas will receive serious attention in this account.

The quest for true religious authority underlay initial Mormon development.[62] In Nauvoo, where the Saints had sufficient time and the concentrated power to put their ideals into practice, the effort to integrate religious and social life soon came to a peak. Five revelations—and four other statements now accepted as revelation by the Utah Church—were given between January 19, 1841, and July 12, 1843. These provided the doctrinal basis for a new worldview that made possible the introduction of plural marriage.[63]

The essence of these revelations was the further extension of Church authority by means of new ceremonies that were seen as linking the living and the dead. There was strong emphasis on the idea that the head of the Mormon Church possessed the powers of Saint Peter to bind and to loose, thereby determining possible relationships in heaven. This was the basis for the doctrine of baptism for the dead, which was believed to make possible the salvation of those who had died without knowledge of the truth. Additionally, special endowment and sealing ceremonies, apparently a revision and elaboration of Masonic ritual,[64] were seen as giving permanence to earthly marriage after death.

Mormons believed that these ceremonies should ideally be performed within a special temple, and they therefore made great efforts to build that temple which would provide tangible sanction for the new doctrinal and social departures. These new beliefs and rituals helped solidify the authority of the Church over its members. Individuals whose lives were often uncertain were provided with a sense of eternal continuity and stability.

Underlying this elaboration of Church authority was a new view of the relationship between the material and spiritual worlds. The central premise of this belief was the close connection between matter and spirit: "All spirit is matter, but it is more fine and pure, and can only be discerned by purer eyes."[65] Smith asserted that "spirit is a substance that is material but that is more pure, elastic and refined matter than the body. . . . It existed before the body, can exist in the body, and will exist separate from the body, when the body will be mouldering in the dust. . . ."[66]

The distance between God and man was also sharply reduced. God was seen as possessing a physical body and subject to the limits of time. Revelation declared that: "The Father has a body of flesh and bones as tangible as a man's. . . ."[67] And Smith made clear that he did not mean this statement metaphorically: "God himself, who sits enthroned in yonder heavens, is a man like unto yourselves, that is the great secret. . . . Adam received instruction, walked, talked, and conversed with him, as one man talks a⌐⏋ communes with another."[68]

This anthropormorphic view, which suggests the popular stereotype of God as the great bearded patriarch on the throne, reflects the extraordinary degree to which Joseph Smith personalized his relationship to God. Implicit in this new view of God was the awesome and intoxicating possibility that men could progress toward full godhood. "As man is, God once was; as God is, man may become" was Lorenzo Snow's succinct summary of this belief.[69]

The key to achieving this highest celestial glory was available to men through the Priesthood and through a "new and everlasting covenant of marriage," which would be most fully described in Smith's last recorded revelation. All these revelations implied that heaven was an accentuation and heightening of the present life. "The same sociality which exists among us here will exist among us there, only it will be coupled with eternal glory, which glory we do not now enjoy."[70] Thus, the afterlife was not merely a matter of concern for the future; the ideal or heavenly pattern could be realized on earth.

The idea that marriage relationships would be eternal when properly sealed by the Church lay at the heart of Joseph Smith's last and perhaps most important revelation on plural and celestial marriage. Marriage was raised to a position of supreme importance as the only means by which the highest status and glory could be achieved in heaven. Neither men nor women could be saved apart from each other in a marriage relationship. Two types of marriage were indicated. The first, ordinary secular marriage or marriage without the proper sealing ceremonies by the Priesthood, would last only "for time." It was thus of an inferior character, for it would be dissolved by the death of either party. In heaven, people who had been married in this way would belong to the lowest order, solitary "ministering angels," a sort of perpetual servant class, unable to progress further toward godhood.

The second, "celestial," form of marriage was "for time and eternity." It had to be properly sealed by the Priesthood, and would endure in heaven as well as on earth. In heaven, men who had contracted such marriages would be great patriarchs having "all power," surrounded by their own families as well as by those unfortunate ministering angels who lacked wives or progeny. Through the "eternal increase" of such godlike patriarchs by means of their children, grandchildren, and so forth, they eventually would move on to rule over whole new worlds, achieving full godhood in conjunction with their wives in what could easily be seen as a kind of cosmic "manifest destiny."

Polygamy or plural marriage was introduced as a particularly exalted form of eternal or celestial marriage. The precondition for polygamy was Smith's belief that God had commanded, or at least sanctioned, the taking of plural wives and concubines by the Hebrew patriarchs Abraham, Isaac, and Jacob, as well as by David and Solomon, and many others. The logic behind the Latter-day Saint version of plural marriage was that if marriage with one wife, sealed under the authority of the Priesthood, could bring eternal progression and ultimate godhood for men, then multiple wives in this life and the next would accelerate the process, in line with God's promise to Abraham that his seed eventually would be as numerous as the sand on the sea shore.

Since the idea of polygamy would obviously be repugnant to many, the bulk of this, as of many previous revelations, was devoted to reminding the Mormons that strict obedience to God's commands was required, even when those commands appeared humanly unreasonable. Thus, when Abraham was prepared if necessary to obey God's command to kill his son Isaac for a sacrifice—even though it is written, "Thou shalt not kill"— he was justified. And likewise, when Abraham, at God's command according to Mormon scripture, took Hagar to wife in addition to Sarah,[71] he was acting under law and was justified. "Go ye, therefore, and do the work of Abraham; enter ye into my law, and ye shall be saved."

Almost no details were given in the revelation as to how polygamy was to be practiced; the revelation did declare, however, that under the authority of the Priesthood,

> If any man espouse a virgin, and desire to espouse another, and the first give her consent, and if he espouse the second, and if they are virgins, and have vowed to no other man, then he is justified; he cannot commit adultery with that that belongeth unto him and to no one else; and if he have ten virgins given unto him by this law, he cannot commit adultery, for they belong to him, therefore he is justified.[72]

Should either party who was sealed under the new and everlasting covenant have sexual relations outside the bounds of Church-supervised law, however, that would be a heinous sin, especially for the woman, who would be destroyed by God.

The extreme arbitrariness of this revelation and the constant emphasis on male prerogatives are characteristic of Joseph Smith's attitudes during this increasingly tense period in Nauvoo. A contemporary scholar, probing to the root of this extraordinary new system, declares: "Mormonism was true to its heritage. It would transgress conventional morality only by claiming the sanction of a higher command. Moral authority must not be questioned in the process.[73]

Reactions to Polygamy

Joseph Smith may have developed an internally consistent theory of plural marriage, but the practical development and workings of the new polygamous system were much more problematical. Even under ideal circumstances, polygamous practices could hardly have been introduced into nineteenth-century Illinois without provoking severe misunderstandings and conflicts. Most people were already suspicious of individual immorality or deviance. To go farther and claim that a deviant practice such as polygamy was authorized and indeed commanded by God seemed to undercut the very basis of moral authority itself.

Some of the most vehement opposition to the new beliefs and practices came from highly placed Mormons, many of whom were appalled at what they considered Joseph Smith's falling away from virtue and the earlier high standards of the Church. The number of Mormons who had first-hand knowledge of the new beliefs before Smith's death was very small. Those who engaged in the practice of polygamy with Joseph Smith's approval were fewer still. Nevertheless, rumors that strange and officially sanctioned practices were being introduced into the Church circulated widely in Nauvoo. These rumors trickled out to nearby newspapers such as the *Warsaw Signal,* which gleefully pounced on such stories as yet another proof of Mormon perfidy. Many of those accounts seemed so improbable that few decent non-Mormons gave them much credence. But within Nauvoo itself, tensions over the introduction of plural marriage created an explosive situation.

Because Joseph Smith assumed ultimate authority and responsibility for everything in the Church, and whatever he supported became more or less official policy, he inevitably became the center around which a storm of dissension swirled. During the last three years of his life, Smith started to prepare the minds of his followers for the introduction of plural marriage, began explicitly advocating polygamous belief and practice to his closest associates, and took a large number of plural wives himself. Thus, be became increasingly vulnerable to discovery and criticism.

Five concentric circles of conflict may be visualized as expanding outward from Joseph Smith. There were tensions within Smith's own psyche; between Smith and his first wife Emma; and between Smith and his closest disciples, including the women he espoused. With the possible exception of Emma, these people comprised an inner core group which knew a good deal about what Smith was trying to do and which supported him, albeit often reluctantly. A much larger outer group of followers sensed that something strange was happening in the Church. Many of these people were disturbed by the direction events were taking. Opposition ranged from those Mormons who engaged in variant polygamous or licentious practices, such as the highly opportunistic John C. Bennett, who distorted a developing religious principle to serve his own personal ends, to sincere believers such as William Law and Austin Cowles, who became convinced that Joseph Smith had become a "fallen prophet" and must be replaced if the Church were to be preserved. Internal and external dissension combined and led, with an almost tragic determinism, to the martyrdom of the Mormon prophet and the exodus of the Mormon community from Illinois.

Joseph Smith himself appears to have been torn by many conflicting impulses. He repeatedly declared to his closest associates that he had decided to introduce plural marriage only with the greatest reluctance because "an angel of God stood by him with a drawn sword, and told him that, unless he moved forward and established plural marriage, his Priesthood would be taken away from him and he should be destroyed."[74] Certainly he was aware of the political explosiveness of the new doctrines, as his numerous carefully veiled remarks and many apparent "feelers" to test Church opinion suggest.[75]

Smith's detractors have not adequately understood the extent to which he was aware of his motives, and how close he may have come to realizing that the doctrine of plural marriage might partly reflect a need for rationalization and sanction of his own impulses and behavior. In a public speech in April 1840, he declared:

> I have my failings and passions to contend with the same as has the greatest stranger to God. I am tempted the same as you are, my brethren. I am not infallible. All men are subject to temptation, but they are not justified in yielding to their passions and sinful natures. There is a constant warfare between the two natures of man.[76]

It is surely no accident that Joseph Smith distinguished between his actions as a fallible man and his role as a prophet or mouthpiece of God,[77] or that revelations frequently rebuked him for his own short-comings or errors in judgment. Several ambiguous statements, including two in the revelation on plural marriage, may even suggest an indirect apology to his wife Emma for possible sexual misconduct.[78] A devoted follower, Joseph Lee Robinson, remembered that Smith once expressed anxiety that he might have committed adultery.[79] Such a concern would suggest either that Joseph Smith may not have been wholly able to leave the old monogamous ways of thinking behind, or else that he himself did not always live up to the standards that he was introducing.

Smith certainly never resembled the stereotype of the hard-nosed Puritan divine; he had a dynamism, sense of humor, and love of life that were contagious. He was proud of both his intellectual and physical prowess. The claim that Smith once told a follower, "Whenever I see a pretty girl, I have to pray for grace," is probably apocryphal,[80] but by Smith's own report a perceptive phrenologist once gave him an extremely high rating for "amativeness."[81] Smith was an immensely popular leader who was idolized by his followers, including many capable and attractive women. Often such women came to him for help with personal, economic, and marital difficulties while their husbands were absent on missions. In such situations, he was exposed to far greater than average pressures and temptations. Had he not been a man of extraordinary energy and need for self-consistency, he probably would never have conceived and introduced the new marriage system that he did.

The bitterness with which Joseph Smith's strong-willed wife Emma reacted to his taking additional wives was another serious difficulty facing the prophet. Emma never became reconciled to plural marriage. The introduction of polygamy was complicated by the deep affection that Emma and Joseph had for each other, a bond which is unmistakably revealed in their personal letters.[82] Emma was jealously devoted to Joseph. He, in turn, showed great love for her. The deep attachment between them must have made the introduction of plural marriage particularly painful. Contemporary accounts from both Mormon and anti-Mormon sources suggest that on at least two or three occasions Emma was on the verge of leaving Joseph altogether because of his polygamous practice.[83] Internal evidence in the 1843 revelation on plural and celestial marriage, as well as affidavits from both the man who recorded it for Smith and the man who made the copy of the original from which the present version is reproduced, support the hypothesis that the immediate occasion for writing the revelation was an attempt to overcome the hatred of Smith's wife for polygamy. According to these accounts, she eventually badgered Smith into giving her the original statement and then proceeded to destroy it, believing there was no other copy.[84]

There is genuine pathos in this strong-willed woman's effort to eliminate the humiliating evidence of her husband's most striking social innovation and in her lifelong attack on the system. Eventually she and her sons by Joseph Smith would become pillars of the schismatic Reorganized Church of Jesus Christ of Latter Day Saints, which held among its primary doctrines opposition to polygamy based on statements in the Book of Mormon and the 1835 Kirtland edition of the Doctrine and Covenants. According to Utah Mormon accounts, Emma's knowledge extended to only a fraction of Joseph's plural marriages.[85] After his death, she apparently attempted to blot out that whole aspect of her life. She said next to nothing about her personal knowledge of polygamy in Nauvoo, even though she continued to hate the practice and all that it represented. Finally, in a posthumously published and highly edited "Last Will and Testament" she admitted that Joseph had talked with her about the possibility that polygamy might be introduced. She said, however, that he had never practiced polygamy and had never had "improper" relations with any other women.[86]

If Joseph Smith faced psychic turmoil and near rebellion from his wife over the introduction of plural marriage, he also encountered great difficulties with the male followers to whom he gradually revealed the system. Brigham Young, who oversaw the introduction of plural marriage after

Smith's death in Nauvoo and in Utah, declared that when he first heard the revelation and thought of all the troubles that would ensue, "it was the first time in my life that I desired the grave."[87] Heber C. Kimball, another of Smith's closest followers, was so distraught after receiving the command to take another wife without his first wife's knowledge that he begged Smith to remove the requirement lest he apostatize and forfeit his salvation. Only after being commanded three times by Smith in the name of the Lord did he obey.[88]

Even more complex was the case of Orson Pratt, who later was chosen to give the first public defense of plural marriage in 1852 and who became its most articulate spokesman in the Church. In 1842, he initally balanced precariously on the verge of apostasy or even madness because of what he felt had been Smith's improprieties toward his wife.[89] And Benjamin F. Johnson, later patriarch of an extensive plural family in Utah, said that he had been horrified when Smith explained plural marriage to him and told Johnson to ask his sister Almera to become Smith's plural wife. Recovering from the shock, Johnson remembered telling Smith that he would try to do as he had been asked but that "if ever I know you do this to degrade my sister I will kill you, as the Lord lives."[90]

Introducing and attempting to institutionalize plural marriage was a risky venture, to say the least. To be sure, a few leaders apparently accepted the new system fairly easily. And perhaps a few of the retrospective accounts may have portrayed their personal reluctance as having been greater than it actually was. Nevertheless, most of Smith's loyal followers appear to have been genuinely distraught when told of the new departure. Smith's personal magnetism, the appeal of his prophetic role, and the attractiveness of the doctrines and rituals he introduced into his Church must have been extraordinarily intense. Even when his followers found the new marriage beliefs and practices personally repugnant, they were still more anxious that if they did not accept them, they might forfeit their eternal salvation.

The acceptance and practice of plural marriage thus came to serve as one of the chief tests of the total loyalty which Smith was coming to demand of his closest followers. Such participation meant there was no turning back. Men or women who had once engaged in polygamous practice were in no position to apostatize, because the air would be blue with stories of their licentious behavior. Likewise, if a man's daughter had been sealed as a plural wife to Joseph Smith or another leader of the Church, effective opposition to the practice became exceedingly difficult. To oppose polygamy under such circumstances would be tantamount to disowning one's own children, as well as everything to which one had previously committed one's whole life.

In addition, polygamy vastly expanded the network of personal loyalties and the range of possible relationships. One Mormon scholar has noted that in Utah the interrelationships in some families became so complex as virtually to defy analysis.[91] By his death at age eighty-eight, for instance, Benjamin F. Johnson was related by blood or marriage to over eight hundred people.[92] For this persecuted group which thought of itself in tribal terms as a "New Israel," such family ties could make an important contribution to social cohesion. There is every reason to believe that an awareness of these factors was an important part of the practical calculations that underlay Joseph Smith's introduction of polygamy and his personal choice of plural wives.

Joseph Smith's Plural Wives

The women whom Joseph Smith took as plural wives encountered extreme emotional and practical difficulties. Their reactions to the new beliefs and practices and their relationships with Smith have never been studied systematically. Most writers have contented themselves with making head counts of Smith's alleged plural wives. The Mormon historian Andrew Jenson listed 27, Fawn Brodie claimed 48, while Stanley S. Ivins found 84.[93] These lists do not adequately distinguish between different types of wives, particularly between those who may have actually lived with Joseph Smith and those who were probably only sealed to him for "eternity." These lists also do not address other important qualitative questions about Smith's relationships.

What were the reactions of women who were asked to become Smith's plural wives? Why and how did they accept the new status, if they did? Did the relationship involve full conjugal rights? If so, why are there no substantiated instances of children born to such unions? Finally, what accounts for the apparent discrepancies between theory and practice in the early development of polygamy, particularly the evidence that Joseph Smith took a number of plural wives who already had living husbands? In an attempt to recover internal Mormon reactions to these controversial developments, this section will primarily rely on Mormon accounts rather than anti-Mormon sources. Anthropological perspectives from other millennial groups will also help to provide a larger context in which to place the problems the Mormons experienced in the process of transition to a new marriage system.

The frank and detailed personal statement of Lucy Walker, who became a plural wife of Joseph Smith and later of Heber C. Kimball, shows many of the characteristic features of Smith's relationships for which we have extensive information.[94] Lucy was born on April 30, 1826, in Peacham, Caledonia County, Vermont. Her family joined the Church shortly after it was founded. They moved frequently with the Mormons, suffered intense persecution in Missouri, and eventually settled in Nauvoo. The family developed a close personal relationship to Joseph Smith. When Lucy's mother died in Nauvoo in 1842, leaving ten motherless children, Lucy's father's health seemed to give way under the strain. Joseph Smith stepped in, suggesting the father seek a change of environment. Smith then temporarily adopted the four oldest children as a part of his own family and household. He went out of his way to help them in every way that he could.

Early in 1843, when Lucy was a lively and attractive sixteen, Joseph Smith had a private interview with her. He told her God had commanded him to take her as a plural wife. Her "astonishment knew no bounds." She felt he was insulting her. Smith asked her if she believed him to be a Prophet of God. She said she did. He explained "the principle of plural or celestial marriage" to her. He said that it was being restored for the good of the human family and that it would "prove an everlasting blessing to my father's house, and form a chain that could never be broken, worlds without end." Lucy was told to pray and that she would receive a personal testimony of the correctness of the principle, but her mind was filled with darkness. She had no father or mother to give her counsel and she was deeply distraught.

Joseph Smith could see her unhappiness. He said that although under the present circumstances he could not publicly acknowledge her as his wife, she would eventually be "acknowledged and honored as my wife." He also told her that if she rejected this message "the gate will be closed forever against you." This threat made her angry. Lucy felt that she was being asked "to place myself upon the alter a living sacrifice—perhaps to brook the world in disgrace and incur the displeasure and contempt of my youthful companions." Unless she knew that God approved her course of action, she would rather die. Smith said she would receive a personal testimony of the truth of the principle. Lucy earnestly desired such a testimony. Shortly before dawn after a sleepless night of fervent prayer, she felt as though her room were "lighted up by a heavenly influence": "Supreme happiness took possession of me, and I received a powerful and irresistable testimony of the truth of plural marriage." On May 1, 1843, she was sealed to Joseph Smith "for time and all eternity" by Elder William Clayton.[95]

Lucy Walker's background and experience are typical of those of many of Joseph Smith's other plural wives. Women who were approached by Smith or his close associates to become plural wives usually were of proven personal and family loyalty to the Church. Frequently they were dependent upon the Church for economic support, and had a variety of strong personal ties to Smith and the other leadership. In an analysis of various relationships among Smith's wives, Vesta Crawford notes that at least eleven of the women were related to prominent Church leaders, five were orphans or otherwise dependent, and seven lived at some time in Smith's home, with some overlapping among these categories.[96] Direct or indirect coercive pressure was placed on the women to accept the overtures to marriage. If they adamantly refused, they were pressured to keep quiet. In the few cases of apparent refusals that became publicly known—such as the tangled cases of Nancy Rigdon, Martha Brotherton, and Sarah Pratt—the characters of the resisting women were thoroughly blackened.

In almost all recorded cases, initial presentation of the belief in plural marriage to either men or women produced shock, horror, disbelief, or general emotional confusion. Those who eventually accepted the principle almost invariably went through a period of inner turmoil lasting from several days to several months. During this period, they might go without adequate sleep, food, or normal social contacts, fervently praying that God would reveal the truth of the new beliefs to them. Those who eventually accepted plural marriage almost invariably had a compelling personal experience revealing the truth of the new standards. Such a drastic step away from established norms demanded more than a purely intellectual assent.[97]

Few contemporary documents have survived which show reactions of supporters of plural marriage within the Mormon community before Joseph Smith's death. One is found in a postscript to a letter of Vilate Kimball to her husband Heber C. Kimball dated "Nauvoo June 24th 1843." She wrote:

> June 27th Since writing the above, I have had a visit from brother Parley [Pratt] and his wife, they are truly converted it appears that J....h has taught him some principles and told him his privilege, and even appointed one for him, I dare not tell you who it is, you would be astonished and I guess some tried. She has ben to me for council, I told her I did not wish to advise in such matters. Sister Pratt has ben rageing against these things, she told me her self that the devel had been in her until within a few days past, she said the Lord had shown her it was all right. She wants Parley to go ahead, says she will do all in her power to help him; they are so ingagued I fear they will run to fast. they asked me many questions on principle I told them I did not know much and I rather they would go to those that had authority to teach. Parley said he and J were interrupted before he got what instruction he wanted, and now he did

not know when he should have an oppertunity. he seamed unwilling
to wate, I told him these were sacred things and he better not make
a move until he got more instruction.—I have a secret to tell you,
but I am almost afrade, it was committed to Sarah and she was
requested not to tell me, but she said she concidered me a part of
her self and she would tell me, and I might tell you for it was just
what you had prophecyed would come to pass. now if you know
what you have said about Sarah Ally then you have got the secret,
for it is even so, and she is ticked about it. and they all appear in
better spirits than they did before. how they will carry it out, is more
than I know, I hope they have got more faith than I have. Brother
nobles folks all send love to you.

In her concluding remarks, Vilate wrote:

> I think you had better burn this, as soon as you can after reading it.
> I should not dare to send it by mail, but I trust it will go safe. if
> Brigham. should go I will write by him. I am as ever your affectionate
> wife Vilate Kimball.[98]

This letter clarifies a number of important points suggested by other
sources. It shows that polygamy was taught and practiced prior to the
formal recording of the revelation on plural and celestial marriage, as the
revelation itself also indicates. As late as 1843, however, polygamy was
practiced only on a very restricted scale even in the top echelons of the
Church, with the exception of Joseph Smith. Recent research by Michael
Quinn on wives of leaders of the Church supports the contention that,
prior to Smith's death, most Mormon leaders had taken at most two or
three additional wives.[99] The taking of large numbers of wives by a few
of the early Mormon leaders would occur largely between Smith's death
and the exodus to Utah. This was a complex period when the transition
to plural marriage was taking place in the Church as a whole.

As this letter indicates, a tendency to go to extremes could easily
develop once earlier patterns of behavior were broken down. Furthermore, the impossibility of finding time and privacy to give detailed instructions even to the twelve apostles, Smith's closest associates, suggests
how difficult it must have been to translate such beliefs into practice for
the general membership. Excesses and confusion were almost certain
to follow. Interestingly, the letter hints at the fact that one of the plural
wives, Sarah Ally, was pregnant. Her child, George Omer Noble, was
born on February 2, 1844, and is generally described as the first child
born into Mormon polygamy.[100] Finally, there is the concluding suggestion
that the letter should be burned. Probably most such documents actually
were.

One other important document which was not burned was a holograph letter of Joseph Smith's dated "Nauvoo, August 18th 1842" to Newel K. Whitney, his wife, "and &c."—presumably their daughter Sarah Ann, who had been married to Smith twenty-two days earlier on July 27, 1842, according to Latter-day Saint accounts. Sarah Ann was said to have been the first plural wife he had taken with the approval of both parents. At the time the letter was written, Smith was hiding in the home of Carlos Granger, hoping to avoid extradition to Missouri.

The letter communicates "Some of my feelings . . . which I want you three Eternally to keep in your own bosoms; for my feelings are so Strong for you Since what has passed lately between us"—presumably a reference to his recent marriage to Sarah Ann. Smith speaks of his great loneliness and need of succor from them. He gives instructions for their coming to see him secretly:

> . . . let Brother Whitney come a little a head, and nock at the south East corner of the house at the window; it is next to the corn-field; I have a room intirely by myself, the whole matter can be attended to with most perfect Safety, I know it is the will of God that you should comfort me now in this time of affliction, or not at all. . . .

Smith continues by saying that the only thing to be careful of is "to find out when Emma comes then you cannot be Safe, but when she is not here, there is the most perfect *Safety.*" He asks them to

> . . . burn this letter as soon as you read it; keep all locked within your breasts, my life depends upon it. one thing I want to see you for is to git the fulness of my blessing Sealed upon our heads, &c. you will pardon me for my earnestness on this subject when you consider how lonesome I must be, your good feelings know how to make every allowance for me, I close my letter. I think Emma wont come to-night if she dont dont fail to come to night, I subscribe myself your most obedient, and affectionate, Companion, and friend. Joseph Smith.[101]

While one cannot be positive about the precise nature of the relationship portrayed in this letter, it certainly was far more than casual friendship. If the possibility of a sexual relationship with his plural wife Sarah Ann is not implied, it is hard to see why the references to Emma were made. According to Mormon and non-Mormon accounts, Emma attempted to keep track of Joseph Smith's possible liaisons and head them off. Why a simple visit from close family friends should be kept secret from her if no sexual element was involved is unclear. The circumstances described and the tone of this letter also suggest the enormous pressures under which Smith was living, pressures which apparently made him desire more than purely intellectual companionship.

It has been hotly contested whether Smith's relationships with his plural wives included full sexual intercourse. Some cases certainly did not. Women who were sealed to Smith only for "eternity" presumably had no physical relationship with him while he was alive, although there may be exceptions to this generalization among some of the women whose names appear in the 1846 Nauvoo Temple Record as sealed to him for "eternity." Following Smith's death a total of some 335 women were sealed to him, many of whom he had not even known.[102] If these two special groups are excepted, however, the almost unanimous testimony of Smith's followers, informed ex-Mormons and anti-Mormons, and his plural wives themselves was that his wives were, indeed, wives in every sense of the word, lacking only public acknowledgement. It is difficult to understand how Smith's followers could have been induced to adopt the new practices if he had not led the way himself.

Although admissions of unorthodox marital relations are obviously a highly personal matter, many of Joseph Smith's plural wives testified explicitly that they had had full sexual relations with him. Emily D. P. Partridge said she "roomed" with Smith the night following her marriage to him, and she also admitted that she had had "carnal intercourse" with him.[103] Melissa Lott testified that she was Joseph Smith's wife "in very deed."[104] Lucy Walker, when asked, "Did you live with Joseph Smith as his wife?" replied in irritation, "He was my husband, sir."[105] Joseph Bates Noble went so far as to claim that he saw Joseph Smith and Louisa Beaman, whom he sealed to Smith, in bed together. When pressed, Noble admitted that he hadn't actually *seen* them in bed together; Smith had told him the next day that they had slept together.[106] Probably Benjamin F. Johnson's statement that he had seen his sister Almera in bed with Smith was an extrapolation similar to that of Joseph Bates Noble.[107]

Perhaps more convincing than the direct testimony of Smith's wives is the tacit assumption underlying almost all major existing accounts—that contemporary sealings to him normally implied full marital relations. Eliza R. Snow's statement clearly makes this assumption and suggests the intellectual process by which the new practice could be accepted. When Eliza first heard that plural marriage was to be introduced into the Church, she found the idea "repugnant." She reflected, however, that "I was living in the Dispensation of the fulness of times, embracing all other Dispensations. surely Plural Marriage must necessarily be included, and I consoled myself with the idea that it was far in the distance, and beyond the period of my mortal existence." Shortly thereafter, however, she heard that the time had come. She was sealed to Joseph Smith for "time and eternity."[108] Eliza's sense of repugnance and her entire statement only make sense if something other than spiritual relationships are being discussed here. Moreover, in order to interpret this in a "spiritual" sense, one would have to assume that marriage sealings for "time and eternity" as practiced in the later Mormon Church had changed since Smith's day.

If Smith did have full conjugal relations with many of his plural wives, why is there no solid evidence of any children born to him by his plural wives? Impotence is not a possible explanation: Emma bore children to Joseph Smith regularly throughout their marriage, even during times of considerable stress. Infrequency of sexual relations with any given plural wife could only provide a partial explanation for the lack of children by the wives. And abortion does not appear to be a plausible explanation. Not only was it in total opposition to Smith's emphasis on polygamy as a means of "raising up a righteous branch," but it also lacks reliable documentary support.

It is significant that despite their strong testimony to being wives of Joseph Smith in the fullest sense of the term, most women who claimed to have been married to him consistently refused, in the face of repeated questioning, to affirm or deny that they or other women had had children by him.[109] This reticence was entirely understandable. If information about Smith's children by plural wives were brought into the open, the line of questioning adopted by often-hostile interrogators would have been even more insulting, and other individuals' names would have been dragged into the discussion. Even if children by Smith's plural wives lived in Utah—as oral and written traditions there suggest—they probably would have borne the names of the family who reared them.[110] Detailed demographic work in progress on the Nauvoo period and early Utah suggests that some children became part of families in which they were not born, under puzzling circumstances.[111]

Evidence for children Smith may have had by plural wives is based largely on oral and family traditions. Mary Rollins Lightner, one of the most articulate and knowledgeable of Smith's plural wives, said: "I know he had six wives and I have known some of them from childhood up. I know he had three children. They told me. I think two are living today but they are not known as his children as they go by other names."[112] Lucy Meserve Smith recalled that her husband George A. Smith told her of going to see Joseph Smith and finding him washing his hands after he had helped Emma—who had served as the midwife—deliver a child by one of his plural wives.[113] Persistent and apparently well-founded family tradition suggests that Eliza R. Snow conceived a child by Joseph Smith and suffered a miscarriage.[114] The *Nauvoo Expositor* of June 7,

1844, published by a schismatic faction in the Church which was attempting to oust Smith from power, alleged that "in order to avoid public exposition from the common course of things," pregnant plural wives "are sent away for a time until all is well; after which they return, as from a long visit."[115]

T. Edgar Lyon, a leading contemporary authority on the Nauvoo period, has related another account of how children by Smith's plural wives may have been handled. When Dr. Lyon was working in Nauvoo in 1968–69, a man introduced himself by saying: "How would you like to meet a descendant of Joseph Smith who has never been out of the Church!" Since none of Smith's children by Emma remained affiliated with the Utah Church, the man's statement showed that he believed himself descended from one of Smith's polygamous unions. The man told Dr. Lyon of three families—Farnsworth, Dibble, and Allred—in each of which lived one of Smith's plural wives. In each case, when the plural wife became pregnant, she and the recognized wife in the household both went into seclusion, as was the practice for visibly pregnant women at the time. After the plural wife's child was born, the recognized wife in the household reappeared and presented the child as belonging to her. At least one of the children was born from these polygamous unions before Smith's death. After his death, these plural wives went to Utah, were married to other men, and had children by them.[116] These and similar traditions can be adduced to suggest that there may well have been children by Joseph Smith's polygamous unions, although indisputable proof of any such descendants is unlikely.

It is less difficult to explain the apparent lack of children born to the plural wives of Joseph Smith's followers prior to his death, since most of them were married for a shorter time and to fewer women in this period. One account of how pregnancies among plural wives of high Church officials were handled was given by Kimball Young, the late sociologist of Mormon polygamy and a descendant of Oscar Young, the first acknowledged child by any of Brigham Young's plural wives. According to Kimball Young, plural wives who became pregnant, including Oscar Young's mother, Harriet Cook, went into seclusion in the second floor of the Erastus Snow home in Nauvoo. The second floor had an entrance that was separate from the remainder of the house. The Snow family was small enough to live entirely on the first floor. Food and other necessities were discreetly brought to the wives who lived on the second floor.[117] The original construction of the Erastus Snow house does correspond with this account of Kimball Young's. In addition, the fact that an unusual 1846 holograph letter from Brigham Young to "Mrs. Hariot Cook" was sent in care of the Erastus Snow home suggests that she may have been living there at the time as well.[118] Quite possibly other arrangements were made in cases of other plural wives, but these examples at least suggest some of the possibilities.

Irregularities and Forgotten Practices

Apparent discrepancies between belief and practice were numerous during the chaotic early days of the development of polygamous practice. Perhaps the most severe conceptual difficulties are raised by the strong evidence that Joseph Smith took as plural wives a number of women who had living husbands and that he asked some of his closest followers to give him their wives as well. Of course some of these marriages may have been only for "eternity," as was apparently the case in two instances in which wives of Smith's closest associates were sealed to him after his death.[119] As the numerous posthumous sealings attest, marriage to Joseph Smith "for eternity" obviously had considerable appeal.

Other allegations that Smith asked married women to become his wives may be instances of what might be called the "Potiphar's wife syndrome," in which women to whom Smith refused his attentions alleged that he had attempted to seduce them. Another possibility is suggested by the charge that Smith's followers leveled against Orson Pratt's wife Sarah, after John C. Bennett's exposé alleged that Smith had commissioned Bennett to ask Mrs. Pratt to become Smith's plural wife. Smith's supporters said that this account was simply a cover for Bennett's own improper relations with Mrs. Pratt. In this, as in almost all other cases, the tangle of allegation and counter-allegation is so complex that one cannot reliably determine exactly what did happen. True or false, such character defamations by both sides did much to disrupt the social atmosphere in Nauvoo. Probably any attempt to secretly introduce and regulate unorthodox marriage practices not sanctioned by law would have led to similar problems, no matter how the process was handled.

When all the contradictory and unreliable evidence about Joseph Smith's plural wives is fully explored and unreliable stories discounted, a hard core of puzzling data remains which demands an explanation if we are to understand the dynamics of the early development of plural marriage. If one accepts Latter-day Saint sources, it seems clear that Smith had full sexual relations with some women who were at the same time legally the wives of other men.[120] Based on such evidence, it is also clear that Smith did ask some of his followers to give him their wives, whatever his motives in such cases may have been.

In a sermon delivered on February 19, 1854, in the Tabernacle in Salt Lake City, Jedediah Grant, second counselor to Brigham Young, discussed the confusion that arose when Joseph Smith asked for the wives of some of his followers:

> When the family organization was revealed from heaven—the patriarchal order of God, and Joseph began, on the right and on the left, to add to his family, what a quaking there was in Israel. Says one brother to another, "Joseph says all covenants are done away, and none are binding but the new covenants; now suppose Joseph should come and say he wanted your wife, what would you say to that?" "I would tell him to go to hell." This was the spirit of many in the early days of this Church.
>
> . . .
>
> If Joseph had a right to dictate me in relation to salvation, in relation to a hereafter, he had a right to dictate me in relation to all my earthly affairs. . . .
>
> . . .
>
> Did the Lord actually want Abraham to kill Isaac? Did the Prophet Joseph want every man's wife he asked for? He did not, but in that thing was the grand thread of the Priesthood developed. The grand object in view was to try the people of God, to see what was in them.[121]

This account suggests a part of the context within which Joseph Smith at least *asked* some of his followers for their wives.

A similar but more concrete statement appears in Orson F. Whitney's biography of his grandfather, Heber C. Kimball. Allegedly Joseph Smith asked Heber to give him Vilate to be his wife, saying that this was a requirement. After enormous inner turmoil, Heber presented Vilate to Smith. At that point, Smith wept, embraced Heber, and said that he had not really wanted Vilate. He had only been determining if Heber's loyalty to him were absolute. There and then, Smith proceeded to seal Heber and Vilate for time and eternity.[122] If this story is an accurate representation of events—and it is hard to believe that there could be any reasonable motive for fabricating such a story and printing it in a standard biography of a respected Mormon leader—it suggests that Smith was showing supremely poor judgment. A number of Mormons whose loyalty to Smith was not so absolute apostatized or began working to undermine his leadership within the Church after they alleged that he had attempted to marry their wives.[123]

How are such actions to be explained? Most non-Mormons and anti-Mormons have simply assumed that Smith was indulging his sexual impulses in these and other cases. Most Mormon writers, on the other hand, have tried to explain the evidence away or ignore it entirely, hoping that it would be forgotten. Neither approach is very satisfactory. What was happening in Nauvoo was considerably more remarkable than a "common sense" point of view is apt to recognize. The process must be judged in terms of its own dynamics, including Joseph Smith's millennial framework and the problems that are inherent in any transitional period between two different and partially incompatible value systems.

The revelation on plural and celestial marriage makes quite clear that marriages based on the standards of the external world were not considered valid for eternity:

> All covenants, contracts, bonds, obligations, oaths, vows, performances, connections, associations, or expectations, that are not made, and entered into, and sealed, by the Holy Spirit of promise, of him who is anointed, both as well for time and for all eternity . . . , (and I have appointed unto my servant Joseph to hold this power in the last days, and there is never but one on the earth at a time, on whom this power and the keys of the priesthood are conferred,) are of no efficacy, virtue, or force in and after the resurrection from the dead; . . . .
>
> . . .
>
> Therefore, if a man marry him a wife in the world, and he marry her not by me nor by my word, and he covenant with her so long as he is in the world and she with him, their covenant and marriage are not of force when they are dead, and when they are out of the world; . . . .[124]

Later Mormon theology has naturally taken this statement as referring to the afterlife. Mormon theology and practice in Nauvoo and early Utah, however, were an attempt to apply presumptive heavenly standards directly on earth. Earthly and heavenly standards were seen as inextricably intertwined; an imminent earthly millennium was to be realized. In marriage, this meant that the standards of "the world" were invalid. Marriage, whether monogamous or polygamous, was only valid under the sanction of the "new and everlasting covenant" *as sealed and practiced on earth.*[125] Mormon initiatory ceremonies, from baptism to the more elaborate temple rites, involved a rebirth into a new and different world that was being created on earth by the Church. Prior to the initiation into the new standards, however, there was a brief but disruptive interregnum when neither set of standards was operative and the basis of social authority was unclear.

Possibly the best analysis of this development in Nauvoo is provided in the following statement by a former member of Smith's secret Council of Fifty, a council which, along with other Church agencies, attempted to regulate the transition:

> About the same time [1842] the doctrine of "sealing" for an eternal state was introduced, and the Saints were given to understand that their marriage relations with each other were not valid. That those

who had solemnized the rites of matrimony had no authority of God to do so. That the true priesthood was taken from the earth with the death of the Apostles and inspired men of God. That they were married to each other only by their own covenants, and that if their marriage relations had not been productive of blessings and peace, and they felt it oppressive to remain together, they were at liberty to make their own choice, as much as if they had not been married. That it was a sin for people to live together, and raise or beget children, in alienation from each other. That there should exist an affinity between each other, not a lustful one, as that can never cement that love and affection that should exist between a man and his wife.[126]

This statement by John D. Lee suggests the interplay between marital dissatisfactions and the larger theological framework that underlay the introduction of plural marriage.

In addition to the larger argument that the revelation on plural and celestial marriage superseded all earthly bonds and covenants, a second argument also suggests why Joseph Smith might have asked for the wives of other men. Speaking before a conference in the Tabernacle on October 8, 1861, Brigham Young is reported to have discussed the ways "in which a woman could leave a man lawfully." The primary valid cause for giving a divorce was: "When a woman becomes alienated in her feelings & affections from her husband, ..." "Also there was another way—in which a woman could leaved [sic] man—if the woman Preferred—another man higher in authority & he is willing to take her. & her husband gives her up—there is no Bill of divorce required in the case it is right in the sight of God."[127]

This passage suggests that in early Utah it may have been possible for a married woman to "move up" in the hierarchy without securing a formal divorce. Could this practice date back to Joseph Smith?[128] If so, it provides a further link which could help to explain otherwise strange early practices. Note that early Mormon belief stressed that wives, just as all other temporal and spiritual blessings, were held as a stewardship or trust from God, subject to the continuing good behavior of the husband. When John Hyde apostatized in the mid-1850s, for example, his wife was considered automatically forfeited, and she was remarried to another worthy man who could ensure her salvation.[129] If Joseph Smith approached wives of some of his followers who were on the verge of apostasy, as numerous allegations suggest, he might have justified that action by the view that since those men had become unworthy and had forfeited their salvation, they had also forfeited their wives. Needless to say, however internally logical such a view might have been, it could only have further embittered Smith's relations with associates whose loyalties were wavering or already lost.

The "all previous covenants suspended" and the "moving up" arguments still fail to cover adequately all possible cases under which Joseph Smith appears to have approached or taken married women as plural wives. A third, extremely conjectural possibility remains. If true, it could probably account for all additional cases for which there is reliable documentary evidence. The earliest basis for this third argument is a passage in the revelation on plural and celestial marriage which declares: "And as ye have asked concerning adultery, verily, verily, I say unto you, if a man receiveth a wife in the new and everlasting covenant, and if she be with *another* man, *and I have not appointed unto her by the holy anointing*, she hath committed adultery and shall be destroyed" [emphasis added].[130] Jason Briggs, who was a bitter anti-polygamist and life-long opponent of the Utah Mormons as well as one of the most intellectually astute early leaders of the RLDS Church, asserted that this passage could be taken to mean that when a polygamist was gone for many years, as sometimes happened, it would theoretically be possible for another man to be appointed by the President of the Church, through the power of the holy anointing, to serve the part of a temporary husband until the return of the first one. The children born under such arrangements would be considered to belong to the first man. Thus, while he was absent in the service of the Church, his "Kingdom," which was heavily dependent on the number of his children, would not suffer loss.[131]

This is, to say the least, an extraordinary allegation. Is it supported by any reliable evidence? Would such a practice have been compatible with early Mormon intellectual and social concerns? It must be noted that no conclusive manuscript evidence explicitly supporting such a practice in the early Church has come to my attention, and that the one statement in printed Mormon sources which suggests the possibility of this practice, is, at best, ambiguous.[132] If any practice of temporal "proxy husbands" ever existed, it must have been on an exceedingly limited scale, and it must have been very soon discontinued as a social experiment. Nevertheless, there exist a small number of early allegations of a practice of appointing proxy husbands which cannot be dismissed out of hand.

The primary source for allegations of proxy husbands is John Hyde, who rose rapidly in the Church and then apostatized during the troubled period of the Reformation of 1856–57, in one of the most bitter of such breaks. Although Hyde frequently exaggerates or fails to understand the deeper spirit underlying Mormon actions, his factual allegations often are surprisingly accurate. Hyde stated:

> As a man's family constitutes his glory, to go on a mission for several years, leaving from two to a dozen wives at home, necessarily causes some loss of family, and consequently, according to Mormon notions, much sacrifice of salvation. This difficulty is however obviated by the

appointment of an agent or proxy, who shall stand to themward [*sic*] in their husband's stead. . . . This is one of the secret principles that as yet is only privately talked of in select circles, and darkly hinted at from their pulpits and in their works. They argue that the old Mosaic law of a "brother raising up seed to his dead brother" is now in force; and as death is only a temporary absence, so they contend a temporary absence is equivalent to death; and if in the case of death, it is not only no crime, but proper; so also in this case it is equally lawful and extremely advantageous! This practice, commended by such sophistry, and commanded by such a Prophet was adopted as early as Nauvoo.

Much scandal was caused by others than Smith attempting to carry out this doctrine. Several, who thought that what was good for the Prophet should be good for the people, were crushed down by Smith's heavy hand. Several of those have spoken out to the practices of the "Saints." [Consider the case of John C. Bennett.] Much discussion occurred at Salt Lake as to the advisability of revealing the doctrine of polygamy in 1852, and that has caused Brigham to defer the public enunciation of this "proxy doctrine," as it is familiarly called. Many have expected it repeatedly at the late conferences. Reasoning out their premises to their natural and necessary consequences, this licentious and infamous dogma is their inevitable result.[133]

Note that Hyde himself described the existence of proxy husbands primarily as a "principle" rather than a present "practice." Hyde's only specific allegation of the practice of such arrangements was the case of Joseph Smith himself, and according to Hyde, Smith did not allow his followers such privileges. Hyde appears correct in his assertion that from a Mormon theoretical and social perspective the practice of a limited arrangement of proxy husbands for some missionaries' wives would have appeared logically consistent. Since logic based on unorthodox premises is a primary characteristic of the early Mormon faith, it would seem unlikely that early Mormon leaders could have avoided *considering* such a possibility, even if they never actually introduced such a practice. If such a practice ever existed, it must have been on a very limited scale and must have soon been discontinued. Intellectually, the idea of a form of proxy marriage, the provisions of which have force only in the afterlife, still remains a part of Mormon belief. Briefly stated, when the husband of a woman who had been sealed to him "for time and eternity" dies, that woman is free to marry another man "for time" only. Mormon theology teaches that in the afterlife the children who had been born on earth to this latter union would be part of the family of the first husband to whom the woman had been sealed for "eternity."[134]

This belief is a highly unorthodox elaboration of the Old Testament

Jewish practice of the levirate. The levirate is based on the Jewish concern for carrying on the family name through a male line. Thus, in Mosaic law, when a man died leaving a widow and no male heirs, it became the duty of the next oldest brother to marry the widow and raise up children to the dead man's name. The much misunderstood "sin of Onan," for which God is said to have slain him, lay in practicing *coitus interruptus* with his brother's widow and thereby failing to fulfill his obligation to raise up children to that family line.[135] That this practice of the levirate, which implies the possibility of polygamy, was widely accepted is evident from the incident in the New Testament in which Jesus was asked about marriage in the afterlife.[136] When the Mormons conceived their unusual elaboration of the levirate, it is possible that they could have linked present and afterlife together in a complex fashion. Likewise, marriage sealings "for eternity" did not refer simply to a future heavenly state; they also made possible new earthly marriage forms, including polygamy. In early Mormonism, the distinction between heavenly ideals and earthly practice is often uncertain.

From a practical point of view, the possibility of appointing a temporary proxy husband, under strict controls, to provide temporal and emotional support for the harassed wives of absent missionaries must sometimes have appeared desirable. Apparent practices of this sort by Joseph Smith himself have led to erroneous allegations that he sanctioned polyandry.[137] If such practices ever occurred, they could be seen as showing compassion for the enormous strains under which wives of missionary elders were placed when they underwent what amounted to prolonged periods of "widowhood." It is known that Mormon men sometimes were assigned to help with the temporal support of women whose husbands were away on missions. Such support, particularly when the woman was actually living in the man's household, would naturally have had a tendency to lead to more intense emotional involvement. Some women must have wondered why, if men could have plural wives, they should not be granted a similar privilege, even if it was only to have a temporary replacement for their absent husband.

Whether this sort of arrangement ever occurred under official sanction remains a matter of conjecture, but if such an intellectual rationale existed, it could provide a satisfactory explanation of documented or highly probable cases in which Joseph Smith sustained relations with married women who continued to remain with their original husbands.[138] Given Smith's mind-set and concern for authority, it seems inconceivable that he could have done what he apparently did without believing that he had a higher justification for his actions.

However appealing an abstract social or intellectual argument for allowing proxy husbands might have been, such arrangements could not have been practiced on any scale without leading to anxieties, jealousies, and uncertainties that would have threatened to tear the Church apart. Perhaps the most judicious assessment of this issue was provided by T. B. H. Stenhouse. He said:

> The Author has no personal knowledge, from the present leaders of the Church, of this teaching; but he has often heard that something yet would be taught which "would test the brethren as much as polygamy had tried the sisters." By many elders it has been believed that there was some foundation for the accusation that Joseph had taught some sisters in Nauvoo that it was their privilege to entertain other brethren as "proxy husbands" during the absence of their liege lords on mission. One lady has informed the Author that Joseph so taught her. All such teaching has never been made public, and it is doubtful if it ever extended very far, if, indeed, at all beyond a momentary combination of passion and fanaticism.[139]

Liminality and Communitas

How is one to explain the many extraordinary early developments associated with the introduction of Mormon polygamy? Taken in isolation, the introduction of new marriage and social forms in the Mormon Church might well appear bizarre or disordered. However, a comparative perspective from anthropology and studies of other millenarian movements suggests that the Mormon experience may in many respects serve as a paradigmatic illustration of such transition states. The discussion presented in Chapter I on the characteristics of the "liminal" phase of rites of passage or larger social transitions is especially applicable to the Mormons. In such an itermediary state, an individual is suspended between two worlds, between an old order that is dying and a new order that is yet to be born. A person's position is then ambiguous: "he passes through a cultural realm that has few or none of the attributes of the past or coming state." A feeling of intense comradeship, egalitarianism, and exhilaration is experienced as a sense of direct personal contact replaces the institutional constraints that normally separate individuals. Men and women become malleable, capable of being molded by their leaders into new cultural forms of great beauty and power.

This tone of feeling and the associated release of powerful emotions, which is so difficult to convey in words, is unmistakably present in the early Mormon experience. That experience shows the passionate involvement, camaraderie, and enthusiasm of the selfless Mormon dedication to what they saw as the supremely important goal of realizing the kingdom of heaven on earth. There is a pervading sense of awe and wonderment that mysteries which had been hid since before the foundation of the world are now to be revealed, and a corresponding heady sense of exhilaration. Whether it be in cases of men leaving wives and children to go bravely into the unknown "without purse or scrip," or of women sacrificing their husbands temporarily and trusting in God to bring them through, the Saints felt an extraordinary closeness as they engaged in a common enterprise that they felt was of cosmic significance. Distinctions between "mine" and "thine" were reduced to an absolute minimum in the face of a common challenge and crisis. In Heber C. Kimball's oft-repeated phrase, Mormons undergoing this transition process were expected to become as "clay in the hands of the potter"; totally subordinating their wills to that of the group, they would allow themselves to be reshaped into a new and more perfect social form as Latter-day Saints.

This intense sense of camaraderie, combined with an implicit trust in the authority of their leaders, is clearly indicated in a letter of Joseph Smith's. This letter appears beyond reasonable doubt to have been sent to Nancy Rigdon by Joseph Smith after she had refused his proposal of marriage.[140] The letter begins by saying that: "Happiness is the object and design of our existence" but that this can only be achieved through "virtue, uprightness, faithfulness, holiness and keeping all the commandments of God. But we cannot keep all the commandments without first knowing them. . . . That which is wrong under one circumstance, may be, and often is, right under another." The letter continues:

> A parent may whip a child, and justly too, because he stole an apple; whereas if the child had asked for the apple, and the parent had given it, the child would have eaten it with a better appetite; there would have been no stripes; all the pleasure of the apple would have been secured, all the misery of stealing lost.
>
> This principle will justly apply to all of God's dealings with his children. Everything that God gives us is lawful and right; and it is proper that we should enjoy his gifts and blessings whenever and wherever he is disposed to bestow; but if we should seize upon those same blessings and enjoyments without law, without revelation, without commandment, those blessings and enjoyments would prove cursings in the end. . . .

The letter concludes:

> Our heavenly Father is more liberal in His views, and boundless in His mercies and blessings, than we are ready to believe or receive; and, at the same time, is more terrible to the workers of iniquity, more awful in the executions of His punishments, and more ready

to detect every false way, than we are apt to suppose Him to be. He will be inquired of by His children. He says: "Ask and ye shall receive, seek and ye shall find;" but, if you will take that which is not your own, or which I have not given you, you shall be rewarded according to your deeds; but no good thing will I withhold from them who walk uprightly before me, and do my will in all things— who will listen to my voice and to the voice of the servant whom I have sent; for I delight in those who seek dilligently to know my precepts, and abide by the law of my kingdom; for all things shall be made known unto them in mine own due time, and in the end they shall have joy.[141]

At a cursory first reading, this statement might be taken for mere sophistry. Such an explanation is too simple, however. When this letter is viewed within the context of Joseph Smith's larger sense of mission and from the perspective of anthropological analyses of the process of change, it clearly reveals an exceptional awareness of the whole basis of social order and human relatedness itself. In a related example, Joseph Lee Robinson remembered that when Smith spoke of polygamy in Turkey or India, he declared: ". . . God dosnt care what laws they make if they will live up to them. . . ."[142] In other words, faced with conditions of extraordinary social fluidity, Joseph Smith appears to have realized at the deepest possible emotional level how variable were the social forms within which certain underlying values may be expressed. The one absolute essential was that authority itself not be questioned. There must be one common basis of belief and practice to achieve unity and avoid social chaos. Joseph Smith felt that he himself was uniquely called by God to exercise that unifying authority and create that consensus of belief for his followers.

This Pauline awareness that the spirit of the gospel can be expressed in a number of different external forms depending upon changing circumstances is a key component of the Mormon concept of authority, particularly in the early period. Joseph Smith frequently acted with remarkable rapidity to introduce new social forms such as the Order of Enoch, yet he could discard such forms equally quickly when they proved ineffective in contributing to the achievement of the underlying goals for which they had been established. What was essential—and what remains essential in the Mormon Church to this day—is that there be a consensus that the head of the Mormon Church is ultimately able authoritatively to determine the specific social forms through which the underlying spirit is expressed as the Church deals with the ever-changing temporal circumstances affecting its existence.

Another side of this concern for authority is the direct personal sense of communion or "communitas" present in the transitional phase between two divergent and partially opposed states of being. Powerful emotions, including sexual emotions, are frequently liberated during this phase. One cannot read for long in the Mormon literature without realizing that Joseph Smith's passionate sincerity and direct emotional engagement with his followers was a key element of his appeal and charisma. But such emotional power was a two-edged sword; it could lead to passionate love or, equally, to passionate hatred. There often seemed to be no middle ground. Either one was for the prophet, or one was against him.

For the most part, the Mormons appear to have attempted to minimize the inevitable disruption of the transition process, just as earlier they had attempted to eliminate some of the more extreme excesses of the revivalistic fervor to which some of their members had been subject. But disruptive phenomena at this stage could not be entirely eliminated. At precisely this critical point in their development, many millennial groups founder. Normal rites of passage within a society are socially sanctioned and have a known end point. In contrast, for millennial groups such as the Mormons the end point and the means of arriving at it are often less clear. Thus such groups frequently disintegrate due to internal dissension or are broken up by an external society that feels threatened by the group's unorthdox behavior and claims. The Mormons skillfully avoided the danger of disintegration at this stage. Effective and often ruthless leadership, maintenance of secrecy at all costs, a generally well-formulated sense of the desired end point—and eventually a forced migration to the relative isolation of the intermountain West—were among the factors that made the successful Mormon transition possible.

The Bennett Scandal

The preceding developments and conflicts were for the most part contained within the circle of Joseph Smith's most intimate followers. But the new beliefs and practices could not long be kept secret from the majority of Church members or from the outside world, as may be seen from the observations of Charlotte Havens, an articulate young non-Mormon resident of Nauvoo.[143] Rumors of strange new standards and unusual behavior soon became widespread, and distorted accounts began circulating. Since the entire movement to introduce plural marriage was carried on secretly, unrecognized by law, and in direct violation of existing moral and religious standards, Mormon authorities must have found it very difficult to check variant interpretations arising within the group. There is necessarily a great difference between polygamy as accepted in a long-established tradition and polygamy when newly introduced into a situation in which people have no previous experience of the practice. In Nauvoo, it was almost inevitable that some irregularities should have occurred and that some individuals within the group should have publicly come out in opposition to the new beliefs and practices.

The controversial adventurer John C. Bennett was the source of some of the most flagrant irregularities, and his was one of the most devastating individual apostasies in the history of the Mormon Church. In a meteoric eighteen-month career between 1840 and 1842, Bennett rose from the rank of a virtual nobody to become the mayor of Nauvoo and Joseph Smith's right-hand man, only to fall from favor, write a lurid exposé of alleged Mormon misdeeds, including polygamy, and become one of the most thoroughly execrated men in Mormon history. In the late spring and early summer of 1842 when Bennett's break with the Church became definite, his exposés began to appear in the *Sangamo Journal* and were widely reprinted throughout the state and elsewhere in the nation. Eventually, in the early fall of 1842, Bennett's account appeared in expanded book form as *The History of the Saints, or, An Exposé of Joe Smith and Mormonism,* with fifty pages of preliminary statements defensively attesting to the uprightness of his own character.

The defection of the second-best-known Mormon in Nauvoo, an intimate friend of Joseph Smith, precipitated a severe crisis for the Church. Bennett charged the Mormon hierarchy with almost every imaginable sin, and presented a highly inflated account of the problems of the early development of polygamy, the first such to appear. Only Bennett's own penchant for polemical exaggeration, together with a carefully orchestrated Church campaign to blacken his character and neutralize his influence, enabled the Mormons to weather the storm his apostasy stirred up. Because of Bennett's inflated rhetoric, his opportunistic and equivocating character, and the understandable hostility his allegations aroused among the Mormons, his role in the early development of polygamy has never been analyzed dispassionately. Without such an analysis, however, the problems associated with the early efforts to introduce this new form of family organization cannot fully be understood.[144]

Bennett's character and political aspirations are the key to understanding his relation to the early development of polygamy. An opportunist *par excellence,* he has been variously described as a "prototypical booster," "a small time Aaron Burr," and "probably the greatest scamp in the western country."[145] Bennett was a man on the make, possessed of immense ambition, undeniable talent, and considerable charm, but never able to decide what he really wanted to do or to carry any project through to completion.[146] He joined the Mormon Church as a means of personal advancement, but when he found himself incapable of wresting control of the organization from Joseph Smith, and perhaps became disgusted with his own profligate behavior, he turned on the Mormons and denounced their entire operation as a monstrous fraud.

Seen with the advantage of hindsight, and with Bennett's personal biases set to one side, his knowledge of the scope of the early development of plural marriage appears to be extremely accurate. Bennett's statements, as recorded in the affidavits of women whom he allegedly had seduced under pretext of the developing polygamous beliefs, are very similar to those reported in some later Utah testimonies and affidavits.[147] But Bennett never really believed the line he was handing out; he thought it was all a hoax, and told William Law that he didn't need Smith's line to seduce women.[148]

Eventually finding that his dreams of unlimited and irresponsible power could not be realized, Bennett turned on Joseph Smith and the Mormons. He decided to make a career of exposure. Then his self-righteousness knew no bounds. But Bennett only told what he thought others were doing; he never was honest about his own feelings or behavior. Contemporary Nauvoo gossip hypothesized that Bennett had fallen as a consequence of moving too fast into polygamy.[149] If the allegations concerning the number of women with whom he had relations are justified, this certainly would appear to be the case. Bennett's indiscretions and excesses threatened the legitimate development of polygamy, as William Smith's behavior would later. Joseph Smith was faced with a dilemma in trying to deal with Bennett. The man knew too much to be summarily thrown out, yet his indiscretions were so great that if he were not thrown out the lid would blow off eventually anyway. Bennett never understood what Joseph Smith was really trying to do. His account is like the reflection in a fun-house mirror, grotesquely elongated or distorted in different directions, although the original object reflected did in fact exist.

How accurate was Bennett's knowledge of developing polygamy? Ironically, once Bennett's factual claims are separated from his lurid personal attacks, many of his statements provide strong corroboration for later Utah Mormon testimony.[150] His identification of Joseph Smith's early plural wives is an example. Almost as an afterthought in his account, Bennett hints at the identities of seven women whom he describes as plural wives of Joseph Smith, using asterisks to indicate omitted letters in the names. One of these women was a "Miss L***** B*****" married to Smith by "Elder Joseph Bates Noble."[151] Some thirty years later, the Mormon Church claimed that a Louisa Beaman had been sealed to Smith by Joseph Bates Noble on April 5, 1841, the first instance of a plural wife for whom definite evidence of a ceremony exists.[152] That the Utah Mormons should have deliberately fabricated this marriage account to corroborate Bennett's claims is highly unlikely—especially since his statement never was put forward to support their testimonies. Most other wives mentioned by Bennett can also be identified from Mormon and apostate accounts.[153]

Bennett's knowledge of polygamy seems to have gone beyond the names of Smith's plural wives, as may be perceived from his straightforward account of the ceremony allegedly used in marrying plural wives. At a key point in this solemn ceremony, the administrator was said to have declared:

> I now anoint you with holy, consecrated oil, in the name of Jesus Christ, and by the authority of the holy priesthood, that you may be fully and unreservedly consecrated to each other and to the service of God, and that with affection and fidelity you may nourish and cherish each other, so long as you shall continue faithful and true in the fellowship of the Saints; and I now pronounce upon you the blessings of Jacob, whom God honored and protected in the enjoyment of like special favor; and may the peace of Heaven, which passeth all understanding, rest upon you in time and in eternity.[154]

This statement is essentially identical to—though slightly more detailed than—the one suggested as the model in a recently published revelation dated July 27, 1842, which was allegedly given through Joseph Smith to Newel K. Whitney at Nauvoo.[155] The wording of the early plural marriage ceremony is also echoed in the testimony of Melissa Lott in the Temple Lot Case many years later.[156] Bennett evidently was much more deeply involved in the early development of polygamy than either he or the Mormon Church later cared to admit.

Possibly Bennett's most controversial and frequently cited allegation was that the marriage system developing sub rosa in Nauvoo divided the women involved into three separate classes. It may be significant that this particular claim did not appear in Bennett's original series of exposés in the *Sangamo Journal,* but was first mentioned in a letter to the *Louisville Journal* from Cleveland, Ohio, dated July 30, 1842. At that point, Bennett's personal indiscretions were being thoroughly aired in the Mormon press. As elaborated in his still later *History of the Saints,* Bennett claimed that the Mormon "Seraglio" consisted of three levels of depravity. From lowest to highest, women in this "Seraglio" were called "Cyprian Saints," "Chambered Sisters of Charity," and "Consecrates of the Cloister" or "Cloistered Saints." Such women were also said to be known as "Saints of the White, Green, or Black Veils," respectively.[157] Bennett is the sole source for the allegation that these terms were used by the Mormons, although other critical contemporary accounts also alleged that some sort of a degree organization for women existed in the Church.[158] Probably these terms were simply invented by Bennett, like the secret "Order of the Illuminati" which he first accused Smith of trying to introduce, but which he himself later introduced under that very name in the schismatic Strangite Mormon sect.

If Bennett's terminology is discounted, however, his concrete allegations demand serious consideration. His basic assertion was that the Mormons had established "a very strictly and systematically organized" secret marriage system "divided into three distinct orders or degrees." At the highest level were women who were married to Smith and a few of his most trusted followers under the ceremony cited above as "secret, spiritual wives."[159] All such marriages had to be approved by Smith himself. A second category of women were married under almost identical provisions, including Smith's necessary approval, but without the benefit of any formal ceremony. The lowest level, which Bennett himself stated was very small and in effect unofficial, was a sort of tolerated prostitution. Probably this last category could best be seen as Bennett's backhanded way of attempting to justify his own irregular behavior. However, some evidence does exist for a two-fold division of plural wives in Nauvoo. The revelation on plural and celestial marriage begins with Smith's inquiry concerning the taking of "wives and concubines" by Old Testament figures. Throughout the revelation "wives and concubines" are again mentioned together. A "concubine" is a wife of lower status and sometimes may be taken without any formal ceremony. Thus "wives and concubines" could well correspond to Bennett's two upper levels of plural wives.[160]

Bennett's information may be of value to historians when carefully analyzed. But his own concerns were almost purely polemical. Very simply, he wanted to destroy Joseph Smith. To this end, Bennett waged a personal vendetta against Smith, calling on many of Smith's associates to "come out" and expose the prophet's iniquities. Some, including George W. Robinson and John F. Olney, did just that. Others, chiefly Orson Pratt and Sidney Rigdon, were extremely disaffected, but took no decisive action. Still others, such as Charles and Francis Higbee, would eventually become associated with the *Expositor* schism in 1844 which led directly to Smith's martyrdom. But in 1842, for the most part, the dam held. This may be credited primarily to Bennett's personal instability and to his betrayal of the personal confidences of his friends. Bennett's penchant for publicly printing the private letters of his associates appears to have angered them more than anything Joseph Smith may have done.

Bennett's lack of consideration for his friends was never more obvious than when he printed detailed accounts of the personal reactions of women whom he alleged had bravely refused to become wives of Smith and other

Mormon leaders. Among the women upon whom Bennett forced this notoriety were Sarah Pratt, wife of apostle Orson Pratt; Nancy Rigdon, eldest daughter of Sidney Rigdon, a long-time associate of Smith's; Mrs. Emmeline White, a non-Mormon; and Martha Brotherton, a young English convert who wrote a detailed affidavit describing how she allegedly had been asked to become a plural wife of Brigham Young. If Bennett assumed that the reputations of these women were beyond reproach, this was a tragic miscalculation. In order to discredit Bennett, the characters of all these women were blackened in varying degrees.

The publication under Church auspices of statements defaming the wife of one of Smith's twelve apostles in very explicit terms indicates the desperate state of affairs, even should the allegations have been true.[161] Bennett had to be discredited at any cost. His defection was especially dangerous because of the dissatisfactions already existing within the Church and his exposé probably did more than any other single factor thereafter to disrupt the social atmosphere in Nauvoo and impede the establishment of a viable polygamous system. Joseph Smith's distress at the backbiting that resulted was heartfelt. In a speech on Febraury 21, 1843, he said: "This biting and devouring each other I cannot endure. Away with it. For God's sake, stop it."[162]

A Pamphlet Defense of Polygamy

As if in response to Bennett's misrepresentations and to attempt to acquaint Mormons with the deeper significance of the new marriage forms which Bennett had failed to comprehend, a remarkable thirty-seven-page pamphlet defending polygamy was printed by the Mormon press in Nauvoo in the late autumn of 1842, little more than a month after the appearance of Bennett's book-length exposé. The pamphlet was represented as two chapters from a larger manuscript—apparently never published—entitled *The Peace Maker, or The Doctrines of the Millennium*.[163] The pamphlet presents a brilliant and often highly unorthodox intellectual and social argument for the "Biblical" basis of divorce and polygamous marriage, which were seen as closely related. This appears to be the only explicit defense of polygamy ever printed under the auspices of the main body of the Mormon Church prior to 1852.

Perhaps because of the explicitness of its argument, the *Peace Maker* seems deliberately vague concerning its authorship. An "Udney Hay Jacob" is indicated as the author. The "Preface" to the account states: "The author of this work is not a Mormon, although it is printed by their press. It was most convenient. But the public will soon find out what he is, by his work." On the title page, however, Jacob was identified as "An

Israelite, and a Shepherd of Israel"—implying a leadership position in the Church. Beneath that was the note: "J. Smith, Printer."

The "Preface" to the *Peace Maker* further indicates that the goal of the pamphlet is "to turn the hearts of the fathers to the children" and vice versa as in Malachi 4:5–6 and that the author of the account professes to stand in relation to the coming millennium as Elijah did to Christ's first coming. These claims are strikingly similar to those Smith was formulating at the time as the rationale for temple sealing ceremonies connected in part with polygamy. And polygamy was one of the last important practices which must be restored before the millennium could be ushered in.[164] In conclusion, the *Peace Maker* exhorts:

> The truth on this important matter is now clearly set before you my countrymen: . . . The question is not now to be debated whether these things are so: neither is it a question of much importance who wrote this book? But the question, the momentous question is; *will you now restore the law of God on this important subject, and keep it?* Remember that the law of God is given by inspiration of the Holy Ghost. Speak not a word against it at your peril. . . . [Emphasis in original.][165]

Coming as it did in the wake of the Bennett allegations, publication of the *Peace Maker* created a brief furor in Nauvoo. A lively retailer of contemporary Nauvoo gossip, Oliver Olney, expressed what must have been a common opinion when he said: ". . . if the pamphlet was not written by the authorities of the Church, it by them was revised in Jacobs [*sic*] name."[166] As a rebuttal to such arguments, Smith mildly dissociated himself from the publication in a brief statement in the *Times and Seasons* on December 1, 1842. He denied that he had seen the pamphlet in advance or that he would have printed it had he known its contents. Significantly, however, Smith defended the author's right to publish such opinions and he did not criticize the pamphlet's extraordinary claims to authority— claims that in effect would have threatened to supersede his own leadership.[167]

In the tense political situation in Nauvoo following the Bennett fiasco, Joseph Smith had moved to centralize all power in his own hands. As part of this effort, he had given control of the Church press to a totally loyal subordinate, John Taylor, replacing Ebenezer Robinson, apparently at least in part because of Robinson's hostility to plural marriage.[168] Under the circumstances, it is hard to imagine how—short of extraordinary and uncharacteristic carelessness—the pamphlet could have been published without the sanction of the leadership of the Church. Probably, as John D. Lee later alleged, the pamphlet was put forward as a "feeler" to test

Church opinion but was disowned when public reaction proved too unfavorable.[169]

Whatever the authorship of the pamphlet and the circumstances of its publication, its primary significance lies in the argument that it presents. The highly unusual argument for divorce put forward in the pamphlet is virtually identical to that used in early Utah. Utah Mormon leaders later explicitly linked their divorce beliefs with those of this pamphlet.[170] In addition, the argument for polygamy presented in the pamphlet, which is an approximation of Old Testament law on the subject, appears largely compatible with early Utah beliefs.[171] Thus it seems possible that the *Peace Maker* may in fact be one of a handful of contemporary accounts providing an insight into some of the larger social purposes which underlay the attempt to introduce Mormon plural marriage.

The complex and sometimes convoluted social argument of the first chapter of the *Peace Maker* may be summarized in three primary assertions. First, patriarchal authority and related patterns of male-female roles in the home and in society must be restored if social chaos is to be avoided. Woman's unnatural usurpation of power in the family has led to ungoverned and ungovernable children, and to male desertion of their families. "Multitudes of families are now in confusion and wretchedly governed. This is a great evil." Second, to establish patriarchal authority and end this social disorder, a true or "Biblical" standard of divorce must be reinstituted. It would allow women whose affections had become irrevocably alienated from their husbands to be divorced by them. Thus the atmosphere of the home would not become posioned because women were held in wedlock against their will. Finally, as a counterpart to restoring the supposedly "Biblical" standard of divorce, polygamy, the "Biblical" form of marriage, must be reinstituted. Polygamy would allow men to reassert their proper authority and leadership. It would free them from the unnatural sexual influence women hold over men in a monogamous system. And it would provide men with an acceptable response to unsatisfactory marital situations short of the socially irresponsible one of divorcing or deserting uncooperative but not fully alienated wives.

Underlying this three-fold social argument is the assumption that only by the reestablishment of such a patriarchal basis for social authority can the true order of Christ's Church on earth be realized. The relationship which should exist between a husband and wife is seen as analogous to the relationship which should exist between Christ and his Church. The inversion of the correct relations between the sexes was a key factor in the thousand-year Great Apostasy from Christ's Church. Such role inversion destroyed the Patriarchal Order, thereby undermining the whole family organization and resulting in social chaos. A restitution of patriarchal authority is thus of overriding importance both for the social order and for Christ's Church on Earth.

Whatever the origin of this argument, it is a coherent theory which plausibly suggests some possible reasons for the preoccupation of Mormon leadership with introducing polygamy, the "patriarchal family system," in Nauvoo.[172]

The Parting of the Ways

With the recording of the revelation on plural and celestial marriage on July 12, 1843, and its presentation by Hyrum Smith before the High Council of the Church on August 12, 1843, the lines of division over this issue began to harden. Previously, Bennett's extreme statements and the obviously biased accounts printed in anti-Mormon newspapers in Illinois such as the *Warsaw Signal* could be dismissed by most Mormons as inaccurate. Indeed, in the long run attacks from such sources may actually have helped solidify Mormon group loyalty and thus strengthened the Church. But when loyal and respected members within the Church who were among the most influential citizens in Nauvoo became disaffected and began building an organization against Smith and his policies in the very heart of the Church, currents were set in motion which led irresistibly to Joseph Smith's death and the temporary disarray of the movement he had started.

The formal recording of the revelation on plural and celestial marriage and its presentation before the High Council signalled unmistakably to leading Mormons the seriousness of Smith's intention to carry through his policy on polygamy. Before this time, not all the leading elements in Nauvoo were aware of this policy, and some may have dismissed it as an aberration or seen it as a negotiable issue. But as Ebenezer Robinson noted, early in the summer of 1843, the "spiritual wife doctrine" was "so closely pressed that I felt that the time was at hand when I must determine whether to accept or reject it."[173] Robinson's course was almost unique: he decided that he could never personally accept the doctrine and practice, but he reserved judgment on what others might do.

Many Mormons took a stronger stand, however. When the revelation was read before twelve members of the High Council, three of them, the president William Marks, Austin Cowles, and Leonard Soby, bitterly opposed it. Cowles, whose daughter Elvira had become one of Joseph Smith's plural wives, wrote in an affidavit on May 4, 1844, that: "This revelation with other evidence, that the aforesaid heresies were taught and practiced in the Church; determined me to leave the office of first counsellor to the president of the Church [in the Nauvoo Stake], inasmuch as I dared not teach or administer such laws.[174] An increasing number of disaffected Mormons supplied material to the anti-Mormon newspapers. One bitter satire entitled "The Buckeye's Lament for Want of More Wives"—which revealed a detailed knowledge of the revelation and of Joseph Smith's plural wives—appeared on February 7, 1844, in the *Warsaw Message*.

Faced with mounting opposition on all sides, Smith broadened his efforts to prepare the minds of his followers for the new marriage standards and for the larger religious and social vision which underlay them. In the winter of 1843–44, he repeatedly preached the spirit of Elijah, and the imminence of an earthly millennium in which the hearts of the fathers would be turned to the children. He warned his followers publicly that some of his closest associates would seek his blood because of the "mysteries" that he had revealed and would reveal to them.

Outwardly, Joseph Smith appeared confident, if not overconfident. On March 10, 1844, he declared in a speech:

> I will make every doctrine plain that I present, and it shall stand upon a firm basis, and I am at defiance of the world, for I will take shelter under the broad wings of the work in which am engaged. It matters not to me if all hell boils over, I regard it only as the crackling of thorns under the pot.[175]

In what has appeared a rather extraordinary move, Smith started a campaign to become President of the United States, eventually sending out more than three hundred followers to preach his candidacy and defend his character. Smith also took action to prepare his inner circle, particularly the Twelve, with a full knowledge of his programs. He set up a secret Council of Fifty on March 11, 1844, to try to handle the increasing problems in Nauvoo and to serve as the secular arm eventually to rule an all-encompassing earthly government. And he pressed forward with the building of the Temple where mysteries hid from before the beginning of the world would be revealed.[176]

Yet underneath the appearance of confidence, if not bravado, Smith seems to have realized the extreme precariousness of his position, the degree to which he was poised, as it were, on the brink of eternity. His moods seem to have fluctuated widely. Between 1841 and 1844, his frustration at his failure to persuade his followers to accept his message and his inability to handle the ever more complex problems besetting him was increasingly apparent. Close followers recalled his deep discouragement on different occasions. Mary Rollins Lightner, one of his plural wives, remembered him saying:

> I am tired, I have been mobbed, I have suffered so much, from outsiders and from my own family. Some of the brethren think they can

carry this work on better than I can, far better. I have asked the Lord to take me away. I have to seal my testimony to this generation with my blood. I have to do it for this work will never progress until I am gone for the testimony is of no force until the testator is dead. People little know who I am when they talk about me, and they will never know until they see me weighed in the balance in the Kingdom of God. Then they will know who I am, and see me as I am. I dare not tell them, and they do not know me.[177]

Although this was recounted many years later, it seems accurately to reflect the spirit of many of Joseph Smith's private statements during his last days. His sermon of April 7, 1844, at the funeral of Elder King Follett may appropriately serve as his own epitaph. In this sermon, he described his glorious vision of men progressing to the achievement of full godlike powers. He declared in his conclusion, which George A. Smith said referred to plural marriage:

You never knew my heart; no man knows my history; I cannot tell it. I shall never undertake it; if I had not experienced what I have, I should not have known it myself. . . . When I am called at the trump of the archangel, and weighed in the balance, you will all know me then.[178]

This statement, it seems to me, reveals a profoundly lonely man, poignantly aware of the inability of the world to understand the underlying significance of his ideas and mission, and seeing with stark clarity that he is about to be overwhelmed by forces which he has helped to set loose, but which are beyond his control. Throughout his life, Smith was painfully aware of his singularity and never able to escape it.

Joseph Smith may have appeared somewhat fatalistic about his own prospects, but to the end he continued to show his characteristic dynamism and commitment to his larger goals for the Church and its welfare. Events began to move rapidly toward their tragic denouement on June 7, 1844, when a group of disaffected Mormons—including William and Wilson Law, Robert D. Foster, Austin Cowles, and Charles and Francis Higbee—published a newspaper, *The Nauvoo Expositor,* which decried polygamy and included a number of affidavits about the practice in Nauvoo which were difficult to dismiss as mere slander. The *Expositor* group was loyal to early Mormon beliefs and sincerely desired to purify the Church. The group thus represented a severe threat to Smith's control.

Knowing that the publication and circulation of such reports would undercut the faith of many members who were as yet unaware that the Church sanctioned and advocated the new practices, Smith acted quickly to have the press of the *Expositor* and any remaining copies of the paper destroyed. Almost inevitably this action brought outside hostility against the Mormons to a fever pitch. Rather than see outright civil war erupt, Smith surrendered himself to the authorities in Carthage, Illinois, to stand trial. There, on June 27, 1844, a mob in collusion with local militiamen entered the jail and shot and killed Joseph and his brother Hyrum.

The martyrdom of the prophet Joseph Smith set the stage for a new phase in the development of plural marriage. Between 1844 and 1852—the period which saw the chaotic final years in Nauvoo, the exodus to the West, and the early years in Utah—what had been largely one man's private vision would be introduced as the ideal model for family life in the whole Mormon Church. We shall now look at this remarkable transformation.

V

"Puritan Polygamy": Brigham Young and the Institutionalization of Mormon Polygamy, 1844-1852

> I have looked upon the community of Latter-day Saints in a vision and beheld them organized as one great family of heaven, each person performing his several duties in his line of industry, working for the good of the whole more than for individual aggrandizement; and in this I have beheld the most beautiful order that the mind of man can contemplate, and the grandest results for the upbuilding of the kingdom of God and the spread of righteousness upon the earth. . . . Why can we not so live in this world?
>
> Brigham Young[1]

The death of the prophet Joseph Smith at the hands of a mob in Carthage, Illinois, on June 27, 1844, could have meant the end of the effort to introduce polygamy among the Mormons. Indeed, Smith's death appeared at first to threaten the survival of the Church itself, for it left many Mormons temporarily adrift and allowed their latent disagreements to break out into the open. Almost at once a many-sided struggle began for control over the remarkable spiritual and temporal organization that Smith had created. Although the legitimate control of power in the Church was at the center of the succession controversy, the most important substantive issue was polygamy, or as its opponents called it, "the spiritual wife system." Polygamy was secretly advocated and practiced by Brigham Young and the main body of the Mormon Church in Nauvoo, while virtually all other factional leaders initially denounced the practice as licentiousness and debauchery—a falling away from the earlier purity of the Church.

Added to the problems within the Church were the continuing difficulties with the outside world, difficulties which had more to do with the Church's politics than with polygamy. At first, Smith's death defused anti-

181

Mormon sentiment, since many anti-Mormons expected the Saints to lose cohesion and disintegrate without their prophet. But by the early autumn of 1845, seeing that the Saints remained active in local politics and that the temple which would serve as the symbol of Mormon unity and singularity neared completion, non-Mormons and anti-Mormons realized that the Saints intended to remain in Illinois. Hostilities, which were most dramatically expressed in the burning of outlying Mormon settlements, quickly became so intense that Mormon leadership realized that co-existence with the other citizens of Illinois would be impossible. The Church would have to move again. Early in February 1846, in icy mid-winter, the first large group of Mormons left Nauvoo for an unspecified destination in the West, trusting only in their leaders and in the faith which had brought them through repeated trials and persecutions before. The survival of the Mormon Church itself seemed problematical, and certainly its controversial new marriage practices (still unknown to many of the members)[2] seemed unlikely to last.

Yet less than a decade later, when the main body of the Saints had settled in the Great Basin region, plural marriage had become a generally accepted part of Mormon patriarchal family arrangements in the West. Although tensions remained throughout the 1850s, the fundamental stability of early Utah social practice was commented upon both by external observers and by practicing Mormons. Writing in 1852, Howard Stansbury of the United States Corps of Engineers stated that, although as an outsider he was unable to see more than "the surface of what is in fact but an experiment, the details of which are sedulously veiled from public view," yet "Peace, harmony, and cheerfulness seemed to prevail, where my preconceived notions led me to look for nothing but the exhibition of petty jealousies, envy, bickerings, and strife."[3] Another early observer, John W. Gunnison, commented that while there were still problems with the regulation of polygamy, "any equal number of persons in the states can hardly exhibit greater decorum."[4] And even Mrs. Benjamin G. Ferris, who stated expressly that she was trying to portray Mormon polygamous society as a "sink of pollution," succeeded only in affixing derogatory adjectives to people whom her own descriptions reveal as generally friendly, hardworking, and sincere in living a difficult system to the best of their capacities.[5]

Internal Mormon accounts from the early 1850s bear out the general acceptance of the new arrangements and the matter-of-fact adjustment of most Mormons to the difficulties and renunciations involved in "living the Principle." In an introspective journal written between 1850 and 1856, the recent convert Martha Spence Heywood recorded in detail her own reactions to becoming a plural wife and the emotional interrelationships among men and women in the upper hierarchy of the Mormon Church.[6] From accounts such as Martha Heywood's it appears that almost at the beginning of the Utah settlement, many of the worst strains of the transition to the new marriage and family practices had already been overcome. In the relative isolation of the Great Basin region, Mormons initially were freed from attack from without. Moreover, many of the individuals most opposed to polygamy had dropped out of the Church during the Nauvoo period and the difficult trek westward, so that the Saints who remained were among the most loyal and dedicated. Finally, the problems of simple survival in the arid and inhospitable intermountain West and the challenges of building a new society with its own cohesive religious, economic, and social patterns left little energy for questioning the validity of the new polygamous arrangements.

How was the transition from polygamy as an idiosyncratic belief and practice of Joseph Smith to polygamy as the ideal and practice of a whole people achieved? What was plural marriage like in early Utah? How was it justified and how did it restructure relations between the sexes? And what was the significance of this effort at marriage and family reorganization within the context of the larger Mormon effort at restructuring all aspects of life in their Great Basin Kingdom?

These are difficult questions, which to date have received only limited scholarly consideration. In this chapter, I shall suggest some of the major issues raised by the effort to institutionalize polygamy and some of the ways in which it affected relationships between men and women in Utah. Not without justification did Brigham Young's non-Mormon biographer M. R. Werner characterize Mormon plural marriage in Utah as "Puritan Polygamy." The Mormons shared with their Puritan forebears the drive to set up a new religiously inspired commonwealth and a strictness and dedication in reorganizing sexual and familial relationships that can perhaps be truly described as "puritan" in spirit.[7]

The Role of Brigham Young

The key figure in this second phase of Mormon history was Brigham Young. By virtue of his presidency of the Council of the Twelve Apostles and his capable management, he rapidly assumed effective power over the Mormons in Nauvoo following Smith's assassination. After December 5, 1847, when the First Presidency of the Church was reconstituted, he assumed the role of President of the Latter-day Saints, as well as "Prophet, Seer, and Revelator," positions which he continued to hold until his death in 1877. Without the steady hand and organizational genius of this Mormon Moses, or a figure of comparable stature, the

history of the Mormon Church and the nature of the achievements of
this second period of its history might have been very different. Surely
polygamy might well have died out or developed very differently under
other leadership.[8]

Brigham Young was born in Whitingham, Windham County, Vermont,
on June 1, 1801. Like many other early Mormon leaders, including
Joseph Smith, he spent his formative years in an economically marginal
family in the Burned-over District of western New York and showed little
initial evidence of any special leadership abilities. Although Young and
Smith shared many similarities in social background, the two men played
strikingly different roles in Mormon development. Smith had been first
of all a man of ideas, and only secondarily an organizer; he had conceived a new way of looking at the world and then had set up the basic
structure of a church to embody that worldview. Beginning as a poverty-
stricken unknown with no following, Smith had made frequent use of
revelations in attempting to establish his authority in the early 1830s.
Highly innovative in both doctrine and practice, he had sought to break
down the old order and to provide a framework for the restoration of
the ideal religious and social relations that he conceived to be those of
the "dispensation of the fullness of time."

Unlike Joseph Smith, Brigham Young was almost solely an organizer;
he showed few original ideas apart from organizational matters, and
initially he felt uncomfortable in the role of "prophet." Whereas Smith
had started his own organization from scratch, Brigham Young stepped
into a powerful existing organization that was in temporary disarray and
sought to pull it together again. Young exercised real power, and he
felt little need to promulgate formal revelations to bolster his authority.
Instead, Young simply told the Saints what to do and expected them
to obey. His concern was to make the organization work, to tighten it up.
Young was thus less interested in intellectual innovation and more concerned with implementing the ideas which had already been developed.

The experiences of more than a decade of loyal association with the
Mormon Church in positions of ever-increasing responsibility had given
Young an excellent preparation for his accession to leadership after
Smith's martyrdom. During the troubled years 1838 and 1839, Brigham
Young and Heber C. Kimball were among the few prominent leaders
of the Church who were on the scene, not in jail, and still loyal, and
who thus could help to oversee the arduous departure from Missouri. In
a small way, this move established guidelines for the much larger exodus
of the Saints to the Rocky Mountains several years later. In the 1840s,
Young became the leader of the Twelve Apostles and played an important
role in organizing the far-flung and effective home and foreign missionary

activities of the Church. By 1846, for example, more than four thousand British converts had come to Nauvoo.[9]

Brigham Young and the Twelve developed an effective working relationship and camaraderie which enabled them to assume increasing importance in Church affairs even before Joseph Smith's death. Because they operated as a group, they were less vulnerable to allegations that they were acting for self-aggrandizement than were the numerous other pretenders to power following Smith's assassination. It was natural for this group to attempt to carry on the policies of the martyred prophet, including the polygamy to which many of them had already become committed by personal action. Plural and celestial marriage was integrally related to other doctrines, ceremonies, and practices, including baptism for the dead and the law of adoption, which sought to irrevocably seal the loyalty of the Mormons to one another and to their Church as a literal extension of the family of God. Out of the last years in Nauvoo and the westward migration, an elaborate patriarchal tribal system modeled on the experiences of the early Hebrews emerged.

Under Brigham Young and the Twelve a symbolic focal point for group loyalty was found in the "gathering" of all the Saints to Nauvoo and in the effort to finish building the Nauvoo temple, where the various priesthood, endowment, and marriage sealing ceremonies were to be performed, especially after December 1845. The building of the temple provided the Saints with a sense of continuity with Joseph Smith's basic program. Smith had emphasized the importance of the temple by revelation as early as 1841. The Saints had been told that unless they completed the temple within an allotted time, they and all their forebears would be rejected by God. Thus an intense emotional commitment was associated with the effort to build the temple. The temple provided a tangible, physical sign of Mormon unity in a troubled period when many Saints felt very much in need of such external validation.[10]

In addition to giving Mormons a sense of continuity with the program of their martyred prophet, the temple-building effort also served important economic functions. Building the temple was, in effect, a massive public works project, absorbing energies, skills, and idealism which might otherwise have dissipated into idleness and other unproductive or antisocial activities. Except for the missionary program, building the temple constituted the primary group-project through which Mormon men of the period could contribute to the common enterprise. Furthermore, the project provided a concrete reason to encourage Saints, both in Nauvoo and abroad, to make unselfish donations of much needed labor, produce, and money. Saints were told that if they did not tithe, they would be ineligible to receive the awesome benefits and powers to be conferred through the temple ceremonies. The capital thus collected by the Church could be used directly on the temple itself, or, as some claimed, it could be diverted to support other Church efforts deemed necessary for the building up of Nauvoo.

Undoubtedly the sense of awe, mystery, and expectation with which the Saints awaited the secret ceremonies of power to be conducted in the completed temple was the most important single function of the temple-building effort. The general membership had no clear idea of exactly what the ceremonies would entail, but few doubted that mysteries hidden since before the foundation of the world were soon to be revealed. The experiences of eternity would be brought directly into earthly life. Keys of power received through the prophet Elijah by the leaders of the Church would be used to link indissolubly the living and the dead. Would the Millennium itself soon follow?

This sense of expectation, combined with the common experience of crisis, was of cardinal importance in preparing the Saints to accept the new celestial and plural marriage system. Between December 1845 and January 1846, various endowment and sealing ceremonies were performed in the nearly completed temple on a round-the-clock basis before the first group of loyal Saints began their exodus west. By the time of the departure of the last major group of the Saints in the spring, more than five thousand ceremonies had been conducted in the temple in Nauvoo. The majority of the marriage ceremonies sealed monogamous marriages for eternity, but some ceremonies sealed polygamous marriages as well. Through these temple rituals, the new Mormon beliefs and worldview were taught, and Saints were strengthened in their sense of the divine authenticity of their Church.[11] By thus building on Smith's work, stressing the gathering, the completion of the temple, and the performing of the temple ceremonies, Brigham Young and the Twelve adopted the most powerful position available to them during their difficult final years in Nauvoo.

Schismatic Challenges to Brigham Young

Although Brigham Young and the Twelve were in a relatively strong position following Joseph Smith's death, they faced a number of other potentially serious contenders for the mantle of the prophet. In the confused aftermath of the assassination, Smith's counselor Sidney Rigdon made an unsuccessful play for the leadership of the Church. Later, Smith's brother William, who was also one of the Twelve Apostles, sought supreme power on family-dynastic grounds. And as the following section will show, the most dangerous challenge of all came from the brilliant charismatic prophet, James J. Strang. Claiming to have Joseph Smith's personal authorization and the support of God, Strang set up a large and well-conceived organization which opposed that of the Twelve. In each of these cases, as in many others, the most important issue was power in the Church, but the conflict over polygamy greatly intensified and complicated that issue. The difficulties of institutionalizing polygamy in the main body of the Mormon Church are vividly suggested by the careers of the most important schismatics who arose after Smith's death.

The first serious challenger to Brigham Young and the Twelve for control of the Mormon organization was Joseph Smith's brilliant if somewhat erratic associate Sidney Rigdon, who had played a major role in the early life of the Church. Rigdon, who had been a prominent Campbellite minister before Smith began to organize his church, had converted to Mormonism in 1831 and brought into the Church with him his sizable personal following at Kirtland, Ohio. Throughout the early and middle 1830s, Smith and Rigdon worked closely together, but by the Nauvoo period the two men had become estranged. Nevertheless, Rigdon's remaining support in the Church was so great that in 1843 Smith did not feel able to remove him from his formal position as the second member of the governing First Presidency. When Joseph and Hyrum Smith were murdered in 1844, Rigdon, as the sole surviving member of the First Presidency, made an abortive bid for the leadership of the Nauvoo Church. After that bid was quashed by the Twelve, Rigdon retreated to his Pittsburgh base to attempt to organize his own counter-movement.[12]

In addition to his legalistic claims to leadership of the Nauvoo Church, Rigdon launched a vitriolic attack on the Twelve, with specific reference to the "spiritual wife system" which he accused the Nauvoo leadership of advocating and practicing. Rigdon's attacks were printed in his revived *Latter Day Saints' Messenger and Advocate* which he published in Pittsburgh between October 1844 and May 1845. The first issue of that paper, dated October 15, 1844, just a month after Rigdon's expulsion from the Church, contained harsh and explicit condemnation of polygamous practices. Rigdon blasted the "desperate lengths" to which the leadership of the Church had been forced to go in order to keep their "corruptions" from the public. He stated that these included character assassinations of uncooperative females (presumably thinking of his daughter Nancy's case), and blatant perjury. Later issues of the newspaper also alleged that counterfeiting and theft were engaged in on a large scale in a desperate effort to support plural wives.[13]

Despite the ferocity of Rigdon's initial attacks on Brigham Young and the Twelve, his efforts soon began to slacken. His newspaper had an extremely limited circulation; he never published a full-length exposé as he had threatened; and by the end of 1846 his organization had almost completely disintegrated. Somewhat ironically, in view of Rigdon's earlier extreme attacks on Nauvoo polygamy, the remnants of his own group apparently for a short time practiced a form of polygamy or marital experimentation under his leadership. At least this allegation is contained in letters in the James J. Strang manuscripts, including one of December 14, 1846, which spoke of Rigdon's revelatory excesses of the period and his introduction of "a system of Wifery on the Battle Ax System or free or common intercourse with the women."[14] Presumably this arrangement was unrelated to that of John Humphrey Noyes, but its precise character and duration is almost as obscure as Rigdon's own career from 1845 until his death in 1876.[15]

If Rigdon's challenge to Brigham Young and the Twelve was simply a flash in the pan, the activities of Joseph Smith's brother William proved far more complex and difficult to handle. Although William's personal instability made him incapable of sustaining a serious challenge to the Twelve, his inconsistent and flagrantly inappropriate behavior caused them endless problems and embarrassment. William had always been the black sheep of the Smith family, a loner who felt neglected in comparison to his more famous brothers and had difficulty taking responsibility for his own life. After the deaths of Joseph and Hyrum Smith on June 27, 1844, and Samuel H. Smith shortly thereafter, William, the only surviving brother of the Smith family, initially cooperated with the governing Council of the Twelve Apostles, of which he was a member. Secretly, however, he began to build up his own power base in an attempt to seize the leadership of the Church. Using a family-dynastic argument, Smith claimed the right to guide the Church, at least until the prophet's young son Joseph III reached his majority. Despite the plausibility of this claim, which continued to bring William supporters into the 1850s, his emotional instability made him incapable of sustaining any concerted independent venture.[16]

In no area was William Smith's instability more evident than in relation to polygamy. Repeatedly he vacillated from total support of the practice to guilt-ridden opposition and then back to support once again. Perhaps the first thing William did that was really damaging to the Church was to attempt, along with George J. Adams and Samuel Brannan, to introduce the doctrine and practice of polygamy in Boston in the late summer and early fall of 1844. Since the Mormon community there numbered only a few hundred members, such a venture would have been pure folly, even had it been conducted with the best of skill and intentions. An outraged John Hardy, respected head of the Boston branch of the Mormon Church before his expulsion by the Smith, Adams, and Brannan faction, wrote an extremely detailed and bitter condemnation of the power play involved and the allegedly disreputable behavior of the three men.[17] Although Hardy's charges would have been highly libelous if false, William Smith declined to deny the accusations directly. He simply said that the criticisms were maliciously put forward with a "false coloring."[18]

This apparently unauthorized effort to introduce polygamy in Boston was only the most extreme of the irregularities which afflicted the vital eastern mission of the Mormon Church between 1844 and 1845. Throughout the eastern mission, whose support was essential to the survival of the Nauvoo organization, overzealous Mormons took it upon themselves to teach polygamy, and sometimes even to practice it. Endless and bitter factional squabbles were the result. Many conservative Saints in the East came to the conclusion that either the teachers of the new doctrines were wicked men or the Church itself had fallen. The Nauvoo leadership had great difficulty in restricting the unauthorized teaching of polygamy and disciplining cases of misbehavior, since they themselves were caught in the inconsistent position of teaching one thing in public and another in private. By the middle of 1845, however, the Nauvoo leadership began to take steps to tighten up the Church, emphasizing that only under proper priesthood authority in Nauvoo could the mysteries of the kingdom be taught or practiced.[19]

A series of unauthorized and highly disruptive activities by William Smith finally led the Nauvoo authorities to discipline him. William's public indiscretions reached their height on August 17, 1845, when he reportedly declared from the stand in Nauvoo that polygamy doctrines and practices were "taught in Nauvoo secretly—that he taught and practiced it, and he was not in favor of making a secret of the matter. He said that it was a common thing amongst the leaders and he for one was not ashamed of it."[20] In conjunction with all of his other misdeeds, this was too much. On October 6, 1845, after a final attempt to get him into line had proved fruitless, the Twelve lost all patience with William and removed him from all leadership positions in the Church. Orson Pratt summarized the two key charges: first, William had been an "aspiring man" who sought to undercut the leadership of the Church so that he could take power himself; second, ". . . while Brother William was in the east, to my certain knowledge, his doctrine and conduct have not had a savory influence; but have produced death and destruction wherever he went."[21]

True to form, William Smith did not go quietly. He proceeded to compose a highly disingenuous diatribe condemning Brigham Young and the Twelve for polygamy, immorality, and hypocrisy. Hearing of this exposé the Twelve excommunicated William on October 19. William's statement was then published as a front-page spread in the bitterly anti-Mormon *Warsaw Signal* on October 27, 1845. It is probable that William Smith's numerous indiscretions and his subsequent five-column exposé made a significant contribution to the violent hostility towards the Nauvoo Mormons that flared up in the late summer and early fall of 1845. William Smith's case graphically illustrates the great difficulty that Brigham Young and the Twelve faced in trying to discipline overzealous or refractory members of the Church. A person who had been privy to Church secrets could not be dealt with too severely, lest he create a public scandal. Only in the isolation of the Great Basin would the Mormons under Brigham Young be able to put the new system of marriage and family organization on a secure footing.

The Prophet Who Failed

Although Sidney Rigdon, William Smith, and other dissidents caused problems for the Nauvoo Mormons, only the prophet-pretender James J. Strang possessed both the intellectual brilliance and organizational talent to mount a serious and sustained challenge to Brigham Young and the Twelve. Strang was without doubt the greatest of the early Mormon schismatics, a man of passionate idealism and driving ambition whom the scholar Klaus J. Hansen has ranked with Joseph Smith as quite possibly one of the two "most creative individuals in Mormon history."[22] Strang's career would seem hard to believe if it were not so thoroughly documented in printed and manuscript sources. Although Strang appears at times to be almost self-consciously replicating Joseph Smith's career, his efforts nevertheless have a distinctive character of their own.[23]

James J. Strang first appeared on the scene when, at the age of thirty-one, he was baptized a Mormon in Nauvoo just four months before Joseph Smith's assassination. Yet only a month after Smith's death, Strang produced a letter ostensibly written to him by Joseph Smith shortly before his death. Strang argued with considerable eloquence that the letter, in conjunction with an angelic ordination that he had received, showed him to be Joseph Smith's true successor. To buttress these claims, Strang began to deliver revelations in Smith's "Thus saith the Lord" style. He denounced polygamy as an utter abomination. He called for Mormons to gather to his headquarters at Voree, Wisconsin, rather than to undertake a foolhardy migration westward. In the presence of four witnesses, in the autumn of 1845 Strang dug up some brass plates near Voree, the inscriptions on which he then "translated." Later he would "translate" a brilliant elaboration and extension of Mosaic Law which he called the *Book of the Law of the Lord*. This work has been described by Strang's skeptical non-Mormon biographer Milo M. Quaife as ". . . a complete framework of government. . . . applicable to any population, however great, and laying down regulations for the most important relations of human society."[24]

In short, Strang appeared to represent everything that the committee, caretaker-type government of Brigham Young and the Twelve did not. He effectively presented himself as a single legal successor to Joseph Smith, a prophet and charismatic, an anti-polygamist carrying on the purity of the early Mormon message, and a supporter of the Mormon gathering who nevertheless opposed the idea of going west. For a newcomer to the Mormon faith, Strang showed great knowledge of Mormon beliefs and an extraordinary sensitivity to Mormon thought patterns.

Even though Strang was new to the Mormon faith and began without any organizational base whatsoever, he soon managed, through force of personality, rhetoric, gimmickry, and organizational skill, to attract most of those dissenting from the policies of Brigham Young and the Twelve. The founders of the Reorganized Church, James C. Brewster's church, William Smith's church, and many other early Mormon factions were first associates of James J. Strang. In the summer of 1846, Strang's highly successful missionary trip to the eastern United States threatened to divert essential support from the Mormon trek westward. By the 1850s, with the main body of the Mormons securely established in the Great Basin, Strang no longer posed a significant threat to Brigham Young and the Twelve. Despite his somewhat narrowed scope of operations, however, he had by 1855 established a community of over 2,500 followers in his "Kingdom" on Beaver Island in Lake Michigan. Contrary to his earlier position, he had also introduced a form of polygamy into his community. Yet when Strang was assassinated by rebellious followers in 1856, his kingdom melted away. Today only a handful of individuals remember this tragic figure, a classic example of a prophet who failed.

What motivated this remarkable man and his decade-long career as a Mormon prophet? How was polygamy related to his initial successes and his eventual failure? And how was his career connected with the development of the Great Basin Mormons? James J. Strang was born on March 21, 1813, at Scipio, New York, in the heart of the Burned-over District. He was an intellectually and emotionally precocious child, painfully attuned to the conflicting currents which swirled around him. His remarkable diary, written between the ages of nineteen and twenty-four, records the complex relation between his passionate idealism and his driving ambition. He could write: "I am resolved to [devote] my life to the service of mankind." Yet he could also refer in cipher to his ambition to "rival Caesar or Napoleon," to be "a Priest, a Lawyer, a Conqueror, and a Legislator," or to contrive some means of marrying the heiress to the English crown (later Queen Victoria).[25]

Perhaps the key to Strang's character and emotional power may be found in the passage which followed his vivid imaginative description of "all the horrors of anarchy and civil war" that he saw growing out of the 1832 South Carolina Nullification Crisis. That crisis was, of course, a precursor of the similar South Carolina crisis that triggered the Civil War. Writing in cipher, Strang initially toyed with the idea of forming some sort of a prankster club. Then he came to the core of his concern. He wrote: "Amidst all the ev[i]ls of the disturbances of our national affairs there is one consolation: that if our government is overthrown some master spirit may form another. May I be the one. I tremble when I write but it is true."[26] In common with the founders of so many of the religious and social movements of the antebellum period, Strang appears to have felt deeply the hopes, fears, and ambitions springing from the breakdown of existing supports. He could not trust his social world; he would have to create another.

Strang's inner sense of his personal mission to construct a new social order runs as a unifying thread throughout his career and gives his words extraordinary emotional power. So great was the cause that almost any methods were justified in its pursuit, and Strang therefore appears to have been willing self-consciously to manipulate the credulity of his followers to achieve his larger ends. Dale Morgan's meticulous research has established beyond reasonable doubt that Strang's so-called "letter of appointment" from Joseph Smith was forged, and almost surely forged by Strang himself.[27] Evidence which need not be detailed here also suggests purposeful manipulation in many of Strang's other ventures, including his revelations, translations, and reversals of position on issues such as polygamy. Yet Strang was far more than a charlatan. One cannot plausibly account for his continuing dedication in the face of all the hardships, poverty, and buffetings he experienced, or the generally well-thought-out and humane quality of his ideals and activities as fraudulent or psychopathological. Why did this brilliant and talented human being apparently feel compelled to forge his credentials for authority?

The most obvious reason was pragmatic. Strang was an unknown who wanted to attract a following among which he could realize his ideals. He evidently saw the potential of the Mormon organization as a vehicle to achieve his objectives, particularly after Joseph Smith's death. Yet he had to find some way of attracting attention and legitimating his authority. Brigham Young and the Twelve had control over the core of the Mormon organization in Nauvoo and no other Mormon faction prior to 1860 even began to offer them a viable organizational challenge. Strang, therefore, was forced to improvise with every means at hand. He attempted to embody in his own life and activities the spirit of Joseph Smith more fully than even the prophet himself had, and he reached out to dissidents, both the best and the worst. Through his own charisma, dedication, and iron will, he attempted to fuse all the disparate elements into a new whole. It was a daring gamble, but it ultimately was too great a task for any one man, no matter how brilliant. While Strang lived, he managed to hold a strong core of followers together, but after his death his personally based organization simply disintegrated.[28]

In no area were the problems and inherent inconsistencies of Strang's approach more evident than in his response to polygamy. Throughout the mid-1840s, Strang inveighed against polygamy publicly and privately with telling effect, stressing his "unchanged" and "unchangeable" opposition to "spiritual wifery" or anything of the kind.[29] Yet in July 1849, Strang reversed his position in practice by privately taking nineteen-year-old Elvira Field as his first plural wife. Dressed in a pageboy's garb and posing as "Charles J. Douglass," Strang's private male secretary, Elvira accompanied Strang east on a missionary trip in 1849–50 to try to induce Mormons to gather at the community Strang was trying to organize on Beaver Island in Lake Michigan. There, in July 1850, Strang publicly announced to the world his firm commitment to polygamy, a full two years before Brigham Young's followers made their similar declaration in Utah.[30]

What accounts for Strang's reversal of his position on polygamy, and how did it affect his struggle with Brigham Young and the Twelve? Certainly Strang's personal attraction to Elvira Field played an important part in his decision. Moreover, Strang had undoubtedly learned by this time of Joseph Smith's own commitment to polygamy, and he may have sought to replicate at least the form of those activities.[31] But Strang's public advocacy of polygamy was based neither on his personal desires nor on Mormon precedent but on a sophisticated social argument. In a powerful rhetorical defense of his position published in his community newspaper, Strang eloquently argued in favor of polygamy primarily as a means of alleviating the problems that women faced in finding husbands and making satisfactory marriages.[32] He noted that although the monogamous practices of his day supposedly granted women their free choice of a husband, in fact women who wanted to marry at all were usually placed under intolerable pressure to taken any man they could get.

> In consequence many talented women find themselves tied for life to puerile men, whom they cannot but despise; and just and amiable women to selfish men, whom they are compelled to dread; and they

set about preaching women's rights, in the hope of finding some relief by relaxing the matrimonial bond as much as possible.

Strang argued that the popular remedy of "making marriage so near
nothing at all, that it shall be only a partnership at will, for propagating
the human species," was not the solution to women's problems in marriage. He did not favor borrowing a husband "for the occasion" or
hiring him as "a lackey or personal attendant," any more than he would
favor casual sex with a woman or hiring a prostitute. Instead, his goal
was to create the best possibility for a marriage relationship of commitment between whole human beings. Polygamy would have the effect
of giving women "a wider range for the selection of husbands" and
more bargaining power.

> Consequently they will accept only such as suit them. Higher talent,
> purer virtues, more constant kindness, more enterprise, better busi-
> ness capacities, a larger share of everything that makes the man the
> gentleman is then requisite to get wives at all.

> Women admire and love every manly excellence, and they are fond
> of each other's society. Take away the feeling of degradation, and
> shame, and a half dozen intellectual, amiable and beautiful women
> would spend their lives far more happily with one man, such as
> either would really choose, than separately with the same number of
> men, such as they can get, in the existing state of society.

Men, too, would benefit if women were given greater freedom of choice
in husbands.

> . . . the worst fault of the system is, that wives being generally
> mated rather than matched to their husbands, treat them without
> affection, and those men who have any degree of kindness acquiesce,
> because they feel that it would be cruel to exact more than the heart
> can feel. Desolate in the want of love, they seek that affection in vile
> places, which is denied at home, and too often their delinquencies are
> returned upon them, and the household made a desolation. The few
> that are really well-matched, are carried away by the prevailing cus-
> tom, and virtuous women are ashamed to show their affection for
> their husbands. It is an unpardonable *weakness*. Thus connubial
> felicity is denied the good and the evil, the well and ill matched.

Was this defense of polygamy simply a debater's ploy, or did it
constitute a serious attempt to deal with pressing social problems? How
well did Strang's system work in practice? Because of the limited extent
and documentation of Strang's polygamy system, these questions can not
be answered in full detail. Out of a Mormon population in 1856 numbering more than 2,500, with probably 500 heads of households, there
never were more than 18 to 20 polygamous families on Beaver Island.

Strang had four wives in addition to his first, L. D. Hickey had three, and all other polygamous families contained but two wives. The limited practice of polygamy appears to have been due to personal disinclination, simple poverty, lack of eligible females, and the more elite character of Strang's system than that which was set up in the Great Basin.[33]

Strang's own family lived together in the same house, with a separate room for each wife. One wife described Strang as judicious and mild, yet a firm leader.[34] Given the crowded circumstances and the other difficulties they faced, Strang's wives appear to have maintained as good relations among themselves as could be expected. Strang made no pretensions that his marriages to his plural wives were legal; he simply said that his wives were women "who I would marry if the law permitted me."[35] Strang's form of polygamous belief and practice was not inconsistent with allowing his wives considerable power. He introduced a Bloomer outfit for women, made his first wife Mary Perce a member of his Governing Council in April 1851, and repeatedly emphasized the importance of a mutual love relationship between husband and wife, as opposed to more pragmatic property and kinship considerations.

As the only Mormon polygamy system outside that of Utah for which anything more than the most superficial documentation exists, the marriage ideals and practices of James J. Strang hold considerable intrinsic and comparative interest. The primary historic importance of Strang's adoption of polygamy, however, lay in its impact on internal Mormon politics. Strang's espousal of polygamy formally signalled his inability or unwillingness to provide a true alternative to the policies of the Great Basin Mormons under Brigham Young. The most devoted and capable of the disaffected Mormons who followed Strang, including William Marks, Zenos Gurley, and Jason Briggs, left him when he followed Joseph Smith's lead in introducing secret societies and polygamy. Marks, Gurley, Briggs, and others would continue to "wander in the wilderness" until the formal establishment of the antipolygamist Reorganized Mormon Church in 1860. To be sure, Strang posed little or no threat to the survival of the Utah Mormons after the late 1840s in any case. Yet, had he not formally introduced polygamy in 1850, he might well have been able to establish the nucleus of a successful non-polygamous branch of the Mormon Church. Instead, Strang retreated to his isolated Beaver Island Kingdom and increasingly became simply a curiosity rather than a dynamic force in history[36]

The Westward Migration and the Law of Adoption

Schismatic challenges by men such as Sidney Rigdon, William Smith, and James J. Strang posed many problems for Brigham Young and the

Twelve, yet these internal difficulties must have seemed minor in comparison to the increasing hostility which they faced in Illinois. As early as 1842, Mormon leadership responded to the external pressures by beginning to consider the possibility that the Saints might once again be forced to migrate to a new location where they would be free to practice and regulate their own distinctive religious and social system in peace. This time, primary consideration was given to locations outside the bounds of what was then the United States, including Texas, California, Oregon, Vancouver Island, and, of course, the Rocky Mountains.[37]

After Smith's death in 1844, the Mormons initially continued to build up their base in Nauvoo, evidently hoping against hope that they would be able to continue to live peacefully in Illinois. As late as the summer of 1845, solid brick houses were still being built in Nauvoo by Mormon leaders. But in the late summer and early autumn of 1845, wide-scale anti-Mormon violence, looting and burning of outlying settlements broke out. The result was an outright civil war between Mormon and non-Mormon in Illinois which even Governor Thomas Ford and his state militia were unable to suppress.[38] To curb the violence, the Church bowed to the inevitable and publicly committed itself to move again. Throughout the fall and early winter of 1845–46, the Saints worked feverishly to prepare for the difficult migration, and in early February 1846, in icy midwinter, the first group of Mormons left Nauvoo to begin the long trek westward.

The epic story of this great Mormon migration to the West, with its heroism, suffering, drama, disappointments, and ultimate much-deserved success, is well known and need not be repeated in detail here. This Mormon exodus was one of the great group movements in history and threw into high relief the remarkable organizational talents of Brigham Young. At the Mormon resting point at Winter Quarters, near what is now Florence, Nebraska, on January 14, 1846, Brigham Young delivered as the "Word and Will of the Lord" an organizational plan which would be a key part of the successful move west.[39] All the Saints were organized in companies with captains of hundreds, fifties, and tens. Some were sent on ahead to plant crops to be harvested later by those coming behind. Additionally, provisions were to be made for the poor, the widows, and the fatherless. By following this plan and using a number of other ingenious expedients, the main body of the Mormons would eventually reach the Valley of the Great Salt Lake.

If one keeps in mind the larger family and kinship model being developed by the Mormons at this time, this great migration becomes both more comprehensible and more impressive. One method of organization which preceded Young's 1847 statement by at least a year and underlay it to some extent was the limited practice of the "law of adoption." The theory underlying the practice of adoption may have gone back as far as the early years of the Nauvoo period. Gordon Irving has characterized the law of adoption as "an experiment" in "the organization of Mormon society along family lines" which was "tried out on a small scale within the families of the leaders."[40] The adoption experiment reached full fruition during the difficult migration westward between 1846 and 1848, though eventually it was largely discontinued.

Through the law of adoption, some Mormon men and their families were literally, as well as spiritually, linked as part of the families of higher Mormon figures such as Brigham Young, Heber C. Kimball, and Wilford Woodruff. These adopted "sons" would in turn sometimes serve as "fathers" by whom other men and their families would be adopted. The belief was that eventually all Mormons would be indissolubly linked in a family relationship to each other, both in this life and in eternity. This adoptionary order was seen as more than simply symbolic; it also entailed temporal rights and obligations. Looking back, thirty years later, John D. Lee characterized the adoptionary system as follows: ". . . I was adopted by Brigham Young, and was to seek his *temporal* interest here, and in return he was to seek my *spiritual* salvation, I being an heir of his family, and was to share his *blessings* in common with his other heirs."[41] When Lee was adopted into Young's family, he chose to emphasize the relationship by signing his name: "John D. Lee Young."[42]

As both a spiritual and a temporal linkage, the adoptionary system might have helped to make the westward trek more orderly and solidify Mormon loyalties to the Church. Problems developed with the new arrangements, however. Conflicts arose over who should have precedence among the adopted "sons" of a particular father. Other conflicts developed between leading figures and those whom they had adopted. Some family leaders came to fear that if they allowed themselves to be "adopted" to another who stood higher in the Church, the size of their own "kingdoms" might suffer in consequence. In many instances, the result was that the practice of adoption aggravated conflict instead of contributing to unity. Since that early form of the law of adoption failed to serve its primary purpose of encouraging unity, it was largely abandoned by the late 1840s.

The law of adoption as practiced during the westward trek was closely connected with the developing Mormon concept of salvation, with sealing ceremonies such as baptism for the dead, and with spiritual marriage and polygamy, as part of a general effort to reestablish spiritual and temporal cohesion within the group. With the adoptionary model in mind, one can more easily understand certain aspects of the development of polygamy just before and during the westward trek. One of the most puzzling features of the development of early polygamy is why many prominent Mormon leaders took large numbers of plural wives just before beginning the exodus or during the migration itself. What relationship did those "wives" have with them? For instance, recent Mormon scholarship verifies that at least fifty-five women can be considered to have been "married" in some sense to Brigham Young, and most of those women were sealed to him in 1846. In addition to the twenty-seven women officially considered to have been Young's wives, there were at least twenty-eight other, evidently non-connubial, wives who have been characterized by the historian Michael Quinn as "lesser-known wives." Although apparently none of these lesser-known wives bore Young any children, the relationship was considered sufficiently binding that there are records of some of the women securing formal divorces before re-marrying.[43] Many other Mormon leaders also took large numbers of wives and "lesser-known wives" in this period. Why did this occur?

One might argue, of course, that these large numbers of plural wives taken in 1846 or during the exodus were a reflection of the confusions and excesses of the period. Putting it crudely, one might assume that the passions when released from normal constraints simply went wild. A more convincing explanation, however, is suggested by the law of adoption. Under the law of adoption, a man could be sealed to his superior as an adopted son. Likewise, it seems likely that as polygamy was practiced during this period, a woman might well have been sealed as the wife of a prominent figure even if she had no sexual relations with him. The Mormons considered marriage essential for full salvation. A single woman going west would face great difficulties and should she die in the exodus she would be alone for all eternity as well. But if she were sealed to a husband, even if only for eternity, should she die in the migration at least her status and relationships in the afterlife would be secure. And during the move west, she could call upon her husband and his family for temporal assistance as well.

Polygamy as practiced in Utah also shows many instances in which wives were taken in order to provide for their temporal support or their eternal salvation, and not for sexual reasons at all. For instance, the most influential leader of women in early Utah, Eliza R. Snow, evidently was married to Brigham Young in name only. She might be characterized as a "married spinster" (or, more properly, "widow"), having the economic security and status of a wife with the freedom of a single woman. In yet another case, John D. Lee married the mother of one of his plural wives only "for her soul's sake" and emphatically did not include her as a wife in a full sense.[44] Thus, polygamy, like adoption, may be considered in important respects as an experiment in social cohesion which is difficult to characterize with existing terminology. Whereas the early adoptionary experiment was soon dropped, polygamy would survive and become a significant social force during nearly forty years of public practice in the Great Basin.

The Public Announcement of Plural Marriage

From the very earliest days of settlement in the Great Basin region, plural marriage was quietly practiced and generally accepted as an integral part of Mormon social life. Not until the belief was openly advocated and defended by the leaders of the Church, however, could the new marriage system be considered to have achieved established status. As long as the practice continued to be secret and was publicly disclaimed, this inconsistency would continue to disturb some members of the Church, and the possibility would remain that polygamy might die out or even be formally discontinued. Thus the public announcement of the Mormon commitment to plural marriage at the special Church conference in Salt Lake City in late August 1852 was an event of the utmost importance. Numerous missionaries were sent out to defend the Church's position to the world. Just as in the past individuals had privately staked their lives and reputations on the new beliefs, so now the Church publicly committed itself to the new marriage and family forms as an integral part of its doctrine and social practice.[45]

It is easy to see why the developing belief and practice of polygamy should have been kept as secret as possible between 1831 and 1847 when the Mormons were living in close contact with a monogamous American society which was extremely hostile toward such variant forms of marriage. But why did the Mormons wait five years after they reached the Great Basin before making public their belief and practice of plural marriage?

The most obvious reason was that the Mormons had difficulties in establishing themselves in the hostile physical environment of the Great Basin and setting up a functioning system of social relations there as well. Survival itself initially took almost all the efforts of most early settlers. Colonization of the region and successful establishment of cohesive group life demanded elaborate organizational efforts in many areas of economic, social, and religious life. Before the Mormons chose to face a hostile world with news of their unorthodox marriage beliefs and practices, it made sense for them to try to put their own house in order so that they could operate from as strong a position as possible.[46]

Another factor was political. The Mormons were eager to gain statehood. Had they been able to achieve such status initially, they would have been much less subject to outside interference. Theoretically, at least, they then could have controlled their own social institutions, including polygamy, much as the Southern states, using a "states' rights" argument, defended their own "peculiar institution" of slavery. The effort to achieve statehood for Utah failed, however, and the region only achieved territorial status in 1850. Moreover, friction between Mormons and gentile appointees sent to the territory, including the famous case of the "runaway judges" in 1851, soon made Mormon polygamy an open secret and removed any advantage of maintaining secrecy about the system.[47]

Finally, the public announcement of polygamy may be seen as serving important internal functions in Utah. The work of Stanley Ivins suggests that periodic revivals of support for polygamy, stimulated by leadership action or as part of a response to external threat, were important in keeping the practice alive.[48] Relatively few polygamous marriages appear to have occurred between the beginnings of the Mormon attempt to establish themselves in the Great Basin in 1847 and the announcement of polygamy in 1852.[49] While this may well have been due to deliberate policy and to the pressure of immediate concerns, it may also have reflected less than enthusiastic support for polygamy among much of the Mormon rank and file. As long as a system about which many were deeply ambivalent was publicly denied, there was always the possibility that the introduction of polygamy might be undermined by disuse and aversion even before it had really begun. The process of institutionalizing polygamy gained support through the completion of a new endowment house in 1851 and the beginning of work on a new temple. Public acknowledgment and defense of the new system, eagerly awaited by its supporters, was an essential final step.[50]

The occasion for the 1852 public announcement of the Mormon belief in polygamy was a special conference of the Church on August 28 and 29 in Salt Lake City. At that time, elders were called to go out on missionary assignments throughout the world. The assignments were difficult, and the men were told that they might last as long as "three to seven years." During that absence from their families, the men were of course expected to maintain strict continence. With typically colorful rhetoric, Heber C. Kimball suggested that Saints might eventually take plural wives as a reward for their renunciation and faithful service in preaching the Gospel, building up the Kingdom of God, and gathering the sheep into the fold: "You are sent out as shepherds to gather the sheep together, and remember that they are not your sheep, they belong to Him that sends you; then do not make a choice of any of those sheep, do not make selections before they are brought home and put into the fold. . . ."[51]

The principle speech in defense of polygamy, later printed under the title "Celestial Marriage," was delivered by Orson Pratt, one of the Twelve Apostles, and the leading intellectual spokesman for the Church. This speech stated, or at least hinted at, every important pro-polygamy argument that would be put forward in the next forty years of public practice of "the Principle." Davis Bitton has said that he can discern "no real *development*" of the Mormon arguments for polygamy in those years. The same themes simply recur with changes of emphasis.[52]

The religious justification for polygamy predominates throughout Pratt's speech and indeed underlies all nineteenth-century Mormon pro-polygamy rhetoric, whether intended for the faithful or for non-Mormon consumption. Pratt began with a lengthy exposition of the Mormon cosmological theory of the stages of human development. Souls began in a pre-existent, "telestial" state before coming to earth. These pre-existent souls were said to be eager to be born into the second, "terrestrial" state, and acquire earthly bodies or "tabernacles." Only by passing through this probationary earthly state could souls progress to the highest, "celestial" world.

Marriage had been ordained by God as a channel by which souls could acquire earthly tabernacles. The first marriage, Pratt declared, was that of Adam and Eve—immortal beings not (initially) subject to death. Human marriages, therefore, ideally should also endure beyond death and through all eternity. Pratt asserted over and over again that the primary object of marriage was procreation, the peopling of this world and other worlds in the hereafter. Polygamy, the blessings of Abraham, Isaac, and Jacob, was a means of raising up a numerous, righteous posterity in the families of the best men, a glorious eternal increase throughout worlds without end.

In addition to the cosmological arguments in favor of polygamy, Pratt dealt with a number of anticipated religious objections to plural marriage. He emphasized that polygamy was not condemned by the Bible. It was practiced under divine sanction in the Old Testament, and was never explicitly disavowed in the New Testament. This fact was not in itself, however, a sufficient justification for the revival of the practice of polygamy by the Mormons. The justification for its present practice was a divine revelation given to Joseph Smith which authorized and indeed commanded Mormons to practice polygamy under special conditions and with special restrictions, as part of the restoration of all things.

The Mormon defense of plural marriage to the outside world was based on the assertion that polygamy was an integral part of Mormon religious belief. Mormons would repeat over and over again, as Pratt did in this sermon, that since the United States Constitution guaranteed "freedom of religion," the government could not justifiably interfere with the Mormon practice of polygamy, which was an essential part of their religion.

Because nineteenth-century Mormons considered polygamy to be inextricably linked to their religious beliefs, they often had difficulty believing that persecution of them by the United States for polygamy *practice* constituted anything more than a roundabout way of attacking their entire religious structure. Even today, many Mormons find it very difficult to understand how profoundly threatened many Americans felt by the existence of a functioning polygamous system within the borders of the continental United States.[53] A recent quantitative analysis by Jan Shipps of attitudes toward Mormons as expressed in American periodical literature between 1860 and 1960 strongly supports the contention that the primary conscious motivation for the nineteenth-century attacks on the Mormons was hostility toward polygamy and other behavior that diverged from American cultural norms, and not toward Mormon religious beliefs as such.[54] Shipps's content analysis shows that there were more objections to polygamy and to the Church's political activities and control than there were to Mormon theology. For many Americans, the question appears to have been to what extent social practices perceived as deeply offensive to public morals could be justified by classifying those practices as part of a religion.

To supplement the religious justification of Mormon polygamy, Orson Pratt in his 1852 speech provided a detailed social defense of plural marriage. This defense was grounded in the perception that even a practice established primarily on religious grounds must also meet human social needs. A special supplement to the *Millennial Star* that printed the minute; of the 1852 conference noted:

> One of the principal faults . . . in the religions of men, is this, they do not reach the social condition, nor meet the needs of the human family; indeed it is the boast of many religious teachers that their religions are "not of this world". . . . The chief excellence of the religion of heaven consists in this, that it meets the needs of man in every condition in which he may be placed, morally, socially, physically, temporally, or spiritually; it blesses him according to his capacity both in this world and in the worlds to come. Time does not comprehend eternity; but eternity comprehends time.[55]

The starting point for the social argument for polygamy put forward by Pratt and so many other Mormons after him was the corrupt and debased state of the wicked external world. Adulteries, fornications, whoredoms, abortion, infanticide, and all manner of evils and irregularities abounded there. Hypocrisy was rampant. Major public figures clucked their tongues in pretended horror at Mormon practices while themselves engaging secretly in extra-marital affairs without any justification or sanction whatsoever.

How is this to be prevented? For we have got a fallen nature to grapple with. It is to be prevented in the way the Lord devised in ancient times; that is, by giving to His faithful servants a plurality of wives, by which a numerous and faithful posterity can be raised up, and taught in the principles of righteousness and truth; and then, after they fully understand those principles that were given to the ancient Patriarchs, if they keep not the law of God but commit adultery and transgressions of this kind, let their names be blotted out from under heaven, that they may have no place among the people of God.[56]

In short, the existing monogamous restrictions were contrary to human nature—or, to be more precise, man's nature. Implicit in this argument was the belief that men were naturally polygamous by inclination. Hence, if the most vigorous and active men were not allowed legitimate and regulated channels to express their sexual drives, the inevitable alternative would be vice and disorder. As a later writer declared:

Man is endowed with polygamic qualities and woman with monogamic ones. This is no question of equality in intelligence or excellence, it turns on uncreated qualities of man's being that enables him to be perfectly one with more than one woman. Woman is not so endowed. She can love many men in a degree, but she can be truly with one only.[57]

Even more importantly perhaps, the primary childbearing function of women was not served by having more than one husband. Men, on the other hand, were capable of having children by a number of different women at the same time, and in a patriarchal and lineage-conscious society, certain knowledge of paternity was an important concern.

What advantages did these formally male-dominated arrangements have to offer to women? Apart from overriding religious commitment, why would many strong-willed and dynamic women have accepted polygamy? Pratt spends little time discussing such questions in this speech. Elsewhere, however, he elaborates on the way in which plural marriage would eliminate the double standard, while allowing every woman the freedom to marry a man of her choice and have children, thereby fulfilling the "measure of her creation." Every woman then would be able to share in the security and status associated with a regularized relationship. Similar arguments based on Biblical grounds, the end of the double standard, and the freedom of choice that plural marriage could provide for women were presented in 1854 in a statement by Belinda Marden Pratt, one of Orson Pratt's plural wives—a statement that has been termed "virtually a classic embodiment of articulate Mormon womanhood's pro-polygamy stance."[58] Later in this chapter some of the ameliorating features that Mormon polygamy held for women and the ways in which it could enable women to develop independence and self-reliance will be discussed more fully.

In conclusion, Orson Pratt emphasized that polygamy could only serve as a means of raising up a righteous posterity and overcoming the evils of a wicked world if practiced under strict controls. Only the President of the Mormon Church held the keys of the sealing power of Elijah and could authorize plural marriages. Any relationship not so authorized, no matter how well conducted, was grievously sinful. This belief is clearly illustrated by a pamphlet defense of polygamy written by Helen Mar Kimball Whitney. She gently but severely criticized a non-Mormon male correspondent who wrote to her for information about the Mormon position on polygamy and to ask her advice concerning his own bigamous relationship. She eloquently defended the divine nature of plural marriage, but at the same time she informed him that he was living in great sin.[59] As always, the issue for Mormons ultimately became one of authority and control. Manuscript evidence from the Brigham Young period shows that every marriage and divorce had to be formally cleared with the President of the Mormon Church, even when the lower levels of the hierarchy made the initial judgment.[60]

The relation of Pratt's intellectual justification of plural and celestial marriage to the actual practice of Mormon polygamy remains somewhat unclear. As in the case of Smith's 1843 revelation, little was said in Pratt's speech about the actual operation of polygamy. Probably the average Mormon was not really concerned about the subtleties of Pratt's reasoning, but was content to know that there *was* a cosmic rationale for the practice. There was considerable latitude for variation in practice within the general limits of the new arrangements.

The Practice of Polygamy

The preceeding section has dealt with the religious and theoretical arguments for polygamy during the early Utah period. Perhaps more interesting is the question of how polygamy worked in practice during this period, how it was related to the reorganization of relations between the sexes, and how it was associated with such larger Mormon concerns as the missionary effort and the settlement of the Great Basin region. Some of these questions have been considered both quantitatively and qualitatively by scholars, including James E. Hulett, Jr., Kimball Young, Stanley Snow Ivins, D. Michael Quinn, and Vicky Burgess-Olson, among others, but the possibilities for the investigation of this rich area of social history still remain largely unexplored.[61] In the remainder of this chapter, the work of these scholars and impressionistic information from diary and journal accounts will be evaluated with particular reference to one early polygamous relationship which illustrates many characteristic features of the early practice of this new form of marriage.

The case in question is that of Jane Snyder Richards, first wife of the Mormon apostle Franklin D. Richards, and herself active in many capacities on behalf of her family and the women of Utah. In 1880 Mrs. Richards spoke at length of her experiences as a plural wife in an interview with a non-Mormon, Mrs. Hubert Howe Bancroft, who was helping her husband collect data on which his monumental history of Utah would be based. Evidently the meeting between the Bancrofts and the Richardses was arranged because it fitted in with the travels of the Richardses and because the Mormon Church felt that this couple would serve as worthy representatives of the best of the Mormon system. The interview with Mrs. Richards, "The Inner Facts of Social Life in Utah," deals sensitively with experiences which span the early development of plural marriage, and indicates the complex adjustments necessary to make polygamy work in even an unusually good relationship. Of Mr. and Mrs. Richards, Mrs. Bancroft wrote:

> He seems remarkably considerate and kind and speaks of her with gratitude and pride, and that he wanted her to enjoy this little visit to California for she has suffered so much affliction and so many hardships. . . . his attentions and kind consideration of her are very marked. She is certainly very devoted to him, and I am imagining this trip and the one they have just returned from East, as a sort of honey-moon in middle life.[62]

Before we focus on some of the characteristic aspects of polygamy illustrated by the Richards case, their relationship and experiences may be briefly sketched. Jane Snyder was born on January 31, 1823, in Pamelia (now Watertown), Jefferson County, New York, one of the younger of eleven children of a prosperous farmer and stock raiser. Her father had not belonged to any church before joining the Mormons; her mother had been a devout Methodist. At age seventeen Jane showed her strength of will when, having decided to join the Mormon Church in mid-winter, she insisted on receiving a proper baptism by immersion out of doors in a lake near her home in La Porte, Illinois.

Franklin D. Richards was born in Richmond, Berkshire County, Massachusetts, on April 2, 1821. The fourth of nine children, he grew up accustomed to hard manual labor on his father's farm, but in his spare time he showed an avid interest in reading and intellectual pursuits. At age ten, Franklin left home to find employment, and for eleven years until his marriage to Jane Snyder in 1842, he traveled from place to place with no fixed abode. After joining the Mormon Church in 1838, Franklin rose rapidly in the hierarchy as he demonstrated his remarkable organizational and proselytizing skills.

Jane Snyder and Franklin Richards met through the Mormon Church. Robert Snyder, Jane's father, was one of Richards's traveling missionary companions. On one occasion, when Franklin become seriously ill, Jane nursed him back to health in the Snyder family home in La Porte. Thereafter, he became a frequent visitor to La Porte, eventually marrying Jane in December 1842. Their first child was born in November 1843, and in the spring of the following year Franklin was called on a mission to England.

As an increasingly prominent member of the Mormon Church, Franklin soon learned of the new belief that polygamous marriage was a necessity for the highest exaltation in the afterlife. About eight months after their marriage, when Jane was in the advanced stages of pregnancy, he approached her about the possibility of taking another wife. She was extremely upset by this suggestion, and probably it was her opposition that caused him to wait more than three years before taking seventeen-year-old Elizabeth McFate as a plural wife in January 1846, eight days after he and Jane had been sealed for "time and eternity" in the new temple.

Though Jane Richards had severe misgivings about polygamy, she found that she and Elizabeth could get along well together. Aware of the awkwardness of the situation, Elizabeth was deferential to Jane and tried hard to be especially considerate and kind. Jane lived in the lower half of the house, while Elizabeth was assigned to the upper story. They divided the labor between them. If Elizabeth did the cooking, for instance, Jane did the washing, and vice versa. To those who were aware of the practice of polygamy, Jane Richards spoke of Elizabeth as Mrs. Elizabeth Richards.

In May 1846, the Richardses reluctantly sold at a great loss the house that they had sacrificed so much to build. Along with the other Mormons who were fleeing the anti-Mormon mobs in Illinois, Jane and Elizabeth Richards began an incredibly arduous journey west. The two women had to assume responsibility for the difficult move, as Mr. Richards was called away on another mission to England at the time of their departure from Nauvoo. During the trip west, Jane Richards gave birth to a second child, who died almost at once. Her first daughter, Elizabeth, whose health had never been robust, then died of "consumption." During the trip Jane Richards was so sick at times that, in her own words, "I only lived because I could not die." Seeing her pitiable state at Winter Quarters, Brigham Young expressed special concern for her, saying that if he had known her situation, he would not have required her husband to go on a mission at that time.

After arriving in Salt Lake, conditions improved somewhat, but life was still extremely hard for Mrs. Richards. In 1849, when her husband Franklin had been back only a short time, he was appointed one of the Twelve Apostles. Shortly thereafter he was called to undertake yet another mission to England, where he was playing an increasingly important role in originating and developing the remarkable Mormon emigration system. Before he left, he was married to Sarah Snyder, a sister of his wife Jane. Sarah's first husband had deserted her and their five children during the trek west, and she was having considerable difficulty managing alone. This appears to have been the principal reason that Franklin Richards married her. Also in 1849, Franklin took Charlotte Fox as a wife.

In the next fifteen years, Franklin received numerous missionary and Church appointments, resulting in long absences from home. Following a highly successful term from 1850 to 1852 as president of the English mission, during which time sixteen thousand people joined the Mormon Church, Richards returned to the Great Basin. He soon took more wives: Susan S. Pierson in 1853, Laura A. Snyder in 1854, Josephine de la Harpe in 1857. After Willard Richards's death in 1854, Brigham Young counseled Franklin to marry some of his uncle's widows, in keeping with the Mormon variant of the Mosiac practice of the levirate. Accordingly, four women, Nancy Longstroth, Mary Thompson, Susannah Bayliss, and Rodah H. Foss, were sealed to Richards by Brigham Young in March 1857.

The various wives saw a wide range of living conditions during the course of their marriages to Franklin Richards. The early years were the hardest. When Franklin was called to go to England in October 1849, Jane Richards was temporarily left in a one-room, floorless, almost roofless house. As soon as possible, she and the other women who married Franklin took steps to improve their condition. To a considerable extent they were left to their own resources, at least until 1869 when Franklin finally returned to live permanently in the Great Basin region after the last of his four important missionary trips to England. Jane Richards eventually established a house in Ogden, while the other wives lived in different Utah cities. In Utah, Franklin Richards continued to call on his enormous reserves of energy and commitment, serving at various times as a judge, as Church Historian, and as President of the Twelve Apostoles. His work still called him away much of the time, but many of the greatest pressures were lifted when he had finally completed his missionary activities abroad.

Jane Richards's interview with Mrs. Bancroft suggests the intense personal commitment and the difficult personal renunciations involved in the practice of polygamy, especially for women, and most especially for the first wife. The new arrangements undercut romantic love for both men and women. Mrs. Richards spoke of her initial "repugnance" when she first learned of polygamy in Nauvoo; how "crushed" she felt when her husband first approached her about the possibility of taking another wife; and of her unhappiness when he married three new wives after returning to Utah from an extended mission to England. Like many other Mormon women, Mrs. Richards was only able to accept polygamy because she convinced herself that it was essential to her salvation and that of her husband. She found that in practice polygamy "was not such a trial as she had feared," and that she and the other wives were able to cooperate effectively. At several points in the interview, Mrs. Richards appeared to be trying to reassure herself that her husband was in fact motivated by a sense of religious duty and not by any lustful desires. Mrs. Bancroft concluded her record of the interview by observing that on the whole it seemed to her that Mormon women considered polygamy

> . . . as a religious duty and schooled themselves to bear its discomforts as a sort of religious penance, and that it was a matter of pride to make everybody believe they lived happily and to persuade themselves and others that it was not a trial; and that a long life of such discipline makes the trial lighter.[63]

Diary and journal entries, the interviews of James E. Hulett, Jr. with individuals from polygamous families, and the recent studies of Vicky Burgess-Olson all support the contention that the principal stated reason of the majority of Mormon men and women for entering into polygamy was religious conviction. Burgess-Olson's quantitative study of early Mormon polygamous families showed that, except for last-and-youngest plural wives—who gave first place to economic concerns and desire for status—first wives, middle wives, and men all gave dedication to religious principle as the primary reason that they entered into the practice of plural marriage.[64] In a moving defense of plural marriage, Helen Mar Kimball Whitney, a plural wife of Joseph Smith and later of Orson F. Whitney, stressed the primary importance of religious renunciation in the service of higher goals as the motivation for entering into polygamy.[65] And the perceptive Annie Clark Tanner, who grew up in a polygamous household and became a plural wife herself, declared:

> I am sure that women would never have accepted polygamy had it not been for their religion. No woman ever consented to its practice without great sacrifice on her part. There is something so sacred about the relationship of husband and wife that a third party in the family is sure to disturb the confidence and security that formerly existed.
>
> The principle of Celestial Marriage was considered the capstone of the Morman religion. Only by practicing it would the highest exalta-

tion in the Celestial Kingdom of God be obtained. According to the founders of the Mormon Church, the great purpose of this life is to prepare for the Celestial Kingdom in the world to come. The tremendous sacrifices of the Morman people can be understood only if one keeps in mind this basic otherworld philosophy.[66]

If the practice of polygamy required great emotional sacrifices from wives, it also demanded significant renunciations from husbands who took on the responsibility of plural wives. The fact that the successful practice of polygamy demanded almost as many renunciations from men as from their wives is illustrated by the experience of Franklin D. Richards. Like other Mormon polygamists studied by Quinn and Burgess-Olson, he was of above average Church and economic status. As a result, he was frequently away from home, either overseas or in difficult assignments in the Great Basin region. Mrs. Richards noted that her husband was away on missions for ten of their first fifteen years of married life. During those extended periods of separation, both Mr. and Mrs. Richards were involved in demanding activities in support of various aspects of the building up of the Mormon kingdom, she largely on the home front and he in the mission field.

Like other leading polygamists, Mr. Richards found that when he returned home he was faced with complex problems of family management that made the expression of romantic love rather difficult. He had to try to avoid favoritism and make an equitable division of his time, money and affections in order to maintain family harmony. According to Mrs. Richards, even her husband's most sincere efforts to treat his wives equally led to frustration and heartache. Even with the best intentions, individuals who had been socialized to monogamous norms found the transition to new patterns of relationships in polygamy difficult.

The diary and journal entries of Mormon men reflect the problems of maintaining impartiality in polygamous families. Male accounts almost never refer to their feelings about their wives, but usually simply give factual information such as "Went to town with Susan." While it is true that men are often less likely than women to record personal emotional reactions in diaries and journals, there is a striking tendency on the part of Mormon men to avoid including such evidence.[67] The omission of personal reactions is probably not accidental. Diaries and journals might some day be read by various wives and children, and it would not do to show any trace of favoritism.[68] Probably the extreme bitterness of some inheritance fights over the estates of polygamists and the embarrassment of Mormons concerning such fights can be traced to the eruption of previously suppressed hostilities or frustrations.[69]

A major result of these sorts of renunciations by both men and women who "lived the Principle" was the sublimation of their sexual impulses into the arduous group enterprise of settling Utah and building up Zion in the wilderness. Men and women were repeatedly enjoined to love their spouses only insofar as their spouses loved the Lord and worked to establish his Kingdom on earth.[70] Although Young spent time with his various plural wives, he slept by himself in a separate room, and once observed: "There are probably but few men in the world who care about the private society of women less than I do."[71] Early polygamy can thus be seen as a means of de-sexualizing and redirecting the husband-wife relationship so that relations between the sexes became first and foremost goal-directed. This is not to say that husbands and wives did not show affection for each other, nor that Mormon men and women did not experience normal pleasure in sexual relations. Procreation, however, rather than pleasure for its own sake, must be the primary purpose of sexual activity. It could be argued that in their practice of polygamy, the Mormons "merely carried conventional morality to an extreme."[72]

In view of the sacrifices inseparable from the Mormon practice of polygamy, it is not surprising that this form of marriage appears never to have become very popular with either men or women in the Mormon areas of settlement in the Great Basin region. Based on a sample of more than six thousand prominent Mormon families, Stanley Ivins estimated that at most 15 to 20 percent were polygamous.[73] Using the subsample of 1,784 polygamous men, Ivins found that a majority, 66.3 percent, married only the one extra wife considered necessary to achieve highest exaltation in the celestial kingdom. Another 21.2 percent married three wives, and 6.7 percent took four wives. The remaining fewer than 7 percent married five or more women.[74] One factor which may have contributed to the relatively limited incidence of polygamy was the limited number of available women. At no time in Utah history did the total number of women outnumber the men.[75] Thus, neither the origin nor the survival of polygamy can be explained simply as a means of finding husbands for surplus women. Finally, according to Ivins's figures, the rate of polygamous marriages was always in overall decline after the early 1856–57 peak. Sporadic increases in the rate of plural marrying occurred during times of internal or external crisis. At such times, polygamy became a rallying point for Mormons who wished to demonstrate their loyalty to the Church, but continued exhortation and group pressure appears to have been necessary to sustain the practice.[76]

Though plural marriage might seem less than appealing in retrospect, in context such arrangements can be viewed as part of the subordination of individual pleasure to long-range group goals which underlay Mormon success in the rapid settlement and development of the intermountain West. Leonard Arrington has observed that initially, "Only a high degree of religious devotion and discipline, superb organization and planning, made survival possible."[77] Mormon men, and particularly those leading Mormon men who were most likely to be polygamists, had to be willing and able to move readily on Church assignments as the demands of the group required. By partially breaking down exclusive bonds between husband and wife and by undercutting intense emotional involvement in family affairs in favor of Church business, polygamy may well have contributed significantly both to the success of the long-range centralized plans set in motion at this time and to the rapid and efficient establishment of religious and communal order.

Status Advantages for Women under Polygamy

The practice of polygamy clearly required difficult emotional sacrifices from both men and women, and tended to weaken, though not to eliminate, emotional attachments based on romantic love. Yet the new marriage arrangements did possess positive features which helped to give them staying power. A good polygamous relationship could well be better than a bad monogamous one, and since individuals who entered into polygamy tended to belong to the religious and economic elite, there were important factors working in favor of good polygamous relationships. Kimball Young's impressionistic study of 110 plural marriages led him to conclude that approximately 53 percent were highly successful or reasonably successful, 25 percent appeared moderately successful, and 23 percent experienced considerable to severe conflict.[78] Previous sections have looked at the ways in which polygamy affected men and some of the positive features that it offered them. This section will consider how polygamy affected women—some of the compensatory advantages which it offered them, how they adjusted to its demands, and some features of the arrangements which helped women to develop self-reliance and independence.

The status advantages accruing to plural wives have seldom been considered. Non-Mormon critics of polygamy have almost invariably assumed that women must have felt degraded under plural marriage. There is very little printed or manuscript evidence from internal Mormon sources that would support this view. Life must have held special difficulties for plural wives, but at least until the 1880s, polygamous wives held higher status through association with the most influential men and through the sense of serving as religious and social models for others. Although first wives like Mrs. Richards, who had married with monogamous expectations, often found it difficult to adjust, many other plural wives had different reactions. In some cases a first wife actively encouraged her reluctant husband to take a plural wife so that they could both reach the highest state of exaltation in the afterlife, or for other more pragmatic economic or personal considerations. As part of the attempt to create a cohesive Mormon community, marriages, plural and otherwise, were sometimes arranged between leading Mormon families.[79] Viewed as an honorable and desirable state, plural marriage could give women a sense of pride and importance.

The most important elevation of woman's status under the patriarchal Mormon marriage system, and polygamy in particular, came through the cosmic importance attached to home and family life. Children were highly valued in Utah. Like outside converts, they provided an essential work force to help settle the new land and build up an essentially agrarian economy in Utah. Mrs. Whitney expressed the extreme importance that Mormons placed on childbearing and childrearing:

> Our children are considered stars in a mother's crown, and the more there are, if righteous, the more glory they will add to her and their father's eternal kingdom, for their parents on earth, if they continue righteous will eventually become as Gods to reign in glory. Nothing but this, and a desire to please our Father in heaven, could tempt the majority of Mormon men or women either, to take upon themselves the burdens and responsibilities of plural marriage.[80]

As Susa Young Gates suggested, the woman chooses to "magnify her sphere" as the man does his.[81] In terms strikingly similar to those used by many of their Victorian contemporaries, Mormons stressed the positive and vital social role that women could play in the home and the family—and, by extension, in the larger community, which, in the Mormon case, was generally coterminous with the family. "Polygamy seemed to introduce no outstanding change in how Mormon women viewed themselves in their home role; the family was often treated in the same sentimental tones used by those who lauded the monogamous family."[82]

By emphasizing the mother-child relationship, the Mormons provided a compensatory emotional outlet for women whose husbands were often absent. Mrs. Richards, like many other plural wives, indicated that her primary emotional involvement was with her children, not her husband. Likewise, children of plural wives generally spoke of their descent through the mother rather than through the father, and had a strong tendency to idealize their mothers. Mrs. S. A. Cooks, who became a Mormon despite her aversion to polygamy, told how Heber C. Kimball's wife Vilate had advised an unhappy plural wife that "her comfort must be wholly in her children; that she must lay aside wholly all interest or thought in what her husband was doing while he was away from her" and simply be as "pleased to see him when he came in as she was pleased to see any friend." In short, the woman was advised to maintain an emotional distance from her husband in order to avoid psychic hurt. Mrs. Cooks concluded: "Mrs.

Kimball interested herself very much in the welfare of others' wives and their children to see that there was plenty of homespun clothing etc for all; and set a noble example to others situated as she was."[83] Similar accounts appeared both in Mormon sources and in accounts of critical former Mormons such as Mrs. T. B. H. Stenhouse.[84]

The emphasis on ties of sisterhood between plural wives also served a compensatory emotional function when the husband was absent. Informal female support networks and cooperation among women developed, especially during such crisis periods as those associated with childbirth, economic hardship, and bereavement. Mormon "sister-wives" were often literally blood sisters. Of Burgess-Olson's sample, for instance, 31.2 percent of the polygamous marriages included at least one pair of sisters.[85] Although this type of polygamy was a departure from Old Testament standards and led to erroneous allegations that the Mormons practiced "incest," such arrangements can be defended on practical grounds. If two sisters were married in polygamy, they might be able to adjust to each other more easily than total strangers could. Formal organizational ties between women, which will be discussed below, also developed through the wide-ranging religious, social, and political activities of the independent-minded Relief Society.

The popular semi-novelistic American stereotype of the plural wife in the Mormon "harem" had almost no basis in fact. Casterline has noted that the cohesive Mormon village society provided many positive features for women:

> As in New England colonial families, the Mormon wife seemed to move with relative ease and frequency between home, neighborhood, and church; the Mormon village plan of settlement allowed a variety of social contacts outside the immediate family. Wives were not cloistered or excluded from the larger society as in a harem, although husbands did seem to have a possessive attitude on the issue of their womenfolk associating with Gentiles.[86]

In point of fact, then, the Mormon wife seems to have had at least as much freedom and independence as her typical non-Mormon counterpart of the period.

Women's independence was encouraged in a variety of ways by social conditions in frontier Utah, including the practice of polygamy. With husbands frequently away on Church missions, wives and their children tended to be thrown back on their own resources. Mrs. Richards said that her husband

> . . . was away so much she learned to live comfortably without him, as she would tell him to tease him sometimes; and even now he is away two thirds of the time as she is the only wife in Ogden, so that

she often forgets when he is home, and has even sat down at meals forgetting to call him. She says she always feels very badly about it when it happens, but that he was more necessary to her in her early life.

Mrs. Bancroft concluded: "And yet she is a very devoted wife, and he is remarkably attentive to her. To see them together I should never imagine either had a thought but the other shared."[87]

Other statements corroborated this tendency for polygamy practice to encourage women's independence. After stating that "plural marriage destroys the oneness of course" and that it "is a great trial of feelings," Mrs. Horne noted that the practice got her away from being "so bound and so united to her husband that she could do nothing without him." She became "freer and can do herself individually things she never could have attempted before; and work out her individual character as separate from her husband."[88] Evidently some women were grateful for the freedom from sexual demands made possible by polygamy; Mary J. Tanner noted: "It is a physical blessing to weakly women."[89] And the feisty Martha Hughes Cannon, who was the first woman state senator in the United States and the fourth wife of a polygamist, argued that a plural wife was in a better position than a single wife: "If her husband has four wives, she has three weeks of freedom every single month."[90]

While this might be the kind of "freedom" that some wives would wish to be freed *from,* it does seem that polygamy and the exigencies of the development of the Great Basin region did force women into new roles and helped to break down certain sex stereotypes, at least temporarily. In the absence of their husbands, women and children ran farms and businesses; some early census reports even reported plural wives as "heads of households."[91] Burgess-Olson's sample showed that in polygamous marriages, husbands and wives exercised approximately equal responsibility in financial management, whereas in her monogamous sample, men exercized greater control.[92] By the late nineteenth century, there was a relatively large class of professional women in Utah. Women dominated the medical profession, for instance, and a sizable number worked as teachers and writers.[93]

Brigham Young and early Church leaders recognized the necessity of utilizing women's abilities and talents in establishing and maintaining the community in the hostile, arid environment of the Great Basin. Mormon leaders encouraged education for women from the very early years, as is indicated by the establishment of the University of Deseret as a co-educational institution in 1850.[94] Women voted earlier in Utah than in any other state or territory in the United States, including Wyoming.[95] And, somewhat ironically in view of the non-Mormon idea of the degradation to which polygamy supposedly subjected women, the efforts of Mormon women in the 1870s and 1880s to organize in support of polygamy served to significantly increase their political awareness and involvement.[96]

The Relief Society provided the major channel for women's expression in the Church. Originally founded in 1842 in Nauvoo, the Relief Society was organized by the women of the Church "under the Priesthood after a pattern of the Priesthood,"[97] to support a variety of activities, including charitable work, cultural betterment, and construction of the temple. During the troubled period following Joseph Smith's death, the Relief Society became largely inactive, but with the reestablishment of the Society in 1855 under the leadership of Eliza R. Snow, it went on to play an important role in Utah social and cultural life, including many economically oriented pursuits.

One of the most impressive achievements of Utah women in the late nineteenth century was the publication of the *Woman's Exponent*.[98] Although it was not officially sponsored or financed by the Church, this newspaper—largely managed, supported, and produced by women—served as the major voice for Mormon women's concerns for the life of its publication between 1872 and 1914. The *Exponent* was the second periodical expressly for women to appear west of the Mississippi. A respectable and well-produced periodical, the *Exponent* reflected the literacy and intelligence of its women contributors and designers. The wide-ranging historical and literary concerns of this publication were by no means limited to sectarian matters.

As suggested by its masthead slogan, "The Rights of the Women of Zion, The Rights of the Women of All Nations," the *Woman's Exponent* provided an important forum for the discussion of many problems of "woman's sphere." Expressing an almost feminist outlook at times, the *Exponent* devoted much attention to the universally inequitable treatment of women in politics, education, and the professions. Not even marriage was put forward as an absolute imperative for women. In the *Exponent*'s wide-ranging discussion of issues, only polygamy, then one of the key elements of Mormon self-definition, failed to receive a critique. Overall, the *Woman's Exponent* portrayed Mormon women as individuals of character, intelligence, and high aspirations. It served an important identity-building function and helped to reinforce a sense of pride and unity among women of the Church.

As Gail Casterline summarized:

> The reinstitution of the ancient custom of polygamy may have in its own subtle ways served as a liberating force for women. This may have occurred by default, with restless or dissatisfied plural wives looking for places to direct their energies, or it may have occurred

through the necessity of a wife's supporting her family. Some women may have welcomed polygamy as a great boon as it decreased some of the demands and divided the duties of the wife role, allowing them more time to develop personal talents. By these quirks in its machinery, plural marriage did in some cases provide a working method for women to achieve independence from men.[99]

Divorce and Polygamy in Utah

Despite certain attractive or at least mitigating factors for both men and women, polygamy was obviously more demanding than monogamy. Even under the best of circumstances, it was difficult to develop and sustain good relationships among husband, wives, and children in polygamous families.[100] How did Mormon families deal with the inevitable tensions arising in plural marriages? The studies of James E. Hulett, Jr., Kimball Young, and Vicky Burgess-Olson reveal great differences in the ways conflict situations were managed in both monogamous and polygamous families, but the general rule was to try to deal with problems within the home as much as possible.[101] Jane Richards noted: "It is making confidants of other women in their domestic disturbances that has brought about most of the trouble in polygamy, and the less people gossip, the better off they are."[102] In the practice of polygamy, as in other aspects of social life in Utah, great stress was placed on unity and consensus, and on the avoidance of public expressions of hostility. This emphasis may help to account for the impressive external order and social harmony described by many of the more openminded visitors to Utah in the nineteenth century.[103]

Even with good will and sincere effort, the attempts to salvage a relationship could fail. In such cases, the possibility of separation or divorce still remained. Jane Richards was quite frank in noting, for instance, that when her husband first talked with her in Illinois about the possibility of taking another wife, she told him that he should do what he felt he had to do and that "if she found they [she and the new wife] could not live without quarreling, she should leave him."[104] This never became necessary for her, but she noted that others had taken such steps: "If a marriage is unhappy, the parties can go to any of the council and present their difficulties and are readily granted a divorce."[105] This was deemed better than insisting that a truly unsatisfactory relationship continue.

How representative were Mrs. Richards's informal observations on Utah Mormon belief and practice in the period? How were problems of divorce handled in early Utah, what were the causes and frequency of divorce, and how was divorce related to the inevitable difficulties of establishing a new marriage and social system? Until recently, this topic has remained almost wholly untouched by scholarship. Here only a few preliminary observations will be made and some possible lines for future scholarly investigation will be suggested.

One starting point for understanding this situation is Utah territorial divorce policy, although—as will be seen below—this policy was not necessarily representative of Mormon Church belief or practice. The Utah divorce law of February 4, 1852, was one of the most liberal in the country. For instance, a divorce could be granted not only to a person who "is a resident of the Territory" but also to a person "who wishes to become one." This proviso presumably allowed the Church flexibility in dealing rapidly with converts who had separated from unbelieving spouses and who needed to be integrated as quickly as possible into the new Mormon society. In addition to the usual causes, a divorce could be granted to the plaintiff in cases in which the defendant was guilty of "absenting himself without reasonable cause for more than one year." Liberally interpreted, this provision could be used to terminate unsatisfactory relationships with missionaries who were gone for extended periods of time. Finally, the territorial law contained an omnibus clause allowing divorce "when it shall be made to appear to the satisfaction of the court, that the parties cannot live in peace and union together, and that their welfare requires a separation."[106]

The primary intention of the Utah divorce law was probably to give maximum flexibility to the Church in handling its own affairs. Marriage and divorce, like all other aspects of social life in Utah, were handled primarily through Church courts and procedures. Thus, an understanding of Mormon belief and practice must be based primarily on Church records. As previously indicated, officially the Mormon Church was strongly opposed to divorce. Marriage was viewed in the light of eternity as a vital part of life which embodied the finest aspects of human relationships. Numerous statements by Brigham Young and other early leaders inveighed against divorce, particularly in cases that involved eternal sealings and when requested by the man.[107] Nevertheless, the official stand of Church leaders was highly complex, shaped by the difficult circumstances of settling the Great Basin and building up a new society. It is sometimes difficult to separate rhetoric from actual practice;[108] much further research will be necessary to recover the full picture of the Utah marriage and divorce policy of the Mormon Church.

Speaking at a Church conference in the Tabernacle on October 8, 1861, Brigham Young made a statement which illustrates the complexity of the early Church's position on divorce. Because of the importance of this statement, the relevant portions are given here in full. Brigham Young

. . . then gave some instructions in relation to sealing He said that
there were many men & women who after having been sealed to
each other for time & all Eternity. Came to him for a Bill of Divorce.
& for the sum of 10 dollars he gave them a Bill Because the Lord
permitted it but it was of no use to them. they might Just as well
tear off a Peice of their shirt tail or have a Peice of Blank Paper for
a divorce. But on account of the hardness of their hearts, the Lord
permitted it. as it was in the days of Moses. But there was a way
in which a woman could leave a man lawfully. When a woman becomes alienated in her feelings & affections from her husband, it is
then his duty to give her a Bill & set her free which would be fornication for the man to cohabit with his wife after she had thus become
alienated from him. the children begotten of such a woman would be
bastards in the true Scriptural term of the word Fornication. for the
crime of adultery a woman (& also men) would be stoned to death
and then come up in the morning of the Resurrection & claim all her
rights and Priviledges in the marrage covenant   Also there was another way—in which a woman could leaved man—if the woman
Preferred—another man higher in authority & he is willing to take
her. & her husband gives her up—there is no Bill of divorce required
in the case   it is right in the sight of God. But if he ever after has
any connexion with her. he is then guilty of committing a very great
sin & will be Punished accordingly   If a Man is faithful & Should
his wife leave him & be married to another without his consent there
is no Power in heaven or on Earth that can Prevent him from claiming her in the Resurection.[109]

The intricacies of this remarkable statement can not be fully discussed here, but one point should be emphasized. As I have shown in
detail in a previous article,[110] this statement is virtually a précis of the unusual argument for divorce put forward in the *Peace Maker,* the extraordinary pamphlet defense of polygamy printed under Mormon auspices in
Nauvoo in 1842. That pamphlet argued that the only legitimate "Biblical"
grounds for divorce was "fornication," which was defined as the alienation
of the affections of the wife from her husband. On the other hand, a man
who was dissatisfied with his wife could not legitimately divorce her; his
option in such a case was to take additional wives. Early Utah practice appears to have been similar to that advocated by the *Peace Maker.* Women
had the primary initiative in determining when to terminate a relationship,
while the husband could not easily divorce his wife if she were opposed.
It was also not difficult for a divorced woman to remarry. Thus in Utah,
while men could practice polygamy, easy divorce gave women the opportunity for what amounted to serial polygamy.

Recently recovered records of 1,645 divorces granted during the Brigham Young period (1847–1877) suggest that divorce was relatively more frequent than previously known in Utah. Although these records have not yet been thoroughly analyzed, it appears likely that the bulk of the divorce cases involved plural marriages.[111] D. Michael Quinn's listing of Mormon Church leaders and their wives between 1832 and 1932 also suggests a high divorce rate among polygamists. A simple analysis of his data shows that the 72 Church leaders who practiced plural marriage had a total of 391 wives, with 54 divorces, 26 separations, and 1 annulment.[112] While this might seem a high number of breakups, one must remember that many of these cases involved non-conjugal wives whose marriage ties had been only symbolic. The extent to which the divorce situation in the Great Basin differed from that of other frontier areas is also uncertain. Nevertheless, there is considerable evidence to support Eugene Campbell's conclusion that "a certain looseness" may have existed in the early practice of polygamy. Evidently the Mormon ideal of eternal marriage relationships was not fully realized in practice.

To understand the significance of these data, the question of divorce must be viewed within the larger context of the development of plural marriage and other early Mormon social institutions. There is much evidence that plural marriage never became fully institutionalized during the relatively brief period when it was publicly practiced in Utah. Hulett, one of the earliest serious scholars to study polygamy, commented that he had "expected to find a variety of behavior but not so great a variety."[113] No fully standardized patterns of handling such needs as shelter, food, clothing, and amusement for polygamous families appeared to have developed, although there were some tendencies toward standardization. Hulett argued that Mormon society of the period remained basically monogamous in its norms and expectations and that "except for the broad outlines, the local culture provided no efficient and detailed techniques for control of the polygamous family; each family in a sense had to develop its own culture."[114] Hulett's sample was taken from the period of extreme stress when polygamy was under heavy attack in the late nineteenth century, but Burgess-Olson also found great variability in her sample from the earlier period between 1847 and 1885.[115] Burgess-Olson, however, placed greater emphasis than Hulett on the evolution of polygamy toward regular social forms.

The variations in polygamy practice as well as the tendency toward crystallization of new behavior patterns can be seen in the housing arrangements of Mormon polygamous families. In most long-established polygamous societies there are definite ways of handling housing. Either all wives live under one roof, or all have separate houses, or there is a standardized pattern of changing arrangements for different stages of the marriage and life cycle. Early Mormon social practice in the Great Basin, however, showed almost every conceivable pattern of housing.

> The same family was usually reported as occupying at different periods quarters ranging from the most uncomfortable and primitive to comparatively spacious and well-built houses on farms or in towns. Individual taste and ability determined the kind of houses a man provided for his wives; the preference most usually indicated, but not always achieved, was that each wife should eventually have her own separate house. . . . .[116]

Housing patterns ranged from the rather atypical example of Brigham Young, second president of the Church, who set up most of his wives and children—with one or two exceptions—in two large houses, each with accommodations for a number of wives, to John Taylor, third president of the Church, who eventually established all of his wives in separate houses.[117] There was also considerable variation in many other aspects of Great Basin marriage practice.

The Crusade against Polygamy

The chief reason that the practice of plural marriage never became fully standardized in Utah was that it only existed there a relatively short period of time before the intense anti-polygamy agitation of the late nineteenth century led the Mormon Church to officially discontinue the practice. Prior to the public announcement of polygamy in 1852, the clandestine practice had only contributed indirectly to tensions between the Saints and the outer world. After that date, however, hostility toward the Saints increasingly focused on polygamy. The first serious anti-polygamy movement began to develop in the mid-1850s, and may partially be blamed for the invasion of Utah by federal troops in 1857. The Civil War and Reconstruction refocused the nation's attention on more pressing matters and gave the Saints a breathing spell, but by the late 1870s and early 1880s, an intense and sustained campaign against Mormon polygamy was under way. This pressure finally caused the Saints in 1890 to declare officially that they would sanction no more plural marriages. Thus polygamy had only 20 to 25 years of relative peace during which to develop and become standardized.[118]

The very existence of polygamy posed a severe cultural threat to many Americans. It was one thing for "lesser breeds without the law" in Asia or Africa to practice such "primitive" and "backward" customs; it was a very different thing for white Anglo-Saxons from Protestant backgrounds to successfully introduce and establish such a practice within the Republic itself. Polygamy in America, practiced by Americans, was much too close to home for comfort. The very existence of polygamy seemed to threaten the validity of the monogamous Victorian family ideal and the nature of the social order. As early as 1856, the Republican Presidential platform linked slavery and polygamy together as "twin relics of barbarism." A year later, in 1857, a series of misunderstandings and political blunders, exacerbated by exaggerated stories of polygamy, led President Buchanan to send twenty-five hundred federal troops into Utah to put down supposed disloyalty. And in 1862, a largely ineffectual anti-bigamy law was passed in Congress, the first direct legislative attack on polygamy to take place at the federal level.

Throughout this period, a new genre of anti-polygamy novels and "true stories of life under polygamy" developed, written primarily by people who had never been near Utah. Although this literature is of little value in describing how polygamy actually was practiced, it does provide insights into the fears and concerns of the larger society. As Leonard Arrington and Jon Haupt have suggested, this anti-polygamy literature is very similar to the anti-Catholic and anti-foreign writings of the antebellum period. It relies heavily on stereotyped characters and seems to constitute a socially sanctioned Victorian form of pornography, pandering to sadistic and prurient interests which were otherwise taboo. For example, looking at one anti-polygamy novel from the 1850s entitled *Boadicea, The Mormon Wife,* Arrington and Haupt observe that it might more appropriately be subtitled "Death Scenes in Utah," for

> . . . in the short space of 97 pages, 17 persons perish. Some are shot, others drowned, some beaten to death, others strangled, one poisoned, one hanged, one beaten with a whip handle, three crushed by a falling rafter, and one succumbs from a broken heart. In addition, there are assorted thrashings, attempted poisonings, successful abductions, and miscellaneous tortures, all of which clutter the lavishly-illustrated pages until the reader is convinced that these tales of Mormon atrocities compare favorably with those told about the German Army during World War I.[119]

Another popular book by a "Maria Ward," entitled *Female Life in Utah,* which went through numerous printings in the nineteenth century, should, Arrington and Haupt suggest, be subtitled "Utah as Torture-Chamber."

> There are no less than thirty-four references to and graphic descriptions of women being physically tortured—with red-hot irons, with tomahawks, with whips, with ice. There are so many examples of the

principle woman character wearing men's clothing and "firing away"
at cowardly males and whimpering females that one suspects Mrs.
Ward had an overpowering desire to dress up like a man and whip
females.[120]

Of course not all the anti-Mormon writings were this crude, but the same
loathing toward polygamy and the Mormon Church's autocratic power
permeates all but a handful of relatively "objective" writings from the
mid-1850s through the turn of the century.

Although a strong current of external hostility toward Mormon polygamy had developed as early as the 1850s, the twenty or so years from the
early 1860s through the late 1870s stand out as an interlude of relative
tranquility, during which time polygamy was quietly introduced and practiced throughout Mormon areas of the intermountain West. In many small,
isolated towns, plural marriage became accepted as a normal part of the
Mormon way of life. Sons and daughters of polygamists came of age and
in some cases entered into the practice themselves.

During the late 1870s, however, changing conditions in the larger society once again led to an upsurge of public hostility toward polygamy.
With the Civil War and Reconstruction over, a rapidly expanding industrial and urban society turned to new crusades against social evils that
were seen as threatening the family, including prostitution and vice, the
liquor traffic, and, of course, polygamy. This time opposition to polygamy
was not limited to a handful of writers, but was effectively organized by
women's groups, religious leaders, politicians, social reformers, and a host
of other individuals. In 1882, the mounting pressures led the United States
Congress to approve the Edmunds Act, which provided severe penalties
both for polygamy and for "unlawful cohabitation." Anyone with a living
husband or wife who subsequently married another was declared guilty of
polygamy and could be sentenced to a $500 fine and five years in prison.
The law also made it impossible for anyone practicing polygamy to perform jury service, to vote, or to hold public office. The Utah Commission
appointed to enforce the law disenfranchised more than twelve thousand
Saints in Utah during its first year in existence.

This legislative and judicial crusade against polygamy created great
problems for Mormons. To avoid arrest and conviction for polygamy,
otherwise law-abiding men were forced to "go on the underground"—that
is, to go into hiding and move frequently from place to place to escape the
federal marshals who were pursuing them. An eleborate network of hide-
outs in homes, barns, and fields were developed to serve as way stations
for fleeing polygamists. Family life was disrupted. With husbands away,
wives and children tended farms and managed family businesses. Women
were sometimes forced to testify in court against their husbands. Church

business became difficult to transact since most Mormon leaders had gone on the underground to avoid arrest.[121]

When all these measures failed to cause the Church to give up polygamy, Congress in 1887 passed the Edmunds-Tucker Act, an astonishingly harsh law which seemed designed to destroy not only polygamy and the Church's influence in Utah political life, but even the Church itself. The act officially dissolved the Church of Jesus Christ of Latter-day Saints as a legal corporation and directed the attorney general to take steps to achieve that end. The Church was required to forfeit to the United States all property in excess of $50,000. The attendance of witnesses at polygamy trials was declared compulsory, and the testimony of a wife against her husband in such cases was declared legal. Woman suffrage was abolished in Utah. No one could vote, serve on a jury, or hold public office unless he signed an oath pledging obedience to and support of the anti-polygamy laws. Children born of plural marriages more than one year after the act was passed were disinherited.

These and other provisions of the Edmunds-Tucker Act created a severe crisis for the Mormon Church. But the final blow came in May 1890 when the United States Supreme Court held in a 5 to 4 decision that the government's actions under the new law had been constitutional. Whereas in 1879, in the earlier Reynolds case, the Supreme Court had upheld attacks on polygamy practice by ruling that constitutional guarantees of religious freedom related only to belief and could not be used as a justification of behavior declared to be illegal by the government, in 1890 the Court went further and sanctioned actions that effectively threatened the destruction of the Mormon religion itself. Faced by a situation in which the Church could not own land or effectively conduct its affairs; in which most of the leaders of the Church were disenfranchised, in prison, or in hiding; and in which no legislative or judicial recourse remained, Wilford Woodruff, the President of the Mormon Church, issued his famous Manifesto on September 25, 1890. In response to press reports that plural marriages were continuing to be sanctioned, Woodruff stated simply that the Mormon Church had already halted the teaching of plural marriage and was not allowing anyone else to enter into the practice. He further declared:

> Inasmuch as laws have been enacted by Congress forbidding plural marriages, which laws have been pronounced constitutional by the Court of the last resort, I hereby declare my intention to submit to those laws, and to use my influence with the members of the Church over which I preside to have them do likewise. . . .
>
> And I now publicly declare that my advice to the Latter-day Saints is to refrain from contracting any marriage forbidden by the laws of the land.[122]

Privately, among his close associates and other Saints, Woodruff discussed the difficult situation in which the Church was placed and why he was acting as he was. He said that plural marriage remained an eternally valid principle, but that since to continue to practice it at that time might lead to the destruction of the Church, polygamy practice must be temporarily discontinued by the Saints. The first priority of faithful Saints must be to preserve the Church so that it would be able to preside over the forthcoming Millennium. In the meantime, the Lord could not require the Saints to fulfill a command that had become impossible to practice because of the persecution of their enemies.[123]

These arguments and the authority of the Church were sufficient to convince the Saints to accept a change in the practices to which they had been so firmly committed publicly for nearly four decades. On October 6, 1890, this support was made explicit when a general conference of the Mormon Church approved the Manifesto, thereby formally committing the Church to stand behind its President. While the promulgation of the Manifesto and its formal acceptance by members of the Church did not answer all the questions of the anti-polygamist forces, it did effectively defuse the most severe of the external pressures on the Saints. During the next two watershed decades, the Mormon Church took further steps to radically change its internal organization and improve its relations with the United States government. Not only did the Church increasingly restrict polygamous relationships that had been established before the 1890 manifesto, but it also moved to formally withdraw from participation in politics as a monolithic force and to cooperate in other ways with the larger society.[124]

The promulgation of the Manifesto in 1890 certainly marked an important shift in Mormon policy, but it also left many questions unanswered, both for the Saints and for the general public. Perhaps the most important of these questions was whether existing polygamous marriages would be broken up. Crusaders against polygamy had long said that they were attacking polygamy in order to preserve the family, yet ironically if they broke up existing polygamous relationships they would, in fact, be disrupting many previously stable families. If polygamy appeared certain to die out eventually anyway, did it make any sense to require that polygamous husbands reject their plural wives and children? In general, the answer was no. Once federal officials were convinced of the Saints' sincerity in ultimately moving away from the practice of plural marriage, they showed considerable leniency in granting amnesty to convicted polygamists and in refraining from rigidly enforcing the laws against plural families that had already been established. Polygamy could be tolerated for a time on a limited scale so long as its eventual extinction seemed certain.

Thus the official Mormon experiment with plural marriage began to draw to a close. Although an underground of disaffected Mormons who supported polygamy would continue to function secretly without Church sanction to the present day, most Mormons gradually came to accept the new standards. The Church showed its continuing vitality by finding new ways of expressing its underlying family ideals in monogamous practice and by creating complex new institutional means of achieving group identity and cohesion. What remained was the memory of the extraordinary commitment and dedication that had accompanied this remarkable Mormon effort to introduce new marriage and family patterns in nineteenth-century America.

VI

Radical Products of the Great Revivals
Reflections on Religion, the Family,
and Social Change

> Revivals breed social revolutions. All the social irregularities reported
> in the papers followed in the train of revivals; and so far as I know,
> all revivals have developed tendencies to such irregularities. . . .
> A worldly wise man might say, that [these facts] show that revivals
> are damnable delusions, leading to immorality and the disorganization
> of society. I should say they show that revivals, because they are
> divine, require for their complement a divine organization of so-
> ciety. . . .
> It is notable that all the socialisms that have sprung from revivals
> have prospered. They are utterly opposed to each other [yet] however
> false and mutually repugnant the religious socialisms may be in their
> details, they are all based on the theocratic principle—they all recog-
> nize the right of religious inspiration to shape society and dictate the
> form of family life.
>
> John Humphrey Noyes[1]

The experiences of the early Shakers, Oneida Perfectionists, and Mormons
raise provocative questions about the relationship of millennial religious
movements to radical social change. This concluding chapter will present
a comparative analysis of some of these questions, highlighting the ways in
which each of these groups was related to the larger American society and
to each other. The introductory section will briefly consider the origin and
development of these ventures, including their complex and often ambivalent connections with their Puritan and antebellum American roots. The
next four sections will focus on the new relationships between men and
women that were established in each of these communities. Special attention will be given to the way sex-role reorganization was related to each
group's attitudes toward religious authority, economic organization, sexual

expression, and ideals of the family, motherhood, and childrearing. The last three sections will analyze the reasons for conflict between these groups and the outer society, the causes of decay or discontinuance of their marriage systems, and the broader issue of how such expressions of intense religious commitment affect society.

In order to understand these three groups, one must grasp a basic paradox: underlying these efforts at radical social change was an essentially conservative religious impulse. In each case, these millennialists were deeply disturbed by the social and religious disorder around them. To overcome that disorder they sought to institute major changes which would subordinate the individual and his concerns to larger group goals. These group goals were seen as the reflection of a higher, divine power whose will was to be realized on earth. The *specifics* of the new religious and social patterns in each of these groups were radically different from those of the outer society, and hence resulted in persecution. The *reason* that the new patterns were introduced, however, was to establish a secure, conservative synthesis that would restore the relation of individual and community as an orderly, harmonious whole.

Socially and intellectually, these efforts had roots in the Protestant Reformation, particularly its English and American Puritan expressions. The Shakers, Oneida Perfectionists, and Mormons shared with their Puritan forebears a concern to restore the faith of early Christianity, a stress on the priesthood of all believers, and a belief that the family was a microcosm of society, the model for the larger social order. The English Puritans had taken an essentially activist approach to the social turmoil of their day, rejecting monastic withdrawal from the world, but demanding an almost monastic degree of commitment to the expression of religious ideals in daily life. The antebellum millennialists, on the other hand, like the American Puritans, temporarily withdrew from the world in almost monastic fashion, yet they too sought within their communities to reunite religious and social life in a new, holistic synthesis.[2] Both the Puritans and the antebellum millennialists struggled with the tensions between the desires of the individual and the demands of the group, seeking to go beyond an exclusive reliance on individual Bible interpretation to achieve a broader religious and social consensus.

The catalysts for the creation of these millennial groups were the powerful emotional, intellectual, and visionary experiences of their prophet-founders. Ann Lee, John Humphrey Noyes, and Joseph Smith all struggled with special intensity to come to terms with their own religious and sexual problems. Unlike most individuals, who simply attempt to reach an accommodation with the larger world, these prophetic figures came to the conclusion that the world itself was wrong and that their own experiences provided a universally valid model for setting the world straight. Possessed by this extraordinary and compelling idea, unable or unwilling to work within what they considered to be an unstable or inconsistent framework, these individuals sought to create new value systems of their own and "to initiate, both in [themselves] as well as in others, a process of moral regeneration."[3] By attracting a following to their ideals and life style, they felt that they had thereby validated their life and message.

The men and women who joined these three millennial groups shared many of the concerns of their prophet-founders with the social and intellectual disorder surrounding them, but their approach to that disorder and their attitudes toward authority were much more conventional. The followers, too, wanted answers, but they looked to others to provide those answers. In another time, many of these individuals would probably have been indistinguishable from their contemporaries, happy simply to fit into the existing social order and to accept both its strictures and rewards. During the rapid changes of the antebellum period, however, many otherwise normal individuals found themselves drifting and sought to discover a new framework of meaning for their lives. Why such seekers should have turned to the Shakers, Oneida Perfectionists, or Mormons, rather than to other groups, is open to question, but it is clear from the record that the millennial approach did have considerable direct and indirect appeal during this period.[4]

Thus, these three movements were characterized by their unusually intense concern to overcome perceived social disorder, their intellectual and social roots in the Protestant Reformation, initial leadership by charismatic or prophetic figures, and a membership which may not have been significantly different from the generality of Americans of their period. The following pages will move beyond the question of origins to present a comparative analysis of how these groups reorganized social and religious life and how they were related to the larger American society before the Civil War.

Women and the Structure of Religious Authority

The ways in which sex roles were restructured in the antebellum Shaker, Oneida Perfectionist, and Mormon communities may be used to illustrate the complex relationship of such communities to the larger society, as well as the powerful internal dynamic leading to change within each group. Perhaps the single issue that most clearly reflects the attitudes toward sex roles within these communities is their approach to religious authority—for religious authority ultimately underlay all other aspects of life within these groups.

The larger society to which these millennial movements responded was undergoing important religious changes during the antebellum period. With the elimination of state support for churches after the Revolutionary War, religious groups had to develop new, revivalistic techniques to attract members. Dramatic preaching styles, mass meetings, exhortations to total commitment, and a variety of other innovative methods were utilized as part of a vigorous competition for new members. Women were especially important in this effort. They constituted a majority of those attending the revival meetings and they were among the most fervent in seeking the conversion of their family and friends. The more traditional churches had generally not allowed women to preach or to participate fully in worship, but revivalists such as Charles Grandison Finney strongly encouraged innovations such as allowing women to pray in mixed public meetings. A few women even became itinerant evangelists. Although most revivalist groups still formally held that women should be subordinate to men, they also provided new institutional means by which women could begin to participate more actively in the larger society. Moral reform groups, missionary organizations, Bible and tract societies, and a variety of other groups all depended heavily on women, and indirectly encouraged them to become involved in the affairs of the society around them.[5]

The Shakers, Oneida Perfectionists, and Mormons all developed out of this broader revivalistic ferment, but they reacted in different ways to the increasing participation of women in religious life. The Shakers, most extreme of the revivalistic groups, both in their ecstatic worship services and in their insistence on celibacy, were also the most extreme in giving women positions of formal equality to men at all levels of their religious structure. Ann Lee, who founded the Shakers, was a woman, and women served as supreme head of the Society at several later stages of its development. Even God, the Shakers believed, was dual in nature, embodying a complementary and equal expression of both male and female elements. Celibacy, the most distinctive feature of Shaker life, was the practice that removed the burden of childbearing and freed women for full participation in all aspects of the religious system. Although no feminist movement as such existed when the Shakers first came to America, the Shakers were sensitive to many issues that would later attract feminists, particularly the sexual exploitation of women by men. Shaker publications, from the earliest hymn books to the later histories such as the one written by Anna White and Leila S. Taylor, stressed the concern for sexual equality as a key part of the effort to attract new members, and numerous capable women did choose to make religious careers with the Shakers.[6]

The Oneida Community, influenced both by Finneyite revivalism and by the Shakers, retained much of the Shaker liberalism with respect to the participation of women in religious life. Although John Humphrey Noyes was the patriarchal head and final authority at Oneida, he encouraged women to participate actively in all aspects of religious and social life in the Community. Noyes did not even exclude the possibility of women receiving revelations or exercising positions of supreme leadership in a religious group, although, all other things being equal, he felt that men should normally fill those roles.[7] Like the Shakers, Noyes believed in a dual Godhead, but unlike the Shakers, his Godhead was composed of the Father and the Son, with the Son subordinate to the Father much as, Noyes argued, women should be subordinate to men. Despite this formal belief in male dominance, Noyes's main concern was not male-female patterns of authority, but his own primacy in leadership. So long as his final authority was acknowledged, he was prepared to delegate power flexibly to both men and women, primarily on the basis of capacity rather than gender. Complex marriage, communal childrearing, and other Community practices helped free women to join in the religious activities at Oneida. While Noyes was sympathetic with many of the concerns of antebellum feminists, he differed with them over the means by which the restrictions and inequities that women faced should be removed. Disturbed by feminist stridency and use of conflict in trying to rectify inequities between the sexes, Noyes felt instead that cooperative solutions should be sought which would serve the interests of all parties.[8]

The Mormons, although they also made changes in women's religious status, were, of the three groups, the most heavily male-dominated and the closest to the attitudes of the outer society about women's role in religion. The Mormon Priesthood as established by Joseph Smith served as the ultimate basis for all religious and social authority and was held solely by men. A woman could only participate in the Priesthood indirectly by marriage to a worthy man and by participating in women's Church auxiliaries such as the Relief Society. Whereas the Shakers actively encouraged women to take a leading role in religious government, and John Humphrey Noyes admitted that women could head a religious group under exceptional circumstances, Joseph Smith flatly denied that women could ever be the legitimate leaders of a religious organization.[9] Polygamy, based in part on a modification of the Old Testament patriarchal marriage system, also underscored the importance of male leadership in religious life. Interestingly, the Mormons, like the Shakers and Oneida Perfectionists, also had a version of a dual Godhead combining both male and female elements. In the Mormon view, God was an exalted man—a man who had progressed to divinity, accompanied by his wife (or wives), who had been similarly exalted. Woman's greatest role was in childbearing and childrearing, so that eventually a great patriarchal family could be established, linking the generations throughout time and eternity. In view of this outlook, it is not surprising that, at least in the religious sphere, the Mormons had little in common with antebellum feminists, but tended to attract women who held a more traditional conception of male-female authority patterns.

These three groups thus represent a range of divergent responses to the revivalistic religious ferment of their day. At one extreme were the Shakers, who gave women total equality in the religious government of their societies. At the other extreme were the Mormons, who formally excluded women from positions of authority in religious affairs. In the middle, as always seeking to maintain a balance between extremes, was John Humphrey Noyes, in certain respects both a conservative and a radical with regard to women's participation in religious life. In short, while revivalism worked as a catalyst helping to break down the old order and make possible the establishment of new authority patterns between the sexes, revivalism as such did not determine *which* new pattern would ultimately be adopted.

Women and Economic Life

Economic life was also in rapid flux during the antebellum period, placing special strains on relations between the sexes. The decades after the end of the Revolutionary War marked the beginning of rapid westward expansion, as well as the first stages of industrialization, with all the attendant challenges and problems. Among the most important structural changes in the economy were the decline of self-sufficient farming, the virtual disappearance of household manufacturing of goods such as cloth, and the growing obsolescence of independent artisans and the apprenticeship system. Society was becoming increasingly complex. Men's and women's economic activities increasingly diverged, with men participating more and more in the larger market economy, while women were increasingly relegated to the home, precisely at the time when many of the home's strictly economic functions were being taken over by the larger society. Although economic self-sufficiency had never been absolute, during the antebellum period all aspects of American life began to be tied to the market economy and to be subject to cycles of boom and bust such as the Panic of 1837. With the changing economic demands on both men and women, there was a need for adjustment to new conditions.[10]

The communitarian impulse that expressed itself in the Shakers, Oneida Perfectionists, and Mormons can be seen as part of an attempt to deal with the economic instabilities arising from unbridled competition in the new market economy. A cohesive group was necessary to provide security from an uncertain world, but once again the three groups developed very different patterns for reorganizing male and female economic roles within their new economic orders. Somewhat paradoxically, the Shakers, although the most egalitarian in dealing with religious authority, were the most traditional in the economic roles that they assigned to men and women. Within their communal system, women did typical women's work—cooking, sewing, cleaning, washing—while men did traditional male tasks in the fields, shops, and similar locations. Why was the most untraditional sexual division of religious authority associated with the most traditional economic relations between the sexes? There are a number of possible explanations. The Shakers originated in the late eighteenth century before the full force of industrialism had begun to change the economic relations between men and women. Thus, once traditional economic roles were institutionalized within Shaker communities, those roles, like the old-fashioned Shaker dress styles, may have been resistant to change. Again, the effort to institutionalize new authority relations in religious leadership had been a difficult, decade-long process, which may have left Shaker leadership with little energy or desire to try to change relations between the sexes in another area. Moreover, the Shakers apparently never viewed female economic activities as inherently inferior to those of men or as inherently exploitative—with the one exception of the disabilities associated with sexual relations and childbearing. In short, the Shakers' main quarrel was with the exploitative consequences of sexual intercourse and with the individualistic economic system, not with any particular division of work roles by sex.[11]

In contrast to the Shakers, the Oneida Community was both in theory and in practice one of the most radical ventures ever attempted in America to reorganize relations between the sexes in economic life. Noyes's ideology called for an end to all sexual distinctions in economic life that were not intrinsic—and there were very few distinctions that he considered intrinsic. He encouraged men and women to work together in vital and rewarding labor; he allowed some women to serve in positions of authority over men; and he let men or women do almost any kind of work they wished to do and could handle effectively. Women could and did, for example, work in the machine shop, while men could and did knit in public meetings, sew their own clothes, and do other work traditionally associated with women.[12] It should be noted that this attempt to avoid sex bias was in some respects a bias toward a single male standard—as in the case of the Bloomer outfit for women, which Noyes instituted in part to encourage woman to become what she ultimately ought to be, "a *female man*."[13] (Emphasis in original.) On the other hand, in many instances differences in sexual reactions were recognized and encouraged. In general, Noyes's main concern in the economic sphere appears to have been to overcome the instabilities and uncertainties encountered in the outer society by creating a cohesive Community home, in which the interests of all could be effectively met. By freeing women from the burdens of unwanted procreation and childcare, Noyes sought to make possible their full participation in the whole range of Community activities.

If the highly traditional economic roles for women in the sexually egalitarian Shakers may appear puzzling, the extremely varied and flexible economic roles for women in the patriarchal, male-dominated Utah Mormon society also demand explanation. Although it is true that the primary economic role for women in frontier Utah remained that of childbearer and childrearer—a vital function for a group attempting to settle and populate an arid and inhospitable new region—women also engaged in an unusually wide range of other activities. They ran farms and retail establishments, dominated the medical profession, participated in numerous economic and social support activities through the Relief Society, and organized, published, and circulated a distinguished women's newspaper, the *Woman's Exponent*. Why did this occur? In the first place, Brigham Young was well aware of the important economic role that women could play in helping to establish a new society in frontier Utah. He therefore sought to make use of women's talents in every possible way. Furthermore, if somewhat ironically, polygamy itself may have helped to free some women for a broader range of activity in society. In many cases, women were required to act independently as the "head of the household" during the temporary absence of a husband, while in other cases, cooperation between plural wives helped free some women from the constraints of the housewife role so that they could engage in other types of work. Although no ideological rationale supported this extension of women's activities, the requirements of life in early Utah allowed, encouraged, and in some cases forced, women to engage in many careers besides that of wife and mother.[14]

These three groups thus show strikingly different responses to the role of women in economic affairs. Though they all shared a communitarian concern to overcome disruptive economic individualism, their sex-role divisions in economic life do not correspond neatly to ideological expectations. The most sexually egalitarian group with regard to religious authority, the Shakers, did next to nothing to modify the traditional economic activities of women, while the more male-dominated Oneida Perfectionists and Mormons made significant changes in women's economic role. Circumstances, not ideology, seem most important in explaining revisions in economic relations between the sexes in these three groups.

Women and Sexual Expression

Sexual expression was yet another aspect of life that was changing for both men and women in the antebellum period. Sex outside of marriage had always been condemned, of course, but in the decades immediately preceding the Civil War, earlier, relatively unrestrictive attitudes toward sexual expression *within* marriage were increasingly giving way to the thoroughgoing restrictiveness that has usually been labeled "Victorian." The reformer Sylvester Graham, who suggested that married couples should have intercourse only once a month (and then only with the intention of procreation), was by no means the most extreme of the popular advisers of the bedroom. The loose-fitting Empire-style dresses worn by middle- and upper-class women during the Napoleonic era were replaced by the restrictive, long-skirted and tightly-corseted Victorian costume which would persist for nearly a century. And the "cult of true womanhood" popularized a view of women as purer than men, free from sexual desires, and responsible for keeping in check the lascivious impulses of the naturally carnal male. While these ideals and styles may not have fully reflected the actual sexual practice of the time, demographic evidence, including a falling birth-rate prior to the widespread availability of artificial means of contraception, suggests that these ideas about sexual self-control were indeed having an effect upon overt behavior. Many individuals appear to have seen the effort to impose control on sexual relations as a part of the larger movement to restore order in a fragmented and fragmenting society.[15]

The Shakers, Oneida Perfectionists, and Mormons were deeply influenced by these new ideals of sexual self-control, and in fact accentuated such concerns within their communities. Shaker celibacy, for example, could be viewed as almost a parody of the literature of marital and sexual advice. The Shakers carried the implications of this literature to their extreme logical conclusion. If sex was basically a dangerous impulse and even in marriage should be expressed only once a month, then why not go further and eliminate it altogether? This was, essentially, what the Shakers did. They sought to completely extirpate all baser, carnal impulses, and replace them with higher, more spiritual ones. Contact between the sexes was restricted and carefully controlled, even in the most minute aspects of daily life. Probably this thoroughgoing separation of the sexes in Shaker communities would not have been workable if the lively meetings for group worship, with singing and dancing, had not provided a means of releasing sexual energies and sublimating such impulses in the service of the group. Perhaps, too, the more vigorous participation of women in such activities may have served, in part, to compensate for the fact that their work was more restricted and sedentary than was that of the men, who could often engage in physically demanding activity in the out-of-doors. Extreme revivalism of the sort found in the Shakers has usually been associated with correspondingly great efforts to hold troublesome sexual impulses in check. In the case of a man such as Issachar Bates, who traveled more than thirty-eight thousand miles, largely on foot, to spread the message of Shakerism, immense energies were channeled into service for the good of the group. And within the more stable, functioning Shaker communities, celibacy helped to maintain an order and cohesion that would have been impossible if family demands and the complications of childbearing had divided the loyalties of men and women.[16]

The Oneida Perfectionists, somewhat surprisingly, illustrate Victorian concerns for control and ambivalence toward sexuality even better than do the Shakers. Although outsiders typically fantasized about the "licentious" behavior that supposedly went on in this "free love" colony, in reality complex marriage at Oneida was associated with control mechanisms that might appear even more restrictive in some respects than Shaker celibacy. Romantic liaisons were systematically broken up; group criticism sessions dealt bluntly with any sexual behavior that did not conform to Community norms; and birth control was accomplished by the highly restrictive and demanding practice of "male continence" or *coitus reservatus*. Although this practice did allow an initial sexual coupling, it denied the full completion of the sex act, as well as any other compensatory sexual outlets, including masturbation. Noyes declared that his system simply required that self-control be exercised one step further in the sexual process than did the Shakers; the Shakers did not allow sexual intercourse at all, while he allowed couples to come together, but did not permit full sexual consummation, except when children were desired.[17] The tightness and effectiveness of these controls at Oneida may be judged from the fact that during 21 years from 1848 to 1869 when male continence was the sole sanctioned method of birth control, at most 31 accidental births took place in a community of approximately 200 adults exchanging partners as often as twice a week.[18] Since manuscript materials dealing with male and female responses to this extraordinary practice have been destroyed or are not generally available at present, it is difficult to know what the reactions to male continence were, but certainly this system did not fit the popular notion of "free love." While it is true that Noyes could wax positively lyrical as he declared that his God was married to matter and committed to human enjoyment of the full wonders of this exquisitely lovely world, he could also assert, speaking of male continence, that "it is the glory of man to control himself and the Kingdom of

Heaven summons him to self-control in ALL THINGS."[19] In the final analysis, Noyes's underlying goal was similar to that of the Victorians— he wanted to help his followers internalize new values of self-control rather than to depend on external social sanctions to direct their behavior.

Mormon sexual attitudes, like those at Oneida, are at least as complex and ambivalent as those of the outer society. On the one hand, the Mormons not only encouraged sex for procreation, they in fact considered such relations one of the chief ends and glories of life. Polygamy, for example, was justified in large measure as a means of allowing the best men to have the largest families and the most influence, both in this life and in eternity. On the other hand—and in contrast to the popular view of polygamy as licentious debauchery—the Mormons were even harsher in their condemnation of unauthorized sexual liaisons than was the larger society. Adultery was viewed as a heinous sin, second only to apostasy. In theory, the only sufficient atonement for adultery after having been sealed in a temple marriage was death—to allow oneself to be slain in such a way that one's blood would run out onto the ground and rise to heaven as a sort of propitiatory sacrifice to God. Although there is little evidence that such "blood atonement" was actually practiced in Utah, the belief underscores the intensity of Mormon antipathy toward sexual transgression and the importance the group attached to totally restricting sexual expression to sanctioned channels.[20] Helping to build the kingdom by begetting and rearing righteous children was the primary purpose of sexual intercourse, not the gratification of base animal instincts. Self-control was stressed constantly. Missions called men away for years of voluntary celibacy, during which no form of sexual release, including masturbation, was permitted. And within marriage, a man was urged not to have intercourse with his wife during her pregnancy or while she was nursing her baby—a restriction which was less onerous for a man with more than one wife. Thus, while plural wives had to forgo the exclusive attentions of their husbands, husbands were also subject to limitations on their sexual expression. Perhaps the restrictive aspects of polygamy, which coexisted with a fundamentally positive attitude toward sex and children, were partly a Mormon effort to demonstrate to themselves and the world that their system was, in fact, a principled one, and not at all the licentious "seraglio" that was portrayed by the non-Mormon world. Surely too, the redirection of sexual relations toward the realization of communal goals must have contributed significantly to the difficult enterprise of building the Mormon Zion in the intermountain West.

Thus, these three groups, whose practices appeared to be so different from those of the larger society, nevertheless shared with that society an extreme concern for controlling any potentially disruptive sexual expression. In each case, sex was a means to an end, not an end in itself, and hence pleasure was not the primary goal of sexual intercourse. Instead the aim was to internalize values of sexual self-control so that individual impulses could be sublimated to the goals of the larger community, however those larger goals might be defined.

Ideals of the Family, Motherhood, and Childrearing

Closely associated with Victorian ideals of sexuality and woman's place was the Victorian idealization of the family, motherhood, and childrearing. One popular Victorian image was of a little white house in the countryside, surrounded by a white picket fence, and inside the house, father, mother, and several well-behaved children gathered together in the family circle, perhaps reading a good book or talking quietly. While such ideals may not have accurately represented the way in which most Americans actually lived in an increasingly urban age, the literature of Victorian America nevertheless placed great emphasis on the nuclear family, on motherhood, and on woman's vital role in shaping a new generation which would in turn shape society. The family was seen as a bastion of security in an uncertain world, a retreat and refuge from the unbridled and unprincipled competition of the larger society.[21] If these were the popular ideals, then how did groups like the Shakers, Oneida Perfectionists, and Mormons, which rejected the conventional nuclear family, justify their departure from the practices of the larger society?

All three groups argued that they were not rejecting the family ideal, but raising that ideal to a higher level. An expanded family and a more broadly-based communal loyalty would prove superior to the narrow nuclear family union. This argument was used even by the celibate Shakers, who called their basic communal units "families," referred to each other as "brother" and "sister," and addressed especially beloved adult members as "father" or "mother." Shaker communities were paternalistic (or maternalistic) oligarchies; decisions were made by the leaders and average members were treated benevolently, if at times rather patronizingly, as though they were children. Family imagery is particularly pronounced in the Shaker hymns, which speak, over and over again, of Mother's (Ann Lee's) love for her loyal children and of her children's love for Mother and for each other. Even more than the revivalistic songs of the larger society, Shaker hymns convey a sense of childlike simplicity, delight, and yearning for unity. Perhaps such imagery reflects the unfulfilled longings of many Shakers for the sort of family life that they had renounced in favor of a broader and more general communal union.[22]

Although the family ideal was strong among the Shakers, the attempt to induct children into their distinctive communal patterns caused severe strains, both within the group and between the group and the outer world. Children beyond the age of weaning generally were separated from their parents and reared communally by specially appointed male and female "caretakers." Although the children were generally well treated, their initial separation from their parents often proved traumatic. Moreover, when a husband or wife decided to leave the Shakers and attempted to regain custody of his or her children, bitter legal fights could ensue, as in the cases of Mary Dyer and Eunice Chapman. Finally, when Shaker children reached puberty, they became increasingly rebellious, and most of them eventually left the Society. Thus, although the family ideal remained strong among the Shakers, many tensions surfaced when they attempted to put that ideal into practice in their celibate communities.[23]

John Humphrey Noyes, a Yale-trained academic, dealt even more skillfully and explicitly than the Shakers did with the problem of how ideal family relations were to be realized in his Oneida Community. Over and over again, Noyes described the Community as an "enlarged family," and he vehemently rejected the claim that he was breaking the family apart. Rather, he declared, he was securing for all individuals in the Community the benefits of a larger group. Whereas romantic love and marriages based on such love encouraged an individualism which undermined communal solidarity, at Oneida "each was married to all" in a complex marriage. In the words of the Community hymn, they "all [had] one home and one family relation."[24] The entire Community lived under one roof in the large, sprawling "Mansion House"; they joined in the daily religious-and-business meetings at which Noyes often delivered didactic "Home Talks"; and they participated in the full range of communal work, rather as though they were living under a feudal manorial system.[25] Only the exclusive sexual, emotional, and economic attachments of the nuclear family were eliminated in favor of a more inclusive communal unity.

Like the Shakers, the Oneida Perfectionists found difficulties in bringing up their children and training them to be fully committed members of the community. The separation of children from their mothers after weaning and their placement in a communal "children's house" were justified as a means of avoiding attachments which might lead to "special love." In some cases, however, such separation was achieved only at the cost of considerable personal unhappiness for both mother and child. After the initial separation, children could see their mothers on specified occasions, and in some cases where too strong an attachment was exhibited, the child and its mother were separated entirely for a time as a sort of penance.[26] As children grew to adulthood, they tended to lack the intense religious commitment of their parents, and a sort of "generation gap" resulted. Eventually, when the "stirpiculture" or eugenics experiment was begun after 1869, only certain individuals were allowed to have children. The resulting resentments and polarization within the group played a significant part in the breakup of the whole Oneida communal marriage system.

The Mormons were considerably closer to the family ideals and practices of the larger society than either the Shakers or the Oneida Perfectionists. In fact, Mormon literature of the polygamy period, whether for internal or external consumption, frequently sounds more Victorian than the writings of the Victorians. Perhaps reacting in part to the intensity of external attacks on their marriage practices, Mormons emphatically denied that they were breaking up the family, demeaning motherhood, or failing to raise up righteous and healthy children. Rather, they argued, polygamy made it possible to bring up more children in the families of the best men. Far from criticizing the ideal of the family, Mormons saw family life and the relationship between family and larger kinship networks as the ultimate basis for all progression, not only on earth but throughout all eternity. To an almost unparalleled extent, the Mormon religion really was *about* the family; earthly and heavenly family ideals were seen as identical.

In spite of the Mormon idealization of family relationships, polygamy and the challenges of frontier settlement created problems in rearing children in early Utah. It was no easy task to graft polygamy onto the monogamous Victorian framework, as may be inferred from the high divorce rate in Utah. Presumably some of the tensions arising in polygamous marriages were also reflected in the lives of Mormon children.[27] Furthermore, since leading polygamists were frequently away from home, special pressures were placed on wives—and often on sister-wives or other relatives as well—to bring up children properly and handle any difficulties which might develop. Both Mormon and non-Mormon observers commented on the rowdiness and petty vandalism of some Mormon youth.[28] These problems appear to have been relatively insignificant in comparison with the adolescent turmoil in the general society at this time,[29] but misbehavior of their youth was nevertheless a cause for concern among Mormon parents. Even in the relative isolation of their Zion in the Mountains, the "making of Saints" was a demanding task for the Latter-day Saints of Utah.

Thus, the Shakers, Oneida Perfectionists, and Mormons all attempted to develop new family ideals, which differed in certain significant respects from those of the larger society. The "family" to these millennialists was far more than the basic biological unit—it represented their entire community and embraced the extended kinship ties between members of that group. Inducting children into the enlarged family-community system posed special challenges, which each group met in different ways and with varying degrees of success.

Relations with the Larger Society

Attempts at radically restructuring relations between the sexes in religious, economic, and social life inevitably created tensions, both within these communities and between the communities and the outside world. If these groups had been truly isolated from the larger society, they might conceivably have been able to set up their new patterns with little outside influence or interference. However, these groups were in reality anything but isolated; they were in constant contact with American society through economic interchange, missionary activities, accession of new members, departure of old members, and visits from outsiders. As we have seen, the celibate Shakers, who depended for their very survival on attracting new members, experienced a membership turnover of greater than 25 percent a year in some communities, and thus almost inevitably were exposed to many of the concerns and enthusiasms of the larger society. Although the Oneida Community did not actively seek new members after 1850, it also stayed in touch with the outer world through trading activities, the influx of weekend visitors, and the wide-ranging interests of its founder John Humphrey Noyes, who traveled extensively and reported his many concerns in the Community newspaper. And the Mormons, vigorously seeking new members to build up their organization in various headquarters from New York, to Ohio, to Missouri, to Illinois, and finally to Utah, remained in close contact with developments in the rest of the United States, and eventually the world. Thus, the actions taken by these groups inevitably influenced and were influenced by events in the outer world.

The degree to which each of these groups came into conflict with the larger American society was determined more by the relative vigor and effectiveness of their proselytizing than by the extent to which their actual beliefs clashed with mainstream American attitudes. Thus the small Oneida Community, whose practices were most radically opposed to American norms, was the least persecuted, whereas the large and rapidly growing Mormon Church, which was closest to conventional American values, was the most heavily and consistently persecuted.

The Shakers supply perhaps the best illustration of the way in which persecution was provoked by the dynamism of the group's evangelism, rather than its beliefs and practices as such. The earliest Shakers, when actively attempting to spread their unorthodox religious and sexual views in New England, suffered violent personal attacks. Similarly, during the Shaker expansion in the Midwest, entire communities such as Union Village in Ohio in 1810 were attacked by hostile mobs. In fact, early Shaker documents often seem to be primarily devoted to detailing the sufferings inflicted on Shaker missionaries, defending the character of their leaders, and countering various legal and extra-legal challenges to the existence of the group.[30] In contrast, after the Shakers had become more established and no longer sought converts so energetically, they encountered less and less hostility. Outsiders began to look with admiration on Shaker achievements in communal living. The Shakers were seen as eccentric but basically decent human beings with the right to live their lives in their own way. Shaker beliefs had remained essentially unchanged during their first seventy-five years, but by the outbreak of the Civil War public attitudes toward the group had been dramatically transformed.

The Oneida Community further demonstrates the relative insignificance of unorthodox beliefs alone as a cause of persecution in the pluralistic American context. Radical though Oneida was, both in theory and in practice, it was virtually free from outside persecution during most of its existence. Only during the introduction of complex marriage in the late 1840s and early 1850s, and during the decay of complex marriage in the late 1870s, were there any significant attacks on the group. The early conflicts with the outside world at Putney and Oneida in the 1840s and 1850s were in large measure due to public relations blunders by the Community and to the activities of dissatisfied members and seceders. By the mid-1850s, when those tensions were resolved and active proselytizing ceased, the Oneida Community was almost totally free from persecution, and remained so for more than twenty years while their complex marriage system quietly continued in full operation. A handful of persistent crusaders against the Community were unable to attract any public support—even Sunday School groups went on excursions to Oneida! Finally, in the mid-1870s, when an intellectual crisis and severe power struggle developed within the Community, Oneidans began to view as a threat the crusading activities of Professor John W. Mears of Hamilton College, which they had previously ignored. Uncertain of the continuing loyalty of its membership, the Community—much to everyone's surprise—suddenly announced in 1879 that it was reverting to monogamy. This move was primarily the result of internal weakness rather than external pressure, which the Community had easily withstood before. Thus, persecution of Oneida after its early expansive phase appears to have had little to do with beliefs, but rather reflected the internal strength or weakness of the group.[31]

The exceedingly complex problem of the causes of Mormon persecution has occupied the attention of many writers and can only be sketched briefly here. Although closest of the three groups studied in this book to general American values, the Mormons were, nevertheless, the most intensely persecuted; indeed, at several points in Mormon history persecution became so severe that the very survival of the group was in doubt. The Mormons migrated from New York, to Ohio, to Missouri, to Illinois, to Utah—each time moving on to escape conflicts with their non-Mormon neighbors and with apostate Latter-day Saints. The varied persecutions which the Saints experienced prior to the departure for Utah appear to have had little to do with polygamy, which was neither widely known nor widely practiced at that time. Instead, hostility during the pre-Utah period was directed at Latter-day Saint religious beliefs, which many non-Mormons viewed as an outrageous hoax, and at the Mormons' extraordinary group solidarity, which was seen by many as a potential political and economic threat. A rapidly expanding movement which claimed to have the only way to truth and the right ultimately to impose its views on others as well was viewed by many as a threat to American democracy. Although the existence of polygamous belief and practice among high figures in the Mormon Church in Illinois did prove to be a disruptive factor *within* the Church, polygamy was insignificant among the reasons for *external* attacks on the group at that time.[32]

After the Mormons moved to the intermountain West and publicly announced their commitment to plural marriage in 1852, hostility toward the group increasingly focused on polygamy, though other factors also continued to create tensions. The internal crisis in Mormon society which accompanied their "reformation" of 1856–57 contributed to and was exacerbated by the invasion of Utah by federal troops to put down supposed Mormon disloyalty to the United States in 1857. Then for some twenty years while the United States was preoccupied with the problems of the Civil War and Reconstruction, the Mormons were largely left alone to work out their own way of life. By the late 1870s and early 1880s, however, with slavery gone, a renewed national campaign was launched to root out the remaining "relic of barbarism"—polygamy. So intense did the persecution become that eventually the question for Mormons was whether to abandon polygamy or see the Church itself destroyed as a legal entity. Thus, in 1890 the President of the Mormon Church declared that no further polygamous marriages would be sanctioned. That decision, along with its elaboration in 1904 in the so-called "second manifesto," which led to the excommunication of recalcitrant polygamists, was associated with fundamental changes in all aspects of Mormon social and religious structure. Hostility toward the group gradually began to be overcome, and today the Mormon public image is as favorable at it once was negative.[33]

Thus, beliefs or practices alone were usually not the primary cause of conflict between any of these groups and the larger American society. Instead, the greatest tensions were a result of the degree of expansionism manifested by the group. American pluralism was prepared to accept even highly unorthodox groups like the Shakers and Oneida Perfectionists— so long as they appeared to pose no serious threat to the larger society. But the Mormons were a different case. They grew too powerful to be ignored. Just as the Republic had been unwilling to countenance the existence of an actively expanding slave system, so, too, it eventually moved to suppress polygamy and to force the Mormons, in practice, to back away from their claims to the exclusive possession of truth. In the late nineteenth century, movements for change within Mormon society combined with external pressure to force the group to give up or severely modify many of its most unorthodox claims and practices. Once a tacit acceptance of American pluralism developed, the Mormons, like the Shakers and Oneida Perfectionists, could become an acceptable part of the larger American society.

Causes of Decline

Eventually each of these three millennial groups either gave up its distinctive marital practices or went into an overall decline in size and the intensity of membership commitment. The Shakers continued to require celibacy, but they lost their earlier dynamism and fire; the Oneida Perfectionists ended complex marriage and their close-knit communal life; and the Mormons gave up polygamy, changed their internal structure, and eventually, as a monogamous group in the post–World War II years, began to expand rapidly again. What accounts for these developments? How were alternative marital and communal systems related to the growth and decline of these movements?

Shaker celibacy served as the defining feature of their group, separating it from other revivalistic movements and requiring a high level of commitment from its members. In Shaker communities, as in monastic organizations, celibacy could be a source of organizational strength, freeing members of the group from the divided loyalties that inevitably result from family life so that they could devote their full energies to the service of the community and God. In the early expansive missionary phase of the group, particularly, celibacy helped to liberate powerful proselytizing energies. Yet celibacy as a practiced by the Shakers also had obvious drawbacks. Whereas Catholic monasticism could always draw on a pool of members from a larger, non-celibate church, the entire Shaker organization was celibate and was thus totally dependent on converts from the outside world. No consistent or reliable system of recruitment was ever developed by the group, and after the Civil War, the organization went into a sharp decline. Requirements for membership were relaxed, and in some cases the Shakers were reduced to advertising that they could provide converts with "a secure home for life."[34] Although much of the early Shaker spirit remained or was rechanneled into new activities, the group increasingly became more a curiosity than a distinctive religious force in the years after the Civil War.

Oneida Community complex marriage, like Shaker celibacy, served important functions within the organization, but it too involved problems that would eventually erode the system itself. Complex marriage and attendant practices such as male continence and mutual criticism demanded a high level of commitment from Community members and produced an almost unshakable loyalty. At the same time, however, complex marriage was, perhaps inherently, self-limiting. Noyes had originally envisioned a network of "associated communes," which would spread throughout the country. He found, however, that it was exceedingly difficult to continue to induct large numbers of new members into the complex marriage system. A system like the one at Oneida, he realized, could only function effectively on a limited scale and under tight controls. As early as 1850, Noyes began to set his sights on doing a "small but safe business," and he eventually gave up all plans for further communal expansion.[35] After a successful quarter-century of small-scale communal living, Oneida itself proved unable to sustain the complex marriage system. Faced with the decline in Noyes's leadership powers, the erosion of old ideals, and a complex variety of sexual tensions including those resulting from the stirpiculture or eugenics experiment, the Oneida Community decided to abandon complex marriage and end its other distinctive patterns of communal living in 1879 and 1880.

Unlike Shaker celibacy or Oneida Community complex marriage, Mormon polygamy was a potentially viable way of organizing marriage and family relations in an ongoing community. In fact, a majority of societies worldwide advocate and practice polygamy in one form or another.[36] Yet in the context of monogamous American society, polygamy, like celibacy or complex marriage, required a high degree of commitment and was inherently self-limiting. For a convinced monogamist to accept the idea of polygamy as divinely inspired demanded a great adjustment, but actually to practice polygamy was even more of a challenge. Even if all Mormons could have fully accepted this practice, external American reactions against polygamy would have created severe and continuing problems for the group. It is conceivable that if Utah had remained sufficiently isolated from American society for a longer period of time, polygamy might have survived as the ideal marital system of the group. But if, indeed, the Mormon Church had not begun to give up the practice of polygamy in 1890, Mormonism could never have achieved any degree of acceptance in America. Instead, the group would have remained at best a deviant and despised subculture, rather than the world-embracing church which it aspires to become.

Thus, in all three of these groups alternative marital beliefs and practices provided a source of initial organizational strength and a means of self-definition which was closely associated with the intense commitment of the transitional, liminal phase of development. In the long run, however, such unorthodox marital systems hampered the continuing growth of each group, causing internal tensions and external conflicts. Only the Mormons appear to have been able to make the successful transition from a persecuted subculture to a mainstream movement in America, and they were only able to achieve that goal by giving up polygamy and modifying those other aspects of their beliefs and practices which were the source of major conflicts with the larger American society.

A "Permanent Revolution"?

What lessons, if any, can we learn from such unorthodox communal experiments? Were these movements simply an American sideshow, a flashy but ephemeral curiosity, or do they have a larger message for us today?

The historian Frank Manuel once aptly observed that: "The utopia may well be a sensitive indicator of where the sharpest anguish of an age lies."[37] Reading through the myriad letters, diaries, and other accounts of these communal experimenters, I, too, have been impressed by their intense concern with social disorder. I have come to see these experimenters not as stick figures but as real men and women facing profoundly human problems. In particular, I have been struck not simply by the acute sensitivity of these men and women to the anguish of their transitional age, but even more importantly, by the sincerity, dedication, and skill with which they attempted to establish a new and more satisfying way of life. The solutions that they initially developed to overcome the religious and social chaos around them did not survive for long, but this is hardly surprising. No social order is static or unchanging, especially when it demands the kind of intense commitment and dedication that these experiments did. For these millennialists, as for their Puritan forebears, the utopian spirit of community almost inevitably was fleeting. Yet though these men and women may have fallen short of their almost impossibly high ideals, in a curious way they succeeded—though perhaps not in exactly the way they originally intended.

Most previous accounts of millennial movements have tended to dismiss them as bizarre, disordered, or pathological—a sick response to sick conditions. Without in any way minimizing the tendency toward pathology in millennial movements or the danger that they may develop in socially destructive ways, I nevertheless think that their potentially healing, restorative side also needs to be emphasized. Surely the three groups studied here are best seen not as cases of psychopathology but as illustrations of a very special process of psychic and social reintegration that has implications for any period of transition or rapid change. The prophet-founders of these groups were individuals who struggled intensely to understand themselves and the troubled world around them. Instead of withdrawing into psychosis or attempting to confront complex social problems directly, they developed a different strategy. They conceived a new way of looking at the world which they felt compelled to share with others, and eventually they attracted a following of individuals who had also been at loose ends emotionally. Working together, prophet and followers internalized a new set of values and then went on to create a functioning communal order based on those values. Eventually, strengthened by such creative withdrawal, members of these groups were able once again to interact creatively with the larger American society. Thus, by means of their new belief system and communal order, both the prophets and their followers achieved a sense of unity and psychic wholeness which had been missing from their lives.[38]

If these groups are not properly seen as cases of psychopathology, should we, then, stand the critical popular view on its head and instead celebrate these ventures and what they stood for? Should we idealize the difficult liminal phase when all believers felt as one and when all things seemed possible? This would not be difficult to do. Many writers have lamented the passing of intense dedication and emotional unity in religious movements after order is restored and the original ideals begin to fade. "Success," particularly economic success, appears to be inversely correlated with idealism in these, as in many other, groups. The Shakers, who have dwindled today to a handful of members, are now left with over two million dollars in assets. The Oneida Community, which reorganized as a joint-stock corporation in 1880 and went on to become one of the most successful small businesses in the country, has largely lost touch with its extraordinary past. And the Mormons, who have given up polygamy and gone on to achieve remarkable economic and social success, have sacrificed much of their original idealism in that process. Is worldly success, then, inevitably a signal of a failure of the spirit?

To bemoan the loss of liminal fervor would, I think, be almost as shortsighted as to bewail the excesses and confusions of that difficult transition period. If Victor Turner is right, then all social systems necessarily experience a continuing dialectical tension between periods of structure and anti-structure, stabilization and renewal. Both aspects of the social process are necessary; neither alone is sufficient for a healthy society. If too much order can be deadening, so can too much change and uncertainty. Human life for its fullest expression, demands both periods of stabilization and renewal. From such a perspective, perhaps the chief significance of these antebellum millennial movements is that they exemplify so starkly the creative tensions between structure and anti-structure, the game of life in all its variety and richness. In an imperfect world, there are no permanent revolutions, only limited and transitory triumphs. But there is, I am convinced, continuing value in the pursuit of an impossible ideal.

Appendix

An exact transcription of the first printed version of the revelation on plural and celestial marriage, as it appeared in the *Deseret News* Extra, September 14, 1852, pp. 25–27.

REVELATION,
Given to Joseph Smith, Nauvoo, July 12th, 1843.

Verily thus saith the Lord, unto you my servant Joseph, that inasmuch as you have enquired of my hand, to know and understand wherein I the Lord justified my servants, Abraham, Isaac, and Jacob; as also Moses, David, and Solomon, my servants, as touching the principle and doctrine of their having many wives, and concubines: Behold! and lo, I am the Lord thy God, and will answer thee as touching this matter: Therefore, prepare thy heart to receive and obey the instructions which I am about to give unto you; for all those, who have this law revealed unto them, must obey the same; for behold! I reveal unto you a new and an everlasting covenant, and if ye abide not that covenant, then are ye damned; for no one can reject this covenant, and be permitted to enter into my glory; for all who will have a blessing at my hands, shall abide the law which was appointed for that blessing, and the conditions thereof, as was instituted from before the foundations of the world: and as pertaining to the new and everlasting covenant, it was instituted for the fulness of my glory; and he that receiveth a fulness thereof, must, and shall abide the law, or he shall be damned, saith the Lord God.

And verily I say unto you, that the conditions of this law [26] are these: All covenants, contracts, bonds, obligations, oaths, vows, performances, connections, associations, or expectations, that are not made, and entered into, and sealed, by the Holy Spirit of promise, of him who is anointed, both as well for time and for all eternity, and that too most holy, by revelation and commandment, through the medium of mine anointed, whom I have appointed on the earth to hold this power, (and I have appointed unto my servant Joseph to hold this power in the last days, and there is never but one on the earth at a time, on whom this power and the keys of this priesthood are conferred,) are of no efficacy, virtue, or force, in and after the resurrection from the dead; for all contracts that are not made unto this end, have an end when men are dead.

249

Behold! mine house is a house of order, saith the Lord God, and not a house of confusion. Will I accept of an offering, saith the Lord, that is not made in my name! Or, will I receive at your hands, that which I have not appointed! And will I appoint unto you, saith the Lord, except it be by law, even as I and my Father ordained unto you, before the world was! I am the Lord thy God, and I give unto you this commandment, that no man shall come unto the Father, but by me, or by my word, which is my law, saith the Lord; and every thing that is in the world, whether it be ordained of men, by thrones, or principalities, or powers, or things of name, whatsoever they may be, that are not by me, or by my word, saith the Lord, shall be thrown down, and shall not remain after men are dead, neither in nor after the resurrection, saith the Lord your God: for whatsoever things remaineth, are by me; and whatsoever things are not by me, shall be shaken and destroyed.

Therefore, if a man marry him a wife in the world, and he marry her not by me, nor by my word, and he covenant with her, so long as he is in the world, and she with him, their covenant and marriage is not of force when they are dead, and when they are out of the world; therefore, they are not bound by any law when they are out of the world; therefore, when they are out of the world, they neither marry, nor are given in marriage, but are appointed angels in heaven, which angels are ministering servants, to minister for those, who are worthy of a far more, and an exceeding, and an eternal weight of glory; for these angels did not abide my law, therefore they cannot be enlarged, but remain separately, and singly, without exaltation, in their saved condition, to all eternity, and from henceforth are not Gods, but angels of God forever and ever.

And again, verily I say unto you, if a man marry a wife, and make a covenant with her for time, and for all eternity, if that covenant is not by me, or by my word, which is my law, and is not sealed by the Holy Spirit of promise, through him whom I have anointed and appointed unto this power, then it is not valid, neither of force, when they are out of the world, because they are not joined by me, saith the Lord, neither by my word; when they are out of the world, it cannot be received there, because the angels and the Gods are appointed there, by whom they cannot pass; they cannot, therefore, inherit my glory, for my house is a house of order, saith the Lord God.

And again, verily I say unto you, if a man marry a wife by my word, which is my law, and by the new and everlasting covenant, and it is sealed unto them by the Holy Spirit of promise, by him who is anointed, unto whom I have appointed this power, and the keys of this priesthood, and it shall be said unto them, ye shall come forth in the first resurrection; and if it be after the first resurrection, in the next resurrection; and shall inherit thrones, kingdoms, principalities, and powers, dominions, all heights, and depths, then shall it be written in the Lamb's Book of Life, that he shall commit no murder, whereby to shed innocent blood; and if ye abide in my covenant, and commit no murder whereby to shed innocent blood, it shall be done unto them in all things whatsoever my servant hath put upon them, in time, and through all eternity; and shall be of full force when they are out of the world, and they shall pass by the angels, and the Gods, which are set there, to their exaltation and glory in all things, as hath been sealed upon their heads, which glory shall be a fulness and a continuation of the seeds forever and ever.

Then shall they be Gods, because they have no end; therefore shall they be from everlasting to everlasting, because they continue; then shall they be above all, because all things are subject unto them. Then shall they be Gods, because they have all power, and the angels are subject unto them.

Verily, verily, I say unto you, except ye abide my law, ye cannot attain to this glory; for strait is the gate, and narrow the way, that leadeth unto the exaltation and continuation of the lives, and few there be that find it, because ye receive me not in the world, neither do ye know me. But if ye receive me in the world, then shall ye know me, and shall receive your exaltation; that where I am, ye shall be also. This is eternal lives, to know the only wise and true God, and Jesus Christ whom he hath sent. I am He. Receive ye, therefore, my law. Broad is the gate, and wide the way that leadeth to the death; and many there are that go in thereat; because they receive me not, neither do they abide in my law.

Verily, verily I say unto you, if a man marry a wife according to my word, and they are sealed by the Holy Spirit of promise, according to mine appointment, and he or she shall commit any sin or transgression of the new and everlasting covenant whatever, and all manner of blasphemies, and if they commit no murder, wherein they shed innocent blood,—yet they shall come forth in the first resurrection, and enter into their exaltation; but they shall be destroyed in the flesh, and shall be delivered unto the buffetings of Satan, unto the day of redemption, saith the Lord God.

The blasphemy against the Holy Ghost, which shall not be forgiven in the world, nor out of the world, is in that ye commit murder, wherein ye shed innocent blood, and assent unto my death, after ye have received my new and everlasting covenant, saith the Lord God; and he that abideth not this law, can in no wise enter into my glory, but shall be damned, saith the Lord.

I am the Lord thy God, and will give unto thee the law of my Holy Priesthood, as was ordained by me, and my Father, before the world was. Abraham received all things, whatsoever he received, by revelation and commandment, by my word, saith the Lord, and hath entered into his exaltation, and sitteth upon his throne.

Abraham received promises concerning his seed, and of the fruit of his loins,—from whose loins ye are, viz., my servant Joseph,—which were to continue, so long as they were in the world; and as touching Abraham and his seed, out of the world, they should continue; both in the world and out of the world should they continue as innumerable as the stars; or, if ye were to count the sand upon the sea-shore, ye could not number them. This promise is yours, also, because ye are of Abraham, and the promise was made unto Abraham, and by this law are the continuation of the works of my Father, wherein he glorifieth himself. Go ye, therefore, and do the works of Abraham,—enter ye into my law, and ye shall be saved. But if ye enter not into my law, ye cannot receive the promises of my Father, which he made unto Abraham.

God commanded Abraham, and Sarah gave Hagar to Abraham, to wife. And why did she do it? Because this was the law, and from Hagar sprang many people. This, therefore, was fulfilling, among other things, the promises. Was Abraham, therefore, under condemnation? Verily, I say unto you, *Nay*; for I the Lord commanded it. Abraham was commanded to offer his son Isaac; nevertheless, it was written, thou shalt not kill. Abraham, however, did not refuse, and it was accounted unto him for righteousness.

Abraham received concubines, and they bare him children, and it was accounted unto him for righteousness, because they were given unto him, and he abode in my law: as Isaac also, and Jacob did none other things than that which they were commanded; and because they did none other things than that which they were commanded, they have entered into their exaltation, according to the promises, and sit upon thrones; and are not angels, but are Gods. David also received many wives and concubines, as also Solomon, and Moses my servant; as also many others of my servants, from the beginning of creation until this time; and in nothing did they sin, save in those things which they received not of me.

David's wives and concubines were given unto him, of me, by the hand of Nathan, my servant, and others of the proph[27]ets who had the keys of this power; and in none of these things did he sin against me, save in the case of Uriah and his wife; and, therefore, he hath fallen from his exaltation, and received his portion; and he shall not inherit them out of the world; for I gave them unto another, saith the Lord.

I am the Lord thy God, and I gave unto thee, my servant Joseph, an appointment, and restore all things; ask what ye will, and it shall be given unto you, according to my word; and as ye have asked concerning adultery, —verily, verily I say unto you, if a man receiveth a wife in the new and everlasting covenant, and if she be with another man, and I have not appointed unto her by the holy anointing, she hath committed adultery, and shall be destroyed. If she be not in the new and everlasting covenant, and she be with another man, she has committed adultery; and if her husband be with another woman, and he was under a vow, he hath broken his vow, and hath committed adultery; and if she hath not committed adultery, but is innocent, and hath not broken her vow, and she knoweth it, and I reveal it unto you, my servant Joseph, then shall you have power, by the power of my Holy Priesthood, to take her, and give her unto him that hath not committed adultery, but hath been faithful; for he shall be made ruler over many; for I have conferred upon you the keys and power of the priesthood, wherein I restore all things, and make known unto you, all things, in due time.

And verily, verily I say unto you, that whatsoever you seal on earth, shall be sealed in heaven; and whatsoever you bind on earth, in my name, and by my word, saith the Lord, it shall be eternally bound in the heavens; and whosesoever sins you remit on earth, shall be remitted eternally in the heavens; and whosesoever sins you retain on earth, shall be retained in heaven.

And again, verily I say, whomsoever you bless, I will bless; and whomsoever you curse, I will curse, saith the Lord; for I the Lord am thy God.

And again, verily I say unto you, my servant Joseph, that whatsoever you give on earth, and to whomsoever you give any one on earth, by my word, and according to my law, it shall be visited with blessings, and not cursings, and with my power, saith the Lord, and shall be without condemnation on earth, and in heaven; for I am the Lord thy God, and will be with thee even unto the end of the world, and through all eternity: for verily, I seal upon you, your exaltation, and prepare a throne for you in the kingdom of my Father, with Abraham, your father. Behold, I have seen your sacrifices, and will forgive all your sins; I have seen your sacrifices, in obedience to that which I have told you: go, therefore, and I make a way for your escape, as I accepted the offering of Abraham, of his son Isaac.

Verily I say unto you, a commandment I give unto mine handmaid, Emma Smith, your wife, whom I have given unto you, that she stay herself, and partake not of that which I commanded you to offer unto her; for I did it, saith the Lord, to prove you all, as I did Abraham; and that I might require an offering at your hand, by covenant and sacrifice: and let mine handmaid, Emma Smith, receive all those that have been given unto my servant Joseph, and who are virtuous and pure before me; and those who are not pure, and have said they were pure, shall be destroyed, saith the Lord God: for I am the Lord thy God, and ye shall obey my voice; and I give unto my servant Joseph, that he shall be made ruler over many things, for he hath been faithful over a few things; and from henceforth I will strengthen him.

And I command mine handmaid, Emma Smith, to abide and cleave unto my servant Joseph, and to none else. But if she will not abide this commandment, she shall be destroyed, saith the Lord; for I am the Lord thy God, and will destroy her, if she abide not in my law; but if she will not abide this commandment, then shall my servant Joseph do all things for her, even as he hath said; and I will bless him, and multiply him, and give unto him an hundred fold in this world, of fathers and mothers, brothers and sisters, houses and lands, wives and children, and crowns of eternal lives in the eternal worlds. And again, verily I say, let mine handmaid forgive my servant Joseph his trespasses, and then shall she be forgiven her trespasses, wherein she hath trespassed against me; and I the Lord thy God will bless her, and multiply her, and make her heart to rejoice.

And again, I say, let not my servant Joseph put his property out of his hands, lest an enemy come and destroy him, for Satan seeketh to destroy; for I am the Lord thy God, and he is my servant; and behold! and lo, I am with him, as I was with Abraham, thy father, even unto his exaltation and glory.

Now as touching the law of the priesthood, there are many things pertaining thereunto. Verily, if a man be called of my Father, as was Aaron, by mine own voice, and by the voice of him that sent me, and I have endowed him with the keys of the power of this priesthood, if he do anything in my name, and according to my law, and by my word, he will not commit sin, and I will justify him. Let no one, therefore, set on my servant Joseph; for I will justify him; for he shall do the sacrifice which I require at his hands, for his transgressions, saith the Lord your God.

And again, as pertaining to the law of the Priesthood;—if any man espouse a virgin, and desire to espouse another, and the first give her consent; and if he espouse the second, and they are virgins, and have vowed to no other man, then is he justified; he cannot commit adultery, for they are given unto him; for he cannot commit adultery with that, that belongeth unto him, and to none else: and if he have ten virgins given unto him by this law, he cannot commit adultery; for they belong to him; and they are given unto him;—therefore is he justified. But if one, or either of the ten virgins, after she is espoused, shall be with another man, she has committed adultery, and shall be destroyed; for they are given unto him to multiply and replenish the earth, according to my commandment, and to fulfil the promise which was given by my Father before the foundation of the world; and for their exaltation in the eternal worlds, that they may bear the souls of men; for herein is the work of my Father continued, that he may be glorified.

And again, verily, verily I say unto you, if any man have a wife who holds the keys of this power, and he teaches unto her the law of my Priesthood, as pertaining to these things; then shall she believe, and administer unto him, or she shall be destroyed, saith the Lord your God; for I will destroy her; for I will magnify my name upon all those who receive and abide in my law. Therefore, it shall be lawful in me, if she receive not this law, for him to receive all things, whatsoever I the Lord his God will give unto him, because she did not believe and administer unto him, according to my word; and she then becomes the transgressor, and he is exempt from the law of Sarah, who administered unto Abraham according to the law, when I commanded Abraham to take Hagar to wife.—And now, as pertaining to this law,—verily, verily I say unto you, I will reveal more unto you hereafter; therefore, let this suffice for the present.—Behold, I am Alpha and Omega:—AMEN.

Notes

Chapter I

1. *First Annual Report of the Oneida Association* (Oneida Reserve, N. Y.: Leonard, 1849), pp. 25, 27 (original numbering removed). This is part of Noyes's "Bible Argument Defining the Relations of the Sexes in the Kingdom of Heaven," the basic statement of his social and sexual theories, written in 1848.

2. For Max Weber's definition of charisma, see his *The Theory of Social and Economic Organization,* ed. Talcott Parsons (New York: Free Press, 1947), pp. 358–59. A critique of the limitations of this concept as applied to millennial movements is in Peter Worsley, *The Trumpet Shall Sound: A Study of "Cargo" Cults in Melanesia,* 2nd ed. (New York: Schocken, 1968), pp. ix–xii. By contrast, the vital role of such leadership is stressed by Kenelm Burridge in "The Prophet," a section of his *New Heaven, New Earth: A Study of Millenarian Activities* (New York: Schocken, 1969), pp. 153–63; and I. C. Jarvie, *The Revolution in Anthropology* (London: Routledge & Kegan Paul, 1964), esp. pp. 74–105. The Old Testament prophetic tradition, which significantly influenced these three groups, is interpreted in Abraham J. Heschel, *The Prophets,* 2 vols. (New York: Harper & Row, 1969).

3. Studies of the social composition of these groups and the reasons that individuals joined such movements still remain to be done in most cases. Only the relatively small Oneida Community has been thoroughly analyzed. See Robert S. Fogarty, "The Oneida Community, 1848–1880: A Study in Conservative Christian Utopianism" (Ph.D. diss., Univ. of Denver, 1968). Some preliminary findings on the sources of Shaker membership are in D'Ann Campbell, "Women's Life in Utopia: The Shaker Experiment in Sexual Equality Reappraised—1810 to 1860," *New England Quarterly* 51 (March 1978): 23–38, and in the Shaker chapter of this study. Speculations on early Mormon membership are in Whitney R. Cross, *The Burned-over District: The Social and Intellectual History of Enthusiastic Religion in Western New York, 1800–1850* (Ithaca, N. Y.: Cornell Univ., 1950), pp. 138–50, and criticized by Mario S. De Pillis, "Social Sources of Mormonism," *Church History* 37 (March 1968): 50–79. Other relevant Mormon studies are discussed in the core chapters of this book.

4. For the general definition of such movements employed as a starting point in this study, see Norman Cohn, "Medieval Millenarism: Its Bearing on the Comparative Study of Millenarian Movements," in *Millennial Dreams in Action,* ed. Sylvia L. Thrupp (New York: Schocken, 1970), pp. 31–43. Cohn suggests that "millenarian" movements look toward a salvation which is to be collective, terrestrial, imminent, total, and accomplished, at least in part, by supernatural or extra-human means. A number of other important works suggest new insights into millennial

movements: Anthony F. C. Wallace, "Revitalization Movements," *American Anthropologist* 38 (April 1956): 264–81; Victor W. Turner, *The Ritual Process: Structure and Anti-Structure* (Chicago: Aldine, 1969); I. M. Lewis, *Ecstatic Religion: An Anthropological Study of Spirit Possession and Shamanism* (Baltimore: Penguin, 1971); Vittorio Lanternari, *The Religions of the Oppressed: A Study of Modern Messianic Cults,* trans. Lisa Sergio (New York: New American Library, 1965); Thrupp, *Millennial Dreams in Action;* Jarvie, *The Revolution in Anthropology;* Peter L. Berger, *The Sacred Canopy: Elements of a Sociological Theory of Religion* (Garden City, N. Y.: Doubleday, 1969); Kenelm Burridge, *New Heaven, New Earth;* and Peter Lawrence, *Road Belong Cargo: A Study of the Cargo Movement in the Southern Madang District, New Guinea* (Manchester, Eng.: University Press, 1971). A detailed bibliography and interpretation of studies of millennial groups is Weston La Barre, "Materials for a History of Studies of Crisis Cults: A Bibliographic Essay," *Current Anthropology* 12 (February 1971): 3–44.

5. Among the more historically oriented accounts of millennialism, see John Gager's provocative study of early Christianity as a millennial movement, *Kingdom and Community: The Social World of Early Christianity* (Englewood Cliffs, N. J.: Prentice-Hall, 1975. A critical analysis of millennial tendencies in Christian history is in Ronald A. Knox, *Enthusiasm: A Chapter in the History of Religion, with Special Reference to the XVII and XVIII Centuries* (Oxford: Clarendon Press, 1951), and Norman R. Cohn, *The Pursuit of the Millennium: Revolutionary Millenarians and Mystical Anarchists of the Middle Ages,* rev. enl. ed. (New York: Oxford Univ., 1970). For a suggestive introduction to the role of millennialism in America, see Ernest Lee Tuveson, *Redeemer Nation: The Idea of America's Millennial Role* (Chicago: Univ. of Chicago, 1968). Also see Ira V. Brown, "Watchers of the Second Coming: The Millenarian Tradition in America," *Mississippi Valley Historical Review* 39 (December 1952): 441–58, and David E. Smith, "Millenarian Scholarship in America," *American Quarterly* 17 (Autumn 1965): 535–49. For an introduction to restorationist/restitutionist thought in its Anglo-American historical context, see the articles in the *Journal of the American Academy of Religion* 44 (March 1976): 3–113. Insights into the nineteenth-century context are in Edwin Scott Gaustad, ed., *The Rise of Adventism: Religion and Society in Mid-Nineteenth-Century America* (New York: Harper & Row, 1974).

6. A discussion of the way in which the study of "deviant" behavior and groups can shed light on the larger society is found in Kai T. Erikson, *Wayward Puritans: A Study in the Sociology of Deviance* (New York: John Wiley, 1966).

7. Bibliographic studies of American communitarianism are given by Arthur E. Bestor, *Backwoods Utopias: The Sectarian and Owenite Phases of Communitarian Socialism in America, 1663–1829,* 2nd enl. ed. (Philadelphia: Univ. of Pennsylvania, 1970), pp. 287–310, and by T. D. Seymour Bassett in *Socialism and American Life,* ed. Donald Drew Egbert and Stow Persons, 2 vols. (Princeton: Princeton Univ., 1952) 2: 91–140. Among the notable works dealing with American communitarian groups other than those discussed in this book are Karl J. R. Arndt, *George*

Rapp's Harmony Society, 1785–1847 (Philadelphia: Univ. of Pennsylvania, 1965), and John F. C. Harrison, *Quest for the New Moral World: Robert Owen and the Owenites in England and America* (New York: Charles Scribner's Sons, 1969). Rosabeth Kanter, *Commitment and Community: Communes and Utopias in a Sociological Perspective* (Cambridge, Mass.: Harvard Univ., 1972), and Dolores Hayden, *Seven American Utopias: The Architecture of Communitarian Socialism, 1790–1975* (Cambridge, Mass.: M.I.T., 1976), present valuable new perspectives on the groups in this study.

For studies suggesting the linkage between the Mormons and more explicitly communitarian groups such as the Shakers and Oneida Perfectionists, see Leonard J. Arrington, "Early Mormon Communitarianism: The Law of Consecration and Stewardship," *Western Humanities Review* 7 (Autumn 1953): 341–69; Leonard J. Arrington, *Great Basin Kingdom: An Economic History of the Latter-day Saints, 1830–1900* (Cambridge, Mass.: Harvard Univ., 1958); Mario S. De Pillis, "The Development of Mormon Communitarianism, 1826–1846" (Ph.D. diss., Yale Univ., 1960); and Leonard J. Arrington, Feramorz Y. Fox, and Dean L. May, *Building the City of God: Community and Cooperation Among the Mormons* (Salt Lake City: Deseret Book Company, 1976).

8. Perry Miller discusses the colonial New England Puritan experiment as "an ideal laboratory":

> It was relatively isolated, the people were comparatively homogeneous, and the forces of history played upon it in ways that can more satisfactorily be traced than in more complex societies. Here is an opportunity, as nearly perfect as the student is apt to find, for extracting certain generalizations about the relationship of thought or ideas to communal experience.

Perry Miller, *The New England Mind: From Colony to Province* (Boston: Beacon, 1961), Foreword.

9. Victor Turner's theoretical discussion of liminality and communitas is in *The Ritual Process*, pp. 94–203. The quotations in the following two paragraphs are from that book, pp. 94–97. Arnold Van Gennep's classic account is *The Rites of Passage*, trans. Monika B. Vizedom and Gabrielle L. Caffee (Chicago: Univ. of Chicago, 1960). Important essays by Victor Turner are found in his *Dramas, Fields, and Metaphors: Symbolic Action in Human Society* (Ithaca, N.Y.: Cornell Univ., 1974).

10. Burridge, *New Heaven, New Earth*, p. 112. Also see Lewis, *Ecstatic Religion*.

11. Burridge, *New Heaven, New Earth*, p. 162. The complexity of the religious prophet's character, experience, and mission is suggested by William James. He writes of individuals in whom a "superior intellect" and a "psychopathic temperament" coalesce, thereby creating

> . . . the best possible condition for the kind of effective genius that gets into biographical dictionaries. Such figures do not remain mere critics and understanders with their intellect. Their ideas possess them, they inflict them, for better or worse, upon their companions or their age. . . . If there were such a thing as inspiration from a higher realm, it might well be that the neurotic temperament would furnish the chief condition of the requisite receptivity.

William James, *The Varieties of Religious Experience: A Study in Human Nature* (New York: New American Library, 1958), pp. 36–37.

12. The study of religious visionary experiences—their origins, character, and significance—remains in its infancy. An indispensable starting point remains James's *Varieties of Religious Experience,* first published in 1902. In the wake of new religious concerns and the widespread use of mind-changing drugs in the late 1960s, a number of important accounts dealing at least tangentially with the psychology of religious experience have appeared. See, for instance, William Braden, *The Private Sea: LSD and the Search for God* (Chicago: Quadrangle, 1966); articles in John White, ed., *The Highest State of Consciousness* (Garden City, N. Y.: Doubleday, 1972), including Kenneth Wapnick, "Mysticism and Schizophrenia," Raymond Prince and Charles Savage, "Mystical States and the Concept of Regression," and Claire Myer Owens, "The Mystical Experience: Fact and Values"; Charles Tart, ed., *Altered States of Consciousness* (Garden City, N. Y.: Doubleday, 1972); and Erika Bourguignon, ed., *Religion, Altered States of Consciousness, and Social Change* (Columbus: Ohio State Univ., 1973). J. A. Hadfield, *Dreams and Nightmares* (Baltimore: Penguin, 1954), suggests the positive role which unconscious processes through dreams can play in psychic integration. In discussing religious visionary experiences as essentially a waking dream formation, Wallace, "Revitalization Movements," suggests an anthropological perspective on such phenomena. The mass movements of the twentieth century point to the enormous potential impact of visionary-prophetic figures, both for good and for ill, when they become directly involved in the political life of the larger society.

13. This optimistic evaluation of Jacksonian America is conveyed in Alice Felt Tyler's *Freedom's Ferment: Phases of American Social History from the Colonial Period to the Outbreak of the Civil War* (New York: Harper & Row, 1962). For other examples of this approach in the extensive literature on Jacksonian America, see Carl Russell Fish, *The Rise of the Common Man* (New York: Macmillan, 1927); Frederick Jackson Turner, *The United States, 1830–1850: The Nation and Its Sections* (New York: Holt, Rinehart & Winston, 1935); and Arthur M. Schlesinger, Jr., *The Age of Jackson* (Boston: Little, Brown, 1945). A recent study in this tradition is Robert V. Remini, *The Revolutionary Age of Andrew Jackson* (New York: Avon, 1977).

14. Ralph Waldo Emerson, "Ode to W. H. Channing," in *The Complete Essays and Other Writings of Ralph Waldo Emerson,* ed. Brooks Atkinson (New York: Random House, 1950), p. 71. For more ambivalent recent interpretations of Jacksonian America, see Edward Pessen, "The Egalitarian Myth and American Social Reality: Wealth, Mobility, and Equality in the Era of the Common Man," *American Historical Review* 76 (October 1971): 989–1034, and Pessen, *Jacksonian America: Society, Personality, and Politics* (Homewood, Ill.: Dorsey Press, 1969). Other interpretations especially useful for this study include Marvin Meyers, *The Jacksonian Persuasion: Politics and Belief* (New York: Vintage, 1960); Fred Somkin, *Unquiet Eagle: Memory and Desire in the Idea of American Freedom, 1815–1860* (Ithaca, N. Y.: Cornell Univ., 1967); Lee Benson, *The Concept of Jacksonian Democracy: New York as a*

Test Case (New York: Atheneum, 1965); Daniel J. Boorstin, *The Americans: The National Experience* (New York: Vintage, 1965); and John Higham, *From Boundlessness to Consolidation: The Transformation of American Culture, 1848–1860* (Ann Arbor: William I. Clements Library, 1969).

15. Austin E. Fife, "Folk Beliefs and Mormon Cultural Autonomy," *Journal of American Folklore* 61 (January–March 1948): 19–30.

16. Arthur E. Bestor, "Patent-Office Models of the Good Society: Some Relationships Between Social Reform and Westward Expansion," *American Historical Review* 43 (April 1953): 505–26.

17. Cross, *Burned-over District, passim.* For a similar treatment of Vermont, see David Ludlum, *Social Ferment in Vermont, 1791–1850* (New York: Columbia Univ., 1939).

18. For an introduction to the rich literature on antebellum reform movements, see Tyler, *Freedom's Ferment;* Cross, *Burned-over District;* John L. Thomas, "Romantic Reform in America, 1815–1860," *American Quarterly* 17 (Winter 1965): 657–81; David Brion Davis, ed., *Ante-Bellum Reform* (New York: Harper & Row, 1967); C. S. Griffin, *The Ferment of Reform, 1830–1860* (New York: Thomas Y. Crowell, 1967); Louis Filler, *The Crusade Against Slavery, 1830–1860* (New York: Harper & Row, 1969); James Brewer Stewart, *Holy Warriors: The Abolitionists and American Slavery* (New York: Hill & Wang, 1976); and Ronald G. Walters, *American Reformers, 1815–1860* (New York: Hill & Wang, 1978).

19. Demographic studies, in particular, clearly suggest how much continuity has existed in many aspects of family social structure. The view that Western Europe moved from a pre-industrial "extended family system" to an industrial-age "nuclear family system" has been largely refuted by recent scholarship. See William J. Goode, *World Revolution and Family Patterns* (Glencoe, Ill.: Free Press, 1963); E. A. Wrigley, "The Process of Modernization and the Industrial Revolution in England," *Journal of Interdisciplinary History* 3 (1972): 225–60; Peter Laslett, *The World We Have Lost* (London: Methuen, 1965); and Peter Laslett and Richard Wall, eds., *Household and Family in Past Time* (Cambridge, Eng.: Cambridge Univ., 1972).

20. For useful overviews of the recent family history literature, see Edward N. Saveth, "The Problem of American Family History," *American Quarterly* 21 (Summer 1969): 311–29; Tamara K. Harevin, "Modernization and Family History: Perspectives on Social Change," *Signs: Journal of Women in Culture and Society* 2 (Autumn 1976): 190–206; Barbara J. Harris, "Recent Work on the History of the Family: A Review Article," *Feminist Studies* 3 (Spring-Summer 1976) 159–72; and Maris A. Vinovskis, "From Household Size to Life Course: Some Observations on Recent Trends in Family History," *American Behavioral Scientist* 21 (November-December 1977): 263–87.

Among the sources which have been especially useful for this study, see Philippe Ariès, *Centuries of Childhood: A Social History of Family Life,* trans. Robert Baldick (New York: Vintage, 1962); Edmund S. Morgan, *The Puritan Family: Religion and Domestic Relations in Seventeenth-Century New England,* new ed., rev. and enl. (New York: Harper

& Row, 1966); John Demos, *A Little Commonwealth: Family Life in Plymouth Colony* (New York: Oxford Univ., 1970); Philip J. Greven, Jr., *Four Generations: Population, Land, and Family in Colonial Andover, Massachusetts* (Ithaca, N. Y.: Cornell Univ., 1970); Edward Shorter, *The Making of the Modern Family* (New York: Basic Books, 1975); Ann Oakley, *Woman's Work: The Housewife, Past and Present* (New York: Vintage, 1974); Theodore K. Rabb and Robert I. Rotberg, eds., *The Family in History: Interdisciplinary Essays* (New York: Harper & Row, 1971); Mary S. Hartman and Lois S. Banner, eds., *Clio's Consciousness Raised: New Perspectives on the History of Women* (New York: Harper & Row, 1974); Michael Gordon, ed., *The American Family in Social-Historical Perspective*, 2nd ed., (New York: St. Martin's, 1978); and Elizabeth Janeway, *Man's World, Woman's Place: A Study in Social Mythology* (New York: Delta, 1971). Also see William J. Goode, *The Family* (Englewood Cliffs, N. J.: Prentice-Hall, 1964), for sociological perspectives, and David M. Schneider, *American Kinship: A Cultural Account* (Englewood Cliffs, N. J.: Prentice-Hall, 1968), for an anthropological analysis. Jean-Louis Flandrin's brilliant study, *Families in Former Times: Kinship, Household and Sexuality*, trans. Richard Southern (New York: Cambridge Univ., 1979), appeared too late to be used in this book.

21. Lois Kimball Mathews, *The Expansion of New England: The Spread of New England Settlement and Institutions to the Mississippi River, 1620–1865* (Boston: Houghton Mifflin, 1909), graphically illustrates this expansion.

22. John Humprey Noyes repeatedly drew this connection. See "Becoming as Little Children," *Spiritual Magazine* 2 (December 22, 1849): 339; "The Social Principle Primary," *Free Church Circular* 3 (September 23, 1850): 249–50; "Egotism for Two," *Circular* 3 (April 11, 1854): 219–20; and "The Family and Its Foil," *Circular* 3 (November 16, 1854): 594. Also see accounts by foreign visitors to America such as Harriet Martineau, Frances Trollope, and Alexis de Toqueville. English reactions are summarized in J. L. Mesick, *The English Traveler in America, 1785–1835* (New York: Columbia Univ., 1922). Probably greater freedom for individuals during courtship had always existed in America than in Europe, but this freedom appears to have been accentuated during the antebellum period.

23. Among the many studies suggesting the range of reactions in this period, see Kathryn Kish Sklar, *Catherine Beecher: A Study in Domesticity* (New Haven: Yale Univ., 1973); John S. Haller and Robin M. Haller, *The Physician and Sexuality in Victorian America* (Urbana: Univ. of Illinois, 1974); Carroll Smith Rosenberg, "Beauty, the Beast and the Militant Woman: A Case Study of Sex Roles and Social Stress in Jacksonian America," *American Quarterly* 23 (October 1971): 563–84; Carroll Smith Rosenberg, "The Hysterical Woman: Sex Roles and Role Conflict in 19th-Century America," *Social Research* 39 (Winter 1972): 652–78; Carroll Smith Rosenberg, "The Female World of Love and Ritual: Relations Between Women in Nineteenth-Century America," *Signs: Journal of Women in Culture and Society* 1 (Autumn 1974): 1–29; Ronald G.

Walters, ed., *Primers for Prudery: Sexual Advice to Victorian America* (Englewood Cliffs, N. J.: Prentice-Hall, 1974); Joseph Kett, *Rites of Passage: Adolescence in America, 1790 to the Present* (New York: Basic Books, 1977); Alice Rossi, ed., *The Feminist Papers: From Adams to De Beauvoir* (New York: Bantam, 1975); and Andrew Sinclair, *The Emancipation of the American Woman* (New York: Harper & Row, 1966).

24. A classic critique of Victorian attitudes toward women is Barbara Welter, "The Cult of True Womanhood, 1820–1860," *American Quarterly* 18 (Summer 1966): 151–74. Also see E. Douglas Branch, *The Sentimental Years, 1836–1860: A Social History* (New York: Hill & Wang, 1965): Walters, *Primers for Prudery;* and Kirk Jeffrey, "The Family as a Utopian Retreat from the City: The Nineteenth-Century Contribution," in *The Family, Communes, and Utopian Societies,* ed. Sallie Te Selle (New York: Harper & Row, 1972), pp. 21–39. The sense of fluidity and the move toward a new order during this period are suggested in Higham, *From Boundlessness to Consolidation;* Stanley M. Elkins, *Slavery: A Problem in American Institutional and Intellectual Life* (Chicago: Univ. of Chicago, 1965); and David J. Rothman, *The Discovery of the Asylum: Social Order and Disorder in the New Republic* (Boston: Little, Brown, 1971).

25. See Welter, "Cult of True Womanhood."

26. Daniel Scott Smith, "Family Limitation, Sexual Control and Domestic Feminism in Victorian America," in Hartman and Banner, *Clio's Consciousness Raised,* pp. 119–36, develops the concept of "domestic feminism," and Sklar, *Catherine Beecher,* describes a leading proponent of such an approach. For the development of concern with contraception and the fall in the birth rate, see Norman E. Himes, *Medical History of Contraception* (New York: Schocken, 1970); Sinclair, *Emancipation of the American Woman,* pp. 132–34; and Yasukichi Yasuba, *Birth Rates of the White Population in the United States 1800–1860: An Economic Study* (Baltimore: Johns Hopkins, 1962).

27. See Kirk Jeffrey, "The Family as a Utopian Retreat from the City."

28. See Rothman, *Discovery of the Asylum.*

29. See Cross, *Burner-over District, passim.*

30. John Humphrey Noyes, *History of American Socialisms* (Philadelphia: J. B. Lippincott, 1870), p. 634. Although the popular view associating revivalism with sexual excess may be overdrawn, an important connection between the two phenomena nonetheless exists. A historical treatment of some of these issues is Charles A. Johnson, *The Frontier Camp Meeting: Religion's Harvest Time* (Dallas: Southern Methodist Univ., 1955). For anthropological and sociological perspectives, see Lewis, *Ecstatic Religion,* and Turner, *Ritual Process.*

31. Three variants of this story are found in Matthew 22:15–22; Mark 12:18–27; and Luke 20:27–40. This analysis does not intend to suggest that these groups developed their conception of marriage from one Biblical passage alone. Rather, in each case, there appears to have been a complex interplay between Biblical exegesis and social concern.

32. Luke 20:34–36.

33. The Shaker interpretation of this passage runs through almost all of their

writings as an underlying theme. The earliest and most authoritative account of Ann Lee's life, activities, and ideas states:

> To the married people, Mother [Ann Lee] said, "You must forsake the marriage of the flesh, or you cannot be married to the Lamb, nor have any share in the resurrection of Christ: for those who are counted worthy to have part in the resurrection of Christ, neither marry nor are given in marriage; but are like unto the angels."

Testimonies of the Life, Character, Revelations, and Doctrines of Our Ever Blessed Mother Ann Lee and the Elders with Her. Collected from Living Witnesses by Order of the Ministry, in Union with the Church (Hancock, Mass.: J. Talcott & J. Deming, Junrs., 1816), p. 17. Hereafter cited as *Testimonies of Mother Ann Lee.*

34. *Handbook of the Oneida Community* (Wallingford, Conn.: Office of the *Circular,* 1867), p. 64.

35. Noyes repeatedly and explicitly contrasted his views with those of the Shakers. In a letter to the Shaker Loren Hollister, for example, he bluntly noted that "marriage and the sexual connection are different things." All animals except man "neither marry nor are given in marriage," yet they nonetheless have sexual connection. Marriage, said Noyes, was a man-made convention and would be done away with in the heavenly state, where love would be universalized among the faithful. *Witness* 1 (September 25, 1839): 80.

> To me, not only the Bible, but all the works of God, from the lowest vegetable to the highest animal, testify that the distinction of the sexes is as universal and perpetual as life. I have never found the slightest valid reason, for the common nebulous impression that heaven is inhabited by a company of non-descript ghosts. I believe that the paradise of redemption, in its elementary constitution, in all respects, except those which involve evil, resembles the paradise of creation.

Witness 1 (September 25, 1839): 77. Also see "The Battle-Axe Letter," *Witness* 1 (January 23, 1839): 50, ftn.; the *Spiritual Moralist* for June 13, 1842, and June 25, 1842; and the "Bible Argument Defining the Relations of the Sexes in the Kingdom of Heaven" in *First Annual Report of the Oneida Association,* pp. 18–42, hereafter cited as "Bible Argument."

36. Although Mormons do not appear to have been particularly concerned to contrast their position with that of the Shakers or the Oneida Perfectionists, their own marriage views nonetheless make explicit use of this same passage. A key strand in the revelation on plural and celestial marriage is based on this statement. See Joseph Smith, Jr., *The Doctrine and Covenants of the Church of Jesus Christ of Latter-day Saints* (Salt Lake City: Church of Jesus Christ of Latter-day Saints, 1971), 132:16–17 (hereafter cited as Doctrine and Covenants). In a detailed early defense of the theological foundations underlying Mormon polygamy, Orson Pratt, *The Seer* 1 (March 1853): 43, also discusses Mormon beliefs in relation to this New Testament passage. A statement by Spencer W. Kimball, current President of the Mormon Church, explains how the Church's

"modern revelation" "clarifies" the passage. Spencer W. Kimball, "Temples and Eternal Marriage," *The Ensign* 4 (August 1974): 2–6.

37. Sidney E. Mead, "The Rise of the Evangelical Conception of the Ministry in America (1607–1850)," in *The Ministry in Historical Perspective*, ed. H. Richard Niebuhr and Daniel D. Williams (New York: Harper & Brothers, 1956), p. 210.

38. A major appeal of the Shakers certainly lay in their well-regulated community life, as the testimony of members and visitors clearly indicates. Fogarty in his "Conservative Christian Utopianism" argues that the primary factor in the appeal of Oneida was its creation of a secure religious and social framework for its members. And the centrality of that theme in Mormonism is also stressed in Mario S. De Pillis, "The Quest for Religious Authority and the Rise of Mormonism," *Dialogue: A Journal of Mormon Thought* 1 (Spring 1966): 68–88. This journal will be cited hereafter as *Dialogue*. For a comparative discussion of the issue of authority in these groups, see Stow Persons, "Christian Communitarianism in America," in Egbert and Persons, eds., *Socialism and American Life,* 1: 125–51.

Chapter II

1. This statement first appeared in [Benjamin Seth Youngs], *The Testimony of Christ's Second Appearing: Containing a General Statement of All Things Pertaining to the Faith and Practice of the Church of God in this Latter Day* (Lebanon, Ohio: John McClean, 1808), pp. 78–79. The version of the statement as quoted here is from the second edition of this work, printed at Albany, New York, by E. and E. Hosford, in 1810, pp. 48–49, which makes one minor spelling and one typographic change. Here all the sentences have been combined into one paragraph. This basic Shaker doctrinal work also was reprinted in 1823, and, in a heavily revised edition, in 1856. All quotations in this book from the *Testimony of Christ's Second Appearing* are from the 1808 edition, unless otherwise indicated.

2. The most authoritative account of Ann Lee's early struggles is in the rare 1816 edition of the *Testimonies of Mother Ann Lee*. Only twenty copies of this work, eight of which are known to be extant, were ever printed. This book was prepared solely for the use of Shaker leadership, not for reading by the general membership or for external polemical purposes. As such, it furnishes an unusually straightforward and comprehensive account of the early development of Shakerism, based on first-hand testimonies. All factual statements about Ann Lee and the early Shakers under her leadership that are not otherwise cited are based on this source. Later printed accounts of Ann Lee's life, with a more apologetic tone, include: *Testimonies Concerning the Character and Ministry of Mother Ann Lee and the First Witnesses of the Gospel of Christ's Second Appearing* (Albany, N. Y.: Packard & Benthuysen, 1827), and *Testimonies of the Life, Character, Revelations and Doctrines of Mother Ann Lee, and the Elders With Her,* 2nd ed. (Albany, N. Y.: Parsons, 1888).

One of the finest accounts of what Mother Ann was like as a person is found in "Incidents Related By Jemima Blanchard of Her Experience with Mother & the Elders," written by Roxalana Grosvenor, in Alonzo Hollister, ed., "Book of Remembrances" (MS, Western Reserve Hist. Soc.; New Lebanon, N. Y., *ca.* 1873), 1: 1–47. All manuscripts cited in this paper are in the Wallace Hugh Cathcart Collection of the Western Reserve Historical Society, Cleveland, Ohio, the finest collection of Shaker manuscripts. Hereafter cited as MS, WRHS. See Kermit J. Pike, *A Guide to Shaker Manuscripts in the Library of the Western Reserve Historical Society: With an Inventory of Its Shaker Photographs* (Cleveland: Western Reserve Hist. Soc., 1974).

3. For a discussion of the relation of Shakerism to these splinter revivalistic sects and to main-line revivalism after the Revolutionary War, see Stephen A. Marini, "Revivalism in Revolutionary New England, 1775–1780" (paper presented at the American Academy of Religion meetings, Chicago, Illinois, November 1975).

4. "Introduction to Records of Sacred Communications, Given by Divine Inspiration in the Church at New Lebanon" (New Lebanon, *ca.* 1843; MS, WRHS), p. 10. Although primarily an account of the remarkable spiritual manifestations among the Shakers in the late 1830s and early 1840s, this official statement also provides a concise historical summary of early Shaker development.

5. According to the ex-Shaker Thomas Brown, *An Account of the People Called Shakers: Their Faith, Doctrines, and Practice* (Troy, N. Y.: Parker & Bliss, 1812), p. 343, in 1803 the New Lebanon, N. Y., and Tyringham, Mass., Shaker communities sent to New York City $300 in specie, 853 pounds of pork, 1951 pounds of beef, 1794 pounds of mutton, 1685 pounds of rye flour, etc. Mayor De Witt Clinton thanked the Shakers for this gift in a letter printed in Edward Deming Andrews, *The People Called Shakers: A Search for the Perfect Society,* new enl. ed. (New York: Dover, 1962), p. 220.

6. Ibid., p. 224, makes this estimate. Statistics on Shaker membership are unreliable, to say the least, but Andrews's figure appears to be a realistic projection based on available manuscript records.

7. Robert Owen's debt to the Shakers was considerable. For instance, his *New View of Society: Tracts Relative to this Subject* (London: Longman, Hurst, Rees, Orme & Brown, 1818), includes a lengthy favorable statement about the Shakers, a group which had buttressed his own faith in the possibility of social reconstruction. In February 1845, Friedrich Engels argued that the Shakers, along with other American communal groups, showed that: "Communism, or life and work in a community where all goods are held in common, is not only possible but, as we shall see, is already being practiced successfully in many communities in America. . . ." Most of Engels's material came from John Finch's travel notes as published in Owen's newspaper, *New Moral World,* shortly after Engels had sent that paper his own analysis of continental communism. See Henri Desroche, *The American Shakers: From Neo-Christianity to Presocialism,* trans. and ed. John K. Savacool (Amherst: Univ. of Massachusetts, 1971), pp. 293–96. In his important history of the American communal movement before the Civil War, John Humphrey Noyes, founder of the Oneida Community and himself no mean social theorist,

described the success of the Shakers as "the 'specie basis' that has upheld all the paper theories, and counteracted the failures, of the French and English schools." See his *History of American Socialisms,* p. 670.

The widespread interest in the Shakers by their contemporaries is indicated in David R. Proper, comp., "Bibliography of Shaker Periodical Literature," *Shaker Quarterly* 4 (Winter 1964): 130–42; 5 (Spring 1965): 26–32; 5 (Winter 1965): 141–44; 8 (Winter 1968): 107–10; and 10 (Winter 1970): 138–40.

8. In addition to the accounts of Mother Ann Lee mentioned in note 2 of this chapter, see the following historical treatments of early Shaker de-development: *Testimony of Christ's Second Appearing,* pp. 17–32; Brown, *Account of the Shakers,* pp. 305–62; and [Calvin Green and Seth Y. Wells], *A Summary View of the Millennial Church or United Society of Believers (Commonly Called Shakers),* (Albany, N. Y.: Packard & Van Benthuysen, 1823), pp. 1–50. A second edition of the *Millennial Church,* with important additions, was printed at Albany, N. Y., by C. Van Benthuysen in 1848.

9. Any direct connection between the Camisards and the Shakers appears tenuous at best. Brown, *Account of the Shakers,* p. 313, claims that both Partington and Hocknell had formerly been "noted men" among the French Prophets. According to Hocknell's daughter Mary, however, he had belonged to the Church of England until he left to join the Methodists. *Testimony of Christ's Second Appearing,* p. 20. Since revivalist groups were highly fluid in their membership, both the Methodists and Camisards could well have influenced the Shakers. Perhaps because the Shaker revivalist activities were more extreme than even those of the early Methodists, the Shakers felt more akin to the Camisards. Given the relatively vague accounts of Shaker origins in England, it is possible that direct connections between the Camisards and the Shakers occurred without being recorded.

10. See Richard T. Vann, *The Social Development of English Quakerism, 1655–1755* (Cambridge, Mass.: Harvard Univ., 1969), a brilliant, succinct use of qualitative and quantitative methods to understand early English Quakerism.

11. For a summary of the classic statement of Quaker theology, see Eleanor Price Mather, *Barclay in Brief: An Abbreviation of Robert Barclay's Apology for the True Christian Divinity* (Pendle Hill, Pa.: Pamphlet Number 28; 1942). To the best of my knowledge, an explicit Quaker formulation of the dual godhead idea was not made in the early period, though hints of such beliefs can be found in the works of George Fox, Margaret Fell, and James Naylor.

12. Even in this early period, Ann Lee's attack on the evils of "lust" went far beyond a simple attack on sexual intercourse per se. As the Shakers further developed their theology and communal organization, they increasingly articulated a broader conception of "carnal" desires as representing all aspects of human rapacity and selfishness that interfered with single-minded devotion to God.

13. This approach is most explicitly formulated in Desroche, *The American Shakers,* although it is also found in other books such as Marguerite Fellows Melcher's *The Shaker Adventure* (Princeton: Princeton Univ.,

1941). Though Desroche's work raises a number of fascinating theoretical perspectives, his analysis sits rather lightly on the facts, seriously over-emphasizing Ann Lee's working-class background and the role of the later brilliant, but far from representative Shaker spokesman, Frederick W. Evans—ex-Owenite, free thinker, and land reformer. See Marius B. Peladeau's review of Desroche in *Shaker Quarterly* 11 (Fall 1971): 122–25.

14. *Testimonies of Mother Ann Lee*, p. 66. Accounts of early Shaker history sometimes carelessly attribute this vision to Ann Lee herself.

15. Some important accounts discussing the relationship of religious concerns to social and intellectual developments in the eighteenth century, par-ticularly the American Revolution, include: Sidney E. Mead, *The Lively Experiment: The Shaping of Christianity in America* (New York: Harper & Row, 1963); Richard L. Bushman, *From Puritan to Yankee: Character and the Social Order in Connecticut, 1690–1775* (Cambridge, Mass.: Harvard Univ., 1967); Clarence G. Goen, *Revivalism and Separatism in New England: Strict Congregationalists and Separate Baptists in the Great Awakening* (New Haven: Yale Univ., 1962); Alan E. Heimert, *Religion and the American Mind from the Great Awakening to the Revolution* (Cambridge, Mass.: Harvard Univ., 1966); Bernard Bailyn, *The Origins of American Politics* (New York: Vintage, 1970); Jack P. Greene, ed., *The Reinterpretation of the American Revolution, 1763–1789* (New York: Harper & Row, 1968); Kenneth Lockridge, "Land, Population and the Evolution of New England Society, 1630–1790; and an Afterthought," in *Colonial America: Essays in Politics and Social Development*, ed. Stanley N. Katz (Boston: Little, Brown, 1971); and Gordon S. Wood, *The Creation of the American Republic, 1776–1787* (Chapel Hill: Univ. of North Carolina, 1969).

16. *Testimonies of Mother Ann Lee*, p. 45.

17. Andrews, *People Called Shakers*, pp. 54–55.

18. An interesting study of this problem from a slightly different perspective is described briefly in David C. McClelland, "Love and Power: The Psychological Signals of War," *Psychology Today* 8 (January 1975): 44–48.

19. Andrews, *People Called Shakers*, pp. 215–16, describes how in 1863, when the Shakers were requesting exemption from the draft or the re-quirement to hire a substitute, they raised the novel argument that there was a sum of money in the national treasury, amounting (with interest) to $439,733, legally belonging to the Society through those who had served in the wars of the Revolution and 1812, which the Society had not claimed because of pacifist convictions.

20. *Testimonies of Mother Ann Lee*, p. 329.

21. Recollections of Thankful Goodrich in Alonzo Hollister, ed., "Book of Immortality" (New Lebanon, 1872; MS, WRHS), pp. 78–79.

22. For the classic expression of this theological liberalism in approaching Ann Lee, see *Testimony of Christ's Second Appearing*. Attitudes toward Ann Lee popularly held in the early nineteenth century are suggested in *Millennial Praises: Containing a Collection of Gospel Hymns in Four Parts, Adapted to the Day of Christ's Second Appearing* (Hancock, Mass.: J. Tallcott, 1812). This was the first hymnal printed by the Shakers. Also

see *Testimonies of Mother Ann Lee*, p. 166, and throughout, for strong evidence that Mother Ann's mystic effusions were frequently taken in a symbolic sense; for example, p. 346, further notes: "When any of the Believers expressed their love to her, she would often reply, 'It is not me that you love, but it is God in me.'"

23. *Testimony of Christ's Second Appearing*, p. 31.

24. Andrews, *People Called Shakers*, pp. 47–49, cites evidence of Shaker communal interest going back at least as far as 1780. The earliest Shaker manuscript extant, a letter from James Whittaker, written in February 1782, concerns communal organization.

25. *Testimonies of Mother Ann Lee*, p. 226. Not surprisingly the woman went off and proceeded to stir up trouble for the Society.

26. Quoted in Constance Rourke, "The Shakers," in her *The Roots of American Culture and Other Essays*, ed. Van Wyck Brooks (New York: Harcourt, Brace, 1942), p. 202. Rourke's fine essay, ibid., pp. 195–237, is the best brief introduction to the Shaker movement. The intensity of Mother Ann's personal horror of sexual relations is suggested by her vision of souls in hell, where "their torment appears like melted lead, poured through them in the same parts where they have taken their carnal pleasure." *Testimonies of Mother Ann Lee*, p. 304.

27. *A Concise Statement of the Principles of the Only True Church, Together With a Letter from James Whittaker to His Natural Relations in England, Dated Oct. 9th, 1785* (Bennington, Vt.: Haswell & Russell, 1790), reprinted as "First Shaker Imprint," in *Shaker Quarterly* 2 (Winter 1962): 144–55.

28. Particularly strong anti-Shaker legal challenges were waged in New Hampshire, New York, Ohio, and Kentucky. Many of the cases were concerned with the Shaker custom of receiving children into the Society accompanied by one parent, usually the father, who had "deserted" the other. Andrews, *People Called Shakers*, pp. 207–12.

29. Hervey Elkins, *Fifteen Years in the Senior Order of Shakers* (Hanover, N. H.: Dartmouth Press, 1853), p. 128.

30. Shaker "families" actually ranged in size from a few individuals to even larger groupings, but approximately 50 was the most common number.

31. Valentine Rathbun, *An Account of the Matter, Form, and Manner of a New and Strange Religion, Taught and Propagated by a Number of Europeans, Living in a Place Called Nisqueunia, in the State of New York* (Providence, R. I.: Bennett Wheeler, 1781), p. 12. This account provides direct corroboration for later Shaker assertions about Ann Lee. Rathbun dated his account December 5, 1780.

32. This succinct statement is found in the version of the Joseph Meacham manuscript edited by Theodore E. Johnson, in the *Shaker Quarterly* 10 (Spring 1969): 26. A longer and more elaborate statement is found in *Testimonies of Mother Ann Lee*, p. 21.

33. "Collection of the Writings of Joseph Meacham Respecting Church Order and Government" (New Lebanon, *ca.* 1850; MS, WRHS).

34. Almost all of the early apostate accounts included criticisms of Ann Lee for being a "witch" and engaging in "witchcraft." Although eighteenth-century America was unfavorable to outright prosecution on such a

count, residual fears of witchcraft may well have contributed to the intensity of the persecutions suffered by the Shakers. Any unorthodox religious group is liable to charges of witchcraft in a culture which believes in the reality of the supernatural, particularly if the group engages in highly emotional religious practices or if it is led by a woman. In our present "enlightened" age, we accomplish the same purposes by freely classing such phenomena as "mental illness."

35. The brutal mobbing at Petersham, Massachusetts, in December 1781, is described in detail in *Testimonies of Mother Ann Lee*, pp. 92–98.

36. First William Lee died at age 44, then Ann Lee at 48, and James Whittaker at 37.

37. Rathbun, *New and Strange Religion*, pp. 10–12.

38. *Testimony of Christ's Second Appearing*, pp. 30–31.

39. The critical, though honest, apostate William J. Haskett, *Shakerism Unmasked* (Pittsfield, Mass.: the author, 1828), notes in a special errata page that he had inadvertently misrepresented a statement by one of his informants. That informant had not asserted that he had seen Ann Lee drunk but rather that he had seen her acting *as if* she were drunk. Shaker sources pointed out that early pentecostal Christians also had been falsely accused of being "drunk with new wine." There can be no question, however, that Ann Lee and the early Shakers did drink wine on occasion, and it is not inconceivable that, faced with extreme stress, they might also have become drunk at times.

40. See William Sargant, *Battle for the Mind: A Physiology of Conversion and Brain Washing* (Garden City, N. Y.: Doubleday, 1957), as well as his many other writings developing this thesis.

41. William J. Samarin, *Tongues of Men and Angels: The Religious Language of Pentecostalism* (New York: Macmillan, 1972).

42. See Lewis, *Ecstatic Religion*, esp. pp. 18–36.

43. For popular treatments of some of these developments, see Braden, *The Private Sea*, and Richard King, "The Eros Ethos: Cult in the Counter Culture," *Psychology Today* 6 (August 1972): 35–39, 66–70. Many varieties of "sensitivity training" and similar therapeutic approaches make use of abreactive techniques.

44. Calvin Green, "Autobiography" (New Lebanon, 1861; MS, WRHS), p. 30.

45. Testimony of Thankful Goodrich in Hollister, "Book of Immortality," pp. 68–69.

46. Amos Tayler, *A Narrative of the Strange Principles, Conduct, and Character of the People Known by the Name of Shakers* (Worcester, Mass.: the author, 1782), p. 10.

47. Ibid., pp. 15–16.

48. Ibid., pp. 11–12.

49. *Testimonies of Mother Ann Lee* shows that Harvard served as the primary base of operations for Mother Ann during the 1781–83 Northeastern missionary trip. For approximately ten years prior to the Shakers' arrival there in 1781, Harvard had been the headquarters of an extraordinary New Light Baptist preacher, Shadrach Ireland, one-time follower of George Whitefield and advocate of Shaker-like doctrines of perfection, celibacy, and the millennium. Ireland appears to have been a rather

emotionally disordered individual. He claimed to be the Messiah, proceeded to desert his wife for a new "spiritual" bride, and then, arguing that he had achieved "perfection," decided that celibacy was to be discarded. As protection from persecution, he and his followers built him a sturdy house with a square roof, a cupola from which he could see when strangers approached, and a trap door with a secret staircase leading from the cupola to the cellar. Ireland boasted that if he died he would arise on the third day. When he did die, a year before the Shakers arrived, his followers faithfully awaited his resurrection, only to become disillusioned as the smell of his putrefying body became intolerable. After the Shakers arrived at Harvard they attempted to provide a more realistic religious base for Ireland's disillusioned but still expectant followers. The Shakers converted many of Ireland's associates and set up the Square House as their headquarters. The Shakers purchased the Square House and property for $536, of which Mother Ann herself was credited with supplying $144.73 in cash. Daryl Chase, "The Early Shakers: An Experiment in Religious Communism" (Ph.D. diss., Univ. of Chicago, 1936), pp. 24–27.

50. Quotations in this and the following two paragraphs are from Calvin Green, "Biographic Memoir of the Life, Character & Important Events, in the Ministration of Mother Lucy Wright" (New Lebanon, N. Y., 1870; MS, WRHS). Also see "Collection of the Writings of Father Joseph Meacham respecting Church Order and Government" (New Lebanon, N. Y., 1791–1796; MS, WRHS). Anna White and Leila S. Taylor, *Shakerism: Its Meaning and Message* (Columbus, Ohio: Fred. J. Heer, 1904), pp. 63–112, discuss Shaker development under Meacham and Wright. This book is the finest later Shaker account of their history and is based on careful use of manuscript sources.

51. See the summary in *Millennial Church,* pp. 58–67.

52. Despite verbal expressions of concern for women's equality, socialists generally have seen the reorganization of the relations between the sexes as subordinate in importance to the reorganization of the economic relations in society. To some extent, the Shakers reversed this order of priority. "In theory and practice, almost all socialists have accorded women more prominence in their organizations than in the contemporary world outside, yet the positions of formal leadership—with the notable exception of the Shakers—have been retained by men." T. D. Seymour Bassett in *Socialism and American Life,* ed. Egbert and Persons, 2: 391.

53. Two standard Shaker accounts of this development are *Millennial Church,* pp. 51–58, and White and Taylor, *Shakerism,* pp. 63–112.

54. Edward Deming Andrews, *The Community Industries of the Shakers* (Albany: Univ. of the State of New York, 1933). See also John Patterson Maclean, *Shakers of Ohio: Fugitive Papers Concerning the Shakers of Ohio, With Unpublished Manuscripts* (Columbus, Ohio: F. J. Heer, 1907); Melcher, *Shaker Adventure;* and Julia Neal, *By Their Fruits; The Story of Shakerism in South Union, Kentucky* (Chapel Hill: Univ. of North Carolina, 1947).

55. Andrews, *Community Industries of the Shakers,* p. 37.

56. Ibid., *passim.*

57. Andrews, *People Called Shakers,* pp. 143–44, notes the frequent obser-

vation of travelers that "the countenances of the sisters often seemed rapt and pallid, their bodies thin, their movements nervous, whereas the brethren looked ruddy, cheerful and healthy."

58. *Testimonies of Mother Ann Lee,* pp. 113–14.

59. The phrase, however, is in the summary of those accounts by Brown, *Account of the Shakers,* p. 362, who observes that "zeal without knowledge, or lack of wisdom and experience, (as they now confess) which caused them to run into many practices which they have now discarded," was common in this period.

60. *Testimony of Christ's Second Appearing,* p. 31.

61. Brown, *Account of the Shakers.*

62. Ibid., p. 334.

63. Ibid., p. 336. Mary Hocknell responded to Brown's question about allegations that during early Shaker development men and women had danced naked together, by saying: "Because the brethren pulled off their coats, or outside garments, to labour, or as the world calls it, dancing; and in warm weather the sisters being lightly clothed, they would report we danced naked." Ibid., p. 47. Throughout both the account of his personal investigation of the Shakers and his history of their development, Brown explains why he finds this sort of statement an inadequate explanation for the widespread stories. He provides names of principals and informants, as well as dates and circumstances, which convinced him beyond any reasonable doubt that both naked dancing and naked flagellant activities occurred during peak periods of early Shaker excitement. For a summary of his conclusions, see ibid., pp. 322–23, 334–36.

64. *Testimonies of Mother Ann Lee,* p. 265. Also see ibid., p. 214. Shaker statements of this sort suggest a level of self-consciousness about the techniques of their revivalism that verges on the secular approach of the later revivalist Charles Grandison Finney in his *Lectures on Revivals of Religion,* 6th ed. (New York: Leavitt, Lord, 1835).

65. *Millennial Church,* p. xii.

66. New Lebanon "Introduction to Records of Sacred Communications," p. 10.

67. Richard McNemar, *The Kentucky Revival; or, A Short History of The Late Extraordinary Outpouring of the Spirit of God in the Western States of America* (Cincinnati: John W. Browne, 1807). This was reprinted in 1808, 1837, and 1846. It also was reproduced in a Shaker periodical, *The Manifesto,* between January 1891 and July 1892.

68. Jerald C. Brauer has suggested the possibility of approaching the Kentucky Revival as an initiation rite. One of Brauer's students, James S. Dalton, attempted to develop this concept in "The Kentucky Camp Meeting Revivals of 1797–1805 as Rites of Initiation" (Ph.D. diss., Univ. of Chicago, 1973). One could, of course, approach any major revival as in some sense both an individual and a social rite of passage. What is remarkable about the Shakers, however, is that their leaders explicitly analyzed their *own* experience from a framework that is almost totally compatible with that of later secular scholarly theorists.

69. McNemar, *The Kentucky Revival,* 1846 ed., p. 89.

70. This development is discussed in detail in John Patterson Maclean, *A*

Bibliography of Shaker Literature, With an Introductory Study of the Writings and Publications Pertaining to Ohio Believers (Columbus, Ohio: F. J. Heer, 1905), pp. 3–20.

71. Ibid., p. 6.
72. Although Shaker concerns with celibacy are voiced throughout the *Millennial Church,* this summary is based on pages 129–43, entitled "The Cause, Nature and Effects of Man's Loss From God."
73. *Millennial Church,* pp. 132–33.
74. Shakers frequently were frustrated by the inability of most outsiders to understand—much less agree with—their celibate system. Richard Pelham expressed such feelings in a pamphlet appropriately entitled *A Shaker's Answer to the Oft-Repeated Question, "What Would Become of the World If All Should Become Shakers"* (Boston: Rand, Avery, 1878). Also see *Testimony of Christ's Second Appearing,* 1810 ed., p. 618.
75. White and Taylor, *Shakerism,* provides a point of entry into the wide range of printed and manuscript Shaker biographical and autobiographical statements. Important printed autobiographical accounts include those of Frederick W. Evans, Mary Antoinette Doolittle, Giles Avery, Henry B. Bear, Jane D. Knight, Henry C. Blinn, and George M. Wickersham. These are primarily late Shaker figures and Shaker "liberals." A more representative cross-section of people is provided by the manuscripts at the Western Reserve Historical Society. See Pike, *Guide to Shaker Manuscripts,* esp. pp. 48–52. Alonzo Hollister's two-volume compilation, "Autobiography of the Saints," is a good entrée into this material. Also see accounts of Issachar Bates, William Leonard, Rebecca Jackson, Proctor Sampson, Calvin Green, Abigail Crossman, Orren N. Haskins, Henry Clough, Rhoda Blake, Richard W. Pelham, and Freegift Wells. Some of these accounts have been reproduced with introductions in the *Shaker Quarterly.*
76. This account is based on Theodore E. Johnson, ed., "A Sketch of Life and Experience of Issachar Bates," in *Shaker Quarterly* 1 (Fall 1961): 98–118; 1 (Winter 1961): 145–63; and 2 (Spring 1962): 18–35.
77. Autobiographical statement of Lucy Brown in Hollister, "Autobiography of the Saints" (New Lebanon, N. Y., *ca.* 1886; MS, WRHS) 2: 318–26. D'Ann Campbell in "Women's Life in Utopia," pp. 28–37, presents evidence on the demographic composition of Shaker communities in New York and Kentucky, as well as some speculations on the reasons why women were attracted to the Shakers. She finds a higher ratio of women to men in Shaker communities than in surrounding areas, although she does not indicate whether Shaker communities had a different proportion of women to men from those of other religious organizations of the area. Using biographical sketches from the Western Reserve Historical Society Library, Campbell suggests some possible factors in Shaker appeal to women. She focuses, in particular, on the role of social dislocation and the desire of converts to find a refuge from problems of the outer society.
78. See Green, "Biographic Memoir of Lucy Wright." Also see White and Taylor, *Shakerism,* pp. 105–9.
79. "Incidents in the Early Life of Elder John Lyon" (Enfield, N. H., 1861; MS, WRHS).

80. Among the most important accounts of seceders and apostates are Rathbun, *An Account of a New and Strange Religion* (1781); Tyler, *Narrative of the Shakers* (1782); Brown, *Acount of the Shakers* (1812); Mary Marshall Dyer, *A Portraiture of Shakerism* (Concord, N. H.: for the author, 1822); Mary Marshall, *The Rise and Progress of the Serpent from the Garden of Eden, to the Present Day* (Concord, N. H.: for the author, 1847); Eunice Chapman, *Account of the Conduct of the People Called Shakers in the Case of Eunice Chapman and Her Children* (Albany, N. Y.: n.p., 1817); Eunice Chapman, *No. 2d, Being an Additional Account of the Conduct of the Shakers in the Case of Eunice Chapman and Her Children* (Albany, N. Y.: I. W. Clark, 1818); Haskett, *Shakerism Unmasked* (1828); David Rich Lamson, *Two Years' Experience Among the Shakers: Being a Description of the Manners and Customs of That People* (West Boyleston, Mass.: the author, 1848); and Elkins, *Fifteen Years in the Shakers* (1853).

81. Mary Marshall (Dyer)'s most important early accounts were her *A Brief Statement of the Suffering of Mary Dyer, Occasioned by the Society Called Shakers* (Concord, N. H.: Joseph C. Spear, 1818) and her *Portraiture of Shakerism* (1822). The Shakers responded in Joseph Dyer, *A Compendious Narrative, Elucidating the Character, Disposition, and Conduct of Mary Dyer* (Concord, N. H.: I. Hill, 1818); [Richard McNemar, et al., comps.], *The Other Side of the Question* (Cincinnati: Looker, Reynolds, 1819); and *A Review of Mary M. Dyer's Publication, Entitled "A Portraiture of Shakerism": Together With Sundry Affidavits Disproving the Truth of Her Assertions* (Concord, N. H.: Jacob B. Moore for the United Society, 1824). Mary Marshall responded with a review of most of her earlier statements in *The Rise and Progress of the Serpent* (1847).

82. Elkins, *Fifteen Years in the Shakers*, p. 128.

83. Andrews, *People Called Shakers*, pp. 207–12.

84. In the programming and statistical aspects of this membership study, Raymond E. Pifer has provided invaluable counsel and assistance. The findings presented here represent only a preliminary foray into the rich Shaker membership materials. I am currently working on a more intensive analysis of the New Lebanon data, an analysis which will utilize census records, qualitative accounts by members of the Second Family, and other membership information on the New York Shakers. By building on Andrews's work in *Community Industries of the Shakers*, which reconstructs the economic life of the New Lebanon community, and on other available manuscript materials, a comprehensive picture of this complex celibate community may be developed. Note that some of the unusual membership characteristics of the New Lebanon Second Family could be explained if that family served as a "gathering order" for the larger New Lebanon community complex.

85. For a valuable account of Shaker life which provides the primary basis for this section, see Andrews, *People Called Shakers*, esp. pp. 94–151, 177–203. Also see the section on the Shakers in Nordhoff, *Communistic Societies of the United States*, and Rourke, "The Shakers."

86. See Irving Goffman, *Asylums: Essays on the Social Situation of Mental Patients and Other Inmates* (Garden City, N. Y.: Doubleday, 1961), pp.

xiii and *passim,* for a provocative discussion of the "total institution," defined as "a place of residence and work where a large number of like-situated individuals, cut off from the wider society for an appreciable period of time, together lead an enclosed, formally administered round of life."

87. William Hepworth Dixon, *New America,* 6th ed., 2 vols. (London: Hurst & Blackett, 1867), 2: 86.

88. Andrews, *People Called Shakers,* pp. 181–82, 185, used by permission.

89. Ibid., p. 126.

90. White and Taylor, *Shakerism,* p. 223.

91. This phase of Shaker history has been described variously as "the new era," "Mother Ann's Second Appearing," "Mother Ann's Work," a period of "spiritual manifestations," the "spiritualist period," or the "wave of mystic symbolism." The phenomena were "spiritualist" in the sense that many were allegedly messages from the dead. The messages expressed a sense of the interconnectedness of the temporal and spiritual worlds, both believed to have a literal existence. Shaker "spiritualist" phenomena occurred prior to the larger nineteenth-century American spiritualist movement and were largely over by the time that movement first achieved general popularity following the table rapping of the Fox Sisters in Hydesville, New York, in 1848. Since the Shaker spiritualist period was primarily a religious revival, I coined the term "spiritualist revival" in an earlier paper to differentiate the period from other revivals in Shaker history in which alleged communications with the dead were not such a prominent feature. A version of this section was presented as a paper at the Shaker Bicentennial Conference in Cleveland, Ohio, on October 10, 1974, entitled: "Shaker Trance and Spirit Possession, 1837–1845: New Perspectives on the Psychology of the Shaker Spiritualist Revival."

For accounts of the larger spiritualist movement with which the Shaker spiritualism was related, see: Cross, *Burned-over District,* pp. 341–52; Slater Brown, *The Heyday of Spiritualism* (New York: Pocket Books, 1972); Geoffrey K. Nelson, *Spiritualism and Society* (London: Routledge & Kegan Paul, 1969); Howard Kerr, *Mediums, and Spirit Rappers, and Roaring Radicals: Spiritualism in American Literature* (Urbana: Univ. of Illinois, 1972); J. Stillson Judah, *The History and Philosophy of the Metaphysical Movements in America* (Philadelphia: Westminster, 1967), esp. "The Mirror of American Culture," pp. 22–49; and R. Laurence Moore, *In Search of White Crows: Spiritualism, Parapsychology, and American Culture* (New York: Oxford Univ., 1977).

92. Eric Rohman's "Words of Comfort, Gifts of Love: Spirit Manifestations Among the Shakers, 1837–1845" (B.A. thesis, Antioch College, 1971), provides one of the few convincing interpretations of this difficult and troubled period. Also see the sociological treatment of Shaker development in John McKelvie Whitworth, *God's Blueprints: A Sociological Study of Three Utopian Sects* (London: Routledge & Kegan Paul, 1974). Whitworth shows how the spiritualist period was pivotal in Shaker development.

93. A patronizing approach is evident throughout many accounts of those fascinated by the externals of Shaker life such as their crafts and architecture, but unsympathetic to the inner meaning of Shaker religious

views and concerns. Even Edward Deming Andrews's great work contains such elements. For the fraud thesis, see John P. Maclean, "Spiritualism Among the Shakers of Union Villiage, Ohio," in his *Shakers of Ohio;* as well as his *A Sketch of the Life and Labors of Richard McNemar* (Franklin, Ohio: printed for the author by the *Franklin Chronicle,* 1905), and Melcher, *Shaker Adventure,* pp. 248–50. The psychopathology thesis has not been systematically developed by serious scholars of Shakerism, but it is an undercurrent in some of the less sophisticated work on the group.

94. John Large's preliminary draft bibliography of the Shaker holdings of the Western Reserve Historical Society has been superceded by Pike, *Guide to Shaker Manuscripts,* which, because of the way it groups the materials, does not suggest the full extensiveness of the holdings from the spiritualist period.

95. The most important Shaker manuscript analyses of this period available at the Western Reserve Historical Society include: New Lebanon "Introduction to Records of Sacred Communications," an invaluable overview of the spiritualist period from the perspective of the leadership at New Lebanon, keyed to the 11-volume official compilation of revelations made there; Alonzo Hollister, "Shakers and Spiritualism" (New Lebanon, n.d.), as well as numerous other collections of spiritualist experiences recorded by his hand; and "A Record of Heavenly Gifts, Messages and Communications" (Watervliet, 1839–1841), a collection of revelations making clear the various social problems and tensions associated with the spiritualist phenomena at Watervliet. Valuable printed Shaker presentations are found in the anonymous account, *A Return of Departed Spirits of the Highest Characters of Distinction* (Philadelphia: J. R. Colon, 1843); Frederick W. Evans, *Autobiography of a Shaker, and Revelation of the Apocalypse* (Mt. Lebanon, N. Y.: F. W. Evans, 1869); Giles B. Avery, *Autobiography* (East Canterbury, N. H.: n.p., 1891); Henry C. Blinn, *The Manifestations of Spiritualism Among the Shakers, 1837–1847* (East Canterbury, N. H.: n.p., 1899); and White and Taylor, *Shakerism.* Indispensable accounts by those who left the Shakers are given in Lamson, *Among the Shakers,* and Elkins, *Fifteen Years in the Shakers.*

96. See the New Lebanon "Introduction to Records of Sacred Communications," pp. 11–13, for a summary of the declension which immediately preceded the 1837 revival. "Remarks on the Necessity of Reforming the Morals and Improving the Religious Condition of our Children" (New Lebanon, 1830; MS, WRHS), written in the same hand as the "Introduction," gives a detailed account of the problems the Shakers were having in keeping children who reached puberty in the Society. Throughout the spiritualist period itself, numerous revelations and writings were directed to the young, possibly the most famous of which was *The Youth's Guide in Zion* (Canterbury, N. H.: n.p., 1842).

97. The major Millerite accessions to the Shakers appear to have occurred between 1844 and 1846. Andrews, *People Called Shakers,* p. 223, notes that in 1846 about two hundred Millerites joined the Midwestern Shaker communities, Whitewater in particular. In the East, Harvard, Canterbury, and Enfield (New Hampshire) were the chief beneficiaries. At the invitation of a Millerite society in Philadelphia, New Lebanon sent mis-

sionaries who organized a Shaker out-family there. Another Shaker group was organized in Philadelphia by a remarkable black woman, Rebecca Jackson, who had ties with the Watervliet community. See Richard E. Williams, "Mother Rebecca Jackson: One of the Black Shakers in Philadelphia," *Shaker Messenger* 1 (Spring 1979): 3–5. Enoch Jacobs, who edited the Adventist *Western Midnight Cry,* which became the *Day-Star,* briefly joined the Shakers, publishing several issues of the *Day-Star* from Union Village, Ohio, between 1846 and 1847. See "On the Second Coming of Christ: Not Personal, but Spiritual and Gradual; Progressive, Like the Rising of the Sun" (n.p.: the compiler, *ca.* 1843?); "Brief Sketches of the Visitations of the Judgments of God to Earth Since 1840; Showing the Fulfillment of Many Prophecies Given in These, Our Days" (New Lebanon?, *ca.* 1848?; MS, WRHS); *Henry B. Bear's Advent Experience* (Whitewater, Ohio: n.p., n.d.); "Diary of Rebecca Jackson" (Watervliet, N. Y., 1849–1861; MS, WRHS): "Autobiography and Testimony of Rebecca Jackson" (New Lebanon, 1877; MS, WRHS); "Sketches of a Conference Meeting Between the Shakers & Adventists held at Enfield, Conn. Feby. 8th 1847" (Enfield, Conn., 1847; MS, WRHS).

98. Andrews, *People Called Shakers,* pp. 248–89, reprints these laws.
99. The New Lebanon, "Introduction to Records of Sacred Communications," pp. 41–44, summarizes the wide range of phenomena observed, as does Elkins, *Fifteen Years in the Shakers,* p. 35.
100. See Lewis, *Ecstatic Religion.*
101. The number of cases of spiritualist phenomena described by the Shakers that would be considered evidence of extrasensory perception by today's standards is miniscule. Walter F. Prince, "The Shakers and Psychical Research: A Notable Example of Cooperation," *Journal of the American Society for Psychical Research* 12 (1918): 61–69, catalogues books on the spiritualist period sent him by Shakers, but barely discusses extrasensory perception. Like most mediums, the Shaker instruments appear primarily to have been unconsciously conveying their personal beliefs and philosophy of life in an almost ministerial sense, using their mediumistic skills as a way of gaining attention for deeply held personal beliefs.
102. Rohmann, "Words of Comfort," suggests the basic typology that I have used here.
103. Blinn, *Manifestation of Spiritualism,* p. 24.
104. Rohmann, "Words of Comfort," pp. 9–11. It is paradoxical that although the manifestations ostensibly were "spiritual," they could, insofar as they represented the repressed desires of average Shakers, contribute to an increasingly secular outlook by giving a sort of supernatural aura to secular ideals. For a discussion of how the larger spiritualist movement also was associated with further secularization, see Judah, *Metaphysical Movements.*
105. "Messages of Mother Ann to the Church at New Lebanon, April 22, 1838, Through Philemon Stuart [*sic*], Sabbath, P.M." (New Lebanon, 1838; MS, WRHS) is a detailed account of this episode. Considerable artificiality does appear to be present in Stewart's presentation, which could easily be seen as having more of a sermonic than an involuntary character. Stewart became a key figure in the orchestration of Shaker spiritualism.

106. Even when deliberately planned or sought, Shaker spiritualist revelations were not seen by the leadership as cynical manipulation, but rather as a part of the normal hierarchical control that they exercised in the Shaker communities. Avery, *Autobiography*, p. 12, illustrates the Shaker attitude. In this book, published by the Shakers, he unselfconsciously describes how he was commissioned to write a book-length revelation. He was unable to work himself into the proper state of mind, so eventually the Ministry gave the assignment to Philemon Stewart—who wanted it. He wrote *A Holy, Sacred and Divine Roll and Book: Sent Forth by the Lord God of Heaven, to the Inhabitants of Earth* (Canterbury, N. H.: United Society, 1843). See Robert F. W. Meader, "The Vision of Brother Philemon," *Shaker Quarterly* 10 (Spring 1970): 8–17, for an account of this strange episode. Avery's account suggests a very different mind-set from our present one. Surely if he had viewed his efforts as cynically manipulative, he would not have reported them straightforwardly as he did. And had the Shakers viewed the information in his autobiography as damaging, presumably they would have deleted it.
107. Blinn, *Manifestation of Spiritualism*, p. 49.
108. Andrews, *People Called Shakers*, pp. 160–61.
109. White and Taylor, *Shakerism*, p. 235.
110. A detailed account of the Mountain Meetings in which he participated is found in Lamson, *Among the Shakers*, pp. 56–74. Composite accounts are given in Andrews, *People Called Shakers*, pp. 161–67, and Rohmann, "Words of Comfort," pp. 24–32.
111. J. P. Maclean discusses this complex episode in his *Richard McNemar*, pp. 61–62. Maclean suggests that some collusion between the medium and Freegift Wells may have been present, at least unconsciously. Compare this interpretation to Freegift Wells's later disillusioned statements about spiritualist phenomena in his "Testimonies, Predictions, and Remarks" (Watervliet, N. Y., n.d.; MS, WRHS), p. 19. The McNemar papers at the Library of Congress also shed much light on this heated conflict. Whatever the conscious intent of the participants in this unfortunate power play, there would seem to be little doubt that the intense division within the Union Village community had a negative effect on its membership. About 1823, that community had reached its peak membership of some 600, rivaling that of New Lebanon. By 1830, its membership had declined to 500. Thereafter it declined slowly to something less than 400 in 1852, and extremely rapidly in the next decade to a mere 100 members in 1862. Whitworth, *God's Blueprints*, p. 78.
112. Andrews, *People Called Shakers*, p. 174.
113. The figures from whom the Shakers received revelations were strikingly similar to the heroes and heroines of the school textbooks of the period as described in Ruth Miller Elson, *Guardians of Tradition: American Schoolbooks of the Nineteenth Century* (Lincoln: Univ. of Nebraska, 1964). This would suggest that the Shakers may have shared much of the common cultural background of their contemporaries.
114. White and Taylor, *Shakerism*, p. 246.
115. Andrews, *People Called Shakers*, p. 267. For purposes of comparison, see the Shaker Laws of 1821 in *Shaker Quarterly* 7 (Summer 1967): 35–58, and the Laws of 1860 in *Shaker Quarterly* 11 (Winter 1971): 139–65.

116. For a discussion of the complex factors leading to Shaker decline, particularly as related to the spiritualist period, see Whitworth, *God's Blueprints*, pp. 48–88.
117. Avery, *Autobiography*, p. 15.
118. "Diary of Rebecca Jackson," page not indicated. The statement appeared in appended comments by Alonzo Hollister.
119. Blinn, *Manifestation of Spiritualism*, pp. 38–39.
120. Freegift Wells, "A Series of Remarks Showing the Power of the Adversary in Leading Honest Souls Astray Through the Influence of Inspired Messages" (Watervliet, N. Y., 1850; MS, WRHS).
121. Prince, "Shakers and Psychical Research," p. 63.
122. Whitworth, *God's Blueprint*, pp. 74–79.
123. Sidney Cohen, *The Beyond Within: The LSD Story* (New York: Atheneum, 1964), p. 62.

Chapter III

1. *Handbook of the Oneida Community,* 1867 ed., p. 64; *Handbook of the Oneida Community,* no. 2 (Oneida, N. Y.: Oneida Community, 1871), p. 56. Italics have been removed from these quotations and from all other quotations in this chapter, except when otherwise indicated.
2. Quoted from Noyes's reprint of the letter and the various responses to it in the *Witness,* January 23, 1839. Noyes first publicly acknowledged his authorship of the letter in print in the *Witness,* September 23, 1837. Numerous reprints and discussions of the letter have appeared, including George Wallingford Noyes, ed., *John Humphrey Noyes: The Putney Community* (Oneida, N. Y.: by the author, 1931) pp. 1–10.
3. The extreme concerns for personal perfection that Noyes and others felt in the antebellum period had precedents going back to the earliest days of the Christian faith. The ideal of eventually overcoming sin and achieving heavenly perfection had always been present in Christianity, of course, but from the beginning there were also those who believed that such total, sinless perfection could and should be achieved at once on earth. Statements such as "You must be perfect, even as your heavenly father is perfect" or "Thy kingdom come . . . on earth as it is in heaven" were viewed by some as showing the possibility, desirability, and even the necessity of immediate earthly perfection. As Christianity developed and became an established religion, particularly after the fifth century, such millennial concerns were largely relegated to an indefinite future. Fringe heretical movements nevertheless kept the millennial tradition alive and the development of Catholic monasticism allowed certain perfectionist tendencies to coexist as part of the Catholic Church's temporal organization.

   With the coming of the Protestant Reformation, particularly the rise of fringe movements such as the Anabaptists, these concerns were revived, for a time, in the sixteenth century. And in nineteenth-century America, similar attitudes were expressed by individuals who reacted against the Calvinist belief that men were totally depraved and could only be saved by the intervention of a mysterious, utterly transcendent God. Instead, many concerned Christians moved toward the Arminian position that men could play an active role in helping to achieve their salvation. Arminianism encouraged perfectionist tendencies such as those reflected in mild form in the teachings of John Wesley and the Methodist church. Methodists saw perfection as an on-going process, and argued that perfection was not absolute, nor Adamic, nor angelic perfection in this life, but rather perfect love as called for by Christ. Though such perfect love was possible on earth and could free those so perfected from all unholy tempers, pride, anger, self-will, and sinfulness, individuals who were moving toward perfection were by no means freed from mistakes, infirmities of judgment, involuntary negligences, and ignorances.

Some individuals influenced by perfectionist ideas carried them one step further, however, and argued for all-or-nothing perfection in this life. Such individuals declared that they were already free from sin—or "perfect"—and that inasmuch as they were perfect, they were free to act as they chose, since God's will and their own were identical. Though Noyes, the Shakers, and similar perfectionists closely approached such beliefs at times, they also recognized the danger of the total individualism and antinomianism that such beliefs could inspire. In attempting to overcome anarchic tendencies, Noyes would create an elaborate theological edifice to buttress his perfectionist ideals. The details of this theological system are not important to this study. The main point is that Noyes eventually was able to develop a framework through which he could affirm the ideal of earthly perfection, while restraining its potential excesses.

For a detailed introduction to the various schools of Christian perfectionist thought, see Frederick Platt, "Perfection," in *Encyclopedia of Religion and Ethics,* ed. James Hastings (New York: Charles Scribner's Sons, 1917), 9: 728–37. The best analytical and documentary introduction to Noyes's perfectionist thought is G. W. Noyes, ed., *Religious Experience of John Humphrey Noyes, Founder of the Oneida Community* (New York: Macmillan, 1923). Merrill Elmer Gaddis, "Christian Perfectionism in America" (Ph.D. diss., Univ. of Chicago, 1929), also places Noyes's perfectionism into its larger intellectual context. John Gager, *Kingdom and Community,* emphasizes the millennial and perfectionist elements in early Christianity.

4. For a study which links many of the historical and intellectual themes of antebellum millennialists and communitarians to those of the contemporary "counter-culture," see Keith Melville, *Communes in the Counter Culture: Origins, Theories, Styles of Life* (New York: William Morrow, 1972).

5. Charles Nordhoff, *The Communistic Societies of the United States: From Personal Visit and Observation* (New York: Harper & Brothers, 1875), p. 271.

6. Alan Estlake [Abel Easton], *The Oneida Community* (London: George Redway, 1900), p. 56.

7. Cross, *Burned-over District,* p. 333.

8. For discussions of Noyes's early life and family relationships see: G. W. Noyes, *Religious Experience,* pp. 1–41 and *passim;* Robert Allerton Parker, *A Yankee Saint: John Humphrey Noyes and the Oneida Community* (New York: G. P. Putnam's Sons, 1935), pp. 3–29; and Robert David Thomas, *The Man Who Would Be Perfect: John Humphrey Noyes*

and the Utopian Impulse (Philadelphia: Univ. of Pennsylvania, 1977), pp. 1–19.

9. The closely knit and somewhat ingrown characteristics of Noyes and his communities have been discussed from the perspectives of Freudian theory and recent ego-psychology in Ernest R. Sandeen, "John Humphrey Noyes as the New Adam," *Church History* 40 (March 1971): 82–90, and in Thomas, *The Man Who Would Be Perfect*.

10. The indispensable source for Noyes's early religious development is his *Confessions of John H. Noyes: Part I: Confession of Religious Experience, Including a History of Modern Perfectionism* (Oneida Reserve, N. Y.: Leonard, 1849). Part II, which was to have described the development of Noyes's social theory, unfortunately never was printed. Excerpts from the *Confessions,* as well as letters and diary entries, are found in G. W. Noyes, *Religious Experience.* Noyes's periodicals also provide insight into many facets of the development of his religious concerns that are not so clearly indicated in other printed sources.

11. *First Annual Report of Oneida Association,* pp. 11–12. A more detailed presentation of Noyes's elaborate theological beliefs is found in his *The Berean: A Manual for the Help of those who Seek the Faith of the Primitive Church* (Putney, Vt.: office of the *Spiritual Magazine,* 1847). Somewhat misleadingly described by some as the "Bible" of the Oneida Community, *The Berean* reprints the core of Noyes's theology as presented in seventy-five articles written and published between 1834 and 1846 in various periodicals which he helped to edit.

12. The idea that faith is more important than works tends to have socially radical implications, as Noyes was well aware. During times of turmoil, in particular, an emphasis on the spirit not the letter of the law may lead reformers to reject institutions which no longer appear to be serving the purpose for which they were created. Hence, St. Paul gave up circumcision and other regulations of Judaism, Martin Luther broke with the Roman Catholic Church, and John Humphrey Noyes, on a much smalller scale, discarded religious and social practices of his day that he considered incompatible with the spirit of early Christianity.

13. The only comprehensive account of this episode is found in Noyes's *Confessions,* pp. 33–47.

14. Ibid., pp. 40–41.

15. Ibid., p. 41.

16. *Witness* 1 (September 25, 1839): 78. The original has copious italics scattered throughout. This statement was part of a reply by Noyes to letters from the Shaker Loren Hollister of New Lebanon, New York.

17. Noyes, *Confessions,* p. 63. Also see *Spiritual Moralist* 1 (June 13, 1842): 7–8.

18. Noyes, *Confessions,* p. 30.

19. G. W. Noyes, *Religious Experience,* pp. 351–54.

20. Ibid., p. 308.

21. Quoted in full in the *Witness* 1 (January 23, 1839): 49. The original emphasis has been restored to this important paragraph.

22. See the *Witness,* September 23, 1837.

23. G. W. Noyes, *Putney Community,* p. 10.

24. *Witness* 1 (January 23, 1839): 56. In his *The Man Who Would Be Per-*

fect, p. 93, Thomas suggests that this marriage proposal, like the Battle-Axe Letter, was an effort by Noyes to "desexualize marriage."

25. "Financial Romance: How the O. C. Got Its Capital," *Circular* 2, n.s. (January 8, 1866): 366.
26. Fogarty, "Conservative Christian Utopianism," p. 66.
27. The only explicit reference to the alcoholism of Noyes's father is found in the "Petition of the Junior Members of the Noyes Family to their Father," dated March 9, 1837, and printed in G. W. Noyes, *Putney Community,* pp. 91–93.
28. Ibid., p. 33.
29. Ibid., p. 25.
30. Noyes's underlying theory of organization and government for his communities was presented in *First Annual Report of the Oneida Association,* pp. 12–14. For the original statement, see *Spiritual Magazine* 2 (July 1, 1847): 57–59.
31. G. W. Noyes, *Putney Community,* p. 33.
32. Fogarty, "Conservative Christian Utopianism." For a summary of this argument, see Robert S. Fogarty, "Oneida: A Utopian Search for Religious Security," *Labor History* 14 (Spring 1973): 202–27. Also see Maren Lockwood Carden, *Oneida: Utopian Community to Modern Corporation* (Baltimore: Johns Hopkins, 1969), pp. 25–26.
33. "Who are the Conservatives?" *Circular* 1 (May 30, 1852): 115. See also Parker, *Yankee Saint,* p. 113.
34. *The Man Who Would Be Perfect.*
35. For discussions of the communitarian concerns in the antebellum period, see as starting points: Noyes, *History of American Socialisms;* G. W. Noyes, *Putney Community,* pp. 151–69; Bestor, *Backwoods Utopias;* Bestor, "Patent-Office Models"; and Stow Persons, "Christian Communitarianism in America," in *Socialism and American Life,* ed. Egbert and Persons, 1: 125–52. John Humphrey Noyes's *American Socialisms* made extensive use of manuscript materials on the Owenite and Fourierist groups collected by A. J. MacDonald, the originals of which are now held by the Yale University Library.
36. Noyes, *American Socialisms,* p. 26.
37. G. W. Noyes, *Putney Community,* p. 168.
38. Noyes, *American Socialisms,* p. 27.
39. Parker, *Yankee Saint,* p. 89.
40. *Handbook of the Oneida Community,* 1867 ed., p. 9.
41. Parker, *Yankee Saint,* pp. 115–16.
42. Benjamin B. Warfield, "John Humphrey Noyes and His 'Bible Communists,'" *Bibliotheca Sacra* 78 (1921): 346–47, argued that Noyes borrowed "the whole formal nature of his system" from the Shakers and that he consistently presented a clear counterpart to major Shaker doctrines, even when he drastically altered them. In my B.A. thesis, "Women and Utopia: The Shaker and Oneida Perfectionist Attempts to Achieve Heaven on Earth by Enlarging the Family to Do Away With Human Selfishness" (Antioch College, 1970), I suggested that Noyes's system, including complex marriage, might, in many respects, best be viewed as a Shaker heresy.
43. "Bible Argument," pp. 38–39.

44. *Handbook of the Oneida Community,* 1867 ed., p. 60. Also see "Marriage—Its Bible Limitation," *Circular* 3 (September 14, 1854): 487.
45. Quoted in "Was Mr. Noyes Ever a Shaker?" *Oneida Circular* 12, n.s. June 28, 1875): 211. The article, in three installments on June 28, July 5, and July 12, 1875, summarizes Noyes's attitudes toward the Shakers by reprinting many of his earlier responses to them and their ideas. Robert Thomas kindly called this article to my attention.
46. "A Word of Warning," *Perfectionist and Theocratic Watchman* 5 (July 12, 1845): 34.
47. Possibly the most interesting debate was the one which Noyes carried on in response to letters of the New Lebanon Shaker Loren Hollister. See *Witness* 1 (September 26, 1839): 80.
48. The substance of this conversation is reported in Parker, *Yankee Saint,* pp. 155–58.
49. "Was Mr. Noyes Ever a Shaker?" *Oneida Circular* 12, n.s. (July 12, 1875): 219.
50. John Humphrey Noyes, *Male Continence* (Oneida, N. Y.: Office of the *Oneida Circular,* 1872), pp. 9, 13, 15. John Humphrey Noyes, *Essay on Scientific Propagation* (Oneida, N. Y.: Oneida Community, 1872?), pp. 21–23.
51. Pierrepont B. Noyes, *My Father's House: An Oneida Boyhood* (New York: Farrar & Reinhart, 1937), p. 144.
52. This "Bible Argument" may have been first printed in the *First Annual Report of the Oneida Association,* pp. 18–42.
53. "Bible Argument," pp. 27–28.
54. Ibid., p. 24.
55. Ibid., p. 25. The internal numbering of the original has been removed.
56. See "Becoming as Little Children," *Spiritual Magazine* 2 (December 22, 1849): 339; and "The Family and Its Foil," *Circular* 3 (November 16, 1854): 594.
57. "Bible Argument," pp. 21–22; Noyes, *American Socialisms,* pp. 626–27. The Freudian implications of this sort of statement are discussed by Sandeen and Thomas from contrasting perspectives. In this regard, Noyes's reaction to Mormon polygamy is illuminating. Noyes recognized that his and the Mormon systems for reorganizing relations between the sexes were akin because they were "masculine products of the Great Revivals." But he argued that complex marriage was different from both monogamy and polygamy. Polygamy, in Noyes's view, *Bible Communism,* p. 84, simply accentuated the worst features of monogamy:

> It is plain that the fundamental principle of monogamy and polygamy is the same; to wit, the ownership of woman by man. The monogamist claims one woman as his wife—the polygamist, two or a dozen: but the essential thing, the bond of relationship constituting marriage, in both cases is the same, namely a claim of ownership.

58. Noyes's concerns for creating an enlarged, unitary family to overcome the sort of fragmentation which he found in the existing American family run throughout his writings. Noyes felt that such concerns were the major preoccupation not only of his own movement, but also of both the Owenite and Fourierist waves of communal excitement, which had for their main idea "the enlargement of home—the extension of family union

beyond the little man-and-wife circle to large corporations." Noyes, *American Socialisms,* p. 23. Some especially revealing articles on this topic include: "The Utility of Combination," *Spiritual Magazine* 2 (October 1, 1847): 131; "Practical Communism," *Circular* 1 (June 13, 1852): 121; "Industrial Marriage," *Circular* 3 (March 18, 1854): 179; "What Communism Offers," *Circular* 3 (October 5, 1854): 522; and "Our Home," *Circular* 3 (October 21, 1854): 550. Excellent analyses of Noyes's concerns for reorganizing the relation of the family and the industrial order are presented in Fogarty, "Oneida," and in Thomas, *The Man Who Would Be Perfect.*

59. G. W. Noyes, *Putney Community,* pp. 37–45.

60. Ibid., p. 46.

61. The first detailed presentation of Noyes's theory and practice of male continence appears in his "Bible Argument," pp. 27–35. About 1866, a four-page letter by John Humphrey Noyes describing the practice to an inquirer was published as a separate leaflet. The letter was reprinted a number of times and finally was included, along with the major summation of Noyes's views on the subject, in his pamphlet, *Male Continence,* in 1872. Noyes's description of the historical roots of the idea first appeared in his *Dixon and His Copyists* (Wallingford, Conn.: Oneida Community, 1872).

62. Noyes, "Bible Argument," pp. 27–28; Noyes, *Male Continence,* p. 6.

63. Noyes, "Bible Argument," p. 33.

64. Noyes, *Male Continence,* p. 16.

65. Ibid., pp. 9–10.

66. Noyes, "Bible Argument," p. 32.

67. Noyes, *Male Continence,* pp. 7, 9.

68. I coined this term in an attempt to capture the paradoxical quality of sexual intercourse without any seminal emission.

69. Noyes, *Male Continence,* p. 8.

70. Noyes, "Bible Argument," p. 32.

71. This is the conclusion reached by Carden, *Oneida,* p. 51. She bases her figures on Hilda Herrick Noyes and George Wallingford Noyes, "The Oneida Community Experiment in Stirpiculture," Scientific Papers of the Second International Congress of Eugenics, 1921, in *Eugenics, Genetics and the Family* (Baltimore: William & Wilkins, 1923), 1: 386. The physiological mechanisms by which male continence was possible have been confirmed in Alfred C. Kinsey, Wardell Pomeroy, and Clyde Martin, *Sexual Behavior in the American Male* (Philadelphia: W. B. Saunders, 1948), pp. 158–61.

72. Constance Noyes Robertson, *The Oneida Community: The Breakup, 1876–1881* (Syracuse, N. Y.: Syracuse Univ., 1972), pp. xi–xiv. Carden, *Oneida,* p. xviii, states that "half a room full" of paper was burned. Some materials which had been thought lost have recently been rediscovered. See Constance Noyes Robertson, *Oneida Community Profiles* (Syracuse, N. Y.: Syracuse Univ., 1977), p. vii.

73. Theodore E. Noyes, M.D., "Report on Nervous Diseases in the Oneida Community" as printed in Noyes, *Scientific Propagation,* pp. 25–32. The "Report" was printed earlier, with high praise as "a model of careful observation and discriminative appreciation," in the *New York Medical*

Gazette, on October 22, 1870. The "Report" presented both general statistics and detailed case examples. It concluded that, although its sample was too small to be statistically significant, the Oneida Community nevertheless had a smaller number of various types of nervous disorders than the society at large. Whatever the significance of male continence in the various cases, it could not be accused of *increasing* the overall number of cases of nervous disorders. For an analysis from a hostile external writer who nevertheless writes favorably about the health of women of the Oneida Community, see Ely van de Warker, "Gynecological Study of the Oneida Community," *American Journal of Obstetrics and Diseases of Women and Children* 17 (August 1884): 755–810.

74. Noyes, *Male Continence,* p. 20.
75. Pierrepont B. Noyes, *My Father's House,* p. 131; Estlake, *Oneida Community,* p. 26.
76. For Noyes's account of the beneficial effects of his system in practice, see his *Male Continence,* pp. 18–21.
77. Carden, *Oneida,* pp. 77–80.
78. Robert Fogarty has called my attention to evidence in T. E. Noyes's "Report" that some members of the Oneida Community remained celibate. P. B. Noyes implies that at least one of the men who took care of the rearing of the Community's children in the Children's House was celibate. See *My Father's House,* p. 150, and elsewhere. There can be no question that celibacy was considered a theoretical alternative to complex marriage at Oneida, although, like worldly marriage, it was considered less desirable. When the Oneida Community announced its final abandonment of complex marriage in August 1879, it stated that the group was advocating "Paul's platform, which allows marriage but prefers celibacy." Robertson, *The Breakup,* p. 160.
79. Thomas, *The Man Who Would Be Perfect,* p. 98.
80. Noyes, *Male Continence,* p. 11.
81. Himes, *Medical History of Contraception,* p. 271.
82. Havelock Ellis, *Sex in Relation to Society,* vol. 6: *Studies in the Psychology of Sex* (Philadelphia: F. A. Davis, 1911), p. 553. This conclusion was based on Ellis's correspondence with an ex-Community member, George Noyes Miller.
83. Carden, *Oneida,* p. 30. Noyes expressed the basis of his commitment in his *Confessions,* p. 41. After his New York experience in 1834, he realized that he would have to reorganize his life around a small number of truths which he "absolutely knew" and could use as the "specie-basis" for all his other beliefs. Everything but those core principles was subject to modification. Noyes's commitment to his basic religious and sexual beliefs and to his sense of personal mission shows exceptional consistency throughout his life, but the way in which those beliefs were expressed in practice varied considerably in the face of altered external circumstances. A similarly intense commitment to basic principles and to a sense of religious mission, but a willingness to innovate radically in specific external forms, also characterized Joseph Smith.
84. Carden, *Oneida,* p. 107.
85. See *Mutual Criticism* (Oneida, N. Y.: office of the *American Socialist,* 1876), esp. pp. 44–69. The major source for personal data of this nature

on Community members was the column inaugurated in the *Spiritual Magazine* on December 22, 1849, entitled "Criticism," p. 346. Like all examples of successfully functioning societies, Oneida operated according to certain underlying shared principles which all members of the group accepted to a large degree, but it also allowed for the interaction of a wide range of character types within that basic framework.

86. Fogarty, "Conservative Christian Utopianism," esp. pp. 105–29. Three appendices to this study, pp. 259–344, print (1) the Oneida Family Register, a manuscript giving the names and personal data on the first 111 people who joined the Community; (2) U. S. census data on Oneida Community members from 1850 through 1880; and (3) maps showing the birthplaces of members. The characteristics of members also are suggested by the first three annual reports of the Oneida Association.

87. In his "The Development of a Utopian Mind: A Psychoanalytic Study of John Humphrey Noyes, 1828–1869" (Ph.D. diss., State Univ. of New York at Stony Brook, 1973), pp. 288–89, Robert David Thomas looks at this popular Community pastime from such a perspective.

88. P. B. Noyes, *My Father's House,* p. 148.

89. Noyes, *Male Continence,* p. 21.

90. The term "criticism" covered more than the relatively formalized procedures described here. Community members were supposed to criticize each other's faults openly and to encourage each other to improve their character, not only in institutionalized sessions, but throughout their daily lives as well.

91. Noyes, *Confessions,* p. 4. Also see *Mutual Criticism,* pp. 4–13.

92. "Criticism," *Circular* 1 (March 21, 1852): 74. This was written by Noyes's sister Harriet.

93. *First Annual Report of the Oneida Association,* p. 11.

94. *Mutual Criticism,* pp. 3, 88. Nordhoff's quotation was from his *Communistic Societies of the United States,* p. 413.

95. According to *Mutual Criticism,* p. 94:

> It is Th[e]ocratic for in recognizing Truth as King, it recognizes God who is the source of all truth, and whose Spirit alone can give power of genuine criticism. It is Aristocratic, inasmuch as the best critics have the most power. It is Democratic, inasmuch as the privilege of criticism is distributed to all classes, and the highest attainments and skill are open to every one.

This statement also appeared in slightly different form in *Bible Communism,* pp. 9–10.

96. G. W. Noyes, *Putney Community,* pp. 196–210.

97. Ibid., pp. 205–7.

98. This was the title of an article in the *Spiritual Magazine* 2 (September 1, 1847): 120.

99. G. W. Noyes, *Putney Community,* p. 202.

100. "Business for the Convention," *Circular* 1 (February 8, 1852): 54.

101. 2 (July 15, 1847): 65 (emphasis in original).

102. G. W. Noyes, *Putney Community,* pp. 276–80.

103. These membership figures are based on the first three annual reports of the Oneida Association.

104. Carden, *Oneida*, p. 77.
105. It is difficult to see how simple social characteristics such as the geographical, occupational, or economic status of Community members could fully account for the attraction of individuals to the group. *Bible Communism*, p. 22, accurately states that "the main body of those who have joined the Association at Oneida, are sober, substantial men and women of good previous character and position in society." Problems with the status anxiety and frustration-aggression models in explaining reform in general and Noyes's efforts in particular are discussed in Thomas, "Psychoanalytic Study," pp. 1–10.
106. *Handbook of the Oneida Community* (Oneida, N. Y.: office of the *Oneida Circular*, 1875), p. 15.
107. *First Annual Report of the Oneida Association*, pp. 8–9.
108. Marlyn Hartzell Dalsimer, "Women and Family in the Oneida Community, 1837–1881" (Ph.D. diss., New York Univ., 1975), pp. 246–47. Ibid., pp. 242–77, gives her complete analysis of women's work at Oneida. The most authoritative treatment of the status of women in the context of Noyes's larger communal goals at Oneida still is found in Parker, *Yankee Saint,* which is based on a comprehensive knowledge of printed and manuscript sources on the Community, including materials which were subsequently destroyed. Parker's basic conclusions are supported by Joseph Kirschner, "Women and the Communal Experience: The Oneida Community, 1849–1877" (prepublication draft of a paper, dated June 6, 1979, read through the courtesy of the author). Kirschner's analysis is one of the few recent studies based on extensive access to surviving manuscript materials. He supports the conclusion that women at Oneida had greater occupational flexibility and chances for personal fulfillment than in the outer society.
109. "Condensation of Life," *Spiritual Magazine* 2 (March 15, 1846): 2. This important article was reprinted in *The Berean*, pp. 487–93. Also see Carden, *Oneida,* pp. 66–67.
110. "Woman's Slavery to Children," *Spiritual Magazine* 1 (September 15, 1846): 109–10.
111. This approach is developed in "Condensation of Life," *Spiritual Magazine* (March 15, 1846): 3–4. Also see "Socialism in Two Directions," *Circular* 3 (April 29, 1854): 250.
112. "Woman's Character," *Circular* 3 (January 14, 1854): 72.
113. Estlake, *Oneida Community,* pp. 74–77.
114. Ibid., p. 35.
115. "Bible Argument," p. 18. Compare this with the Shaker analysis of the process of transition.
116. Letter of August 1847, printed in the *Spiritual Magazine* 2 (September 1, 1847): 126. In this same issue, p. 124, Miller wrote an article entitled "The Soldier Spirit," which presented the same line of argument as Noyes's later statement in the "Bible Argument," p. 18.
117. "A Memoir of Charlotte Miller," *Oneida Circular* 12, n.s. (May 1875): 170.
118. *Circular* 3 (January 17, 1854): 75. This was an irregular column.
119. "Brooklyn and Oneida," *Circular* 1 (November 16, 1851): 6 Noyes wrote:

> The Brooklyn Company which is engaged in the business of this paper has heretofore been *called* sometimes a *branch* of the Oneida Association—strictly speaking however it is an independent company; and so far as there is any affiliation between the two, the Oneida Association is the Branch [italics in original].

120. Fogarty, "Conservative Christian Utopianism," p. 162. Noyes characteristically went to New York City, or, later, to the Wallingford, Connecticut, branch community. Robert Thomas commented wryly to me that instead of retreating from the bustle of the city to a rural haven in times of stress, Noyes instead went from a rural base to the city.

121. Parker, *Yankee Saint,* pp. 187–89.

122. "Plans and Prospects," *Free Church Circular* 3 (October 21, 1850): 281. Fogarty, "Conservative Christian Utopianism," pp. 182–83.

123. "Editorial Correspondence," *Free Church Circular* 3 (October 21, 1850): 281.

124. In his Home-Talk, "Disasters and Successes of Perfectionism," *Spiritual Magazine* 2 (January 10, 1850): 353–57, Noyes discussed at great length the various betrayals through "bad partnerships" and "false fellowships" which had continually undercut his efforts and had resulted in negative publicity for his cause. He concluded: "The consequence, or result of this antagonism of disaster and success has been to limit our operations to a rather small compass—we have been doing a small but safe business."

125. "A Complaint Answered," *Free Church Circular* 3 (October 3, 1850): 270. The letter was from a Charles Degroff of Wisconsin.

126. The immediate occasion for the move was the accidental burning of the printing office at Oneida in November 1851. The decision to relocate in Brooklyn rather than to rebuild at Oneida, may well have been due to a number of factors, including the insecure position of the Community at Oneida and Noyes's desire to have his press located closer to the centers of public opinion.

127. "The Past, Present and Future," *Circular* 1 (March 7, 1852): 66. The *Observer's* campaign contributed to severe local problems for the Community, as well as larger public relations difficulties.

128. See "The Second Course," *Circular* 1 (April 4, 1852): 82; "Past Enjoyments," *Circular* 1 (April 4, 1852): 83; "Hints to the Peaceable," *Circular* 1 (May 2, 1852): 98; "Things Proved," *Circular* 1 (May 23, 1852): 110. This last article declares:

> The Oneida Community has in a certain sense, discharged its mission, and may be looked upon as in the past. By its change of position last winter, it surrendered the distinctive and peculiar characteristics which constituted its individuality and fell back within the lines of worldly toleration, and under the forms of selfish law. Of course it is no longer, as to outward force and feature, the original Oneida Association.

In a conclusion suggesting a sort of forced cheerfulness, the article asserts that at least the past accomplishments of the Community are a part of history and can "never be touched, or blotted out, or forgotten." These accomplishments prove that this kind of unselfish association is possible.

129. Robertson, *The Breakup,* p. 161.

130. Estlake, *Oneida Community,* pp. 40–41.

131. "The Second Course," *Circular* 1 (April 4, 1854): 82.
132. It is significant that many of these articles coupled the terms "disease and death." For Noyes's basic statement on the topic, see "Abolition of Death" in *The Berean*, pp. 476–86.
133. *Circular* 1 (February 1, 1852): 51.
134. "The Rival of Christ," *Circular* 1 (April 4, 1852): 82; "A Bible Contest," *Circular* 1 (April 11, 1852): 87. These articles were written by Noyes's sister Harriet.
135. If one can "break the code" used during this tense period of Noyes's communal experimentation, all the parts fit together like pieces in a jigsaw puzzle. By writing about the Oneida Community in terms of Biblical characters, the paper could operate simultaneously on two levels. On the simple, public level, a person would see articles of moral exhortation. On a more private level, those who knew more about the inner details of the Community could find out what was going on there.
136. *Bible Communism*, p. [4]. The reprint of this book by Porcupine Press prints this dedication, but the AMS Press reprint inexcusably omits it. Note that Noyes could use any of the various Marys in the New Testament in referring symbolically to Mary Cragin. No identity is being established here between a particular Biblical character and a particular follower of Noyes, any more than Noyes's own self-identification with Christ in many of the articles is intended in a literal sense. The Bible stories are freely adapted to say important things about the present.

The intense veneration for Mary Cragin at Oneida is suggested in "Community Journal," *Circular* 5 (October 19, 1868): 245, as quoted in Carden, *Oneida*, p. 70. In 1868, practical considerations made it appropriate to rebury Mary Cragin's remains. Looking at her skull, "all who knew her, recognized the contour—so beautifully feminine. [Her son George] expressed a wish that the skull might be retained. The wish was unanimous. It is to be varnished and preserved."
137. "The Message," *Circular* 1 (August 1, 1852): 150.
138. *Circular* 1 (August 4, 1852): 150.
139. *Circular* 1 (August 29, 1852): 170. The capitalization of the original has been eliminated in this quotation from the "Theocratic Platform."
140. *Circular* 3 (April 15, 1854): 226.
141. Carden, *Oneida;* P. B. Noyes, *My Father's House;* Parker, *A Yankee Saint.* Constance Noyes Robertson, ed., *The Oneida Community: An Autobiography, 1851–1876* (Syracuse, N. Y.: Syracuse Univ., 1970), captures the richness of Community life through excerpts from its newspapers.
142. Noyes, *American Socialism*, p. 642.
143. Handbook of the *Oneida Community*, 1867 ed., p. 5.
144. P. B. Noyes, *My Father's House*, p. 138.
145. "A Panoramic View," *Oneida Circular*, August 18, 1873, as quoted in Dalsimer, "Women and Family in the Oneida Community," pp. 318–19. The original quotation was a single paragraph.
146. Parker, *Yankee Saint*, pp. 253–54. Presumably Bible Communism, as printed in 1848, is the same text as the "Bible Argument" printed in *First Annual Report of the Oneida Association*.
147. See Carden, *Oneida*, p. 63. She bases her figures on H. H. Noyes and G. W. Noyes, *Eugenics, Genetics and the Family*, 1: 378.

148. An indispensable presentation of the conflicts associated with the dissolution of complex marriage is Robertson, *The Breakup*. This could serve
as a model for a similar scholarly study of the dissolution of Mormon
polygamy. Among the other important discussions of stirpiculture and
the breakup, see Parker, *Yankee Saint*, pp. 254–91; Fogarty, "Conservative Christian Utopianism," pp. 200–49; and Carden, *Oneida*, pp. 61–65,
89–111.
149. Robertson, *The Breakup*, p. 160.
150. Ibid., p. 161.
151. *Bible Communism*, p. 6.
152. G. W. Noyes, *Religious Experience*, p. 306. This is a part of the larger
portion of Noyes's letter to George Harrison which was not printed by
Theophilous Gates as part of the Battle-Axe Letter.
153. "The Liberty of Union," *Circular* 1 (January 4, 1852): 86.
154. "Liberty to Change," *Circular* 3 (August 8, 1854): 422.

Chapter IV

1. Speech of October 6, 1854. Reported in *Journal of Discourses*, 26 vols.
(Liverpool, Eng.: F. D. Richards and others, 1854–1886), 2: 90. These
volumes, based on stenographic reports of the speeches of early Mormon
leaders, are an invaluable source for understanding many early developments in the Latter-day Saint movement.
2. Numerous printed versions of the revelation on plural and celestial marriage exist. The minutes of the conference of the Mormon Church in
Salt Lake City at which the revelation was first read publicly, appeared
as a *Deseret News* Extra for September 14, 1852, and were reprinted as a
supplement to vol. 15 of the *Millennial Star* in 1853. Another early reprinting of this revelation is found in the *Millennial Star* 15 (January 1,
1853): 5–8. The earliest printed versions of this revelation are untitled.
This is also true of the two manuscript versions of the revelation, photo-
copies of which I have carefully examined in the Archives of the Historical Department of the Church of Jesus Christ of Latter-day Saints in
Salt Lake City, Utah. Hereafter cited as Church Archives. The strong
contemporary evidence that this revelation existed in Nauvoo and was
dictated by Joseph Smith will be presented in the course of this chapter.
The handwriting of the two manuscript versions of the revelation in the
Church Archives has been established by Danel W. Bachman in "A
Study of the Mormon Practice of Plural Marriage Before the Death of
Joseph Smith" (M.A. thesis, Purdue University, 1975), pp. 208–11. This
is a thorough analysis of the origins of plural marriage from a Mormon
perspective. Although Bachman and I worked independently of each
other and started from somewhat different sets of assumptions, we reached
conclusions that are compatible on most issues. The full text of the first
printed version of the revelation on plural and celestial marriage will be
found in the appendix to this book.
   Note that technically the term "polygamy" refers either to "polygyny,"
a man having more than one wife, or to "polyandry," a woman having
more than one husband. The Utah Mormons practiced a form of polygyny, never polyandry; however, in deference to the almost universal

usage of both Mormons and non-Mormons, the term polygamy will be used in this book.

3. The sermon by Orson Pratt which presented the initial Mormon defense of their marriage system to the world appeared in the *Deseret News* Extra of September 14, 1852, and the supplement to vol. 15 of the *Millennial Star*. It was also reprinted under the title "Celestial Marriage" in *Journal of Discourses*, 1: 53–66.

4. Charles A. Shook, *The True Origin of Mormon Polygamy* (Cincinnati: Standard Publishing Co., 1914), reproduces and skillfully analyzes most of the early evidence—including statements by almost every early leader of the RLDS Church—which links Joseph Smith beyond any reasonable doubt to the intellectual genesis and practice of polygamy. The first issue of the *True Latter Day Saints' Herald* in January 1860 included statements by Isaac Sheen, William Marks, and others, admitting that Joseph Smith had been actively involved in introducing polygamy, but claiming that he had repented of his errors prior to his death. As individuals who had had a personal knowledge of Joseph Smith's polygamy activities died, the RLDS Church increasingly tended to react to the polygamy issue as a bad dream; the official stance was to deny that the whole affair had ever taken place—but always with the significant proviso that *even if* Smith had taught or practiced polygamy, it still was wrong. For instance, see *Joseph Smith III and the Restoration*, ed. Mary Audentia Anderson and condensed by Bertha Audentia Anderson Holmes (Independence, Mo.: Herald Publishing House, 1952), pp. 152–54; and Maurice L. Draper, *Marriage in the Restoration: A Brief Historical Doctrinal Review* (Independence, Mo.: Herald Publishing House, 1968).

The primary LDS arguments for the thesis that Joseph Smith was responsible for introducing the theory and practice of polygamy into the Mormon Church are summarized in John A. Widtsoe, "Evidences and Reconciliations: CX. Did Joseph Smith Introduce Plural Marriage?" *Improvement Era* 49 (November 1949): 721, 766–67; and Joseph F. Smith, Jr. [Joseph Fielding Smith], *Blood Atonement and the Original Plural Marriage: A Discussion* (Salt Lake City: Deseret News, 1905). Also see the article by Andrew Jenson, LDS Church Historian, giving affidavits and a list of twenty-seven women who allegedly were sealed to Joseph Smith, primarily during the last three years of his life, "Plural Marriage," *Historical Record* 5 (May 1887): 219–34. Note that such "sealings" did not necessarily involve full conjugal relations. I have carefully examined the many published and unpublished affidavits and other personal statements in the Church Archives in Salt Lake City. The hypothesis of fraud cannot possibly account for this entire body of material which represents so many different perspectives and biases.

5. Although accounts of knowledgeable apostates generally fail to present the spirit which underlay Smith's efforts, such accounts are indispensable if one is to reconstruct the complex early development of polygamy. Later Mormon writings often prefer to forget some of the early difficulties. Among the accounts which must be seriously considered in making a historical reconstruction of the early development of polygamy, see: John C. Bennett, *The History of the Saints, or, An Exposé of Joe Smith and Mormonism* (Boston: Leland & Whiting, 1842); Oliver H. Olney, *The*

Absurdities of Mormonism Portrayed (Hancock County, Ill.: n.p., 1843); *The Nauvoo Expositor* (June 7, 1844); John Hyde, Jr., *Mormonism: Its Leaders and Designs* (New York: W. P. Fetridge, 1857); T. B. H. Stenhouse, *The Rocky Mountain Saints: A Full and Complete History of the Mormons* (New York: D. Appleton, 1873); John D. Lee, *Mormonism Unveiled, or, The Life and Confessions of the Late Mormon Bishop, John D. Lee,* ed. W. W. Bishop (St. Louis: Byran, Brand, 1877); and Wilhelm Wyl, *Joseph Smith, The Prophet: His Family and Friends; A Study Based on Facts and Documents* (Salt Lake City: Tribune Printing and Publishing Company, 1886). Such accounts based on first-hand documentation should not be confused with the vast body of nineteenth-century anti-Mormon treatments which are semi-novelistic in character and usually historically valueless for understanding the early development of polygamy. Analyses of this latter genre are provided in Leonard Arrington and Jon Haupt, "Intolerable Zion: The Image of Mormonism in Nineteenth Century American Literature," *Western Humanities Review* 22 (Summer 1968): 243–60, and Charles A. Cannon, "The Awesome Power of Sex: The Polemical Campaign Against Mormon Polygamy," *Pacific Historical Review* 43 (February 1974): 61–82. The results of a far-reaching content analysis of changing attitudes toward Mormons in major American magazines are summarized by Jan Shipps in "From Satyr to Saint: American Attitudes Toward the Mormons, 1860–1960" (paper presented at the 1973 annual meeting of the Organization of American Historians, Chicago, Illinois).

6. The complex process by which Joseph Smith received and interpreted revelation has not yet received adequate scholarly analysis. Some starting points for such a treatment are found in the Doctrine and Covenants, esp. sections 6 through 10; Joseph Smith, Jr., *History of the Church of Jesus Christ of Latter-day Saints: Period I: History of Joseph Smith the Prophet,* ed. Brigham H. Roberts, 6 vols., 2nd ed. rev. (Salt Lake City: Deseret Book Company, 1948), 5: xxxiv–xlvi; Eduard Meyer, "The Nature and Mechanism of Smith's Revelations," in his *The Origin and History of the Mormons,* trans. Heinz F. Rahde and Eugene Seaich (Salt Lake City: [Univ. of Utah], 1961), pp. 30–38; Richard P. Howard, *Restoration Scriptures: A Study of Their Textual Development* (Independence, Mo.: Herald Publishing House, 1969); and Jan Shipps, "The Prophet Puzzle: Suggestions Leading Toward a More Comprehensive Interpretation of Joseph Smith," *Journal of Mormon History* 1 (1974): 4–20.

7. Some important examples of psychological reductionist approaches are Isaac Woodbridge Riley, *The Founder of Mormonism: A Psychological Study of Joseph Smith, Jr.* (New York: Dodd, Mead, 1902); Bernard De Voto, "The Centennial of Mormonism," *American Mercury* 19 (January 1930): 1–13; and Fawn Brodie, *No Man Knows My History: The Life of Joseph Smith, the Mormon Prophet,* 2nd ed. rev. and enl. (New York: Alfred A. Knopf, 1972), pp. 418–21. Marvin Hill, "Secular or Sectarian History? A Critique of *No Man Knows My History,*" *Church History* 33 (March 1974): 78–96, analyzes a number of weaknesses in Brodie's assumptions and criticizes the tendency toward psychological reductionism that is present in her revised account. A recent biography

which qualifies but does not supersede Brodie's work is Donna Hill, *Joseph Smith: The First Mormon* (Garden City, N. Y.: Doubleday, 1977).

8. "The Prophet Puzzle."

9. T. Edgar Lyon informed me, in a letter dated May 18, 1978, of his research showing that the population of Nauvoo was second to that of Chicago in 1845.

10. Millennial themes continue to run through Joseph Smith's life, becoming especially important during times of crisis such as the late Nauvoo period. Tuveson, *Redeemer Nation,* pp. 175–86, notes that Mormon millennialism can not easily be fitted into the pessimistic pre-millennial or the optimistic post-millennial categories. For instance, the *Millennial Star,* official organ of the British mission, carefully detailed various natural disasters which presumably presaged the end of the world when God would miraculously intervene to set things straight. Yet the Mormons also showed a strong sense that they could mold a glorious future themselves and take fate into their own hands. Like most millennialists, the Mormons combined both optimism and pessimism. Sometimes these attitudes fluctuated in an almost manic-depressive manner.

11. There are both positive and negative early accounts of the activities of Joseph Smith and the Smith family. On the sources for the Smith family's ill repute, the non-Mormon scholar Whitney Cross observes:

> Every circumstance seems to invalidate the obviously prejudiced testimonials of unsympathetic neighbors (collected by one hostile individual whose style of composition stereotypes the language of numerous witnesses) that the Smiths were either squatters, or shiftless "frontier drifters." Many an honest and industrious farmer followed their identical experience, pursued by bad luck or poor judgment, and sought a new fling at fortune further west. No doubt the Smiths, like many of their fellows, wasted valuable time hunting gold at the proper turn of the moon. One of the potent sources of Joseph's local ill repute may well have been the jealousy of other persons who failed to discover golden plates in the glacial sands of the drumlins.

Burned-over District, pp. 141–42. Smith, like many other individuals in the Burned-over District, was searching for "hidden treasure"—treasure in both the literal and symbolic sense. Whether the "golden plates" which he eventually claimed to have found ever actually existed or were only the product of his creative imagination is not the most important question; the *content* of his work is of far greater importance than its origin. In any case, whether or not the golden plates ever had an actual existence can probably never be established to the full satisfaction of those who take opposing points of view.

12. *History of the Church,* 1: 3.

13. For texts and analyses of the various accounts of the "first vision," see Dean C. Jesse, "The Early Accounts of Joseph Smith's First Vision," *Brigham Young University Studies* 9 (Spring 1969): 275–94. *Brigham Young University Studies* will be cited hereafter as *BYU Studies.* Also see *History of the Church,* 1: 2–8, and Doctrine and Covenants, section 2. Numerous articles in *Dialogue* and *BYU Studies* during the past decade

have addressed issues connected with the first vision. See esp. James B. Allen, "The Significance of Joseph Smith's First Vision in Mormon Thought," *Dialogue* 1 (Autumn 1966): 28–45; Wesley P. Walters, "New Light on Mormon Origins from the Palmyra Revival," *Dialogue* 4 (Spring 1969): 60–81, with Richard L. Bushman's reply and Walters's response, ibid., pp. 82–100. Because of certain polemical considerations, Mormon historiography has placed excessive emphasis on the precise *date* of Joseph Smith's first vision, instead of analyzing the more important values and concerns underlying those visions. Smith's visions were neither unique nor culturally aberrant. Visionary phenomena of all sorts were a common part of the revivalistic religion of the period. Smith's visions were significant because, unlike similar phenomena experienced by many of his contemporaries, his visions led to socially significant actions—specifically, his decision to "translate" the Book of Mormon, and his larger, long-range concern to found his own church. For a starting point in analyzing the larger context of prophetic visionary experiences such as those that led to the "translation" of the Book of Mormon, see Wallace, "Revitalization Movements."

14. Joseph Smith, Jr., *The Book of Mormon: An Account Written by the Hand of Mormon, Upon Plates Taken from the Plates of Nephi* (Palmyra, N. Y.: E. B. Grandin for the author, 1830), was the first edition of this basic Mormon work. Subsequent editions have undergone considerable modification, largely of a stylistic nature. As only one example, the first edition identifies Joseph Smith, Jr., as the "Author and Proprietor" of the work, while subsequent editions state that he was the "Translator." See Howard, *Restoration Scriptures,* pp. 24–69. Quotations from the Book of Mormon will be taken from the first edition, but for reader convenience citation will also be given based on Orson Pratt's division of the text into chapter and verse in 1879: Joseph Smith, Jr., *The Book of Mormon: An Account Written by the Hand of Mormon Upon Plates Taken from the Plates of Nephi* (Salt Lake City: Church of Jesus Christ of Latter-day Saints, 1963).

15. I have not considered it either necessary or desirable in this book to present an extended evaluation of the various interpretations of the origin of the Book of Mormon. In these notes, however, it may be useful to suggest some of the sources that could contribute to the development of a comprehensive naturalistic explanation of the Book of Mormon—an explanation which could go beyond the conventional Mormon view that it is a literal history translated by Joseph Smith or the conventional anti-Mormon view that it is a conscious fraud.

On some possible nineteenth-century sources for factual and thematic elements in the Book of Mormon, see Thomas F. O'Dea, *The Mormons* (Chicago: Univ. of Chicago, 1957), pp. 22–49; Hal Houghey, *"A Parallel": The Basis of the Book of Mormon* (Concord, Calif.: Pacific Publishing Company, 1963); and Brodie, *No Man Knows My History,* pp. 1–82, 405–25, 442–56. Michael Coe, "The Mormons and Archaeology: An Outside View," *Dialogue* 8 (1973): 40–48, summarizes the various positions on "the Book of Mormon archaeology" from a critical non-Mormon point of view. For an important Mormon evaluation of the problem of evidence and interpretation relating to "the coming forth of the

Book of Mormon," see Edward H. Ashment, "The Book of Mormon: A Literal Translation?" *Sunstone* 5 (March-April 1980): 10–14. The extensive literature on the Joseph Smith papyri and the Book of Abraham, which suggest the way in which the Book of Mormon might also have been "translated," is discussed in *Dialogue* 3 (Summer 1968): 66–105, a special issue on the topic, as well as in articles in *Dialogue* for Autumn 1968 and Summer 1969, and in *BYU Studies* between 1968 and 1971.

The greatest single weakness of most previous interpretations of the origin of the Book of Mormon has been their failure to take into account comparative perspectives on revelatory and trance phenomena similar to those associated with the production of the Book of Mormon. For an introduction to the comparative literature on such phenomena, see Wallace, "Revitalization Movements," and Burridge, *New Heaven, New Earth,* as well as other references to cargo cults and millennial movements indicated in the notes for Chapter 1 and in the Essay on Sources following these notes. Also see the literature on religious visionary experiences cited in note 12 of Chapter I. For an introduction to such phenomena in the American context, see Slater Brown, *The Heyday of Spiritualism,* esp. pp. 242–44, which treats the activities of the gifted American trance poet, Thomas Lake Harris.

A problem second only to the lack of comparative perspectives on the origin of the Book of Mormon is the failure of both Mormon and non-Mormon writers to attempt seriously to understand the process of "translation" as Smith himself used the term. Edward Ashment, "The Book of Mormon: A Literal Translation?" p. 12, observes:

> . . . it is germane to discuss what the term "translate" actually meant to Joseph Smith for it is true that he used the term in a sense not commonly understood. Possibly the best evidence of that comes from his description of facsimile number two of the Book of Abraham in which the prophet expressly avoided any of the portions which contained written text, confining his descriptions to the vignettes. He called the interpretations a "translation." In fact, evidence from elsewhere suggests that the prophet never actually required a physical text from which to translate. For example, he "translated" a record which was written "on parchment" and hidden away by the ancient apostle John that he saw only through the medium of the urim and thummim. His revision of the Bible was consistently termed "translations" even though he "did not at any time use Biblical manuscripts," with the result that it should therefore "be more appropriately interpreted to mean 'revision.' " Furthermore, the recent evidence of the Joseph Smith papyri has demonstrated that there is no "evidence that Joseph Smith knew Egyptian, in fact, [there is] evidence that he did not, and when we read descriptions of his translating which came as inspiration rather than efforts to understand a foreign language, we are hard pressed to see the connection between the papyri and the Book of Abraham."

An indication of how Joseph Smith may have "translated" the Book of Mormon is provided in a revelation of April 1829 given through Smith to Oliver Cowdery, the chief scribe to whom he dictated the Book of Mormon, in Doctrine and Covenants, section 9. Verses 7 through 10 of this section offer instructions to Cowdery on how he, too, could have participated in the "translation" of the Book of Mormon:

> Behold, you have not understood; you have supposed that I would give it unto you, when you took no thought save it was to ask me.
>
> But behold, I say unto you, that you must study it out in your mind; then you must ask me if it be right, and if it is right I will cause that your bosom shall burn within you; therefore, you shall feel that it is right.
>
> But if it be not right you shall have no such feelings, but you shall have a stupor of thought that shall cause you to forget the thing which is wrong; therefore, you cannot write that which is sacred save it be given you from me.
>
> Now, if you had known this you could have translated; nevertheless, it is not expedient that you should translate now.

Also important for understanding the process of "translation" of the Book of Mormon is the statement of Joseph Smith's wife Emma, who also served as a scribe to whom he dictated part of the work. "Last Testimony of Sister Emma," *Saints' Herald* 26 (October 1, 1879): 289–90. Although this statement was made nearly fifty years after the publication of the book and was printed following her death, it raises a number of questions worthy of further investigation. Speaking to her son Joseph III, Emma stated:

> In writing for your father I frequently wrote day after day, often sitting at the table close by him, he sitting with his face buried in his hat, with the [seer] stone in it, and dictating hour after hour with nothing between us. . . . The plates lay on the table without any attempt at concealment, wrapped in a small linen table cloth, which I had given him to fold them in. I once felt of the plates, as they lay on the table, tracing their outline and shape. They seemed to be pliable like thick paper, and would rustle with a metalic sound when the edges were moved by the thumb, as one does sometimes thumb the edges of a book. . . . My belief is that the Book of Mormon is of divine authenticity—I have not the slightest doubt about it. I am satisfied that no man could have dictated the writing of the manuscript unless he was inspired; for, when acting as his scribe, your father would dictate to me hour after hour; and when returning after meals, or after interruptions, he would at once begin where he had left off, without either seeing the manuscript or having any portion of it read to him. This was a usual thing for him to do. It would have been improbable that a learned man could do this; and for one so ignorant and unlearned as he was, it was simply impossible.

This statement and others like it, have led me to the conclusion that the Book of Mormon is probably best understood, at least in part, as a trance-related production. The use of the seer stone or of the urim and thummim (two stones set in silver bows, which could be fastened to a breast plate), the evidence that the plates themselves (if they existed) were not even visible to Joseph Smith during much of the time he was "translating" them, and the fact that Smith could engage in skillful dictation of a highly complex work for hours on end, suggest that Smith was acting as an unusually gifted trance figure, perhaps one of the most gifted such figures in the history of religion. Available evidence, in my opinion, is thus most nearly compatible with the idea that the Book of Mormon should properly be viewed, like the Doctrine and Covenants, as what Mormons would describe as a work of "inspiration" or "revelation" rather than as a literal translation or history in any sense. From a Mormon perspective, the book could then be described as "divinely inspired"; from a non-Mormon viewpoint, it could be seen as an unusually sophisticated product of unconscious and little-known mental processes. In either case, the focus of attention could shift from the unrewarding and ultimately irrelevant question of whether any golden plates with inscriptions ever existed or whether the Book of Mormon was a literal history to the far more important and fascinating question of the content and meaning of this most extraordinary religious document.

16. Original quotation from the *New Yorker* as cited in *Iowa Territorial Gazette and Advertiser*, Burlington, I. T., February 13, 1841, as quoted in Cecil A. Snider, "Development of Attitudes in Sectarian Conflict: A Study of the Mormons in Illinois in Contemporary Newspaper Sources" M.A. thesis, State Univ. of Iowa, 1933), p. 3, in the documentary appendix. For a recent study suggesting the complexity of the Book of Mormon as a literary composition, see Wayne A. Larsen, Alvin C. Rencher, and Tim Layton, "Who Wrote the Book of Mormon?: An Analysis of Word Prints," *BYU Studies* 20 (Spring 1980): 225–51. The article concludes that an analysis of what it calls "wordprints" in the Book of Mormon shows "conclusively that there were many authors who wrote the Book of Mormon" (p. 245). This conclusion appears premature. The divergence of styles that this article identifies in the Book of Mormon could also have been produced if, as I suggest in note 15 above, the work was a complex, trance-related production by Joseph Smith. For an able discussion of the major issues that future Mormon and non-Mormon scholarship on the Book of Mormon will need to address, see Mark Thomas, "Scholarship and the Future of the Book of Mormon," *Sunstone* 5 (May–June 1980): 24–29.

17. "The Book of Mormon Reviewed and Its Divine Pretensions Exposed," *Painesville Telegraph*, March 15, 1831, reprinted in Alexander Campbell, *Delusions: An Analysis of the Book of Mormon, With An Examination of Its Internal Evidences, and a Refutation of Its Pretences to Divine Authority* (Boston: Benjamin H. Greene, 1832), p. 13.

18. For studies emphasizing the early formulation of basic Mormon beliefs and practices, see Marvin Hill, "The Shaping of the Mormon Mind in New England and New York," *BYU Studies* 9 (Spring 1969): 351–72, and his larger study, "The Role of Christian Primitivism in the Origin and Development of the Mormon Kingdom, 1830–1844" (Ph.D. diss., Univ. of Chicago, 1968). Other writers have placed greater stress on the developmental aspects of Mormon religion. See especially Mario S. De Pillis's "Quest for Religious Authority" and "Social Sources of Mormonism." The distinctive form of Biblical "literalism" underlying the early Mormon worldview is ably delineated by Gordon Irving, "The Mormons and the Bible in the 1830's" *BYU Studies* 153 (Summer 1973): 473–88, based on his more detailed study, "Mormonism and the Bible, 1832–1838" (Honors B.A. thesis, Univ. of Utah, 1972).

19. Book of Mormon, 1830 ed., p. 127, cited as Jacob 2:31, 35, in the current

edition of the Book of Mormon, which makes slight changes from the original quoted here.

20. Doctrine and Covenants, 2:2–3.

21. Book of Mormon, 1830 ed., p. 127, cited as Jacob 2:24, 26, in the current edition of the Book of Mormon. O'Dea, *The Mormons,* p. 269, n. 30, observes that the following verses of the Book of Mormon contain definite antipolygamous doctrine: Jacob 1:15; 2:23, 24, 27, 28, 32, 35; 3:5; Mosiah 11:2, 4, 14; and Ether 10:5.

22. Book of Mormon, 1830 ed., p. 127, cited as Jacob 2:27–28, 30, in the current edition of the Book of Mormon which makes the change indicated in brackets. Compare that statement with the one Smith is said to have written on October 5, 1843:

> Gave instructions to try those persons who were preaching, teaching, or practicing the doctrine of plurality of wives; for, according to the law, I hold the keys of this power in the last days; for there is never but one on earth at a time on whom the power and its keys are conferred; *and I have constantly said no man shall have but one wife at a time, unless the Lord directs otherwise* [emphasis in original].

History of the Church 6: 46.

23. *Millennial Star* 21 (January 8, 1859): 19. Italics removed. The standard Mormon account of the genesis of polygamy is found in Brigham H. Roberts, *A Comprehensive History of the Church of Jesus Christ of Latter-day Saints: Period I,* 6 vols. (Salt Lake City: Deseret News Press, 1930), 2: 108–10.

24. *Saints' Herald* 21 (October 1, 1874): 584. Briggs was an early leader of the RLDS Church.

25. Orson Pratt, *The Bible and Polygamy,* 2nd ed. (Salt Lake City: Deseret News Steam Printing Establishment, 1877), p. 80; from a speech delivered on October 7, 1869.

26. Denials of polygamy belief and practice took a wide range of forms, which are fully described in Shook, *Origin of Mormon Polygamy.* Frequently, Mormons denied that they believed in or practiced a "spiritual wife system," this being taken to denote John C. Bennett's corruption of the proper Mormon form of plural marriage. Sometimes individuals denied that the (whole) Church believed in or sanctioned polygamy. Strictly speaking, this was true, since belief in polygamy was not known by or enjoined upon the majority of the membership of the Church while Joseph Smith was alive. Smith himself most characteristically made indirect denials of polygamy in which he said simply that such statements were too ridiculous to be believed. But he always carefully refrained from saying that such statements weren't *true.* Although many individuals were cut off from the Church for teaching polygamy publicly, their error lay not in what they taught but in the premature disclosure of the principle without prior Church sanction. Such cases continued to occur throughout the late 1840s and early 1850s when there can be no doubt that polygamy was being taught and practiced at the highest levels of the Church.

27. Roberts, *Comprehensive History,* 2: 95–96. A summary of such statements and an analysis of the evidence for Joseph Smith's belief in and

limited practice of polygamy during the Kirtland-Missouri period is found in Max H. Parkin, "The Nature and Cause of Internal and External Conflict of the Mormons in Ohio Between 1830 and 1838" (M.A. thesis, Brigham Young Univ., 1966), pp. 162–74, and in Bachman, "Plural Marriage Before the Death of Joseph Smith," pp. 47–103.

28. Ezra Booth, one of the first apostates from the Mormon Church to make extensive public disclosure of its alleged misdeeds, wrote in a letter printed in the *Ohio Star* of December 8, 1831: "In addition to this, and to cooperate with it, it has been made known by revelation, that it will be pleasing to the Lord, should they form a matrimonial alliance with the natives: . . ."; quoted in Jerald and Sandra Tanner, *Mormonism Like Watergate?* (Salt Lake City: Modern Microfilm, 1974), p. 9.

29. The text of this revelation as quoted in this paper is based on a typescript prepared by Andrew Jenson, the LDS Church Historian, from the earlier of the two manuscript copies in the handwriting of W. W. Phelps, which are held in the Church Archives. The most readily available source for copies of the two manuscript versions of this revelation is Jerald and Sandra Tanner, *Mormonism Like Watergate?* pp. 7–8. According to scholars in the LDS Church Historical Department, the two extant manuscript copies are in the handwriting of W. W. Phelps, and both date from some time in the Utah period. The later copy was sent as a letter to Brigham Young, dated August 12, 1861. It is impossible to date the first copy, but the paper is definitely not of an 1830s vintage. The paper used for the first version is of the same rule and size as that used for the 1861 letter, though considerably more worn and discolored. The original copy is marred by numerous corrections and changes.

The introduction to the revelation indicates that it was not written down on the date that Joseph Smith gave it orally because they lacked pen and paper on that occasion. Given the detail with which the revelation is recorded and W. W. Phelps's appended note that he asked Smith about the meaning of the revelation three years later, one would assume that probably the revelation had been taken down shortly after Smith gave it orally. Present on the occasion were Joseph Smith, Oliver Cowdery, W. W. Phelps, Martin Harris, Joseph Coe, Ziba Peterson, and Joshua Lewis.

30. Jerald and Sandra Tanner, *Mormonism Like Watergate?* p. 9. In understanding the development of early Mormon family attitudes and practice, an especially valuable source is Herbert Ray Larsen, " 'Familism' in Mormon Social Structure" (Ph.D. diss., Univ. of Utah, 1954).

31. *Chardon Spectator and Geuga Gazette,* October 30, 1835, as cited in Parkin, "Internal and External Conflict," p. 176.

32. *History of the Church,* 2: 320.

33. The revelation is printed ibid., 1:167–69, and as section 49 of the current Doctrine and Covenants. For a detailed account of the negative Shaker reaction to the Mormon proselytizing at North Union, see Robert F. W. Meader, "The Shakers and Mormons," *Shaker Quarterly* 2 (Fall 1962): 83–96.

34. *Latter Day Saints' Messenger and Advocate* 1 (June 1835): 10, as cited in D. Michael Quinn, "Organizational Development and Social Origins of the Mormon Hierarchy, 1832–1932: A Prosopographical Study" (M.A.

thesis, Univ. of Utah, 1973), p. 148. Quinn's brilliant study is indispensable for serious scholarship on Mormon family patterns.

35. Evidence of the premature practice of polygamy before Nauvoo is slight, although I have not worked extensively with manuscript material from the period. Such evidence is suggested in the detailed retrospective comments recorded by Smith's close associate Benjamin F. Johnson, Letter to George F. Gibbs, 1903. The original manuscript and various typescript copies with slightly different pagination are in the Church Archives. Some subsequent allegations were made that Jared Carter, Warren Parish, and Oliver Cowdery practiced polygamy in the period, but these allegations are unconvincing. See Parkin, "Internal and External Conflict," pp. 167–71.

Later Mormon writers frequently charged that Cowdery had made early attempts to practice polygamy without Joseph Smith's sanction. For an exhaustive detailing of this argument and the sources for it, see Robert Glen Mouritsen, "The Office of Associate President of the Church of Jesus Christ of Latter-day Saints" (M.A. thesis, Brigham Young Univ., 1972), pp. 78–111. This argument is not convincing. No contemporary evidence that Cowdery practiced polygamy appears to exist. In fact, contemporary sources show that Cowdery strongly opposed Joseph Smith's polygamous practice and was cynical about Smith's motives. For Cowdery and several close friends in Missouri, polygamy appears to have been one of the factors contributing to their apostasy from the Church. See the Oliver Cowdery Letterbook held at the Huntington Library, San Marino, California, especially his letter to Warren Cowdery from Far West, Missouri, on January 21, 1838; as well as the "Far West Record," a record book containing minutes of meetings in Kirtland and in Far West, Missouri, p. 117. Significantly, in Cowdery's excommunication trial on April 11, 1838, in Far West, Missouri, no charges of any sexual indiscretions on his part were made. Instead, one of the chief charges against him was "For seeking to destroy the character of Joseph Smith, Jun., by falsely insinuating that he was guilty of adultery." *Elders' Journal* 1 (July 1838): 45. If Cowdery's character in this regard had been anything but spotless, there can be little doubt that he would have been thoroughly vilified for his indiscretions. Probably later Mormon writers may have confused Cowdery's and Smiths's actions in this period. I am indebted to Marvin Hill for suggesting that Cowdery probably did not practice polygamy.

36. *Journal of Discourses,* 9: 294.

37. See the card index entries for "Polygamy Before 1841" in Stanley Snow Ivins, Notebooks and Transcripts. The original manuscripts are held by the Utah State Historical Society Library, Salt Lake City, Utah. An example of the statements that appear to be based on solid knowledge is the letter entitled "The Nauvoo Block and Tackle" which appeared anonymously in the *Warsaw Signal* on April 26, 1844.

38. *Saints' Herald,* vol. 2, no. 1 (January 1861), as cited in Ivins, Notebook 4: 37–38.

39. Mosiah Hancock, "Letter to the Editor," *Deseret News Daily* 17 (February 21, 1884): 4.

40. Joseph Smith, Jr., *Doctrine and Covenants of the Church of Latter-Day Saints; Carefully Selected from the Revelations of God and Compiled by Joseph Smith, Junior, Oliver Cowdery, Sidney Rigdon, Frederick G.*

Williams [*Presiding Elders of Said Church*], (Kirtland, Ohio: F. G. Williams, 1835), p. 251. This was the first edition of the Doctrine and Covenants, and it differs slightly from the current edition to which citation is made elsewhere in this book.

41. Note the possibly ambiguous wording of the statement itself, which does not actually prohibit a man from having *more* than one wife. The statement "one man should have one wife" is not parallel to "and one woman *but* one husband." Stenhouse, *Rocky Mountain Saints*, p. 193, states that he heard Brigham Young say in a public meeting that the appendix on marriage "was written by Oliver Cowdery against Joseph's wishes, and was permitted to be published only after Cowdery's incessant teasing and Joseph's warning to him of the trouble which his course would create."

42. Hostility resulting from attempts to introduce polygamy may have been a contributing factor in the anti-Mormon sentiment that led the Mormons to leave Kirtland in 1837. A number of apostate sources refer to problems with polygamy in this period. Furthermore, Mormon theology identifies the dedication of the Kirtland Temple in April 1836 as the first time when Joseph Smith had full divine authority given him to introduce polygamy. For instance, in introducing polygamy belief to the world in 1852, the apostle Orson Pratt declared that Joseph Smith held

> . . . the sealing keys of power, or in other words, of Elijah, the Prophet, who held many keys, among which were the keys of sealing, to bind the hearts of the fathers to the children, and the children to the fathers; together with all other sealing keys and powers, pertaining to the last dispensation. They were committed by that Angel who administered in the Kirtland Temple and spoke unto Joseph the Prophet, at the time of the endowments in that house.

Journal of Discourses, 1: 64.

43. *Latter-Day Saints' Messenger and Advocate* 3 (June 1837): 510–11.
44. *Elders' Journal* 1 (November 1837): 28; and 1 (July 1838): 43.
45. *History of the Church*, 3: 230–33. This letter of December 16, 1838, was in part a response to "foul and libelous reports" that Joseph Smith had allegedly committed adultery. Communitarian and cooperative ventures have frequently received criticism, both real and imaginary, for introducing unorthodox marital practices. Smith was almost certainly aware of some of those ventures. For instance, between November 9 and 11, 1835, a self-styled prophet, Robert Matthias, stayed at Joseph Smith's house. At that time, Matthias was achieving notoriety for a variety of reasons, including his efforts at establishing a community of property and of wives. Matthias's marriage system allowed each of his male followers one wife, but made him alone a husband to all the women. See *Memoirs of Matthias the Prophet*, cited in Ivins, Notebook 7: 157–60. Since Joseph Smith took the rare step of telling Matthias about his first vision on the occasion of the visit, it is reasonable to assume that considerable rapport and personal openness existed between the two men. A slightly altered account of their exchange is published in *History of the Church*, 2: 304–7.

46. Johnson, Letter to George Gibbs, p. 12; Jenson, "Plural Marriage," p. 233. Exactly what constituted a "marriage" is unclear in this as in many other early instances in which Smith is said to have taken plural wives.

A number of early Mormon writers evidently viewed a sexual connection as tantamount to a "marriage," particularly in the cases of Joseph Smith's plural wives. There is no evidence that any plural marriage ceremony was performed by or for Joseph Smith prior to April 5, 1841.

47. Cowdery Letterbook, especially the letters for February 24, 1838, and January 21, 1838. Johnson, Letter to George Gibbs, p. 10, states that "I was afterwards told by Warren Parrish, that he himself and Oliver Cowdery did know that Joseph had Fannie Alger as wife, for they were spied upon and found together." Also see the July 1872 letter of William E. McLellan to Joseph Smith III, the original copy of which is in the archives of the Reorganized Church of Jesus Christ of Latter Day Saints at Independence, Missouri; called to my attention by James E. Elliott.

48. Among those whose disaffection may have been connected in part with opposition to polygamy were Oliver Cowdery, David Whitmer, Lyman E. Johnson, Warren Parrish, Jared Carter, and W. W. Phelps. Utah Mormon accounts suggest that an important factor in the apostasy of Thomas Marsh, head of the Quorum of the Twelve, may have been his opposition to polygamy. When Marsh returned to the Church in 1857 following his wife's death, he was ridiculed in public speeches: as a broken down man, he would not have to worry about polygamy any more. See *Journal of Discourses,* 5: 28–29, 115, 206–9, for references relating to Marsh's return. In a sermon on July 12, 1857, Heber C. Kimball said that Marsh's problem was sustaining his wife in preference to Joseph, and that Emma had been involved in the same sort of opposition to Joseph over polygamy. See Journal History, July 12, 1857, pp. 1–2. The Journal History, located in the Church Archives, contains excerpts from diaries, journals, letters, and newspapers, which give a day-by-day account from the founding of the Church in 1830 to the present. At least four of Joseph Smith's closest associates—Oliver Cowdery, Thomas Marsh, John C. Bennett, and William Law—apparently apostatized at least in part over polygamy.

49. Parkin, "Internal and External Conflict," p. 174.

50. The best, and possibly the definitive, treatment of Mormon Nauvoo as a Jacksonian boom town is found in Robert Bruce Flanders, *Nauvoo: Kingdom on the Mississippi* (Urbana: Univ. of Illinois, 1965). Useful overview analyses of the period also appear in a special issue of *Dialogue* 5 (Spring 1970): 7–79, on "The Mormons in Early Illinois," ed. Stanley B. Kimball. Recently, Mormon scholars have been placing greater stress on the religious than on the economic motivations for social life in Nauvoo. As an example, see Marvin Hill, "Mormon Religion in Nauvoo: Some Reflections," *Utah Historical Quarterly* 44 (Spring 1976): 170–80.

51. In "The Nauvoo Charter: A Reinterpretation," *Journal of the Illinois State Historical Society* 64 (Spring 1971): 66–78, James L. Kimball, Jr., shows that the city charter granted to the Nauvoo Mormons actually was very similar to those granted other Illinois cities of the period. The only uniqueness of the Nauvoo Charter lay in the way it was used by the Mormons. Kimball's article is based on his more detailed analysis, "Study of the Nauvoo Charter, 1840–1845" (M.A. thesis, Univ. of Iowa, 1966).

52. O'Dea, *The Mormons,* pp. 53–54.

53. A dramatic first impression of the extremes of wealth and poverty in Nauvoo is given in a letter of Charlotte Haven, dated January 3, 1843, as quoted in William Mulder and A. Russell Mortensen, eds., *Among the*

Mormons: Historic Accounts by Contemporary Observers (New York: Alfred A. Knopf, 1958), pp. 115–17.

54. This informal estimate was made by Kenneth W. Godfrey, "Some Thoughts Regarding an Unwritten History of Nauvoo" (paper presented at the Mormon History Association Meetings, Nauvoo, Illinois, April 1974), p. 2, footnote. This figure apparently is based on an extrapolation rom the total number of obituaries in the popular Nauvoo newspaper, he *Wasp,* during part of 1842. As T. Edgar Lyon suggested to me, there are several reasons why this is probably a high estimate. In 1842, a large influx of British immigrants who were highly susceptible to malaria-caused disease and death came to Nauvoo. Furthermore, deaths varied on a seasonal basis in Nauvoo, so one cannot extrapolate a total figure from only part of a year. Finally, the *Wasp* printed obituaries for Mormons anywhere in the United States who were known to the residents of Nauvoo. Although Godfrey's estimate is thus undoubtedly high, he has correctly identified a major factor contributing to social dislocation in Nauvoo.

55. Letter of Parley P. Pratt to Mary Ann Frost Pratt, dated July 6, 1840, Parley P. Pratt Papers, Church Archives, box 1, folder 6.

56. Letter of Eunice B. Shurtliff, dated December 24, 1842, as recorded in Luman Andros Shurtliff, Biographical Sketch; a typescript copied from the original by the Federal Writers Project of Ogden, Utah. Copy in the Huntington Library, San Marino, California, pp. 58–59.

57. S. George Ellsworth, ed., *Dear Ellen: Two Mormon Women and Their Letters* (Salt Lake City: Univ. of Utah Library, 1974), p. 42, records a letter from Ellen Pratt McGary to Ellen Spencer Clawson on April 12, 1857. It refers to her mother's independent management of family affairs while her husband, Addison Pratt, was away on a mission from June 1, 1843, to September 28, 1848, as "her five year widowhood." During that period, Mrs. Pratt successfully organized her family's move from Illinois to Utah.

58. Klaus J. Hansen, *Quest for Empire: The Political Kingdom of God and the Council of Fifty in Mormon History* (East Lansing: Michigan State Univ., 1967), pp. 155–58, provides evidence that Joseph Smith may have had himself crowned King, at least symbolically, of his evolving Political Kingdom of God. Some information on the possible origins and significance of Smith's concerns with the political kingdom is presented in Reed C. Durham's 1974 Mormon History Association Presidential Address, " 'Is There No Help for the Widow's Son': Mormonism and Masonry," printed as pp. 6–8 of the unauthorized typescript transcription of the talk circulated by Mervin B. Hogan, Salt Lake City, Utah.

59. George Q. Cannon, *The Life of Joseph Smith, The Prophet* (Salt Lake City: Juvenile Instructor Office, 1888), p. 401.

60. Mary Rollins Lightner, one of Smith's plural wives, stated that he recognized that his death might be a necessary precondition for the successful establishment of his religion, including plural marriage. Smith is said to have declared that "this work will never progress until I am gone for the testimony is of no force until the testator is dead." Mary Elizabeth Rollins Lightner, Speech Given at Brigham Young University, April 14, 1905, p. 5; copy in Brigham Young University Special Collections.

61. Elkins, *Slavery,* brilliantly argues this case.

62. De Pillis, "Quest for Religious Authority," is the classic statement of this argument.

63. The statements are printed as sections 124 through 132 of the Doctrine and Covenants.

64. Like almost every feature of Mormonism connected with the introduction of polygamy, the origin of the endowment ritual remains a point of considerable sensitivity in Mormon circles. An outsider reading the early accounts is struck by the remarkable similarities between certain aspects of Masonic ritual and the endowment ceremony, both of which began to be introduced in Nauvoo by Joseph Smith at almost exactly the same time. See William J. Whalen, *The Latter-day Saints in the Modern-day World: An Account of Contemporary Mormonism* (New York: John Day, 1969), pp. 145–206. In his judicious evaluation, O'Dea, *The Mormons*, p. 57, stated simply:

> To find appropriate materials for ritual development, his [Joseph Smith's] own non-liturgical background made it necessary to look outside strictly religious practices. Joseph went to Masonry to borrow many elements of ceremony. These he reformed, explaining to his followers that the Masonic ritual was a corrupted form of ancient priesthood ceremonial that was now being restored.

This line of interpretation is supported by a letter of Heber C. Kimball to Parley P. Pratt and his wife, dated Nauvoo, June 17, 1842, in the Church Archives, which states: ". . . there is a similarity of preast Hood in masonry. Br Joseph Ses Masonary was taken from preasthood but has become degenerated. But menny things are perfect. . . ." To introduce new marriage practices such as polygamy in nineteenth-century Illinois obviously necessitated some means of maintaining strict secrecy and determining who had first-hand knowledge of the new practices from those who did not. Some form of secret society thus was a pragmatic necessity. For important scholarly Mormon interpretations of this issue, see Durham's "Mormonism and Masonry," and Kenneth W. Godfrey, "Joseph Smith and the Masons," *Journal of the Illinois State Historical Society* 64 (Spring 1971): 66–78.

65. *History of the Church,* 5: 393.

66. Ibid., 6: 573. From an editorial in the *Times and Seasons* on April 1, 1842; punctuation modified for purposes of clarity.

67. Doctrine and Covenants, 130:22; given on April 2, 1843.

68. *Millennial Star* 5 (November 1844): 88–89.

69. Although it is unclear whether Lorenzo Snow actually was the first to coin this striking phrase, his name has become firmly linked to it.

70. *History of the Church,* 5: 323.

71. Doctrine and Covenants, 132:65. The cosmological framework which helped to prepare the minds of Mormon believers for the acceptance of polygamy is suggested in the Book of Abraham, which was "translated" by Joseph Smith in 1842. It was printed in Joseph Smith, Jr., *The Pearl of Great Price: Being a Choice Selection from the Revelations, Translations, and Narratives of Joseph Smith, First Prophet, Seer, and Revelator to the Church of Jesus Christ of Latter-Day Saints* (Liverpool: F. D. Richards, 1851). The Pearl of Great Price is now printed together with the Doctrine and Covenants by the Utah branch of the Mormon Church.

72. Doctrine and Covenants, 132:61. This is possibly the most frequently cited passage from the revelation, both in contemporary Nauvoo Mormon apostate attacks on Joseph Smith and in later accounts critical of polygamy.
73. O'Dea, *The Mormons,* p. 61.
74. Eliza R. Snow, *Biography and Family Record of Lorenzo Snow* (Salt Lake City: Deseret News, 1884), pp. 69–70. Accounts of the "angel with a drawn sword" story are widespread, although manuscript versions of such a story apparently do not exist from the period when Joseph Smith was still alive. The earliest manuscript evidence of this story known to me dates from 1846 in Joseph Lee Robinson, Autobiography and Journal (original manuscript in Brigham Young University Special Collections), p. 25. Whether or not Joseph Smith ever made this particular statement, his actions in attempting to introduce polygamous belief and practice among his followers in Nauvoo suggest that he was, indeed, operating under a sense of extreme inner compulsion.
75. Attempts to prepare the minds of his followers for plural marriage were numerous and varied. As early as November 21, 1841, prior to the return of the Twelve from England, Smith gave a public speech before a large assemblage of Saints in Nauvoo. He asked what the Mormons should do if they converted polygamous men in Turkey or India, where polygamy was legal. Would the Mormons force such converts to break up their families if they came to America? The answer was No. And the implication was clear: that polygamy might eventually be practiced by American Mormons also. Mormon women responded so negatively to this sermon that in the afternoon Smith got up and retracted the remarks he had made in the morning. Robinson, Journal, pp. 24–27. Smith's many sermonic references to the "mysteries" yet to be revealed also led to a mood of expectancy conducive to the introduction of plural marriage. These "mysteries" were associated with new doctrines and sealing ceremonies. If one becomes sensitized to the possible meaning of such references, many of the standard accounts of the Nauvoo period can be seen in a new light. It is no accident that the RLDS Church later rejected all the new Nauvoo doctrines and sealing ceremonies except baptism for the dead, for they provide an intellectual and emotional framework within which polygamy is a logical if not inevitable development.
76. Lee, *Mormonism Unveiled,* p. 111.
77. On February 8, 1843, he made clear that "a prophet was a prophet only when he was acting as such." *History of the Church,* 5: 265.
78. Following a series of statements saying that Emma must accept Joseph's plural wives or "be destroyed," the revelation reads: "And again, verily I say, let my handmaid forgive my servant Joseph his trespasses. . . ." Doctrine and Covenants, 132:56. And Doctrine and Covenants, 132:60, further declares: "Let no one, therefore, set on my servant Joseph; for I will justify him; for he shall do the sacrifice which I require at his hands for his transgressions, saith the Lord your God."
79. Robinson, Journal, p. 22, declares:

> I Joseph Lee Robinson do verily know it [the LDS gospel] is true, so help me God. my love for the Prophet Joseph was truly Stronger than death it was greater than for any man that Ever lived Except

> Jesus the first Begotten of the Father. . . . we allso heard him
> [Joseph Smith] say that God had revealed unto him that any Man
> that Ever Committed Adultery in Either of his Probations that that
> man could never be raised to the highest Exaltation in the Celestial
> Glory, and that he felt anxious with regard to himself that he en-
> quired of the Lord, that the Lord told him that he Joseph had never
> commited Adultery . . .

Similar allegations were made by William Law and others shortly before
Smith's death, and drew his usual indirect denial: such allegations were
too absurd to be believed. The revelation on plural and celestial marriage
itself shows great concern for distinguishing between sanctioned sexual
behavior and behavior defined as adulterous.

80. Coming from Wyl, *Mormon Portraits,* p. 55, this statement is understandably suspect.

81. *History of the Church,* 5: 53.

82. Even in the Nauvoo period, these letters continue to show great personal
warmth.

83. A summary of contemporary accounts is provided in Raymond T. Bailey,
"Emma Hale: Wife of the Prophet Joseph Smith" (M.S. thesis, Brigham
Young Univ., 1952), p. 104. Bailey's account of Emma's reaction to
polygamy, pp. 50–111, is the most complete assessment of the evidence
on the subject yet available. Typical of the gossip about Smith's marital
difficulties which circulated in the Illinois press was a note in the *Warsaw
Signal* for April 24, 1844, which alleged that Emma Smith had gone
down the river on a boat trip and that before she left she "became reconciled to Joe, who last week turned her out of his house."

  Joseph Lee Robinson, a brother of Ebenezer Robinson who was writing
on July 14, 1846, in Nauvoo as a loyal member of the Church, indicated
that the involvement of Ebenezer's wife Angeline in watching Joseph
Smith's movements for Emma infuriated him and precipitated a family
crisis that almost led Emma to go home to her parents. Apparently
Ebenezer's support of his wife's stand in the matter was a contributing
factor in his sudden removal from the editorship of the *Times and Seasons,* the official Church newspaper, in February 1842. Robinson, Journal,
p. 49. Writing many years later in *The Return,* a retrospective newspaper
that he published, Ebenezer Robinson skirted the whole issue, which
apparently was still painful to him.

84. A convenient summary of the relevant affidavits on the subject is found
in Roberts, *Comprehensive History,* 2: 105–7. The original affidavit by
William Clayton, Joseph Smith's secretary who swore that he wrote down
the revelation, is in the Church Archives in a slightly longer version than
that which is commonly printed. Bachman, "Plural Marriage Before the
Death of Joseph Smith," pp. 208–11, corroborates these affidavits.

85. According to Utah Mormon accounts, Emma had personally approved
Joseph Smith's marriages to four women—Eliza M. and Emily Dow
Partridge, and Maria and Sarah Lawrence. In all probability, such approval was given with extreme reluctance. Emma may also have known
of her husband's relations with a few of his other plural wives as well.
Even Joseph Smith's close associates knew only a small number of his
plural wives by name, and, depending on their range of contacts, the

wives whom they knew as such varied. Evidently the extent of Joseph Smith's plural marriages was even kept secret from most of his trusted followers.

86. The statement was printed as "Last Testimony of Sister Emma," *Saints' Herald* 36 (October 1, 1879): 289–90. Apparently the questions had been carefully prepared in advance and may have been seen by Emma prior to her being asked them for the record. The questions were asked her at an unspecified time or times during a seven-day period. Frequently they were asked her in the presence of her second husband Major Lewis C. Bidamon, who was in and out of the sitting room where the conversation took place. It is unclear how much of the original conversation is printed in this account or what qualifying or linking statements may have been edited out. The hostility of the questioners toward polygamy was palpable; Joseph Smith III prefaces the account by saying that they were fearful what Emma might have to say on the subject, but that they swallowed their fears and decided "whatever the worst might be, we would hear it." Before asking Emma the questions, they apologized to her for asking about polygamy. The questions about polygamy show an ambiguity in wording that is probably not accidental. Despite her apparent flat denial that Joseph Smith had taught or practiced polygamy, Emma did admit that he had discussed the possibility of plural wives in a "chat" with some of his followers, and that he had supposedly said: "Well such a system might possibly be, if everybody was agreed to it and would behave as they should . . ." Emma's statement was taken informally, not under oath, and it was not published until after her death. I do not believe that any of Emma's statements contained therein were deliberately fabricated, but how it was edited is unclear. Even less convincing than Emma's "Last Testimony" is her reported statement to Jason Briggs in an interview of April 1867, which denies, simply, that her husband ever taught *her* the "principles of polygamy" or that she knowingly *burned* the original revelation. *Messenger* 1 (April 1875): 23. Knowing Emma's passionate hatred of polygamy, it is difficult to imagine why she refused throughout her entire life to personally issue any public denials or affidavits refuting Joseph Smith's involvement with polygamy, unless, as the evidence overwhelmingly shows, she knew that he had in fact taught and practiced polygamy during his lifetime. Important insights into Emma's reactions to polygamy are provided in statements of December 1876 in the Emily D. P. Young Journal; a typescript is in the University of Utah Library Special Collections, but the original in the Church Archives is not currently available to researchers.

87. *Journal of Discourses*, 3: 266; speech of July 14, 1855.

88. Orson F. Whitney, *Life of Heber C. Kimball, An Apostle: The Father and Founder of the British Mission* (Salt Lake City: Kimball Family, 1888), p. 336.

89. For a consideration of this problem, see Thomas Edgar Lyon, "Orson Pratt—Early Mormon Leader" (M.A. thesis, Univ. of Chicago, 1932), pp. 34–44.

90. Benjamin F. Johnson, *My Life's Review* (Independence, Mo.: Zion's Printing and Publishing Company, 1947), p. 94.

91. Quinn, "The Mormon Hierarchy," p. 159.

92. Johnson, *My Life's Review*, p. 388.
93. Exactly what relationship existed between Joseph Smith and the twenty-seven women listed as his plural wives in Jenson, "Plural Marriage," pp. 233–234, is unclear. Of this list, full marriage dates are given in ten cases; no date is given in the cases of two women who presumably were married to Smith before Nauvoo; and no dates are given for the marriages of ten women who presumably were sealed to him in some fashion in Nauvoo. Of the list of forty-eight plural wives of Joseph Smith presented in Brodie, *No Man Knows My History*, pp. 335–36, 457–88, approximately one third appear to have been sealed to him for "time and eternity"; another one third may or may not have been sealed to him for "time and eternity"; and approximately one third were presumably sealed to him only "for eternity," or else are of such dubious and unsubstantiated character that little can be said about them. Brodie makes use of a number of apostate accounts in drawing up her list. Some of these may contain important information, while others, such as William Hall's account, are of extremely dubious accuracy and must be evaluated with the caution used in evaluating any malicious gossip. Stanley Snow Ivins's list of eighty-four alleged plural wives is found in a Miscellaneous Folder in his collection at the Utah State Historical Society, and is most readily available in Jerald and Sandra Tanner, *Joseph Smith and Polygamy* (Salt Lake City: Modern Microfilm, n.d.), pp. 41–47. Again, the precise nature of the relationship, if any, that Joseph Smith had with these women is unclear. Ivins includes eleven women in his list who were sealed by proxy to Joseph Smith long after his death, but who, he says, *might* have been married to Smith during his life.

The major primary and secondary accounts on which this analysis of Joseph Smith's plural wives is based include Jenson, "Plural Marriage," pp. 219–34; Joseph F. Smith, Jr., *Blood Atonement and the Origin of Plural Marriage;* Temple Lot Case [U.S. Circuit Court (8th Circuit)] in Church Archives, printed in abbreviated form as *Complainant's Abstract of Pleading and Evidence . . . The Reorganized Church of Jesus Christ of Latter-Day Saints, Complainant, vs. The Church of Christ at Independence, Missouri . . .* (Lamoni, Iowa: Herald Publishing House, 1893), hereafter cited as *Abstract of the Temple Lot Case;* Shook, *Origin of Mormon Polygamy;* Brodie, *No Man Knows My History*, esp. pp. 297–322, 334–47, and 457–588; Jerald and Sandra Tanner, *Joseph Smith and Polygamy;* and Vesta P. Crawford Papers, Univ. of Utah Special Collections. Bachman's "Plural Marriage Before the Death of Joseph Smith" is the most comprehensive Mormon analysis of the affidavits concerning Joseph Smith's plural marriages, and must be consulted by all serious scholars concerned with these issues. Since the closing of the records on Joseph Smith's marriage sealings in the Genealogical Archives in Salt Lake City to researchers, that data is available for the use of historians and genealogists in Thomas Milton Tinney, "The Royal Family of the Prophet Joseph Smith, Junior: First President of the Church of Jesus Christ of Latter-day Saints" (typescript, 1973; a copy is held in the Utah State Historical Society Library and the University of Utah Library, both in Salt Lake City). Many important primary anti-Mormon sources exist, but their use has been de-emphasized in this section. Insofar as most of these sources, whether Mormon or non-Mormon, tend to focus on Smith's personal behavior, they tend to ignore the important social issues that are of most interest to historians. As Brigham Young stated emphatically in *Journal of Discourses,* 4: 78, a prophet's personal conduct is not necessarily a measure of the validity of his general program.

94. The chief source used here for Lucy Walker's experience is a typescript copy of her account made by the Federal Writer's Project in 1940. This version is almost identical to that held in manuscript in the Church Archives, except that the latter contains a fuller account of Lucy Walker's experiences following Joseph Smith's death. A version omitting almost all references to plural marriage was printed in the *Woman's Exponent* 39 (1910): 31, and *passim.* The testimony in the Temple Lot Case also should be consulted.

Some of Joseph Smith's other plural wives for whom extensive documentation exists include Eliza R. Snow, Mary Elizabeth Rollins Lightner, Sarah Ann Whitney, Emily and Eliza Partridge, Helen Mar Kimball, and Melissa Lott.

95. Since Lucy Walker's accounts were written many years after the events she describes, her lack of clarity in giving dates is understandable. According to Joseph F. Smith, Jr., *Blood Atonement and the Origin of Plural Marriage,* p. 55, William Clayton's Private Journal for May 1, 1843, states: "At the Temple. At 10 married Joseph to Lucy Walker." The whereabouts of Clayton's Journal is not currently known.

96. Typescript analysis of various characteristics of Joseph Smith's plural wives as indicated in Vesta P. Crawford Papers.

97. Compare this type of experience to conventional rites of passage as described in Van Gennep, *Rites of Passage,* and Turner, *Ritual Process.*

98. Vilate Kimball, Letter dated June 24, 1843, to Heber C. Kimball, in Winslow Whitney Smith Papers, box 5, folder 2, Church Archives. This was called to my attention by Jan Shipps. This letter was also printed, in part, with slight modifications, in Helen Mar Kimball Whitney, "Scenes and Incidents in Nauvoo," *Woman's Exponent* 11 (September 15, 1882): 58.

99. See Quinn, "The Mormon Hierarchy," pp. 246–91.

100. *Historical Record* 6 (May 1887): 237.

101. Letter of Joseph Smith's, dated August 18, 1842, in Joseph Smith Collection, Church Archives. This letter has been photographically reproduced, along with a line by line transcription, in H. Michael Marquart, *The Strange Marriages of Sarah Ann Whitney to Joseph Smith the Mormon Prophet, Joseph C. Kingsbury and Heber C. Kimball* (Salt Lake City: n.p., n.d.), pp. 6–9. Marquart's accompanying text provides background information and a suggestion of the fluidity of marital relationships during the early development of polygamy in Nauvoo.

102. See Tinney, "Royal Family," for a full reproduction of the relevant temple sealing records. This list includes all women who are known to have been sealed to Joseph Smith, either during his life or after his death. Unfortunately, it is little more than a listing of evidence and fails to ask most of the historically interesting questions.

103. Temple Lot Case (complete transcript), pp. 364, 367, 384.

104. Affidavit of Melissa Willes, August 3, 1893, as reproduced in Bailey, "Emma Hale," pp. 98–100. In the Temple Lot Case (complete tran-

script), p. 98, 105, Melissa Willes emphatically stated that she was married to Joseph Smith for time and eternity, even if it was not officially so recorded, and she gave the room number in Smith's home where she allegedly spent the night with him.

105. Ibid., p. 451.

106. Ibid., p. 427.

107. Johnson, Letter to George Gibbs, p. 12.

108. The original "Sketch of My Life" by Eliza R. Snow is held by the Bancroft Library, Berkeley, California. The portions dealing with polygamy were reprinted in Spencer J. Palmer, "Eliza R. Snow's 'Sketch of My Life': Reminiscences of One of Joseph Smith's Plural Wives," *BYU Studies* 12 (Autumn 1971): 125–30.

109. Typical of such statements in the Temple Lot Case (complete transcript), pp. 96–97, 99, Melissa Willes denied that she had any children by Joseph Smith but she refused to say anything about other children that he may have had because "I told you that I couldn't swear to any body else's children but my own. . . ."

110. Even Joseph Smith's acknowledged plural wives went by the names of the men whom they remarried, or, as in the atypical case of Eliza R. Snow, who was remarried to Brigham Young but had no children by him, retained their maiden names. Children born to wives of Joseph Smith who had been sealed to him for eternity bore the names of their natural father even though Mormon theology taught that the children would belong to Joseph Smith's family after they died. Thus, it may be assumed that if Smith had children by any of his plural wives, they would have borne the surnames of the families which reared them.

111. James L. Kimball, Jr., who is making a detailed demographic reconstruction of Nauvoo based on census records and other information, expressed his personal puzzlement to me at a number of cases of children who appear in early Utah census records but not in those from Nauvoo. Their age in Utah would have suggested that they should have been counted in the Nauvoo census also. This discrepancy in the record could be due to errors by the census takers, to various forms of "adoption" by the Mormons, or to factors connected with the early development of polygamy.

112. Mary E. Rollins Lightner, Remarks at Brigham Young University, April 14, 1905, p. 5.

113. Handwritten statement by Lucy Meserve Smith, dated May 18, 1892, in the George A. Smith Papers, University of Utah Special Collections; called to my attention by Robert Flanders.

114. See Brodie, *No Man Knows My History*, pp. 345–46, 470–71. Part of Brodie's unidentified documentation for her assertion in this case is found in a handwritten letter of John R. Young to Vesta P. Crawford in April 1931, Vesta Crawford Papers; called to my attention by Robert Flanders.

115. This is part of a low-keyed description of the manner in which plural wives were said to have been taken by Mormon leaders in Nauvoo. This statement in the *Expositor* is compatible with other Mormon and apostate accounts. In fact, if anything, it is understated.

116. Personal conversation with T. Edgar Lyon, June 27, 1974. This account

could easily be reconciled with that of the *Expositor,* above, which indicated that pregnant plural wives disappeared from public view. Although there are a number of family traditions in Utah of children by plural wives of Joseph Smith, I have not been able to investigate them closely enough to determine their possible validity. If Smith had children by women who were legally married to other men, such children obviously would not have been publicly acknowledged. For examples of such allegations, see Brodie, *No Man Knows My History,* pp. 301–8, 334–47.

117. Personal conversation with T. Edgar Lyon, July 19, 1974. Also see T. Edgar Lyon, "The Development of Church Organization and Doctrine, 1839–1846" (Mimeo, LSD Institute of Religion talk, March 1, 1968), p. 9.

118. This letter, dated June 23, 1846, was sent by Brigham Young to his plural wife, "Mrs. Hariot [*sic*] Cook." On the cover of the letter, its destination is indicated as "Snow House." Reproduced in full in Fawn M. Brodie, "A Letter from the Camp of Israel, 1846," *Princeton University Library Chronicle* 33 (Autumn 1971): 67–70.

119. Mary Ann Frost Pratt, first wife of Parley P. Pratt, was sealed to Joseph Smith "for eternity" in February 1846, and Nancy Marinda Johnson Hyde, first wife of Orson Hyde, was sealed to Joseph Smith "for eternity" on July 31, 1857. It cannot be positively determined whether or not early cases of sealings "for eternity" were for eternity *only.*

120. One example of a seemingly clear case based on LDS sources is that of Zina Diantha Huntington Jacobs. In an interview with J. W. Wight on October 1, 1896, in the Zina D. H. Young Papers in the Church Archives, Zina was unwilling to give the date or even the year of her marriage to Joseph Smith. When asked how she could have been married to Joseph Smith "for time and eternity," as she asserted, while she was at the same time the wife of Henry Jacobs for "time," she became very upset and said: "I do not wish to reply. I only know that this is the work of God upon this earth, and I know by testimony from God that Joseph Smith was a Prophet." This interview is reproduced in Elder D. Stead, *Doctrines and Dogmas of Brighamism Exposed* (Independence, Mo.: Reorganized Church of Latter-Day Saints, 1911), pp. 212, 216. The Mormon writer Vesta Crawford lists eight other cases of Joseph Smith's plural wives who were married women with living husbands, Vesta Crawford Papers. See Bachman, "A Study of Plural Marriage Before the Death of Joseph Smith," for details on many of these cases.

121. *Journal of Discourses,* 2: 13–14.

122. Whitney, *Life of Heber C. Kimball,* pp. 333–35. According to Whitney, Joseph Smith asked Heber for Vilate in this manner prior to acquainting him with the implications that the idea of celestial marriage had for the practice of plurality of wives. When Heber was informed about plural marriage and commanded to take a plural wife himself, Joseph Smith told him not to tell Vilate about the situation for fear she would not accept it. Actions of this sort were almost certain to lead to serious misunderstandings, particularly in cases of individuals whose loyalty was not so total as was that of Heber and Vilate Kimball. For a more detailed description and analysis of the reactions of members of the Kimball family to the introduction of polygamy, see Stanley B. Kimball, "Heber C. Kim-

ball and Family: The Nauvoo Years," *BYU Studies* 15 (Summer 1975): 447–79. Also see my paper/response, " 'Puritan Polygamists': The Strains and Challenges of the Transition to Polygamy in the Heber C. Kimball Family"; presented at the Mormon History Association session of the Organization of American Historians meetings in St. Louis on April 8, 1976.

123. A classic case was reported in the affidavit of M. G. Eaton on March 27, 1844, printed in the *Nauvoo Neighbor* on May 15, 1844. The affidavit describes in detail Robert D. Foster's allegations that Smith had tried to seduce his wife. Although the affidavit does not mention Smith by name, other sources make clear that he was the person whom Foster was accusing. Some of the other individuals who joined the *Expositor* group also became disaffected due in part to similar misunderstandings.

124. Doctrine and Covenants, 132:7, 15.

125. In denying the allegations made by the *Expositor* concerning polygamy, Hyrum Smith "referred to the revelation read to the High Council of the Church, which has caused so much talk about a multiplicity of wives. . . ." He said "that said Revelation was in answer to a question concerning things which transpired in former days [see Doctrine and Covenants, 132:1–2], and had no reference to the present time." The first part of this statement was correct. The second part appears to have constituted an elaborate evasion of the issue: the *question* was in reference to former times, not to the present; the *practice* which arose out of the answer to that question about former times, however, most certainly did have implications for the present—but *only* when a person was apprised of the revelation and commanded by Joseph Smith to enter into the practice. Then the practice of polygamy became mandatory and very much a part of this world. See *Nauvoo Neighbor* Extra, June 17, 1844. The text of the Extra is also reprinted in the *Nauvoo Neighbor* on June 19, 1844.

126. Lee, *Mormonism Unveiled*, pp. 146–47.

127. James Beck Notebooks, 1859–1865, vol. 1, in Church Archives; report of a speech by Brigham Young on October 8, 1861.

128. In the original stenographic report of Brigham Young's speech of October 8, 1861, he states that he and a few others learned this belief from Joseph Smith himself. Brigham Young Addresses, box 49, folder 8, in Church Archives. An unauthorized transcription of this speech has been reproduced by present-day schismatic Mormons in Dennis R. Short, *For Men Only: The Lord's Law of Obedience* (Salt Lake City: Dennis R. Short, 1977), pp. 85–90.

129. *Journal of Discourses,* 4: 165.

130. Doctrine and Covenants, 132:41.

131. *Messenger* 1 (March 1875): 17.

132. One source with a bearing on these issues is the letter of Brigham Young to Mrs. M. R., a Mormon woman of Manti, Utah, dated March 5, 1857; typescript copy of the original letter in my possession. On the face of it, the letter would appear to imply at least theoretical approval by Brigham Young of a form of temporal proxy arrangement. A closer analysis of the letter and an investigation of additional evidence, however, suggest that such an interpretation can not be conclusively established. Seen in context, a number of ambiguities arise. The where-

abouts of the woman's earlier letter to Brigham Young on February 22, 1857, is apparently not known. Thus we cannot be sure what the nature of her husband's dysfunction was, concerning which Brigham Young responded in the letter of March 5th: ". . . if I was imperfect and had a good wife I would call on some good bror. to help me. that we might have increase; that a man of this character will have a place in the Temple, receive his endowments and in eternity will be as tho' nothing had happened to him in time." In addition, the couple had already had two children (in 1841 and 1846) prior to their conversion to Mormonism in 1853, so the two children born subsequently to the letter (on October 13, 1858, and on January 26, 1861, both in Manti) need not be explained as due to any extraordinary circumstances. It is highly significant that, according to the autobiography of the first child born in Manti, the relationship between him, his father, and his younger brother was extremely warm. Finally, it is always possible that this letter represents an example of Brigham Young's exaggerated rhetoric. Even if the letter means what it appears on the surface to mean, it is significant that the relationship, whatever it may have been, was an honorable one and fully sanctioned by the Church.

Like this letter, the one passage with which I am familiar in official printed Mormon sources which might be construed as a reference to a practice of assigning temporal proxy husbands is also ambiguous. In a public speech on October 4, 1857, Erastus Snow first stressed the importance of each woman's doing her best to cooperate with her husband honor him as Lord. He then declared:

> I ask can you get into the Celestial Kingdom without him? Have any of you been there? You will remember that you never got into the Celestial Kingdom without the aid of your husband. If you did, it was because your husband was away, and someone had to act proxy for him.

Journal of Discourses, 5: 291. Although at first reading this passage might appear to refer to the type of hypothesized temporal proxy arrangement suggested here, the use of the past tense in the passage suggests that Snow was probably referring to the temple endowment ceremony instead. Similar confusion regarding public references to the endowment ceremony may account for some of the other allegations that the Church sanctioned temporal proxy arrangements during this period.

A statement by an ex-Mormon who was evidently well informed about the events of the Mormon Reformation of 1856–57, alleged that in a public speech during that period Heber C. Kimball had presented an argument for temporal proxy husbands, and that when a group of angry women descended on Brigham Young the next day to ask whether he endorsed such beliefs or not, he simply parried them with an evasive answer. This statement appeared as an open letter to Brigham Young signed "A Mormon and Defender of the Truth" in *Christian Advocate* of March 1877, as quoted in Ivins, Notebook 8: 233–34. For another statement giving such allegations, see the account of John Benjamin Franklin, as recorded in Ivins, Notebook 1: 113–14. In contrast to the highly polemical and obviously imaginary accounts characteristic of many semi-novelistic exposés of Mormon polygamy, the relatively few allegations of temporal proxy husbands that appear in the literature are usually given in an essentially straightforward manner by individuals who appear basically accurate in their other statements.

133. Hyde, *Mormonism*, pp. 87–88.

134. For an early description of the various categories of marriage sealings, see Orson Pratt's comments in the *Seer*, pp. 141–43. A contemporary doctrinal statement of Mormon marriage beliefs about plural and celestial marriage is found in Bruce R. McConkie, *Mormon Doctrine* (Salt Lake City: Bookcraft, 1958), in several different articles.

135. Genesis 38:8–10.

136. Matthew 22:15–22; Mark 12:18–27; and Luke 20:27–40. For information relating to allegations of a relationship between Emma Smith and William Law, see Wilhelm Wyl, *Mormon Portraits, or The Truth about the Mormon Leaders, 1830–1886* (Salt Lake City: Tribune Publishing Co., 1886), p. 108; and Wilhelm Wyl's interview with William Law, as reported in *Salt Lake Tribune*, July 3, 1887.

137. For instance, see Brodie, *No Man Knows My History*, esp. pp. 301–4, 335–37. Also consider the puzzling relationship of Willard Richards to Orson Hyde's wife, Nancy Marinda Johnson Hyde. Jerald and Sandra Tanner, *Joseph Smith and Polygamy*, pp. 80–87.

138. Vesta Crawford lists nine women she says were married to Joseph Smith while still having living husbands; see Vesta Crawford Papers. Fawn Brodie lists twelve such alleged cases, at least one of which is highly conjectural; see *No Many Knows My History*, pp. 335–36. There is strong reason to believe that in at least some of the cases cited by Crawford and Brodie, the women remained with their original husbands while they also sustained a sexual relationship with Joseph Smith. The most clear-cut such case is that of Zina D. Huntington Jacobs, who remained with Henry Jacobs until 1846. Also consider the complex cases of Elvira Cowles and Sara Ann Whitney. For additional evidence on puzzling cases of this kind, see Bachman, "A Study of Plural Marriage Before the Death of Joseph Smith."

139. Stenhouse, *Rocky Mountain Saints*, p. 301.

140. The letter was first printed in Bennett's *History of the Saints*, pp. 243–45. Bennett stated that Smith had proposed marriage to Nancy Rigdon and had been refused. After that refusal, Smith had allegedly dictated the letter through his secretary, Willard Richards, to Nancy Rigdon. In a roundabout and equivocal statement, the Mormon paper, the *Wasp*, stated on August 27, 1842, that the letter was more moral than anything that Bennett would write, but that Smith was not the author. In the *Wasp* on September 3, 1842, Nancy's father, Sidney Rigdon, asserted that the use of the letter was not authorized by his daughter and that he considered its publication a violation of the "rules of gallantry." Rigdon also noted that the letter was not in Smith's hand but rather in the hand of another person. In an affidavit of July 28, 1905, Nancy Rigdon's brother, John W. Rigdon, confirmed the truth of Bennett's allegations and commented on the hard feelings between the Rigdon family and Joseph Smith that the episode had produced. Joseph F. Smith, Jr., *Blood Atonement and the Origin of Plural Marriage*, pp. 83–84. The letter is

currently printed in the *History of the Church,* 5: 134–36, with wording identical to Bennett's version, as an essay on "happiness" that was given by Joseph Smith under unspecified circumstances. Even apologetic contemporary Mormon scholarship now accepts as fact that the letter was authorized by Joseph Smith after his marriage proposal to Nancy Rigdon had been rejected. For instance, see John J. Stewart, *Joseph Smith, The Mormon Prophet* (Salt Lake City: Mercury Publishing Company, 1966), pp. 170–71.

141. *History of the Church,* 5: 136.

142. Robinson, Journal, p. 24.

143. Mulder and Mortensen, *Among the Mormons,* pp. 116–23, print some of her letters.

144. Two important and as yet largely untouched sources providing a more positive perspective on Bennett's activities are the Ralph V. Chamberlain Papers and the Martin Wilford Poulson Papers in the Brigham Young University Special Collections. Arriving at a realistic assessment of Bennett's role is extraordinarily difficult. Later Mormon historiography has tended to assume that Bennett did not really know the factual details of the development of polygamy in Nauvoo. This seems highly improbable. Given Bennett's pivotal position in the secular life of Nauvoo and his high position in the Church as an "Assistant President" (an office which apparently was created just for him and which was discontinued after his apostasy), it strains credulity to believe that Joseph Smith would not have taken the man into his full confidence. B. H. Roberts, *The Rise and Fall of Nauvoo* (Salt Lake City: Deseret News, 1900), p. 136, succinctly stated a major reason why Joseph Smith initially became attracted to Bennett: "Joseph said Bennett was the first man who'd do exactly what he wanted done, the way it should be done, and at once." Bennett was capable, imaginative, and initially something of a sycophant, but as soon as he had created his own power base, he became an extraordinarily disruptive figure. The social disorganization in Nauvoo which could allow a man like Bennett to rise and fall so rapidly deserves serious historical attention.

145. These were the evaluations, respectively, of Kimball, "Study of the Nauvoo Charter," p. 25, ftn. 21, which sees Bennett as an excellent example of the "booster type" described in Daniel J. Boorstin, *The Americans: The National Experience* (New York: Vintage, 1965); personal conversation with Robert Flanders in summer 1974; and Thomas Ford, *History of Illinois* (Chicago: S. C. Griggs, 1859), p. 263.

146. The anti-Bennett exposés and the Poulson and Chamberlain Papers suggest how incapable Bennett was of staying with a single project for any length of time. Bennett's religious affiliations ranged from the Campbellites to the Methodists, the Mormons, and the Stangite Mormons. As summarized by the medical historian Frederick C. Waite, Bennett's medical career included writing a short book on gynecology, establishing a number of short-lived colleges, making use of medical innovations in his private practice, and helping to found several state medical societies. Following Bennett's Mormon interlude, which included a brief and similarly stormy affiliation with the Strangite organization, he returned to secular life to reestablish a successful medical practice, write an important treatise

on the raising of poultry, and develop a strain of the Plymouth Rock chicken.

147. Bennett's actions as described in the Mormon affidavits against him differ in two respects from the later Mormon accounts of the way in which plural marriage was introduced. First, if Bennett had relations with as many women as the accounts against him indicate, it seems virtually impossible that he could have taken all of them with Joseph Smith's official sanction. In 1842 there is evidence of only a very limited practice of polygamy among Joseph Smith's closest associates. If Bennett was taking women without Joseph Smith's sanction and going through an external form in which he did not really believe, he was corrupting the new practices.

Second, Mormon affidavits against Bennett indicate that he promised the women whom he tried to seduce that if they became pregnant he would give them medicine to produce abortions. Whether or not such charges are true, such practices would seem plausible in view of Bennett's background in medicine and midwifery, and his later printed advertisements in 1846 stressing his knowledge of various remedies for women's private ailments. If Bennett did provide abortions for women in Nauvoo, such actions would have been fundamentally inconsistent with the development of plural marriage, which always stressed that the primary purpose of polygamy was to raise up a numerous progeny in the families of righteous men. Bennett's perversion of plural marriage seems to have left Joseph Smith apoplectic. See his comments in the *Wasp* Extra for July 27, 1842. Although allegations of abortions in Nauvoo appear in both the manuscript and printed sources for the period, it is probably impossible to determine the accuracy, or lack thereof, of the accounts.

148. See William Law's affidavit of July 20, 1842, printed in the *Wasp* Extra of July 27, 1842.

149. Oliver Olney's private journal, the original of which is in the Coe Collection at the Beinecke Library, Yale University, New Haven, Connecticut, notes in an entry for June 16, 1842: "They [Joseph Smith and John C. Bennett] have moved together hart and hand in all their windings. If Bennett had not moved quite so fast all would have been well now, as I look at things with them."

150. Mormon scholarship has already shown that Bennett was factually accurate in some of his other allegations which appeared grossly inflated at the time. For example, see Hansen's *Quest for Empire*, for an account making serious use of Bennett's testimony regarding Mormon political aspirations. Given Bennett's closeness to major development in the Church, it strains credulity to believe that he could have produced an account of polygamy devoid of all truth, even had he wanted to do so.

151. Bennett, *History of the Saints*, p. 256.

152. Jenson, "Plural Marriage," p. 221. Affidavit of Joseph Bates Noble taken on June 6, 1869.

153. See Brodie, *No Man Knows My History*, p. 302, ftn.

154. Bennett, *History of the Saints*, p. 224. Bennett concludes this straightforward description of the plural marriage ceremony with his own typically extreme personal reaction, p. 225: "The above is a faithful and unexaggerated account of the most enormous and detestable system of depravity that

was ever concocted by the corrupt heart of a human being." Evidently Bennett eventually reached a point at which the only way he could intellectually comprehend what Joseph Smith was doing was by viewing it as a monstrous fraud—at it would have been had he been setting up such a program without Smith's sense of religious mission and compulsion.

155. See Marquart, *Strange Marriages*, p. 23, for the text of the alleged revelation. The instructions to Newel K. Whitney include:

> These are the words which you shall pronounce upon my servant Joseph and your daughter S. A. Whitney. They shall take each other by the hand and you shall say, You both mutually agree, calling them by name, to be each other's companion so long as you both shall live, preserving yourselves for each other and from all others and also throughout eternity reserving only those rights which have been given to my servant Joseph by revelation and commandment and by legal authority in times passed . . . Let immortality and eternal life hereafter be sealed upon your heads forever and ever.

Compare this with Orson Prat's description of the plural marriage ceremony in Utah as printed in the *Seer* 1 (February 1853): 31–32.

I have not verified the accuracy of Marquart's unauthorized printing of the July 27, 1842, revelation with scholars in the Church Historical Department. However, the fact that such a revelation did exist is corroborated by Orson F. Whitney's statement in *The Contributor* 6 (January 1885): 131.

156. In *Abstract of the Temple Lot Case*, p. 314, Melissa Lott Willes stated:

> As nearly as I can remember or understand it, the marriage ceremony at the time I married Joseph Smith is as follows: "You both mutually agree to be each other's companion, husband and wife, observing the legal rights belonging to this condition, that is, keeping yourselves wholly for each other, and from all others, during your lives."

The puzzling references to "keeping yourselves wholly for each other, and from all others," a statement apparently left from the earlier Mormon marriage ceremony, would seem to be directed primarily at the woman. Also, note the stress on companionship.

157. Bennett, *History of the Saints*, pp. 217–25.

158. Durham, "Mormonism and Masonry," pp. 5–6.

159. Bennett's references to "spiritual wives" and to the "spiritual wife system" must be clarified. Although the use of such terminology was almost universal by knowledgeable ex-Mormons, anti-Mormons, and schismatic Mormons during the Nauvoo period, the Mormon Church at the time and subsequently has consistently denied that such terminology was ever used to refer to its *own* form of plural marriage. The phrases are almost invariably taken to be a shorthand for the irregularities of Bennett and others. In fact, however, there can be little doubt that Bennett was using terminology that also was being used by contemporary Mormons to refer to polygamy. That the term "spiritual wife" was used by Nauvoo Mormons is clear from a statement in the *Nauvoo Neighbor*, January 1, 1845, which responded to part of Governor Ford's message on the disturbances in Hancock County:

> To relieve the Governor's mind, on this subject, we will just say
> that the meaning of spiritual wives is to be married for eternity,
> instead of natural lifetime; and should a man die after they have
> been married, they have a legal right to get married again; and
> should they do it for eternity, especially a man, he must have spiritual
> wives.

What this statement does not say is that when this doctrine was translated into temporal terms, it served as a justification for polygamy. In
a defense of polygamy in 1882, Helen Mar Kimball Whitney, a former
plural wife of Joseph Smith's, described the use of the term "spiritual
wife" during the early development of polygamy in Nauvoo: "At that time
spiritual wife was the title by which every woman who entered into this
order was called, for it was taught and practiced as a spiritual order
and not a temporal one though it was always spoken of sneeringly by
those who did not believe in it. . . ." *Plural Marriage as Taught by the
Prophet Joseph* (Salt Lake City: Juvenile Instructor Office, 1882), p. 15.
I have almost never encountered the term "plural marriage" or "celestial
marriage" in Mormon or non-Mormon accounts from the Nauvoo period,
although the term "spiritual wife system" was in common usage. When
the Mormon Church finally admitted in 1852 that it had been practicing
polygamy (which it had vehemently denied earlier), the Church evidently
decided to replace the pejorative term "spiritual wife system" with
"celestial marriage," which also had a "spiritual" sound but lacked the
negative connotations associated with the earlier expression.

160. D. Michael Quinn has identified a number of wives of General Authorities whom he calls "lesser known wives" because they apparently sustained
some sort of marriage relationship with early Church leaders but were
not publicly acknowledged as their wives. Apparently a marriage ceremony was performed for these women, and some definitely secured a
divorce before remarrying, but the precise status of this group of women
remains ambiguous. Quinn, "The Mormon Hierarchy," pp. 154–56.

161. After over one hundred years of non-productive contention about the
veracity or falsehood of Bennett's allegations about these women, it is
obvious that establishing exactly what did happen in these cases is impossible. Based on my research, I believe that whether or not Bennett's
allegations are true, none of his statements regarding Martha Brotherton,
Nancy Rigdon, and Sarah Pratt are implausible. But to document this
point of view would convince no one who was unwilling to be convinced. The Mormon Church was extremely successful in obscuring what
was really going on in this period. If one looks at polygamy from the
standpoint of its political impact, as I have done here, one might possibly
be able to bypass the endless character defamations and counter-
defamations which make this period of Mormon history so unpleasant.
For a summary of much of the evidence supporting Bennett's contentions
in these cases, see Jerald and Sandra Tanner, *Joseph Smith and Polygamy*, pp. 62–75.

162. *History of the Church*, 5: 286.

163. The title page of the pamphlet reads as follows: *An Extract, From a
Manuscript Entitled The Peace Maker, or the Doctrines of the Millennium: Being a Treatise on Religion and Jurisprudence. Or a New System*

of Religion and Politicks. For God, My Country, and My Rights. By Udney Hay Jacob. An Israelite, and a Shepherd of Israel. Nauvoo, Ill. J. Smith, Printer, 1842.

To the best of my knowledge, there are only two extant copies of this extremely rare document. The one to which references are made in this book is found in the William Robertson Coe Collection of the Beinecke Library at Yale University, New Haven, Connecticut. A photocopy made from this pamphlet is found in the Library of the LDS Church Historical Department in Salt Lake City, Utah. The other copy of this document is in the Everett D. Graff Collection of the Newberry Library, Chicago, Illinois. A typescript made from this copy by Dale Morgan is located in the Utah State Historical Society Library, Salt Lake City, Utah.

164. Hyrum L. Andrus, *Doctrines of the Kingdom: Volume III, Foundations of the Millennial Kingdom of Christ* (Salt Lake City: Bookcraft, 1973), esp. pp. 1–19 and 439–89, discusses the context within which the restoration of the patriarchal order and plural marriage was conceived of by nineteenth-century Mormons as part of a necessary prelude to the coming of the millennium.

165. *Peace Maker,* p. 37.

166. Olney, *Absurdities of Mormonism,* p. 10.

167. The complete statement as printed in the *Times and Seasons* 4 (December 1, 1842): 32, read:

> NOTICE: There was a book printed at my office, a short time since, written by Udney H. Jacobs [*sic*], on marriage, without my knowledge; and had I been apprised of it, I should not have printed it; not that I am opposed to any man enjoying his privileges; but I do not wish to have my name associated with the authors [*sic*] in such an unmeaning rigmarole of nonsense, folly and trash. JOSEPH SMITH.

This is one of the mildest of all Joseph's Smith's carefully worded apparent denials of polygamy. Far stronger denials were made of beliefs and practices which contemporary apostate and later Utah Mormon sources clearly verify existed with official sanction in Nauvoo. Note the possible *double entendre* in the phrase: "not that I am opposed to any man enjoying his privileges." From an initial reading, this statement could be taken to mean that Joseph Smith would not oppose publication of the pamphlet. But in later Utah Mormon usage, statements about men exercising or enjoying their privileges often referred to polygamy. And there is some evidence that Joseph Smith may have made similar oblique references to polygamy in some of his statements. Thus, this phrase could also have been a word to the wise that even if Smith was disavowing this particular pamphlet for the record, he was not opposing properly sanctioned polygamy. Since polygamy was illegal in Illinois at this time, any explicit public statement in its support was hardly to be expected from Mormon leaders.

168. See note 83 in this chapter.

169. Lee, *Mormonism Unveiled,* p. 246.

170. For instance, on October 10, 1895, at a meeting of the First Presidency and the Quorum of the Twelve, Abraham H. Cannon records:

> Joseph F. Smith holds that where the President gives a divorce it dis-unites the couple for time and eternity, for the same power which unites them together dissolves the bond. No man is justified in putting away his wife, however, save for fornication, and this, as explained in a pamphlet issued in the days of Joseph the Prophet, is alienation.

Called to my attention by D. Michael Quinn. The original of the Cannon Journal is in the Brigham Young University Special Collections.

171. See the evidence presented in my article, "A Little-Known Defense of Polygamy from the Mormon Press in 1842," *Dialogue* 9 (Winter 1974): 21–34.

172. The social argument of the *Peace Maker* is integrally connected with and receives its intellectual justification from an argument for the nature of true religious authority. A discussion of the relationship of the religious and social argument of the *Peace Maker* to contemporary Mormon values is presented in C. Jess Groesbeck, "Psychosexual Identity and the Marriage Relationship," *Dialogue* 2 (Spring 1967): 130–35.

173. *The Return* 3 (February 1891): 29.

174. *Nauvoo Expositor,* June 7, 1844.

175. *History of the Church,* 6: 253.

176. Hansen, *Quest for Empire,* pp. 72–89.

177. Remarks at Brigham Young University, April 14, 1905, p. 5.

178. *Millennial Star* 5 (November 1844): 93. See the letter of George A. Smith to Joseph Smith III, dated October 9, 1869, as reproduced in Bailey, "Emma Hale," p. 84.

Chapter V

1. *Journal of Discourses,* 12: 153; Speech of January 12, 1868.

2. Based on manuscript accounts, it appears that not until the encampment of the main body of the Latter-day Saints at Winter Quarters (now Florence, Nebraska) in late 1846 did knowledge of polygamy practice become general within the group. Considerable sifting out of less committed members apparently took place at this time.

3. Howard Stansbury, *An Expedition to the Valley of the Great Salt Lake of Utah* (Philadelphia: Lippincott, Grambo, 1852), pp. 137–38.

4. J. W. Gunnison, *The Mormons, or Latter-day Saints, in the Valley of the Great Salt Lake* (Philadelphia: Lippincott, Grambo, 1852). Gunnison was also a member of the United States Corps of Topographic Engineers with Howard Stansbury. Gunnison's account shows much the same sensitivity to mid-nineteenth-century Mormon culture and experience that O'Dea showed in his mid-twentieth-century treatment, *The Mormons.* For other useful accounts by non-Mormons, see William Kelly, *Across the Rocky Mountains* (London: Simms & M'Intyre, 1852); William Chandless, *A Visit to Salt Lake and Mormon Settlements in Utah* (London: Smith Elder, 1857); Burton, *City of the Saints;* and [William E. Waters], *Life Among the Mormons and a March to Their Zion* (New York: Moorehead, Simpson & Bond, 1868). Burton's account is the most important example of the early travel literature. Though Waters

frequently is inaccurate, his account provides many conceptual insights worthy of further investigation.

5. Mrs. Benjamin G. Ferris, *The Mormons at Home* (New York: Dix & Edwards, 1856), pp. 122–64. Mrs. Ferris's resolute determination to find negative adjectives to describe positive characteristics of individuals she met becomes almost laughable at times.

6. Juanita Brooks, ed., *Not By Bread Alone: The Journal of Martha Spence Heywood, 1850–56* (Salt Lake City: Utah State Historical Society, 1978).

7. M. R. Werner, *Brigham Young* (New York: Harcourt, Brace, 1925).

8. Important overview perspectives on the early role of Brigham Young and the Twelve Apostles, particularly during the succession controversy, are provided by T. Edgar Lyon, "Nauvoo and the Council of the Twelve," in F. Mark McKiernan, Alma Blair, and Paul Edwards, eds., *The Restoration Movement: Essays in Mormon History* (Lawrence, Kan.: Coronado Press, 1973), pp. 167–205; D. Michael Quinn, "The Mormon Succession Crisis of 1844," *BYU Studies* 16 (Winter 1976): 187–233; and Quinn's earlier work in "The Mormon Hierarchy," pp. 40–78. The Spring 1978 issue of *BYU Studies* contains important articles on Brigham Young.

9. Lyon, "Nauvoo and the Twelve," p. 173.

10. The enormous importance that building the temple had for Mormons of the period can be seen in numerous articles in the *Times and Seasons* and other Church publications. For a treatment emphasizing economic factors, see Flanders, *Nauvoo,* pp. 190–210. Smith's revelation of January 19, 1841, on building the temple is printed in Doctrine and Covenants, section 124.

11. The details of the temple ceremonies are not important for our purposes here, although the content of those ceremonies has been frequently described by apostates. The sociologist Thomas F. O'Dea observed that: "These rites were once described in lurid terms or surrounded by hints and innuendo in the writing of some apostates, but there is actually nothing more to them than a ritualization of the beliefs that Joseph taught in Nauvoo. . . ." Controversy was generated not so much by the rites themselves as by the new beliefs which the rites served to introduce and by the fact that the rites were conducted in secrecy. For O'Dea's account of the temple ceremonies, see his *The Mormons,* pp. 57–60. A more detailed account, which practicing Mormons have confirmed as an essentially accurate description of the current temple ceremonies, is found in Whalen, *The Latter-day Saints in the Modern-day World,* pp. 158–94. The early ceremonies, which appear to be virtually identical to those of the present, are described by I. M. Van Deusen, *A Dialogue Between Adam and Eve, the Lord and the Devil, Called the Endowment* (Albany, N. Y.: C. Killmer, 1847), and Hyde, *Mormonism,* pp. 89–101. For a bibliography of published accounts of the temple ceremonies, prepared by Wesley P. Walters, see Jerald and Sandra Tanner, *The Mormon Kingdom,* 2 vols. (Salt Lake City: Modern Microfilm, 1969), 1: 170–72.

12. For the account of Rigdon's trial and excommunication, see the *Times and Seasons* for September 15, October 2, and October 15, 1844.

13. For some sources on Rigdon see his *Latter Day Saints' Messenger and Advocate;* the Sidney Rigdon-Stephen Post Papers in the Church Archives;

other papers on Rigdon held in the Brigham Young University Special Collections; Daryl Chase, "Sidney Rigdon—Early Mormon" (M.A. thesis, Univ. of Chicago, 1931); and F. Mark McKiernan, *The Voice of One Crying in the Wilderness: Sidney Rigdon, Religious Reformer, 1793–1876* (Lawrence, Kan.: Coronado Press, 1971.)

14. For the disorders associated with the disintegration of the Rigdonite faction, see the following letters in the Strang Papers: Benjamin Chapman to James J. Strang, March 24, 1846; Hazen Aldrich to Strang, April [14?], 1846; James Smith to Strang, May 16, 1846; and Peter Hess to Strang, December 14, 1846. This important source was called to my attention by D. Michael Quinn. None of these letters provides conclusive evidence of the practice of polygamy among the Rigdonite faction. Shook, *Origin of Mormon Polygamy,* p. 183. states categorically, however, "That Sidney Rigdon did advocate a spiritual wife system of his own will not be denied. . . ." President Joseph Smith of the RLDS Church wrote in a letter to Joseph Davis, dated October 13, 1899, that Sidney Rigdon had one form of polygamy "practiced by but a few, and that spasmodically, as an outburst of religious fervor rather than as a settled practice." Ibid., p. 194.

15. Rigdon's personal relationship to the development of polygamy in the early 1830s also remains an unanswered question. Is it possible that Rigdon himself could have played a significant role in the formation of Joseph Smith's beliefs on polygamy? An affirmative answer to this question is suggested by two pieces of evidence. First, Joseph Smith is usually said to have conceived the idea of reintroducing polygamy during the period when he was engaged in his inspired "translation" of the Bible—a "translation" conducted in close association with Rigdon. If polygamy beliefs were formulated at this time, might not such beliefs have been stimulated by the intellectual interaction of these two men? Second, two dates were commonly mentioned in LDS accounts as the origin of polygamy belief. It is said that Smith *may* have conceived the idea of polygamy "as early as 1831"—evidently an extrapolation from the revelation of July 17, 1831, cited in note 29 of the preceding chapter. More commonly, however, men who were close associates of Joseph Smith during the early period stated that the origin of polygamy belief occurred "in early 1832."

What could have been the occasion of this latter date? In the public announcement of the belief and the practice of polygamy to the world in the *Deseret News* Extra for September 14, 1852, and in the reprint of that information in a supplement to the *Millennial Star* for 1853, two revelations are cited in full. One of these, of course, is the revelation on plural and celestial marriage itself, dated July 12, 1843. The other statement (a somewhat more puzzling choice)—which was read in full by Brigham Young to prepare the minds of the Latter-day Saints for the polygamy revelation—was a revelation received by Joseph Smith and Sidney Rigdon in Hiram, Ohio, on February 16, 1832. This revelation, now section 76 of the Utah Mormon Doctrine and Covenants, promises eventually to "reveal all mysteries; yea, all the hidden mysteries of my Kingdom from days of old. . . ." It also declares that Smith and Rigdon then saw and understood all "things of God, even those things which were from the beginning before the world was. . . ." As a hypothesis for further investigation, I would suggest that perhaps on this occasion "in early 1832" not only the basic Mormon cosmology with its telestial, terrestrial, and celestial stages may have been formulated, but also that the idea of polygamy as an integral part of the "restoration of all things" may first have been conceived by Joseph Smith and Sidney Rigdon.

16. For a more detailed account of William Smith's activities, see the treatment in my dissertation, "Between Two Worlds," pp. 301–7. Major LDS, Strangite, and RLDS printed and manuscript accounts are in basic agreement on William Smith's instability and the erratic character of his activities. For the writings of William Smith's faction of the Church, see Dale Morgan's bibliography in *Western Humanities Review* 7 (Summer 1953): 131–38. Among the numerous LDS sources, see the Church newspapers such as the *Times and Seasons* and the *Prophet*, the testimony of William's alleged plural wife Mary Ann West in *Abstract of the Temple Lot Case*, pp. 379–84, as well as Quinn, "The Mormon Hierarchy," p. 280, which identifies several of his alleged plural wives, their dates of marriage and separation, and related information. The James J. Strang Papers in the Coe Collection at the Beinecke Library, Yale University, New Haven, Connecticut, hereafter cited as Strang Papers, are perhaps the richest single manuscript source on William Smith. These papers contain many of his letters and much other information on his activities. Early leaders of the RLDS Church such as Jason Briggs and Issac Sheen, who for a time were close associates of William Smith, also left testimony about their split with him over his advocacy and practice of polygamy. For instance, see Jason Briggs's reminiscences in *The Messenger* 2 (November 1875): 1. That William Smith was initiated into the knowledge of the temple ceremonies is asserted in his exposé in the *Warsaw Signal*, October 29, 1845, and by Reuben Miller, *James J. Strang, Weighed in the Balance and Found Wanting* (Burlington, Wisconsin Territory: n.p., September 1849), p. 19. Also see John K. Sheen, *Polygamy, or the Veil Lifted* [York, Nebraska: n.p., 1889]. This prints the full title page of the manuscript *Elders' Pocket Companion*, allegedly written in 1844 by William Smith, as well as the passages in one of the sections of that work justifying and explaining the rationale for polygamy. The *Elders' Pocket Companion* appears to be authentic. John K. Sheen was the son of Isaac Sheen who, with William Smith, edited the *Melchisedek* [sic] *and Aaronic Herald* in Covington, Kentucky, between February 1, 1849 and April 1, 1850. When Sheen broke with William Smith, in part because he discovered that Smith secretly advocated polygamy, he secured a number of Smith's papers.

17. John Hardy, *History of the Trial of Elder John Hardy, Before the Church of Latter Day Saints in Boston, for Slander, in Saying that G. J. Adams, S. Brannan and William Smith Were Licentious Characters* (Boston: Conway, 1844). Hardy's trial was on October 22, 1844.

18. One rejoinder by William Smith was printed in the *Prophet*, February 8, 1845. Another letter that he wrote in self-defense appeared in the *Nauvoo Neighbor*, May 14, 1845. Wilford Woodruff had several encounters with Smith, Adams, and Brannan, and reported his adverse judgment on them to the Twelve in Nauvoo. Lyon, "Nauvoo and the Twelve," p. 203, citing Journal History, September and October 1844, as well as Wilford Woodruff letters in the George J. Adams and Brigham Young Letter Files, Church Archives.

19. For a discussion of some of these problems, see my dissertation, "Between

Two Worlds," pp. 307–10. Major RLDS sources on this difficult period include Joseph Smith III and Heman C. Smith, *The History of the Reorganized Church of Jesus Christ of Latter Day Saints, III, 1844–1872* (Independence, Mo.: Herald House, 1952); Inez Davis Smith, *The Story of the Church,* 4th ed. rev. and enl. (Independence, Mo.: Herald House, 1948); Robert Bruce Flanders, "The Mormons Who Did Not Go West: A Study of the Emergence of the Reorganized Church of Jesus Christ of Latter Day Saints" (M.A. thesis, Univ. of Wisconsin, 1954); and Alma R. Blair, "The Reorganized Church of Jesus Christ of Latter Day Saints: Moderate Mormonism," in McKiernan, *Restoration Movement,* pp. 207–30.

20. *Warsaw Signal,* September 3, 1845. Needless to say, this speech resulted in widespread gossip. William Smith was still trying unsuccessfully to live down this part of his past late in his life when he wrote an undated statement to Joseph Smith III, which is preserved in the Archives of the Reorganized Church of Jesus Christ of Latter Day Saints, the Auditorium, Independence, Missouri.

21. *Times and Seasons* 6 (November 1, 1845): 1008.

22. Klaus J. Hansen, "James J. Strang and the Amateur Historian," *Dialogue* 6 (Spring 1971): 76.

23. Among the major sources consulted for this section are: Milo M. Quaife, *The Kingdom of Saint James: A Narrative of the Mormons* (New Haven: Yale Univ., 1930), the only scholarly biography of Strang; Dale L. Morgan, "A Bibliography of the Church of Jesus Christ of Latter Day Saints [Strangite]," *Western Humanities Review* 5 (Winter 1950–51): 42–114, an exhaustive annotated bibliography of all known early Strangite publications; and the Strang Papers at Yale University, an extremely rich source comprising 544 lots, most of which are four-page letters in foolscap, but many of which are documents of greater length or lots that contain several related letters. I am grateful for the hospitality of Klaus and Joan Hansen and their family, which made possible extensive research in this superb collection. Strang's own writings are an essential source, since he is his own most eloquent interpreter. See Mark A. Strang, ed., *The Diary of James J. Strang: Deciphered, Transcribed, Introduced and Annotated* (Ann Arbor: Michigan State Univ., 1961); the Strangite newspapers, the *Voree Herald* and the *Northern Islander;* Strang's *The Diamond: Being the Law of Prophetic Succession, and a Defense of the Calling of James J. Strang as Successor to Joseph Smith* (Voree, Wis.: Gospel Herald, 1848); Strang's *The Prophetic Controversy: A Letter from James J. Strang to Mrs. Corey* (Saint James, Mich.: Cooper & Chidester, 1856); and Wingfield Watson, ed., *The Revelations of James J. Strang* (Boyne, Mich.: [Wingfield Watson?], 1885). Essential, too, is Strang's eloquent *Book of the Law of the Lord* (Saint James, Mich.: Royal Press, 1856). This book was reprinted by the present-day Strangite remnant in 1948. See also George Miller, *Correspondence of Bishop Miller* (Burlington, Wis.? 1916?). These letters were first printed in the *Northern Islander* in 1855. Only a handful of secondary treatments are of more than historiographic interest. Among these, see Henry E. Legler, *A Moses of the Mormons* (Milwaukee: Parkman Club Publications, nos. 15 and 16, 1897), which was reprinted by Michigan Pioneer and Historical Collections, 1902, vol.

32, pp. 180–224; Dale L. Morgan's fine, unsigned and undated typescript, "Summary Description of the Strang Manuscripts," which introduces those manuscripts in the Coe Collection; and Klaus J. Hansen, "The Making of King Strang: A Re-Examination," *Michigan History* 46 (September 1962): 201–19. O. W. Riegel's fictional *Crown of Glory: The Life of James J. Strang, Moses of the Mormons* (New Haven: Yale University Press, 1935) is disappointing in its treatment of Strang's motives. Other recent interpretations show superficiality of research and conceptualization.

24. Quaife, *Kingdom of Saint James*, p. 138.

25. Mark A. Strang, *Diary of James J. Strang*, pp. 9, 17, 19, 22.

26. Ibid., p. 32. It is interesting that Joseph Smith had a similar visionary sense of impending Civil War at the time of the 1832 South Carolina Nullification Crisis. Both Strang and Smith were extraordinarily sensitive to major currents of their time, and showed an ability to see such events within a framework of cosmic significance.

27. In his Calendar of the Strang Papers, pp. 21–28, Dale L. Morgan points out a number of factors which suggest a forgery. First, the letter is hand printed. No other extant letter ever written or dictated by Joseph Smith was hand printed. Second, the signature of the letter, written by the same hand as the text of the letter, bears not the slightest resemblance to Joseph Smith's distinctive signature. Finally, the content of the letter itself is extremely uncharacteristic of Joseph Smith's writing style, but it is strikingly similar to a beautiful passage in Strang's own diary for March 20, 1833. For these and a number of other complex reasons, Morgan concludes that the letter was probably a forgery by Strang. I have carefully examined the original "letter of appointment" and fully concur with Morgan's judgments.

28. For a more detailed evaluation of Strang's motivation and career, see my dissertation, "Between Two Worlds," pp. 340–56.

29. Quaife, *Kingdom of Saint James*, p. 98, quoting the *Voree Herald*, August 12, 1847.

30. For Quaife's analysis of the development of Strang's polygamy system, see *Kingdom of Saint James*, pp. 96–115.

31. The profound impression that Joseph Smith made on James J. Strang, as well as on so many other followers, cannot be more clearly shown than by the fact that almost every important faction of the Mormon Church before 1850, and many unattached individuals as well, introduced or attempted to introduce some form of polygamy practice. Such efforts were made by the main body of the Mormons in Nauvoo, as well as by Lyman Wight, Sidney Rigdon, William Smith, and James J. Strang, among others. See Shook, *Origin of Mormon Polygamy*, p. 194.

32. One of the most detailed presentations of Strang's social argument for polygamy is found in his defense of *The Seer*, Orson Pratt's detailed argument for Utah polygamy, in the *Northern Islander*, March 2, 1854. The description of Strang's argument for polygamy which follows is taken from this source. In his *Book of the Law of the Lord*, pp. 318–28, in an extended footnote elaboration of the text of the book itself, Strang uses Old Testament sources to justify polygamy, in addition to presenting a social argument similar to that found in the *Northern Islander*. Interest-

ingly, not a single passage in the original, unamplified *Book of the Law of the Lord* directly supports polygamy. Striking though Strang's arguments for polygamy are, they seem almost exclusively to be an after-the-fact justification, rather than an outgrowth of prior religious belief.

33. For a treatment of the practical operation of Strang's polygamy system on Beaver Island, see Quaife, *Kingdom of Saint James*, pp. 106–10.

34. Ibid., pp. 107–8. Statement of Strang's last surviving wife, Mrs. Sarah A. Wing, in an interview with Quaife in the summer of 1920.

35. Ibid., p. 101, quoting Strang's statement in the *Northern Islander*, October 11, 1855.

36. Despite Strang's many failings and failures, his life and mission have elements of undoubted grandeur. It has not been possible here adequately to suggest Strang's remarkable human sensitivities which are so starkly revealed in his personal letters and the articles in his newspapers, as well as the extremely high calibre of so many of the people whom he attracted. Dale L. Morgan writes of the Strang Papers as a whole in his Introduction to them, p. 17: "They are so full of human hope, fear, mistrust, and anger, often sad and as often exalted, that to read them is to be given a fresh understanding of Mormonism, what it brought into the lives of its believers, and what they suffered in the cause. . . ." Like Joseph Smith himself, James J. Strang profoundly affected the people with whom he had been associated.

37. Writing as early as July 20, 1842, in a manuscript account, Oliver Olney recorded the stories that a plurality of wives was being taught by commandment of God "to raise up a righteous branch," and that the Saints were about to start west as far as the Rocky Mountains and there raise up a righteous branch without being molested by the laws of the land. Oliver Olney Papers, in the Coe Collection at the Beinecke Library, Yale University, New Haven, Connecticut. Numerous reports of explorations in different parts of the West appeared in the *Wasp* and *Nauvoo Neighbor*, probably to acquaint Mormons with information about possible locations for settlement. Special expeditions, such as the one by Lyman Wight to Texas, also suggest the concern of Mormon leaders to locate a new site for a possible Mormon settlement.

38. For a discussion of some of the factors that led to polarization between Mormons and non-Mormons at this time, see my dissertation, "Between Two Worlds," pp. 330–40.

39. Doctrine and Covenants, section 136. This statement is the only directive of Young's to be included along with Smith's revelations in the Doctrine and Covenants.

40. Gordon Irving, "The Law of Adoption: One Phase of the Mormon Concept of Salvation, 1830–1900," *BYU Studies* 14 (Spring 1974), p. 297. Irving's fine analysis, ibid., pp. 291–314, is the primary basis of the brief discussion which follows.

41. Lee, *Confessions*, p. 197; emphasis in the original.

42. Irving, "The Law of Adoption," p. 296.

43. See the discussion in Quinn, "The Mormon Hierarchy," pp. 154–56.

44. Lee, *Confessions*, p. 289.

45. The full minutes of the conference were first printed as a *Deseret News* Extra for September 14, 1852, and were reprinted as a supplement to

vol. 15 of the *Millennial Star* in 1853. It it interesting to note that the Mormon Church did not make a full public commitment to plural and celestial marriage until 1876, when the revelation finally was included in the Doctrine and Covenants, and the 1835 Kirtland statement on marriage was removed.

46. For the best introduction to Mormon settlement of the Great Basin region under Brigham Young, see Arrington, *Great Basin Kingdom,* pp. 38–231. Also see Leland Hargrave Creer, *The Founding of an Empire: The Exploration and Colonization of Utah, 1776–1856* (Salt Lake City: Bookcraft, 1947); Milton R. Hunter, *Brigham Young, the Colonizer* (Salt Lake City: Deseret News, 1940); Dean May, "The Making of Saints: The Mormon Town as Setting for the Study of Cultural Change," *Utah Historical Quarterly* 15 (Winter 1977): 75–92; D. W. Meinig, "The Mormon Culture Region: Strategies and Patterns in the Geography of the American West, 1847–1864," *Annals of the Association of American Geographers* 55 (1965): 191–220; Lowry Nelson, *The Mormon Village: A Pattern and Technique of Land Settlement* (Salt Lake City: Univ. of Utah, 1952); Joel E. Ricks, *Forms and Methods of Early Settlement in Utah, 1847–1877* (Logan: Utah State Univ., 1964); and Ray B. West, Jr., *Kingdom of the Saints: The Story of Brigham Young and the Mormons* (New York: Viking, 1957). A proposed study of a later period with important implications for early Mormon settlement is Melvyn Hammarberg, "Designing a Sample for Mormon Society, 1880" (Unpublished Working Paper No. 1, Great Salt Lake Basin Culture Area Project—copy courtesy of the author).

47. For a brief discussion of the politics of early Utah, with special reference to the relationship of the politics of polygamy and the politics of slavery, see Richard D. Poll, "The Mormon Question Enters National Politics, 1850–1856," *Utah Historical Quarterly* 25 (1957): 117–31. Also see Norman F. Furniss, *The Mormon Conflict, 1850–1859* (New Haven: Yale Univ. 1960), and Andrew Love Neff, *History of Utah, 1847–1869,* edited and annotated by Leland Hargrave Creer (Salt Lake City: Deseret News, 1940). The "runaway judges" were three non-Mormon officials who left Utah late in 1851 in a state of high dudgeon and proceeded to make lurid allegations of polygamy, treason, and Church-inspired murder.

48. Stanley Snow Ivins, "Notes on Mormon Polygamy," *Western Humanities Review* 10 (Summer 1956): 229–39, provides an overview of the development of polygamy in Utah. Ivins notes that according to his data, which is based on some 2,500 polygamous marriages covering the whole period of the experiment, peak periods during which polygamous marriages occurred were the winter of 1845–46 in Nauvoo, 1852, 1856–57, 1862, 1868–69, and 1883–84. Overall he finds a decline in the taking of plural wives following the period of the 1856–57 Reformation.

49. Ibid., p. 231. Jane Snyder Richards, first wife of Franklin D. Richards, stated that "in the first two or three years [in Utah] polygamy was not much entered into." Reminiscences of Mrs. F. D. Richards, p. 35, in Hubert Howe Bancroft Collection of Mormon Manuscripts in the Bancroft Library, University of California at Berkeley, California; hereafter cited as Bancroft Collection.

50. In his diary on August 29, 1852, after the revelation on plural and celestial

marriage was first read in public, Hosea Stout recorded "the great joy of the Saints who have looked forward so long and so anxiously for the time to come when we could publicly declare the true and greatest principles of our holy religion and the great things which God has for his people to do in this dispensation." Juanita Brooks, ed., *On the Mormon Frontier: The Diary of Hosea Stout, 1844–1861*, 2 vols. (Salt Lake City: Univ. of Utah, 1964), 2: 449–50. While many Mormons responded with enthusiasm to the public announcement of plural marriage in 1852, an undercurrent of hostility to the practice appears to have remained strong throughout the 1850s among some Mormons, particularly Mormon women. Numerous statements suggesting such dissatisfaction appear in the early issues of the *Journal of Discourses*. Heber C. Kimball noted in the *Deseret News* 5 (October 6, 1855): 274, that some women had had a revelation "that when this time passes away, and they go through the vale, every woman will have a husband to herself." Such opposition never became formally organized.

51. Supplement to vol. 15 of the *Millennial Star,* p. 3; emphasis in original removed.
52. David Bitton, "The Polygamy Controversy: A Study of 19th-Century Polemic" (unpublished paper—read through the courtesy of the author).
53. Recent Mormon historiography has increasingly taken note of such concerns by analyzing the images of the Mormons held by other Americans. For examples of such studies, see: Leonard J. Arrington and Jon Haupt, "The Missouri and Illinois Mormons in Ante-Bellum Fiction," *Dialogue* 5 (Spring 1970): 37–50; Arrington and Haupt, "Intolerable Zion"; David Brion Davis, "Some Themes of Counter-Subversion: An Analysis of Anti-Masonic, Anti-Catholic, and Anti-Mormon Literature," *Mississippi Valley Historical Review* 47 (September 1960): 205–24; Cannon, "The Awesome Power of Sex"; Gail Farr Casterline, " 'In the Toils' or 'Onward for Zion': Images of the Mormon Woman, 1852–1890" (M.A. thesis, Utah State Univ., 1974); Neil Lambert, "Saints, Sinners and Scribes: A Look at the Mormons in Fiction," *Utah Historical Quarterly* 36 (Winter 1968): 63–77; Dennis Leo Lythgoe, "The Changing Image of Mormonism in Periodical Literature" (Ph.D. diss., Univ. of Utah, 1969); Jan Shipps, "From Satyr to Saint"; and Edwina Jo Snow, "Singular Saints: The Image of the Mormons in Book Length Travel Accounts, 1847–1857" (M.A. thesis, George Washington Univ., 1972).
54. See Shipps, "From Satyr to Saint," esp. pp. 22–28.
55. Supplement to vol. 15 of the *Millennial Star,* p. 63.
56. Ibid., pp. 24–25.
57. Statement by the editor of the *Utah Magazine,* October 2, 1869, as quoted in Kimball Young, *Isn't One Wife Enough?: The Story of Mormon Polygamy* (New York: Henry Holt, 1954), p. 44. Helen Mar Kimball Whitney, *Why We Practice Plural Marriage* (Salt Lake City: Juvenile Instructor Office, 1884), pp. 50–53, makes this argument at some length.
58. Casterline, "Images of the Mormon Woman," p. 101. Belinda Marden Pratt's defense was originally printed in pamphlet form as an anonymous *Defence of Polygamy, by a Lady in Utah, In a Letter to Her Sister in New Hampshire* (n.p., n.d.). The letter was dated "Great Salt Lake City, Jan. 12, 1854" and was addressed to "Mrs. Lydia Kimball, Nashua, N. H." The letter was reprinted in Burton, *City of the Saints,* pp. 484–93.

59. Helen Mar Kimball Whitney, *Why We Practice Plural Marriage*, pp. 4–22.
60. I am grateful to Ron Esplin for allowing me to see uncatalogued marriage and divorce requests which were approved by Brigham Young.
61. The first scholarly study of the dynamics of polygamous family life was made by James Edward Hulett, Jr., "The Sociological and Social Psychological Aspects of the Mormon Polygamous Family" (Ph.D. diss., Univ. of Wisconsin, 1939). Hulett's study was based on interviews with 78 individuals who had lived as husbands, wives, or children in 47 polygamous families that were established in the late nineteenth century prior to the 1890 manifesto which ended public Church support of the practice. Two important articles which Hulett wrote based on his study were "Social Role and Personal Security in Polygamy," *American Journal of Sociology* 5 (January 1940): 538–49, and "The Social Role of the Mormon Polygamous Male," *American Sociological Review* 8 (June 1943): 279–87. Hulett's dissertation advisor, Kimball Young, wrote an impressionistic popular treatment of polygamy based on Hulett's work and some additional research, entitled *Isn't One Wife Enough?* in 1954. Copies of Young's notes and other materials collected by Hulett and other interviewers are held in the Huntington Library, San Marino, California, and the Garrett Theological School Library in Evanston, Illinois. After years of assiduously collecting data on all aspects of polygamy, Stanley Snow Ivins wrote an article, "Notes on Mormon Polygamy," which remains possibly the best overview treatment of the subject. The work of Ivins is elaborated and qualified in James E. Smith and Philip R. Kunz, "Polygyny and Fertility in Nineteenth-Century America," *Population Studies* 30 (1976): 465–80. D. Michael Quinn's prosopographical study of "The Mormon Hierarchy" between 1832 and 1932 provides an invaluable source on family relationships among the leading families of the Mormon Church. Vicky Burgess-Olson, "Family Structure and Dynamics in Early Utah Mormon Families—1847–1885" (Ph.D. diss., Northwestern Univ., 1975), uses survey research techniques to analyze historical documents on early Mormon families.
62. Interview of Mrs. Hubert Howe Bancroft with Mrs. F. D. Richards, "The Inner Facts of Social Life in Utah," p. 11; Bancroft Collection. Also see "Reminiscences of Mrs. F. D. Richards" and "Narrative of Franklin Dewey Richards" in the Bancroft Collection. For a bibliographic sketch and family data on Franklin D. Richards, see Andrew Jenson, comp., *Latter-day Saint Biographical Encyclopedia*, 4 vols. (Salt Lake City; Andrew Jenson History Co., 1901), 2: 115–21; Quinn, "The Mormon Hierarchy," p. 271; and Connie Duncan Cannon, "Jane Snyder Richards: The Blue-White Diamond" in Vicky Burgess-Olson, ed., *Sister Saints* (Provo: Brigham Young Univ., 1978), pp. 173–98. Also see Franklin L. West, *Life of Franklin D. Richards, President of the Council of the Twelve Apostles of the Church of Latter-day Saints* (Salt Lake City: Deseret News Press, 1924). Hubert Howe Bancroft's study appeared as *History of Utah, 1540–1886* (San Francisco: History Company, 1889).
63. "Social Life in Utah," p. 18. This attitude runs throughout many accounts written by Mormon women. For instance, see Helen Mar Kimball Whitney's *Why We Practice Plural Marriage*.
64. Burgess-Olson, "Early Utah Mormon Families," pp. 69–82, 131.
65. *Why We Practice Plural Marriage*.

66. Annie Clark Tanner, *A Mormon Mother: An Autobiography* (Salt Lake City: Univ. of Utah, 1969), pp. 116 and 1.

67. After reading and surveying hundreds of diaries of Mormon men and women, Davis Bitton indicates that only a handful of the diaries and journals of Mormon men practicing polygamy discuss their emotional reactions to their plural wives. For the sources surveyed, see Davis Bitton, *Guide to Mormon Diaries and Autobiographies* (Provo: Brigham Young Univ., 1977).

68. Mormon folklore would be an interesting source to use in beginning to understand the problems of achieving equal treatment of wives under polygamy. As starting points, see Austin and Alta Fife, *Saints of Sage and Saddle: Folklore Among the Mormons* (Bloomington: Indiana Univ., 1956), and the Record of J. Golden Kimball Stories and Brother Peterson Yarns (Sharon, Conn.: Folk Legacy Record FTA–25).

69. Hulett, "The Mormon Polygamous Family," includes a long section analyzing such conflicts, pp. 118–64, and reports one complex case in an appendix, pp. 426–33.

70. Such references were made in the supplement to vol. 15 of the *Millennial Star* and were repeatedly made in the early issues of the *Journal of Discourses.*

71. *Journal of Discourses,* 5: 99.

72. Werner, *Brigham Young,* pp. 300–301. On Mormon sexual attitudes, see the special issue of *Dialogue,* v. 10, no. 2 (Autumn 1976), on "Sexuality and Mormon Culture," edited by Harold T. Christensen and Marvin V. Rytting, as well as Marvin V. Rytting, "Struggling with the Paradoxes of Mormon Tradition" (paper presented at the Annual Meeting of the Society for Values in Higher Education, South Bend, Indiana, August 1978; copy secured through the courtesy of the author). Strictly speaking, Mormon repressive attitudes toward sexual expression are better described as "Victorian" rather than "puritanical." The Puritans were more tolerant of sexual expression in moderation than were their Victorian successors.

73. Ivins, "Notes on Mormon Polygamy," p. 230. Ivins's source for these calculations was Frank Esshom's massive *Pioneers and Prominent Men of Utah* (Salt Lake City: Utah Pioneers Book Publishing Co., 1913; reprinted by Western Epics, 1966).

74. Ivins, "Notes on Mormon Polygamy," p. 233.

75. United States census figures for the Utah Territory between 1850 and 1890 show an approximately equal balance of men and women, always with a slightly higher number of men. Whether these figures would necessarily mean that there were a preponderance of *eligible* men over eligible women is an interesting question. Smith and Kunz, "Polygyny and Fertility," p. 470, address this question, noting, "The larger number of females aged 20 to 29 relative to males aged from 30 to 39 would permit a significant amount of polygyny among those males." There is some evidence that due to the lack of women, young men may occasionally have found difficulty in securing wives, although this never appears to have been a significant problem. The relatively equal sex ratio in Utah did, however, make polygamy a possible option. Had Utah had an extreme excess of men over women, it is difficult to imagine that polygamy could have been successfully established.

A related question is the possible appeal of polygamy to women who came to Utah from other areas where they had been having difficulty finding husbands. For example, William Mulder, *Homeward to Zion: The Mormon Migrations from Scandinavia* (Minneapolis: Univ. of Minnesota, 1957), indicates that although slightly more Scandinavian men than women migrated to Utah, the proportion was very nearly equal. In contrast, Scandinavian migration to other parts of the United States during the period showed a significant preponderance of men. Evidently Mormon polygamy made possible the migration of more than the usual number of single women. Frequently, these women were from the poorest and most exploited servant class which found any marriage a step upward. More demographic work needs to be done before we can begin to gain a full understanding of the social factors which contributed to the development of polygamy.

76. Ivins, "Notes on Mormon Polygamy," pp. 231–32. I am informed that unpublished research by S. George Ellsworth on the demography of early Cache County, Utah, shows that relatively high concentrations of polygamous families occurred in certain parts of the county, while other areas were almost exclusively monogamous. If this variation in the concentration of monogamists and polygamists also occurred elsewhere in the Great Basin, it could suggest that polygamists felt more comfortable in areas where there were significant numbers of polygamists and that in other areas of Mormon settlement there may have been undercurrents of opposition to the practice.

There are several organized groups of present-day Mormon "fundamentalists," i.e., Mormons practicing polygamy despite the refusal of the main body of the Latter-day Saints to sanction such a practice. It is difficult to determine the numbers of individuals involved in such groups, but the fundamentalists put out a considerable though often highly ephemeral printed literature. For an entrée into such literature and arguments, see Dennis R. Short, *Questions on Plural Marriage, With A Selected Bibliography and 1600 References* (Salt Lake City: Dennis R. Short, 1975); [Gilbert A. Fulton, Jr.], *The Most Holy Principle*, 4 vols. (Murray, Utah: Gems Publishing Co., 1970–1975); and the numerous writings and publications of Ogden Kraut. The reaction of Gilbert A. Fulton, Jr.'s first wife, who left him after he became a polygamist, is found in Melissa Merrill (pseud.), *Polygamist's Wife* (Salt Lake City: Olympus Publishing Co., 1975). The most important of the periodicals issued by the various fundamentalist groups was *Truth,* a magazine which appeared in 21 volumes between June 1935 and May 1956. Insights into the strains of life in polygamy after the Manifesto of 1890 are provided in two semi-fictionalized accounts by Samuel W. Taylor: *Family Kingdom* (New York: McGraw-Hill, 1951) and *I Have Six Wives* (New York: Greenberg, 1956). For a critique of fundamentalist claims from the perspective of the main body of the Mormons, see Dean C. Jesse, "A Comparative Study and Evaluation of Latter-day Saint and 'Fundamentalist' Views Pertaining to the Practice of Plural Marriage" (M.A. thesis, Brigham Young Univ., 1959). Although several other studies of such groups have been put out in refutation of their claims to authority, a social analysis of the persistence of such groups and their relation to the emotional and intellectual upheavals caused when the main body of the Mormons gave up polygamy in the late nineteenth and early twentieth centuries remains to be written.

77. Arrington, *Great Basin Kingdom,* p. 38. It would be interesting to compare the voluntarily accepted strains on family life that were part of the early Mormon settlement of the Great Basin with the many involuntary pressures on the family that were generated by the relatively unplanned developments and dislocations of the early industrial revolution.

78. Young, *Isn't One Wife Enough?* pp. 56–67. Young's criteria for judging the degree of success of polygamous marriages are somewhat unclear. It would appear that his sample may be biased by the exclusion of many cases of plural marriages which resulted in divorce.

79. Quinn, "The Mormon Hierarchy," discusses the many ways in which kinship relationships were used to strengthen the cohesion of the group, creating a sort of Mormon "dynasticism." For a discussion of one specific example suggesting an "arranged marriage," see ibid., pp. 167–69.

80. Whitney, *Why We Practice Plural Marriage,* p. 53. Of course, children were stars in the crown of the monogamous mother as well. Furthermore, there is evidence that polygamously married women had a smaller total number of children per wife, on the average. The objective of polygamy was not to produce the largest number of children per wife, but rather the largest total number of children in the families of the best men, where presumably they would be reared under the most advantageous circumstances. See Ivins, "Notes on Mormon Polygamy," pp. 236–37; Quinn, "The Mormon Hierarchy," pp. 246–91; Burgess-Olson, "Early Utah Mormon Families," pp. 100–104; and Smith and Kunz, "Polygamy and Fertility," p. 471.

81. Susa Young Gates and Leah D. Widtsoe, *The Life Story of Brigham Young* (New York: Macmillian, 1930), pp. 295–96.

82. Casterline, "Images of the Mormon Woman," pp. 85–86.

83. Mrs. S. A. Cooks, "Theatrical and Social Affairs in Utah" (Salt Lake City, 1884), pp. 5–6; original MS in Bancroft Collection.

84. Mrs. T. B. H. Stenhouse, *A Lady's Life Among the Mormons: A Record of Personal Experience as One of the Wives of a Mormon Elder During a Period of More than Twenty Years,* 2nd ed. (New York: American News, 1872), pp. 147–48.

85. Burgess-Olson, "Early Utah Mormon Families," pp. 87–90. Ivins, "Notes on Mormon Polygamy," p. 234, observes that of a sample of 1,642 polygamists, ten percent married one or more pairs of sisters. The issue of female support networks and the sense of female solidarity in the past has recently become a topic of much scholarly interest. One important analysis is Carroll Smith Rosenberg's "The Female World of Love and Ritual." A Mormon analysis from a similar perspective is Maureen Ursenbach Beecher, "Sisters, Sister Wives, and Sisters in the Faith: Support Systems Among Nineteenth Century Mormon Women" (paper presented at the Conference on the History of Women, sponsored by the Women Historians of the Midwest and the Chicago Area Women's History Conference, St. Paul, Minnesota, October 22, 1977).

86. Casterline, "Images of the Mormon Woman," p. 71.

87. Mrs. F. D. Richards, "Social Life in Utah," pp. 13–14.

88. Mrs. Joseph Horne, "Migration and Settlement of the Latter Day Saints"

(Salt Lake City, 1884), pp. 34–35; original MS in Bancroft Collection. Mary Isabella Horne was Relief Society President of the Salt Lake Stake and a prominent woman in her own right.

89. Letter of Mrs. Mary J. Tanner, Provo City, Utah, 1880, in Bancroft Collection, pp. 5–6. See Casterline, "Images of the Mormon Woman," p. 103, for a discussion of the Mormon women's argument that polygamy freed them from masculine demands and allowed for a healthy continence. It also made possible continence during gestation as recommended by nineteenth-century medical theory, and therefore was seen as making for healthier, better-spaced babies.

90. *San Francisco Examiner,* November 8, 1896, as quoted in Cannon, "The Awesome Power of Sex," p. 76, ftn. For accounts of this remarkable woman, see Jean Bickmore White, "Dr. Martha Hughes Cannon: Doctor, Wife, Legislator, Exile," in Burgess-Olson, *Sister Saints,* pp. 383–97; and Barbara Hayward, "Teaching the Slavish Virtues: The Public Life of Martha Hughes Cannon," *Century 2: A Brigham Young University Student Journal* 2 (Winter 1978): 1–5.

91. Ivins, Notebook 4: 276, indicates that the 1851 census described some plural wives as heads of households.

92. Burgess-Olson, "Early Utah Mormon Families," p. 135.

93. See Casterline, "Images of the Mormon Woman," p. 77; Keith Calvin Terry, "The Contribution of Medical Women During the First Fifty Years in Utah" (M.A. thesis, Brigham Young Univ., 1964); and Leonard J. Arrington, "Women as a Force in the History of Utah," *Utah Historical Quarterly* 38 (Winter 1970): 3–6.

94. Shauna Adix, "Education for Women: The Utah Legacy," *Boston University Journal of Education* 159 (August 1977): 38–49, is critical of the limitations on such education in early Utah. Similar limitations also existed, however, at other early coeducational institutions such as Oberlin College.

95. Although Wyoming in 1869 was the first territory to pass a bill granting woman suffrage, women in Utah actually went to the polls in 1870, under a similar bill passed that year, and cast their votes before women in Wyoming did. Among the articles on this topic, see Thomas G. Alexander, "An Experiment in Progressive Legislation: The Granting of Woman Suffrage in Utah in 1870," *Utah Historical Quarterly* 38 (Winter 1970): 20–30; Beverly Beeton, "Woman Suffrage in Territorial Utah." *Utah Historical Quarterly* 46 (Spring 1978): 100–120; Jean Bickmore White, "Woman's Place is the Constitution: The Struggle for Equal Rights in Utah in 1895," *Utah Historical Quarterly* 42 (Fall 1974): 344–69; and T. A. Larson, "Woman Suffrage in Western America," *Utah Historical Quarterly* 38 (Winter 1960): 7–19.

96. The development of political awareness and involvement among Mormon women as they organized themselves to support polygamy is discussed in Casterline, "Images of the Mormon Woman," pp. 94–100. For general accounts of the vital role that women played in the development of Utah, see Susa Young Gates and Leah D. Widtsoe, *Women of the "Mormon" Church* (Salt Lake City: Deseret News, 1926), and Leonard J. Arrington, "Blessed Damozels: Women in Mormon History," *Dialogue* 6 (Summer 1971): 22–31.

97. General Board of the Relief Society, *A Centenary of the Relief Society, 1842–1942* (Salt Lake City: General Board of the Relief Society, 1942), p. 14.

98. Casterline, "Images of the Mormon Woman," pp. 83–94; Sherilyn Cox Bennion, "The *Woman's Exponent:* Forty-Two Years of Speaking for Women," *Utah Historical Quarterly* 44 (Summer 1976): 222–39; and Carol Cornwall Madsen, " 'Remember the Women of Zion': A Study of the Editorial Content of the *Woman's Exponent,* A Mormon Woman's Journal" (M.A. thesis, Univ. of Utah, 1977). For another Mormon women's publication of the period, see *Young Woman's Journal,* published between 1889 and 1929.

99. Casterline, "Images of the Mormon Woman," pp. 80–81.

100. Eugene Campbell's unpublished paper "Mormon Polygamy—A Loose Marriage System?: Preliminary Impressions" raises some important questions which deserve further investigation; called to my attention by David J. Whittaker. These issues are further developed and elaborated in Eugene E. Campbell and Bruce E. Campbell, "Divorce Among Mormon Polygamists: Extent and Explanations," *Utah Historical Quarterly* 46 (Winter 1978): 4–23.

101. Hulett, "The Mormon Polygamous Family," pp. 308–403; Burgess-Olson, "Early Utah Mormon Families," pp. 117–19. Also see Young, *Isn't One Wife Enough?* pp. 191–225.

102. Mrs. F. D. Richards, "Reminiscences," p. 47.

103. May, "The Making of Saints," provides an analysis of the ways in which the Mormons handled conflict situations and developed communal solidarity. May compares the Mormon experience with the New England Puritan experience as described in recent studies of the New England town.

104. Mrs. F. D. Richards, "Social Life in Utah," p. 1.

105. Mrs. F. D. Richards, "Reminiscences," p. 55.

106. The Utah territorial divorce law is printed in *Acts, Resolutions and Memorials, Passed at the Several Annual Sessions of the Legislative Assembly of the Territory of Utah* (Great Salt Lake City: Joseph Cain, 1855), pp. 162–64.

107. For examples of Brigham Young's strong official disapproval of divorce, see *Journal of Discourses,* 17: 119, and Historian's Office Journal, 1858–1859 Book, p. 11 (December 15, 1858). Ibid., p. 15 (December 17, 1858), Brigham Young told a man who asked him for a divorce: "It is not right for the brethren to divorce their wives the way they do. I am determined that if men do not stop divorcing their wives, I will stop sealing. I am determined men shall not abuse the gifts of God & privileges of the Priesthood the way they are doing"; called to my attention by D. Michael Quinn. On the other hand, note that Young was relatively flexible in granting divorces requested by women. For instance on October 5, 1861, Young ". . . remarked he liked a woman to live with her husband as long as she could bear with him and if her life became too burdensome then leave and get a divorce." Brigham Young's Office Journal, 1858–1863, p. 300; called to my attention by David J. Whittaker. For secondary discussions of Utah Mormon divorce policy and practice, see Larsen, "Mormon Social Structure," pp. 201–5, and Young, *Isn't One Wife Enough?* pp. 226–40.

108. An example of Brigham Young's rhetorical statements on divorce, given during one of the most troubled periods of Utah history, is found in *Journal of Discourse,* 4: 55–56.
109. Recorded with all spelling, capitalization, and punctuation as in the original. James Beck, Notebooks, 1859–1865, I, in Church Archives. Beck's account is an accurate summary of the original speech given by Brigham Young and stenographically recorded by G. D. Watt, in Church Archives.
110. "A Little-Known Defense of Polygamy."
111. Campbell and Campbell, "Divorce Among Mormon Polygamists," pp. 5–6, present this information on divorces under Brigham Young. They note that since Brigham Young had no authority to grant civil divorces terminating monogamous marriages, and since as president of the Church he alone had the right to sever polygamous relationships, probably most of the 1,645 divorce certificates were issued to polygamists.
112. Ibid., p. 6, based on information in Quinn, "The Mormon Hierarchy" pp. 248–91.
113. Hulett, "The Mormon Polygamous Family," p. 11.
114. Ibid., p. 406.
115. Burgess-Olson, "Early Utah Mormon Families," pp. 59–68.
116. Hulett, "The Mormon Polygamous Family," p. 42. This is supported by Burgess-Olson, "Early Utah Mormon Families," pp. 129–30.
117. Hulett, "The Mormon Polygamous Family," p. 42. For a discussion of Brigham Young's remarkable household organization, see Clarissa Young Spencer and Mabel Harmer, *Brigham Young at Home* (Salt Lake City: Deseret News Press, 1947), esp. pp. 15–80.
118. An extensive literature exists on the political campaign against Mormon polygamy. For bibliographic starting points, see James B. Allen and Glen M. Leonard, *The Story of the Latter-day Saints* (Salt Lake City: Deseret Book Company, 1976), pp. 681–87, and Davis Bitton, "Mormon Polygamy: A Review Article," *Journal of Mormon History* 4 (1977): 106–11. Some of the most useful studies include Ray Jay Davis, "The Polygamous Prelude," *American Journal of Legal History* 6 (January 1962): 1–27; Richard D. Poll, "The Mormon Question, 1850–1865"; Orma Linford, "The Mormons and the Law: The Polygamy Cases," *Utah Law Review* 9 (Winter 1964–Summer 1965): 308–370, 543–591; Richard D. Poll, "The Twin Relic: A Study of Mormon Polygamy and the Campaign by the Government of the United States for Its Abolition, 1852–1890" (M.A. thesis, Texas Christian Univ., 1939); Gustive O. Larson, *The "Americanization" of Utah for Statehood* (San Marino, Calif.: Huntington Library, 1971); and Henry J. Wolfinger, "A Reexamination of the Woodruff Manifesto in the Light of Utah Constitutional History," *Utah Historical Quarterly* 39 (Fall 1971): 328–49.
119. Arrington and Haupt, "Intolerable Zion," p. 249.
120. Ibid., p. 254.
121. Accounts conveying the personal flavor of this difficult period include Tanner, *A Mormon Mother;* Juliaetta Bateman Jensen, *Little Gold Pieces* (Salt Lake City: Stanway Printing Co., 1948); Larson, *"Americanization" of Utah for Statehood;* Young, *Isn't One Wife Enough?* pp. 300–442; and George Q. Cannon, "The Prison Diary of a Mormon Apostle," *Pacific Historical Review* 16 (November 1947): 393–409.

122. Quoted from Larson, *"Americanization" of Utah for Statehood*, pp. 263–64.
123. See ibid., pp. 243–64, and Allen and Leonard, *Story of the Latter-day Saints*, pp. 413–16.
124. This difficult transition period still remains to be adequately assessed. As starting points, see ibid., pp. 401–64; Hansen, *Quest for Empire*; Kenneth L. Cannon II, "Beyond the Manifesto: Polygamous Cohabitation among LDS General Authorities after 1890," *Utah Historical Quarterly* 46 (Winter 1978): 24–36; and Jan Shipps, "Utah Comes of Age Politically: A Study of the State's Policies in the Early Years of the Twentieth Century," *Utah Historical Quarterly* 35 (Spring 1967): 91–111.

Chapter VI

1. Condensed, with changes in paragraphing and capitalization, from William Hepworth Dixon, *Spiritual Wives*, 2 vols. (London: Hurst & Blackett, 1868), 2: 176–85. This was part of a letter that Noyes wrote Dixon in March 1867. The core of the letter is also printed in Tyler, *Freedom's Ferment*, pp. 193–94.
2. A succinct summary and interpretation of the different varieties of Puritanism is presented in Alan Simpson's *Puritanism in Old and New England* (Chicago: Univ. of Chicago, 1955). Kenneth A. Lockridge, *A New England Town, The First Hundred Years: Dedham, Massachusetts, 1636–1736* (New York: W. W. Norton, 1970), treats one New England town as "utopian" in much the same sense that the antebellum millennialists might be described as "utopian."
3. Burridge, *New Heaven, New Earth*, p. 162.
4. It has frequently been argued that social movements such as these can be explained in economic or class terms—though the specific explanations have varied widely. Either such movements are a product of the upward striving of the poor and dispossessed, or they result from the activism of the middle classes, or they are a response to the fear of loss of status by threatened elites. None of these explanations by itself adequately accounts for the appeal of the overall millennial style of these three groups. Whereas the Mormons drew most of their membership from the lower classes, many early Shakers appear to have come from middle-class backgrounds, and the Oneida Perfectionists were heavily based on the educational and financial elite. Thus, although one could argue that each of these groups was especially appealing to a particular social and economic segment of American society, the appeal of the broader millennial impulse which they shared transcended simple economic or class boundaries, Also see John L. Thomas, "Romantic Reform in America, 1815–1865," *American Quarterly* 17 (Winter 1965): 656–81. Much further work must be done before any direct causal connections can be made between specific social, economic, or political backgrounds and the appeal of these groups.
5. For discussions of these issues, see Mead, *The Lively Experiment*; Bernard A. Weisberger, *They Gathered at the River: The Story of the Great Revivalists and their Impact on Religion in America* (Chicago: Quadrangle, 1966); and Cross, *Burned-over District*.
6. Edward Deming Andrews, *The Gift to Be Simple: Songs, Dances and*

Rituals of the American Shakers (New York: Dover, 1962), provides an introduction to these themes in Shaker music. White and Taylor, *Shakerism,* is oriented toward the concerns of feminists, and convincingly portrays Shaker history from such a perspective.

7. "Try the Spirits," *Perfectionist* 3 (September 15, 1843): 59.
8. See my paper, "Free Love and Feminism: John Humphrey Noyes and the Oneida Community," for an analysis of Noyes's attitude toward the antebellum women's movement. This paper was delivered at the Conference on Communes and Utopias at Omaha, Nebraska, on October 13, 1978. A complementary analysis of the way Noyes's ideals were reflected in the practice at Oneida is provided by Kirschner, "Women and the Communal Experience: The Oneida Community, 1849–1877."
9. Joseph Smith's 1831 revelation criticizing the Shakers is printed in *History of the Church,* 1: 167–69, and a more detailed attack on women exercising any formal leadership role in the church is presented, ibid., 4: 577–81.
10. For an overview of some of these trends, see Alan Barker, *The Civil War in America* (Garden City, N. Y.: Doubleday, 1961).
11. Andrews, *Community Industries of the Shakers,* presents an illuminating case study of the economic organization of the New Lebanon, New York, Shaker community.
12. For discussions of the range of work open to women, see Parker, *A Yankee Saint;* Carden, *Oneida;* and Dalsimer, "Women and Family in the Oneida Community."
13. *First Annual Report of the Oneida Association,* p. 41.
14. Leonard J. Arrington's pathbreaking article, "The Economic Role of Pioneer Mormon Women," *Western Humanities Review* 9 (Spring 1955): 145–64, has been qualified by the comparative analysis which Maureen Ursenbach Beecher presented in "Women's Work on the Mormon Frontier" (paper delivered at the Berkshire Conference on Women's History, August 24, 1978). On Brigham Young's attitudes toward women, see Jill Mulvay Derr, "Woman's Place in Brigham Young's World," *BYU Studies* 18 (Spring 1978): 377–95.
15. See Stephen W. Nissenbaum, "Careful Love: Sylvester Graham and the Emergence of Victorian Sexual Theory in America, 1830–1840" (Ph.D. diss., Univ. of Wisconsin, 1968); Walters, *Primers for Prudery;* and Haller and Haller, *The Physician and Sexuality in Victorian America.*
16. The question of whether revivalistic excesses necessitated extreme measures of sexual self-control or whether extreme sexual self-control necessitated the outlets provided by revivalistic activities remains a chicken-and-egg proposition which is open to continuing debate. Clearly both elements were closely related.
17. Noyes, *Male Continence,* p. 9.
18. Carden, *Oneida,* p. 51.
19. "Asceticism Not Christianity," *Circular* 1 (November 23, 1851): 11; Home Talk no. 71, *Circular* 1 (November 30, 1851): 16; Noyes, *Male Continence,* p. 16.
20. The doctrine of blood atonement was widely preached in early Utah, and numerous sermons in the *Journal of Discourses* deal with this belief. For examples, see *Journal of Discourses,* 3: 235; 4: 53–54; 4: 219–20. For statements on blood atonement that may be considered to represent

authoritatively the nineteenth-century Mormon position, see Charles W. Penrose, *Blood Atonement, As Taught by the Leading Elders of the Church of Jesus Christ of Latter-day Saints* (Salt Lake City: Juvenile Instructor Office, 1884), and Joseph F. Smith, Jr., *Blood Atonement and the Origin of Plural Marriage.* The possibility that blood atonement might be used against two specific individuals was discussed in a meeting of the Mormon Council of Fifty on March 3, 1849. Robert Glass Cleland and Juanita Brooks, eds., *A Mormon Chronicle: The Diaries of John D. Lee,* 2 vols. (San Marino, California: Huntington Library, 1955): 1: 98. The assiduous anti-Mormon writers Jerald and Sandra Tanner have collected a few examples of slayings in Utah that were carried out in the classic blood atonement style, but they have been unable to establish authoritatively whether or not any of these killings were actually authorized by the Mormon Church itself. Jerald and Sandra Tanner, *The Mormon Kingdom,* 2 vols. (Salt Lake City: Modern Microfilm, 1971), 2: 134–69. For an evaluation of the problem of blood atonement and its relations to the broader American hostility toward sexual transgression, see my dissertation, "Between Two Worlds," pp. 335–40.

21. Jeffrey, "The Family as a Utopian Retreat from the City."
22. Andrews, *Gift to Be Simple.* The first published Shaker hymnal, *Millennial Praises,* uses extensive family imagery.
23. Andrews, *People Called Shakers,* pp. 186–94. Elkins, *Fifteen Years in the Shakers,* provides a fairminded and analytical account of his experience growing up among the Shakers.
24. The most readily accessible source for the Oneida Community hymn is Nordhoff, *Communistic Societies of the United States,* pp. 299–300.
25. "Practical Communism," *Circular* 1 (June 13, 1852): 121.
26. See *Circular* 3 (September 21, 1854): 499; Corinna Ackley Noyes, *The Days of My Youth* (Kenwood, N. Y.: by the author, 1960), p. 16; and Pierrepont B. Noyes, *My Father's House.*
27. See Kimball Young, *Isn't One Wife Enough?* pp. 191–260; and Campbell and Campbell, "Divorce Among Mormon Polygamists."
28. Davis Bitton, "The Mormon Child: Growing Up on the Mormon Frontier" (paper presented in Indianapolis, Indiana, on March 31, 1978, at the Conference on Childhood in American Life).
29. Kett, *Rites of Passage,* pp. 51–61.
30. Andrews, *People Called Shakers,* pp. 204–23. In an important study published too late to be used in writing this section, Carol Weisbrod, *The Boundaries of Utopia* (New York: Pantheon, 1980), describes and analyzes the relationship between the Mormons, Shakers, Oneida Community, Harmonists, and Zoarites and the larger society.
31. For treatments of this period, see Robertson, *The Breakup;* Parker, *A Yankee Saint;* Fogarty "Conservative Christian Utopianism"; and Carden, *Oneida.*
32. The Stanley Snow Ivins notebooks show that relatively few attacks on the Mormons prior to 1852 focused on polygamy, while the attacks after 1852 were predominantly directed against polygamy.
33. A convenient and well-presented overview of some of these changes may be found in Allen and Leonard, *Story of the Latter-day Saints.*
34. As quoted in Persons, "Christian Communitarianism in America," p. 139.

35. "Disasters and Successes of Perfectionism," *Spiritual Magazine* 2 (January 10, 1850): 353–57.

36. Of George P. Murdock's world ethnographic sample, 193 out of 234 societies held polygamy as the ideal. Goode, *The Family*, p. 46. A provocative account of contemporary African polygamy, with many comparative insights for the Mormon case, is Remi Clignet, *Many Wives, Many Powers: Authority and Power in Polygynous Families* (Evanston: Northwestern Univ., 1970).

37. Frank E. Manuel, "Toward A Psychological History of Utopias," in *Utopias and Utopian Thought,* ed. Frank E. Manuel (Boston: Beacon, 1967), p. 70.

38. Wallace, "Revitalization Movements," suggests that the process of individual psycho-social reintegration is analogous to the process by which a whole society can be revitalized by a millennial movement.

Essay on Sources

All sources used directly in this book are cited in the notes. In addition, a detailed bibliography including other materials consulted in preparing the study is available in my Ph.D. dissertation, "Between Two Worlds: The Origins of Shaker Celibacy, Oneida Community Complex Marriage, and Mormon Polygamy" (Univ. of Chicago, 1976). Rather than duplicate such information, this essay will simply highlight a few of the most valuable printed and manscript materials useful in understanding these groups and their marital experimentation.

General Conceptual and Historical Sources

The most important conceptual frameworks for the study of millennialism are found in anthropological literature. Particularly suggestive treatments are Anthony F. C. Wallace, "Revitalization Movements," *American Anthropologist* 38 (April 1956): 264–81; Kenelm Burridge, *New Heaven, New Earth: A Study of Millenarian Activities* (New York: Schocken, 1969); and Victor W. Turner, *The Ritual Process: Structure and Anti-Structure* (Chicago: Aldine, 1969). The theoretical problems of explaining Melanesian cargo cults are laid out in I. C. Jarvie, *The Revolution in Anthropology* (London: Routledge & Kegan Paul, 1964). Women's role in millennial movements is discussed in I. M. Lewis, *Ecstatic Religion: An Anthropological Study of Spirit Possession and Shamanism* (Baltimore: Penguin, 1971). Weston La Barre, "Materials for a History of Studies of Crisis Cults: A Bibliographic Essay," *Current Anthropology* 12 (February 1971): 3–44, provides a detailed bibliography and interpretation of existing studies.

For the American context of antebellum millennial and communitarian movements, essential starting points are Whitney R. Cross, *The Burned-over District: The Social and Intellectual History of Enthusiastic Religion in Western New York, 1800–1850* (Ithaca, N. Y.: Cornell Univ., 1950), and Arthur E. Bestor, *Backwoods Utopias: The Sectarian and Owenite Phases of Communitarian Socialism in America, 1663–1829,* 2nd enl. ed. (Philadelphia: Univ. of Pennsylvania, 1970). Bestor's book also includes his important essay "Patent-Office Models of the Good Society: Some Relationships Between Social Reform and Westward Expansion," as well as a general bibliography of studies of antebellum communitarian movements. John Humphrey Noyes, *History of American Socialisms* (Philadelphia: J. B. Lippincott, 1870), and Charles Nordhoff, *The Communistic Societies of the United States: From Personal Visit and Observation* (New York: Harper & Brothers, 1875), are two classic nineteenth-century studies which complement each other. Accounts of related movements are presented in Karl J. R. Arndt, *George Rapp's Harmony Society, 1785–1847* (Philadelphia: Univ. of Pennsylvania, 1965), and John F. C. Harrison, *Quest for the New Moral World: Robert Owen and the Owenites in England and America* (New York: Charles Scribner's Sons, 1969). Broad-ranging recent interpretations are Rosabeth Kantor, *Commitment and Community: Communes and Utopias in a Sociological Perspective* (Cambridge, Mass.: Harvard Univ., 1972), and Dolores Hayden, *Seven American Utopias: The Architecture of Communitarian Socialism, 1790–1975* (Cambridge, Mass.: MIT, 1976). Ronald G. Walters sketches the larger context of antebellum reform in his *American Reformers, 1815–1860* (New York: Hill & Wang, 1978).

Perspectives on the antebellum ferment in marriage and family relationships are found in Barbara Welter, "The Cult of True Womanhood, 1820–1860," *American Quarterly* 18 (Summer 1966): 151–74; Carroll Smith Rosenberg, "The Hysterical Woman: Sex Roles and Role Conflict in 19th-Century America," *Social Research* 39 (Winter 1972): 652–78; and John S. Haller and Robin M. Haller, *The Physician and Sexuality in Victorian America* (Urbana: Univ. of Illinois, 1974). More positive treatments of the factors leading toward Victorian family patterns are presented in Nancy F. Cott, *The Bonds of Womanhood: "Woman's Sphere" in New England, 1780–1835* (New Haven: Yale Univ., 1977); Kathryn Kish Sklar, *Catherine Beecher: A Study in American Domesticity* (New Haven: Yale Univ., 1973); and Daniel Scott Smith, "Family Limitation, Sexual Control and Domestic Feminism in Victorian America," in Mary S. Hartman and Lois Banner, eds., *Clio's Consciousness Raised: New Perspectives on the History of Women* (New York: Harper & Row, 1974), pp. 119–36. Kirk Jeffrey suggests some parallels between Victorian family concerns and the appeal of communitarian ventures in the mid-nineteenth century in his article, "The Family as a Utopian Retreat from the City: The Nineteenth Century Contribution," in Sallie Te Selle, ed., *The Family, Communes, and Utopian Societies* (New York: Harper & Row, 1972), pp. 21–39.

Shaker Sources

The printed and manuscript sources on the Shakers are extensive. Mary L. Richmond has compiled and annotated *Shaker Literature: A Bibliography,* 2 vols. (Hanover, N. H.: University Press of New England, 1977), a comprehensive bibliography of printed sources by and about the Shakers which supersedes all previous reference works of its kind. For each printed item, Richmond lists the major repositories at which it may be found. She also includes information on collections of manuscripts. The most extensive single Shaker manuscript collection is catalogued in Kermit J. Pike, *A Guide to Shaker Manuscripts in the Library of the Western Reserve Historical Society* (Cleveland: Western Reserve Historical Society, 1974). Both the printed and manuscript holdings of that indispensable collection are available for purchase on microfilm from the Microfilming Corporation of America, Glen Rock, New Jersey. The Library of Congress and a half-dozen other repositories also have significant Shaker manuscript holdings. *The Shaker Quarterly,* edited by Theodore E. Johnson, provides bibliographic essays and reprints many manuscript items which otherwise are not readily available.

Among the numerous secondary treatments of the Shakers, the most important are the various studies by Edward Deming Andrews, particularly his *The People Called Shakers: A Search for the Perfect Society,* new enl. ed. (New York: Dover, 1963). Andrews's work complements the earlier, somewhat more impressionistic account by Marguerite Fellows Melcher, *The Shaker Adventure* (Princeton: Princeton Univ., 1941). Also of special interest are the essays in John Patterson MacLean, *Shakers of Ohio* (Columbus, Ohio: F. J. Heer, 1907). The most sensitive appreciation of the Shakers is Constance Rourke's "The Shakers," in her *The Roots of American Culture and Other Essays,* ed. Van Wyck Brooks (New York: Harcourt Brace, 1942), pp. 195–237. An ambitious but not fully successful attempt to treat the Shakers within a larger theoretical context is Henri Desroche, *The American Shakers: From Neo-Christianity to Presocialism,* trans. and ed. John K. Savacool (Amherst: Univ. of Massachusetts, 1971).

Of Shaker writings, the most important doctrinal and theoretical overviews are [Benjamin Seth Youngs], *The Testimony of Christ's Second Appearing* (Lebanon, Ohio: John McClean, 1808), and [Calvin Green and Seth Y. Wells], *A Summary View of the Millennial Church or United Society of Believers (Commonly Called Shakers)* (Albany, N. Y.: Packard & Van Benthuysen, 1823). Particularly valuable on earliest Shakerism is the rare *Testimonies of the Life, Character, Revelations, and Doctrines of Our Ever Blessed Mother Ann Lee and the Elders with Her* (Hancock, Mass.: J. Tallcott & J. Deming, Junrs., 1816). On Shakerism in the Midwest, an indispensable source is Richard McNemar, *The Kentucky Revival* (Cincinnati: John W. Browne, 1807). Anna White and Leila S. Taylor, *Shakerism: Its Meaning and Message* (Columbus, Ohio: Fred. J. Heer, 1904), provides a thorough and sensitive history of the Shakers from a late-nineteenth-century perspective.

Accounts by seceders and apostates present valuable information on many aspects of the early Shaker movement. Most comprehensive and historically oriented is Thomas Brown, *An Account of the People Called Shakers: Their Faith, Doctrine, and Practice* (Troy, N. Y.: Parker & Bliss, 1812). Also perceptive and fairminded are David Lamson, *Two Years' Experience Among the Shakers* (West Boyleston, Mass.: the author, 1848), and Hervey Elkins, *Fifteen Years in the Senior Order of Shakers* (Hanover, N. H.: Dartmouth, 1853). The most vitriolic and persistent apostate from the Shakers was Mary Marshall Dyer, whose major exposé was *A Portraiture of Shakerism* (Concord, N. H.: for the author, 1822).

Among the most important of the many manuscripts in the Western Reserve Historical Society collections, see the books of biographical sketches compiled by Alonzo G. Hollister, the various community membership records, and the extensive writings from the period of spiritual manifestations in the 1830s and 1840s.

Oneida Sources

Printed materials by and about the Oneida Community are numerous. An annotated bibliography of almost all the printed sources is found in Lester G. Wells, *The Oneida Community Collection in the Syracuse University Library* (Syracuse, N. Y.: Syracuse Univ. Library, 1961). The Syracuse holdings, which include both monographs and articles, can be purchased on microfilm through the Microfilming Corporation of America, Glen Rock, New Jersey. Most of the manuscript records of the Oneida Community either have been destroyed or are not presently available for scholarly research.

Among the secondary accounts on Oneida, the most important still remains the biography by Robert Allerton Parker, *A Yankee Saint: John Humphrey Noyes and the Oneida Community* (New York: G. P. Putnam's Sons, 1935). A recent social-psychological study of Noyes which suggests new perspectives is Robert David Thomas, *The Man Who Would Be Perfect: John Humphrey Noyes and the Utopian Impulse* (Philadelphia: Univ. of Pennsylvania, 1977). Maren Lockwood Carden, *Oneida: Utopian Community to Modern Corporation* (Baltimore: Johns Hopkins, 1969), provides a sociological analysis which also deals with events after the breakup of the Community itself. Robert Fogarty's thesis on the sources of membership is presented in his article, "Oneida: A Utopian Search for Religious Security," *Labor History* 14 (Spring 1973): 202–27. The best account of the end of the Community is Constance Noyes Robertson, *Oneida Community: The Breakup, 1876–1881* (Syracuse, N. Y.: Syracuse Univ., 1972).

The most important primary source on John Humphrey Noyes and his various communal efforts is found in the periodicals that he and his associates published between 1834 and 1879. These periodicals went by many different titles, including *The Circular* (Brooklyn and Oneida, N. Y., and Wallingford, Conn., 1851–1864). No study which does not make use of these materials can be considered authoritative. Supplementing the newspapers are two rich collections of primary documents edited by George Wallingford Noyes: *The Religious Experience of John Humphrey Noyes, Founder of the Oneida Community* (New York: Macmillan, 1923), and *John Humphrey Noyes: The Putney Community* (Oneida, N. Y.: by the author, 1931). Also valuable for this study were the first three annual reports from Oneida, published between 1849 and 1851. *The First Annual Report of the Oneida Association* (Oneida Reserve, N. Y.: Leonard, 1849) includes the "Bible Argument Defining the Relations of the Sexes in the Kingdom of Heaven," the core statement of Noyes's social and sexual theories. This "Bible Argument" was elaborated in final form in *Bible Communism: A Compilation of the Annual Reports and Other Publications of the Oneida Association and Its Branches* (Brooklyn, N. Y.: Office of the *Circular*, 1853).

Monographs by John Humphrey Noyes are another essential source on Oneida. Noyes's unorthodox religious theories are set out in his *The Berean: A Manual for the Help of Those Who Seek the Faith of the Primitive Church* (Putney, Vt.: Office of the *Spiritual Magazine*, 1847). The religious turmoil which led to those religious theories is laid out in his *Confessions of John H. Noyes: Part I: Confessions of Religious Experience, Including a History of Modern Perfectionism* (Oneida Reserve, N. Y.: Leonard, 1849). Part II, which was to have been a Confession of Social Experience, was never published. Informal sermons by Noyes on a variety of topics are found in *Home Talks by John Humphrey Noyes*, ed. Alfred Barron and George Noyes Miller (Oneida, N. Y.: Oneida Community, 1875). Noyes's extraordinary birth-control theories are described and defended in his *Male Continence* (Oneida, N. Y.: Office of the *Oneida Circular*, 1872), while his eugenics views are put forward in his *Essay on Scientific Propagation* (Oneida, N. Y.: Oneida Community, 1872?)

Other accounts also suggest broader perspectives on Oneida. The journalist William Hepworth Dixon, *Spiritual Wives*, 2 vols. (Philadelphia: J. B. Lippincott, 1868), presents interesting interpretive approaches, but sometimes is factually inaccurate. In addition to Noyes's own interpretation in his *History of American Socialisms*, cited above, Oneida member William Alfred Hines attempted to place Oneida within the larger context of similar nineteenth-century experimentation in his *American Communities* (Oneida, N. Y.: Office of the *American Socialist*, 1878). Allan Estlake [Abel Easton], a former Community member, provided reminiscences after the breakup in his *The Oneida Community: A Record of an Attempt to Carry Out the Principles of Christian Unselfishness and Scientific Race Improvement* (London: George Redway, 1900). Noyes's son, Pierrepont B. Noyes captures the flavor of growing up at Oneida in his memoir, *My Father's House: An Oneida Boyhood* (New York: Farrar & Reinhart, 1937). Unfortunately, no anti-Oneida or apostate accounts are of significant historical merit.

Mormon Sources

The literature on Mormonism, both printed and manuscript, is vast, complex, and often highly polemical. Because the Latter-day Saints have been assiduous in collecting and recording information on their past and because much of that material is now becoming available for serious research, the scholar is faced in some instances with almost an embarrassment of riches. An entreé into this rich literature and into contemporary Mormon historiographic concerns is furnished by articles in *Dialogue: A Journal of Mormon Thought, Brigham Young University Studies,* and *Sunstone.* An invaluable aid to the location of early Mormon and Mormon-related imprints is Chad Flake, ed., *A Mormon Bibliography, 1830–1930: Books, Pamphlets, Periodicals, and Broadsides Relating to the First Century of Mormonism,* intro. Dale L. Morgan (Salt Lake City: Univ. of Utah, 1978). This monumental annotated bibliography identifies all known printed sources during the first century of Mormonism, as well as the major repositories at which they may be found. A similarly thorough and indispensable source for Mormon manuscripts is Davis Bitton, *Guide to Mormon Diaries and Autobiographies* (Provo: Brigham Young Univ., 1977). Bitton provides a synopsis of the contents of each of the manuscripts and notes where the originals and copies may be found.

Some of the major repositories of Mormon printed and manuscript materials are cited in the acknowledgements. Special mention must be made, however, of the exceptionally fine collection held in the Library and Archives of the Historical Department of the Church of Jesus Christ of Latter-day Saints in Salt Lake City, Utah. This collection, which dwarfs all others in the size, range, and quality of its holdings, is now open to serious scholarly research, both by Mormons and non-Mormons. Any comprehensive study of Mormon history must make use of this extraordinary resource. Among the important bibliographies available in the Church Library and Archives, see the following: *A Catalogue of Theses and Dissertations Concerning the Church of Jesus Christ of Latter-day Saints, Mormonism, and Utah* (Provo: College of Religious Instruction at Brigham Young Univ., 1971): Beth Oyler, comp., *Index to the Millen-*

nial Star, 4 vols. (unpublished photocopy, n.d.); and indices to other important Mormon periodicals, including the *Times and Seasons,* the *Journal of Discourses,* and the *Woman's Exponent.* The Journal History, a huge scrapbook in more than 750 volumes covering events of Mormon history chronologically from 1830, is another well-indexed resource in the Church Archives.

The most important single source for this study is the thoroughly indexed Notebooks and Transcripts of Stanley Snow Ivins, held by the Utah State Historical Society, and available on microfilm. Indispensable for the study of early Mormon schismatics are the annotated bibliographies by Dale L. Morgan on the Strangite, Green Oak, and other churches of the dispersion, published in *Western Humanities Review* 4 (Winter 1949–50); 5 (Winter 1950–51); and 7 (Summer 1953). Because of the frequency with which reprints of early Mormon manuscript and printed items are issued in altered form, serious scholarly work on Mormonism must go back to the original manuscript sources or to first editions whenever possible.

The best introduction to the Mormon experience is found in two pathbreaking studies, Thomas F. O'Dea, *The Mormons* (Chicago: Univ. of Chicago, 1957), and Leonard J. Arrington, *Great Basin Kingdom: An Economic History of the Latter-day Saints, 1830–1900* (Cambridge, Mass.: Harvard Univ., 1958). Also important for understanding themes of the early period are Mario S. De Pillis, "The Quest for Religious Authority and the Rise of Mormonism," *Dialogue: A Journal of Mormon Thought* 1 (March 1966): 68–88; Marvin S. Hill, "The Shaping of the Mormon Mind in New England and New York," *Brigham Young University Studies* 9 (Spring 1969): 351–72; Jan Shipps, "The Prophet Puzzle: Suggestions Leading Toward a More Comprehensive Interpretation of Joseph Smith," *Journal of Mormon History* 1 (1974): 4–20; and Marvin S. Hill, "The 'Prophet Puzzle' Assembled: or, How To Treat Our Historical Diplopia Toward Joseph Smith," *Journal of Mormon History* 3 (1976): 101–5. The standard Mormon account of the early period is Brigham H. Roberts, *A Comprehensive History of the Church of Jesus Christ of Latter-day Saints: Century I,* 6 vols. (Salt Lake City: Deseret News Press, 1930). A thorough chronological narrative of Mormon development, with an up-to-date bibliography of major scholarly studies, is James B. Allen and Glen M. Leonard, *The Story of the Latter-day Saints* (Salt Lake City: Deseret Book Company, 1976). Major themes in Mormon history are analyzed in Leonard J. Arrington and Davis Bitton, *The Mormon Experience: A History of the Latter-day Saints* (New York: Alfred A. Knopf, 1979).

Among the other essential secondary accounts of the early period, the most important still remains Fawn Brodie's controversial *No Man Knows My History: The Life of Joseph Smith, the Mormon Prophet,* 2nd ed. rev. (New York: Alfred A. Knopf, 1971). Brodie's pathbreaking study, first published in 1945, has been qualified but not superseded by Donna Hill, *Joseph Smith: The First Mormon* (Garden City, N. Y.: Doubleday, 1977). An interpretation with ramifications for many aspects of early Mormon history is Klaus J. Hansen, *Quest for Empire: The Political Kingdom of God and the Council of Fifty in Mormon History* (East Lansing: Michigan State Univ., 1967). For political and social developments during the Mormon stay in Illinois, see Robert B. Flanders, *Nauvoo: Kingdom on the Mississippi* (Urbana: Univ. of Illinois, 1965). The development of Mormon communitarian and cooperative enterprises in the nineteenth century is discussed in Leonard J. Arrington, Feramorz Y. Fox, and Dean L. May, *Building the City of God: Community and Cooperation among the Mormons* (Salt Lake City: Deseret Book Company, 1976). Despite sometimes questionable editing, the most important primary source for Joseph Smith is his *History of the Church of Jesus Christ of Latter-day Saints: Period I,* ed. Brigham H. Roberts, 6 vols., 2nd ed. rev. (Salt Lake City: Deseret Book Company, 1948). A scholarly biography of James J. Strang, the most influential early Mormon schismatic, is Milo M. Quaife, *The Kingdom of Saint James: A Narrative of the Mormons* (New Haven: Yale Univ., 1930).

For the Utah period, the starting point is Arrington's *Great Basin Kingdom,* cited above. No satisfactory biography of Brigham Young currently exists, but two conflicting approaches are presented in M. R. Werner, *Brigham Young* (New York: Harcourt, Brace, 1925), and Susa Young Gates and Leah D. Widtsoe, *The Life Story of Brigham Young* (New York: Macmillan, 1930). Biographical materials on early Mormon leaders are found in Andrew Jenson, *Latter-day Saint Biographical Encyclopedia,* 4 vols. (Salt Lake City: Andrew Jenson History Co., 1901–1936), and in Frank Esshom, *Pioneers and Prominent Men of Utah: Comprising Photographs, Genealogies, Biographies* (Salt Lake City: Utah Pioneers Book Publishing Co., 1913). Much valuable material is also included in biographies of other Mormon figures, including Andrew Karl Larson, *Erastus Snow: The Life of a Missionary and Apostle of the Early Mormon Church* (Salt Lake City: Univ. of Utah, 1971), and Juanita Brooks, *John Doyle Lee: Zealot, Pioneer Builder, Scapegoat* (Glendale, Calif.: Arthur H. Clark, 1961). Important primary sources are edited in Robert Glass Cleland and Juanita Brooks, eds., *A Mormon Chronicle: The Diaries of John D. Lee, 1848–1876,* 2 vols. (San Marino, Calif.: Huntington Library, 1955), and Juanita Brooks, ed., *On the Mormon Frontier: The Diary of Hosea Stout, 1844–1861,* 2 vols. (Salt Lake City:

Univ. of Utah, 1964). A useful anthology based on primary sources is William Mulder and A. Russell Mortensen, eds., *Among the Mormons: Historic Accounts by Contemporary Observers* (New York: Alfred A. Knopf, 1958).

On Mormon women, three essential studies are Ileen Ann Waspe, "The Status of Women in the Philosophy of Mormonism from 1830 to 1845" (M.A. thesis, Utah State Univ., 1942); Leonard J. Arrington, "The Economic Role of Pioneer Mormon Women," *Western Humanities Review* 9 (Spring 1955): 145–64; and Gail Farr Casterline, " 'In the Toils' or 'Onward for Zion': Images of the Mormon Woman, 1852–1890" (M.A. thesis, Utah State Univ., 1974). Useful topical and biographical essays are found in Claudia Bushman, ed., *Mormon Sisters: Women in Early Utah* (Cambridge, Mass.: Emmeline Press Limited, 1976), and Vicky Burgess-Olson, ed., *Sister Saints* (Provo: Brigham Young Univ., 1978). An ambitious and controversial recent book by Marilyn Warenski, *Patriarchs and Politics: The Plight of the Mormon Woman* (New York: McGraw-Hill, 1978), presents an overview of the changing role of Mormon women in the nineteenth and twentieth centuries. Another approach to the process of change in Mormon women's status is my article, "From Frontier Activism to Neo-Victorian Domesticity: Mormon Women in the Nineteenth and Twentieth Centuries," *Journal of Mormon History* 6 (1979): 3–21. Extremely positive interpretations are presented in Susa Young Gates and Leah D. Widtsoe, *Women of the "Mormon" Church* (Salt Lake City: Deseret News Press, 1926); Edward Wheelock Tullidge, *The Women of Mormondom* (New York: n.p., 1877); and Augusta Joyce Crocheron, *Representative Women of Deseret: A Book of Biographical Sketches* (Salt Lake City: J. Graham, 1877). An invaluable source for women's own perceptions is the *Woman's Exponent,* a periodical by and for women published between 1872 and 1914. For a review of the range of materials available on Mormon women, see David J. Whittaker and Carol C. Madsen, "History's Sequel: A Source Essay on Women in Mormon History," *Journal of Mormon History* 6 (1979): 123–45.

Scholarly studies of Mormon polygamy are analyzed in Davis Bitton, "Mormon Polygamy: A Review Article," *Journal of Mormon History* 4 (1977): 101–18. For the development of polygamy prior to the assassination of Joseph Smith, the first detailed study by a non-Mormon based on full access to the relevant materials in the LDS Church Library and Archives is found in my dissertation, "Between Two Worlds," cited above, which has been incorporated into the text of this book. Danel W. Bachman, "A Study of the Mormon Practice of Plural Marriage before the Death of Joseph Smith" (M.A. thesis, Purdue Univ., 1975), provides a detailed treatment of the early development of polygamy from a Mormon perspective. These two analyses, done independently and from different theoretical perspectives, are, nevertheless, essentially complementary in their overall conclusions. The best published study on polygamy before Utah is Charles E. Shook, *The True Origin of Mormon Polygamy* (Cincinnati: Standard Publishing Co., 1914). Shook conclusively establishes Joseph Smith's responsibility for the introduction of the practice. Also see Joseph F. Smith [Joseph Fielding Smith], *Blood Atonement and the Origin of Plural Marriage* (Salt Lake City: Deseret News Press, 1905). On a possible social rationale for early polygamy, see my article, "A Little-Known Defense of Polygamy from the Mormon Press in 1842," *Dialogue: A Journal of Mormon Thought* 9 (Winter 1974): 21–34.

For polygamy in Utah, a starting point is Stanley S. Ivins, "Notes on Mormon Polygamy," *Western Humanities Review* 10 (Summer 1956): 229–39. The Ivins interpretation is elaborated and qualified in James E. Smith and Philip R. Kunz, "Polygyny and Fertility in Nineteenth-Century America," *Population Studies* 30 (1976): 465–80. Kimball Young, *Isn't One Wife Enough?: The Story of Mormon Polygamy* (New York: Henry Holt, 1954), is still the best book-length study. It is based in part on James Edward Hulett, Jr., "The Social and Social Psychological Aspects of the Mormon Polygamous Family" (Ph.D. diss., Univ. of Wisconsin, 1939). An exceptionally valuable source on all aspects of Mormon kinship is D. Michael Quinn, "Organizational Development and Social Origins of the Mormon Hierarchy, 1832–1932: A Prosopographical Study" (M.A. thesis, Univ. of Utah, 1973). Quinn includes 114 pages of appendices with family data on all members of the Mormon hierarchy during the century his work covers. Also suggestive is Vicky Burgess-Olson, "Family Structure and Dynamics in Early Utah Mormon Families, 1847–1885" (Ph.D. diss., Northwestern Univ., 1975). Insights into women's perceptions of life under polygamy are found in S. George Ellsworth, ed., *Dear Ellen: Two Mormon Women and Their Letters* (Salt Lake City: Univ. of Utah Library, 1974), and Juanita Brooks, ed., *Not by Bread Alone: The Journal of Martha Spence Heywood, 1850–56* (Salt Lake City: Utah State Historical Society, 1978). Powerful defenses of polygamy from the nineteenth century are found in *The Seer,* a periodical edited and published by Orson Pratt in Washington, D. C., between 1853 and 1854, and in Helen Mar Kimball Whitney, *Why We Practice Plural Marriage* (Salt Lake City: Juvenile Instructor Office, 1884).

Anti-polygamy writings of the nineteenth century can be loosely divided into those that have a significant factual basis and those that are primarily fictional or so general in their treatment as to be of little direct use to the historian. Among the apostate writings which must be taken seriously by scholars seeking to understand the development of polygamy, see John C. Bennett, *The History of the Saints, or, An Exposé of Joe Smith and Mormonism* (Boston: Leland & Whiting, 1842); John Hyde, Jr., *Mormonism: Its Leaders and Designs* (New York: W. P. Fetridge, 1857); T. B. H. Stenhouse, *The Rocky Mountain Saints: A Full and Complete History of the Mormons* (New York: D. Appleton, 1873); Fanny Stenhouse, *"Tell It All": The Story of A Life's Experience in Mormonism* (Hartford, Conn.: A. D. Worthington, 1874); and John D. Lee, *Mormonism Unveiled, or, The Life and Confessions of the Mormon Bishop, John D. Lee,* ed. W. W. Bishop (St. Louis: Bryan, Brand, 1877).

The vast majority of the anti-polygamy works of the nineteenth century are semi-novelistic in character. They reveal little or nothing about how polygamy was practiced, but much about the fears and fantasies of their authors. For analyses of this latter genre, see Leonard J. Arrington and Jon Haupt, "Intolerable Zion: The Image of Mormonism in Nineteenth Century American Literature," *Western Humanities Review* 22 (Summer 1968): 243–60; David Brion Davis, "Some Themes of Counter-Subversion: An Analysis of Anti-Masonic, Anti-Catholic, and Anti-Mormon Literature," *Mississippi Valley Historical Review* 47 (September 1960): 205–24; Charles A. Cannon, "The Awesome Power of Sex: The Polemical Campaign against Mormon Polygamy," *Pacific Historical Review* 43 (February 1974): 61–82; and Casterline, "Images of the Mormon Woman," cited above. A relatively moderate example of this anti-polygamy genre is Jennie Anderson Froiseth, ed., *The Women of Mormonism, or, The Story of Polygamy as Told by the Victims Themselves* (Detroit: C. G. Paine, 1882). For the crusade against Mormon polygamy, the best single scholarly source is Gustive O. Larson, *The "Americanization" of Utah for Statehood* (San Marino, Calif.: Huntington Library, 1971). Two Mormon accounts which deal frankly with life under polygamy during the difficult period of persecution in the late nineteenth century are Annie Clark Tanner, *A Mormon Mother: An Autobiography* (Salt Lake City: Univ. of Utah, 1969), and Juliaetta Bateman Jensen, *Little Gold Pieces* (Salt Lake City: Stanway Printing Co., 1948).

Mormon manuscript sources are extensive and are fully cited in the text of this book, so only a few outstanding collections will be highlighted here. Essential for this study were the numerous but often poorly catalogued affidavits on polygamy held in the Church Archives in Salt Lake City. Also valuable were the many diary and journal accounts in the Church Archives which dealt with polygamy. Outside the Church Archives, the James J. Strang Papers in the Coe Collection of the Beinecke Library at Yale University in New Haven, Connecticut, are the most important single manuscript collection on Mormon development before Utah. Insights into the lives of women under polygamy are suggested in the Hubert Howe Bancroft Collection of Mormon Manuscripts held at the Bancroft Library of the University of California at Berkeley, available on microfilm in the Church Archives. The Kimball Young Papers, which include interviews by James E. Hulett, Jr., and others with individuals who grew up in polygamous families, are available both at the Huntington Library, San Marino, California, and the Garrett Theological Seminary Library, Evanston, Illinois.

Index

From the earliest days of settlement to the present, Americans have experimented with varied forms of communal living, alternative marriage and sexual patterns, and other unorthodox lifestyles. During the turbulent decades before the Civil War in particular, thousands of Americans joined communally oriented religious groups which rejected existing family and sex-role patterns. In *Religion and Sexuality,* Lawrence Foster analyzes the origin, early development, and institutionalization of three such alternative systems—Shaker celibacy, Oneida Community complex marriage, and Mormon polygamy. These three experiments highlight the process by which individuals and groups can radically change an entire belief system and way of life.

Based on extensive research in the primary sources—including the first work ever conducted by a non-Mormon with full access to the central Mormon archival holdings on polygamy in Salt Lake City—*Religion and Sexuality* breaks new ground both factually and conceptually. Foster presents his findings in case studies, sympathetically yet critically describing the development of each experiment. A comparative introduction and conclusion link the groups to each other and to the antebellum crisis in marriage and family life that led eventually toward more